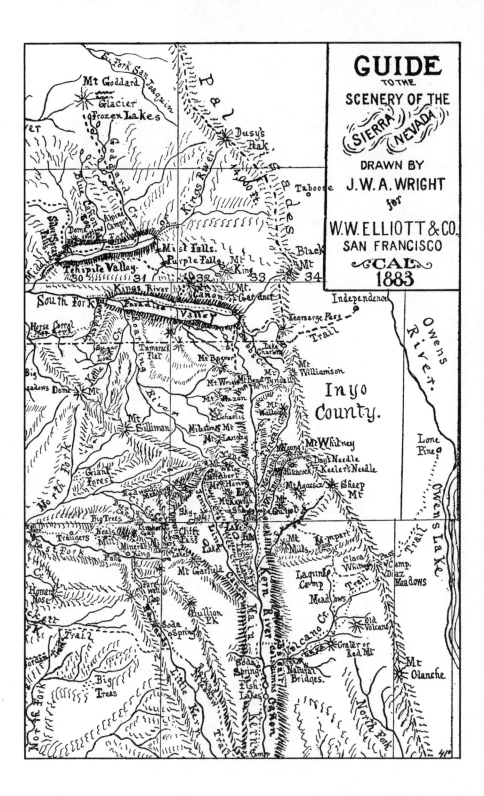

GUIDE
TO THE
SCENERY OF THE
SIERRA NEVADA
DRAWN BY
J. W. A. WRIGHT
for
W. W. ELLIOTT & CO.
SAN FRANCISCO
CAL
1883

PLACE NAMES
of the
SIERRA NEVADA

From Abbot to Zumwalt

Peter Browning

WILDERNESS PRESS · BERKELEY

Copyright © 1986 by Peter Browning

Design by Thomas Winnett
Cover design by Larry Van Dyke and Noelle Liebrenz
Cover photo courtesy The Sierra Club
Photos courtesy The Bancroft Library

Library of Congress Card Catalog Number 84-52655
International Standard Book Number 0-89997-047-8

Manufactured in the United States of America

Published by Wilderness Press
    2440 Bancroft Way
    Berkeley, CA 94704
    Write for free catalog

Library of Congress Cataloging-in-Publication Data

Browning, Peter, 1928–
 Place names of the Sierra Nevada.

 Bibliography: p.
 1. Sierra Nevada Mountains (Calif. and Nev.)—
Gazetteers. I. Title.
F868.S5B76 1986   917.94′4′00321   84-52655
ISBN 0-89997-047-8

Introduction

None of the place names in the Sierra Nevada has been handed down from antiquity. The names that we have come to regard as fixed and permanent are of relatively recent origin. They are not eternal, nor is there anything necessarily correct or appropriate about them. Were we to begin anew to apply names to this mountain range and to the multitude of features in it, we would achieve a radically different result.

Pedro Font, on an April day in 1776, described the range as *una gran sierra nevada*—and that became the name. The Spanish priests and soldiers named remarkably few features in the Sierra Nevada. Their interest in converting Indians to Christianity led them to explore the Central Valley and the foothills of the Sierra. In the course of these explorations they named the major westward-flowing rivers, such as the Merced and the Tuolumne. Other rivers originally named by the Spanish for saints or religious feast days were later renamed by American explorers (e.g., the Kern) or for a rebellious Indian (the Stanislaus), or were given Indian names of questionable authenticity and meaning (the Tule and the Kaweah). The Spanish had no interest in exploring the mountains. There were no converts to be had at high altitude, nor did the mountains offer anything that could be transformed into wealth or articles of use.

No one has suggested that the Indians of any tribe had a name for the entire mountain range, or that they named the high peaks and major lakes. In only one limited area—Yosemite Valley and vicinity—has a considerable number of Indian names survived. Most of those names are mispronounced due to the difficulties of phonetic spelling, are applied to the wrong features because of the ignorance and arrogance of the white namers, and have been subjected to multiple interpretations. Many of the major features of Yosemite Valley were given their present names during the space of a few days in March and April of 1851 by Lafayette H. Bunnell and other members of the Mariposa Battalion.

From 1861 to 1865 the members of the first California Geological Survey (the Whitney Survey) engaged in the first spate of naming based on need—the need for identifiable features to place on maps. Most of the objects of their attention were mountains, which they named for one another and for prominent geologists and other scientists of the time.

From the middle 1860s until about 1900, sheepmen and cattlemen named meadows and streams as they took their flocks and herds ever deeper into the mountains. Many a meadow became known by the name of the sheepman who made it his summer camp.

Simultaneous with the sheepmen came the early homesteaders. Seldom were meadows and creeks formally named for them; the names simply came to be in common use by local people. When the first official maps were made, the government surveyors inquired locally about names, and accepted what was in use.

Theodore S. Solomons and Joseph N. LeConte were the most prominent individual namers during the 1890s and early 1900s. Various other Sierra Club members—especially Chester Versteeg—have named numerous features since the club's founding in 1892.

From 1889 to 1914 the US Geological Survey conducted the first comprehensive survey and mapping of the entire area covered by this book, and published a series of 30-minute topographic maps on a scale of 1:125,000. Several hundred names appeared for the first time. Some were names of common use, others were created by the surveyors and cartographers who prepared the maps. Foremost among the namers was Robert B. Marshall, who named peaks and lakes for family members, friends, and their wives and daughters.

William W. Forsyth, acting superintendent of Yosemite National Park from 1909 to 1912, named a number of features within the park—many of them for fellow army officers.

Packers contributed many names from about 1920 through 1950, often naming lakes for people or events on the occasions when they stocked the lakes with fish. Dozens of lakes were given names during the 1940s and 1950s by the California Department of Fish and Game. Their need was the same as that of surveyors and cartographers: it is more convenient to identify a lake or other feature by name rather than to assign it a number.

There are hundreds of place names in the Sierra Nevada whose origin is not known. They were created informally many years ago by people who kept no written records. The sources of information I consulted are cited in the individual entries. Of particular interest to researchers are the records of the General Land Office at the Bureau of Land Management on Cottage Avenue in Sacramento. These homestead and patent documents, preserved on microfilm in the "control document index" files, are records of when land left control of the federal government. The "Lake Survey" reports of the Department of Fish and Game in Fresno provided information on many lake names, especially in Fresno County.

James T. Gardiner (Gardner) of the Whitney Survey spelled his last name both ways at different times in his life (see **Gardiner, Mount**). I have used the spelling "Gardiner" throughout, except when it appears as "Gardner" in quoted matter.

The US Geological Survey does not use periods, apostrophes, or diacritical marks in names on topographic maps, lest they be mistaken for other map symbols. Therefore some of the names in this volume do not have apostrophes where they normally would be.

For many peaks and a few lakes, two elevations are given. The first is from the 7½-minute quadrangle and the second from the 15-minute quadrangle. The Geological Survey is in the process of mapping the entire United States on 7½-minute quadrangles, a project that will be completed by 1990. There are two large parts of the area covered by this volume that have not yet been mapped on the 7½-minute scale: most of Yosemite National Park and vicinity, and the Giant Forest area and much of the nearby southern Sierra Nevada. The names of these future maps are already established, but because they will not be published until 1988 and 1989 they have not been included.

The 7½-minute quadrangle maps of the Sierra Nevada published from about 1983 to 1990 are "provisional" editions. The topographic details are correct, but elevations have been hand-lettered. Contours and elevations are in meters, a circumstance the mountain traveler will have to adjust to, since the future maps will also be metric. On these maps control elevations are shown to the nearest 0.1 meter, and other elevations to the nearest meter. To convert meters to feet, multiply by 3.2808. To convert feet to meters, multiply by 0.3048. If and when "standard" editions of these 7½-minute quadrangles are published, it will certainly not be until after 1990.

The US Board on Geographic Names has officially defined the Sierra Nevada as extending from the gap south of Lassen Peak, on the north, to Tehachapi Pass, on the south. The region covered by this volume, however, is limited on the north by roughly the northern boundary of Alpine County, on the south by Walker Pass and Lake Isabella, on the east by US 395 and the Nevada state line, and on the west by several things: elevation, major roads, permanent settlements, map boundaries, and the author's arbitrary decisions.

Francis P. Farquhar's 1926 *Place Names of the High Sierra* provided the nucleus of this book. Without his pioneering efforts, the origin of many names in the Sierra Nevada would not be known. Marjory Farquhar allowed me complete freedom to delve into the files that her husband had accumulated over many years.

I received much generously given assistance and advice from many people: the staff of the Bancroft Library in Berkeley; Barbara Lekisch at the Sierra Club library in San Francisco; Ted Inouye and others at the US Geological Survey in Menlo Park; June English of Fresno and Pat Stewart of Bishop, historical researchers of the first order; Heyward Moore of Fresno; Mary Vocelka and Linda Eade at the Yosemite National Park research library; Bob Ehlers and Phil Pister, California Department of Fish and Game; Mr. and Mrs. Art Schober, Round Valley, California; Pam Conners, Stanislaus National Forest, Sonora; Kathy Moffitt, Sierra National Forest, Fresno; and Rich Weaver, Inyo National Forest, Bishop.

I am eager to receive new information on Sierra Nevada place names. If any reader can provide factual details on names not contained in this book or additional information on the existing entries, or thinks that some of the entries are incorrect, please write. Address your letters to the author in care of Wilderness Press.

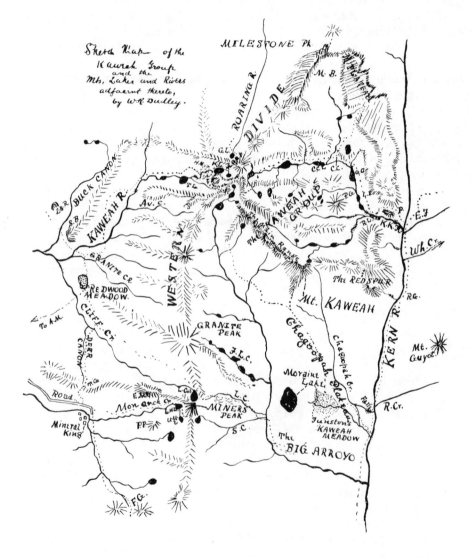

Sketch Map of the
Kaweah Group
and the
Mts, Lakes and Rivers
adjacent thereto,
by W.R. Dudley.

MILESTONE Pk.

ROARING R.

DIVIDE

M.B.

WESTERN

BUCK CAÑON

KAWEAH R.

Av. C.

G.L.

C.C. C.C.

G.C.

THE KAWEAH GROUP

GRANITE CR.

REDWOOD
MEADOW

To A.M.

CLIFF Cr.

DEER
CAÑON

Road

Mineral
King

P.P.

Monarch Cr.

GRANITE
PEAK

J.I.C.

E.

L. Col.

MINERS
PEAK

L.C.

S.C.

FG.

Mt. KAWEAH

The RED SPUR

Chagoopah Cr.

Chagoopah Falls

Moraine
Lake

Funston's
KAWEAH
MEADOW

The
BIG ARROYO

KERN R.

R.G.

R.Cr.

Mt.
Guyot.

Wh Cr.

E.J.

P.

R.G. K.K.C.

Abbot to Zumwalt

Abbot, Mount (13,704–13,715)   *Mt. Abbot 15′* and *7½′*
Named by the Whitney Survey in 1864. Henry Larcom Abbot (1831–1927), a soldier and engineer. He graduated from West Point in 1854, and served for two years as assistant on the survey for a Pacific railroad through California and Oregon. In the early 1900s he was a member of the American committee to plan the Panama Canal. The name was incorrectly spelled "Abbott" on many early maps and references to the mountain.
First ascent July 13, 1908, by J. N. LeConte, James Hutchinson, and Duncan McDuffie. "Then the rope was brought into play, and, after two or three ugly places, we finally climbed over the edge once more, this time at the extreme summit, and Mount Abbott was conquered." (*SCB* 7, no. 1, Jan. 1909: 13.) (INF, SiNF)

Acker Peak (11,015)   *Tower Peak 15′*
William Bertrand Acker was in charge of national park affairs in the Department of the Interior before the National Park Service was created in 1916. The name was given by the Geological Survey, and first appeared on the *Dardanelles* 30′ map of 1912. (Farquhar: R. B. Marshall.) (YNP)

Ackerson Meadow, Creek, Mountain   *Lake Eleanor 15′*
Named for James F. Ackerson, a '49er. (Paden, 207.) The meadow was called "Wade's or Big Meadows" on Hoffmann and Gardiner's map, 1863–67. (On that same map, "Wade's Ranch" was midway between the present "Ackerson Meadow" and "Sawmill Mtn," and the present "Bald Mtn" was called "Wade's Mt.") The creek was called "Big Meadow Creek" on the 1880 GLO Plat. Ackerson homesteaded 160 acres in sec. 24, T. 1 S., R. 19 E. in 1882. He patented another 180 acres in secs. 24 and 25 in 1884. (StNF)

Adair Lake   *Merced Peak 15′*
Charles F. Adair (1874–1936), a Yosemite National Park ranger from 1914 to 1935. He introduced golden trout into this lake, which gave him the right to name it after himself. (Bingaman, *Guardians,* 91.)

Aeolian Buttes   *Mono Craters 15′*
Named in the early 1880s by Israel C. Russell. ". . . for convenience of description we may name them Aeolian Buttes. They are fragments of the older history of the region. . . ." (Russell, *Quaternary,* 388.) (INF)

1

Agassiz, Mount (13,893–13,891); **Agassiz Col**   *Mt. Goddard 15',*
North Palisade 7½'
Louis Agassiz (1807–1873), a naturalist, geologist, and teacher. He was born in Switzerland, came to the United States in 1846, and became a professor of zoology at Harvard in 1848. Lilbourne A. Winchell, in 1879, gave the name "Agassiz Needle" either to this peak or to what is now Mount Winchell, a truly needlelike peak 0.7 mile southeast of Mount Agassiz. (Winchell, 160.) The name change from "Agassiz Needle" to "Mount Agassiz" was proposed by the Sierra Club in the 1930s. (SC records in BL.) The name "Agassiz Col" first appeared on the 1948 *Mt. Goddard* 15' map. (KCNP, INF)

Agnew Grove   *Tehipite Dome 15'*
For Jesse Agnew, "an ardent protector of Big Trees." (Fry and White, 102.) (SeNF)

Agnew Meadows   *Devils Postpile 15', Mammoth Mtn. 7½'*
Agnew Pass   *Devils Postpile 15', Mt. Ritter 7½'*
Agnew Lake (8,508)   *Mono Craters 15'*
Theodore C. Agnew, a miner, settled in the meadow named for him in 1877. "Agnew's House" is marked on the 1885 GLO plat. He tried several times to patent the land, but was refused because there was no accepted survey of that township. The survey that ostensibly was made in 1885 was declared fraudulent by the Department of the Interior in 1899. It was one of many so-called barroom surveys. The surveyor sat in the tranquillity of a tavern, safe from the elements and hard work, and composed fictional field notes. Agnew performed valuable service by guiding army troops who were patrolling Yosemite National Park. (Farquhar.) (INF)

Ahart Meadow   *Huntington Lake 15', Nelson Mtn. 7½'*
John *Earthart* patented 160 acres in secs. 32 and 33, T. 10 S., R. 27 E. in 1892. The name "Ahart," which has been on maps since the 1904 *Kaiser* 30' sheet, is due to an obvious error in spelling or pronunciation. (SiNF)

Ahwahnee   *Yosemite 15', Yosemite Valley 1:24,000*
"A-wa'-ni, a large village standing directly at the foot of Yosemite Fall. This was the ruling town, the metropolis of this little mountain democracy, and the giver of its name, and it is said to have been the residence of the celebrated chief Ten-ai'-ya." (Powers, 365.)
"Ten-ie-ya . . . responded rather loftily: 'I am the descendant of an Ah-wah-ne-chee chief. His people lived in the mountains and valley where my people have lived. The valley was then called Ah-wah-nee. Ah-wah-ne-chee signifies the dwellers in Ahwahnee." (Bunnell, *Discovery,* 1911, 72.) "When these facts were communicated to Captain Boling, and Ah-wah-ne was ascertained to be the *classical* name, the captain said that name was all right enough for history or poetry, but that we could not now change the name Yosemite, nor was it desirable to do so." (Ibid., 73.)
Galen Clark said the name meant "deep grassy valley." Although it may have been the Indians' name for Yosemite Valley, it now applies only to the

Ahwahnee Hotel and a bridge on a park road. Construction of the hotel began in the spring of 1926; it was opened on July 14, 1927. (Sargent, *Innkeepers*, 89–93.) (YNP)

Ahwiyah Point   *Hetch Hetchy 15', Yosemite Valley 1:24,000*
    This was originally the Indian name for Mirror Lake (various spellings were used by early writers). Now applied to a spur on the south wall of Tenaya Canyon below Half Dome, overlooking Mirror Lake. Galen Clark said the name meant "quiet water." Some earlier names that fortunately do not survive were "Acorn Peak," "The Old Piute," and "Old Man Mountain." Although this is an old name, it did not appear on the *Yosemite Valley* map until the edition of 1938. (YNP)

Ainslee Meadow   *Mt. Morgan 7½'*
    Ainslee was a homesteader who lived in the vicinity in the early 1900s. (USGS.)

Airola Peak (9,942–9,938)   *Dardanelles Cone 15' and 7½'*
    John and Emma Airola homesteaded 160 acres at Frogtown in the 1890s. The Airola family has been in the cattle business since 1909. (StNF files.) (StNF)

Alabama Hills   *Lone Pine 15', Mt. Langley 7½'*
    "In the early 60's the Hitchcock boys discovered a mine in these hills which they called the 'Old Abe' mine, and they called their district the 'Alabama District.' They were Rebels and in those days 'Old Abe' was a term of ridicule. But they named the district in honor of the Confederate Cruiser 'Alabama.' These hills are now called the 'Alabama Hills.' " (Thomas Keough, "Over Kearsarge Pass in 1864," *SCB* 10, no. 3, Jan. 1918: 342.)
    The CSS *Alabama* was a British-built ship, with Southern officers and a British crew, that destroyed a total of 64 American merchant ships in the Atlantic and Indian oceans during the Civil War. She was sunk by the USS *Kearsarge* off the port of Cherbourg, France, in June 1864. (See **Kearsarge.**)

Albanita Meadows   *Monache Mtn. 15'*
    A combining and modifying of the Spanish "agua bonita," meaning "beautiful water." (*Los Tulares,* no. 60, March 1964: 3.) Origin unknown. The name appeared on the 1904 *Olancha* 30' map. (SeNF)

Alder Creek   *Yosemite 15'*
    A tributary of the South Fork of the Merced River; crossed by the Wawona Road five miles south of Wawona. "Undoubtedly named for a native species of alder, *Alnus rhombifolia.*" (YNP files.) A common name, but one might speculate that it was named by the members of the Whitney Survey who passed this way in the summer of 1864, since the name first appeared on the 1863–67 Hoffmann and Gardiner map. (YNP)

Alger Lakes, Creek   *Mono Craters 15'*
    R. B. Marshall of the USGS named the one lake (two lakes narrowly joined) in 1909 for John Alger, a packer for the Geological Survey. The creek name

derives from the lakes. It was called "North Fork" (of Rush Creek) on the 1914
Mt. Lyell 30' map. (Farquhar: R. B. Marshall.) (INF)

Alice, Mount (3,541 m.–11,630)   *Big Pine 15', Split Mtn. 7½'*
This name was originally given to what is now called "Temple Crag," a
higher peak two miles to the southwest. (See **Temple Crag**; also BGN, *Sixth
Report,* 748.) (INF)

Alpine Col   *Mt. Goddard 15', Mt. Darwin 7½'*
Mrs. Art Schober of Round Valley, California, said that the Sierra Club
named this pass in the 1930s or 1940s. (KCNP, SiNF)

Alpine, Lake (7,303)   *Big Meadow 15', Tamarack 7½'*
                                        Dardanelles Cone 15', Spicer Meadow Res. 7½'
The lake was created by Pacific Gas and Electric building a dam across
Silver Creek. The valley was called "Silver Valley" in a GLO surveyor's field
notes in 1879.

Alsace Lake   *Mt. Tom 7½', Mt. Hilgard 7½'*
Ralph Beck of the DFG in Bishop named this lake in 1954. The DFG was
asked by the USGS whether the lakes in the basin at the head of French Canyon
had names. They didn't, but Beck saw his chance. He had been in France during
the Second World War, so he provided names for this lake and several others
that were French or had a French association. (Phil Pister of the DFG in
Bishop.) (SiNF)

Alta Meadow, Peak (11,204)   *Triple Divide Peak 15'*
"In 1876, W. B. Wallace, Tom Witt, and N. B. Witt, on their way from Big
Meadow to Mineral King, camped at Alta Meadow and gave it its name because
it was higher than any other meadow in the vicinity." (Farquhar: G. W.
Stewart.)
"It is suggested that 'Alta Peak' be substituted as a name for what is
denominated Tharp's Peak on the present Club map. It is a most conspicuous
crag eastward from the Giant Forest, as seen from Three Rivers. We climbed it
in 1896, when, so far as we know, it had no name. The name 'Alta Peak' then
given from the long-named Alta Meadow on its slope, has been almost
universally adopted by the Three Rivers people and the frequenters of the Giant
Forest. Besides, it is euphonious and appropriate." (William R. Dudley, "Near
the Kern's Grand Canyon." *SCB* 4, no. 4, June 1903: 306–7.) (SNP)

Amelia Earhart Peak (11,982)   *Tuolumne Meadows 15'*
The name was proposed by the Rocketdyne Mountaineering Club for
Amelia Earhart Putnam, who disappeared over the Pacific on an around-the-
world flight in 1937. Approved by the BGN in 1967. The name is not on the first
edition of the 15-minute quad. The peak is about 0.7 mile east by south from
Ireland Lake. (YNP)

Amphitheater Lake (10,734–10,706)   *Mt. Goddard 15',*
                                                    North Palisade 7½'
Named by J. N. LeConte in 1902 while exploring a route to the Palisades.

"Far below lay another desolate lake walled in by gigantic cliffs to the east, and the outlet, which entered a deep gorge, was evidently a tributary of Palisade Creek. . . . At the shore of our Amphitheater Lake we stopped a moment to rest and enjoy the wild outlook . . . ." (*SCB* 5, no. 1, Jan. 1904: 8.) (KCNP)

Amphitheater Lake *Mineral King 15'*
Named by W. F. Dean in 1889. (Farquhar: W. F. Dean.) (SNP)

Anderson Canyon, Ridge *Silver Lake 15', Bear River Reservoir 7½'*
Edward M. Anderson patented 160 acres in sec. 18, T. 9 N., R. 16 E. in 1892—about one mile north of these two features. Mary M. Anderson homesteaded 160 acres in secs. 19, 20, and 30 in 1905, a homestead that is exactly on the features. (ENF)

Andrews Camp *Mt. Goddard 15'*
F. K. Andrews bought the property from S. J. Newlan expressly for the purpose of building a summer resort. (INF files: *Inyo Register,* Oct. 17, 1907.) The resort no longer exists; the name is not on the *Mt. Thompson 7½'* quad. (INF)

Angora Mountain (10,202), **Creek** *Kern Peak 15'*
The mountain was called "Sheep Mountain" on the *Olancha* 30' map from 1907 through the fifth edition, 1931. The name was changed by a 1928 BGN decision; it appeared as "Angora Mountain" on the 1939 edition.
"Named by a sheepman honoring the leader of his flock, an Angora goat." (*Newsletter* 1, no. 1, Oct. 1968: 5.) (SeNF)

Anna Lake *Tower Peak 15'*
Probably named for Anna Mack, whose parents lived at Hardy Station, near the junction of US 395 and State Route 108. This was the presumption of Senator Maurice Mack of Nevada, her brother. (Maule.) The peak (11,144) just west of the lake is not named "Anna," but is marked as the location of the "Anna VABM." (See also **Emma, Mount.**) (TNF)

Anna Mills, Mount (12,064) *Kern Peak 15'*
Named for Anna Mills Johnston, who on August 3, 1878, was one of the first four women to climb Mount Whitney. The name was suggested by Leonard Daughenbaugh in 1984, and approved by the BGN in 1985.
"Walking over to the monument, we planted the Stars and Stripes on its topmost point . . . then we sang the 'Star-Spangled Banner' and 'Nearer, my God, to Thee.' " (Anna Mills Johnston, "A Trip to Mt. Whitney in 1878," *MWCJ* 1, no. 1, May 1902: 18–28.) Not named on the 15-minute quad. The mountain is 2.5 miles south of Mount Guyot and 2.5 miles northwest of the Rocky Basin Lakes. (SNP)

Anne Lake *Mt. Abbot 15', Graveyard Peak 7½'*
Possibly named by William A. Dill of the DFG in 1943. (DFG Survey.) (SiNF)

Ansel Lake   *Mineral King 15'*
   For Ansel Franklin Hall, a ranger in Sequoia National Park, 1916–17, and
later information officer at Yosemite. (SNP)

Ansel Adams, Mount (over 11,760)   *Merced Peak 15'*
   Ansel Adams (1902–1984) was the preeminent American landscape
photographer of the 20th century. His wilderness portraits of Yosemite, the
Sierra Nevada, Big Sur, and the Southwest awakened three generations to the
unparalleled beauty of the American West. Adams had his greatest influence as
a conservationist, using his photographs to demonstrate the need to preserve the
remaining wild areas in the West. He was a director of the Sierra Club for 37
years, and was the author of seven portfolios of original prints and more than 30
books. In his book *These We Inherit,* Adams wrote: "Our time is short, and the
future terrifyingly long. . . . With reverence for life, and with restraint enough to
leave some things as they are, we can continue approaching, and perhaps can
attain, a new society at last—one which is proportionate to nature."
   Adams first saw and photographed this peak in September 1921, when he
described it as "undoubtedly inaccessible." On a Sierra Club outing in 1934, the
peak was climbed for the first time by three men, who unofficially named it for
Adams. Two days later, July 13, 1934, dedication ceremonies were conducted
on the summit by a party of 15, including Ansel Adams and his wife, Virginia.
(*SCB* 11, no. 3, 1922: 315–16, photo opp. p. 258; and *SCB* 20, no. 1, Feb.
1935: 104–5, photo plate VI.)
   The name remained unofficial, since BGN regulations do not permit naming
a geographic feature for a living person. It was approved by the BGN in
December 1984. The name does not appear on present USGS maps, but will be
on the *Mt. Lyell* 7½' map when it is published. The peak is at the headwaters of
the Lyell Fork of the Merced River, ¾ mile NE of Foerster Peak. (YNP)

Aperture Peak (13,265)   *Mt. Goddard 15', North Palisade 7½'*
   The name was used informally by climbers for a number of years; it was
made offical by a BGN decision in 1969. The peak is not named on early editions of the 15-minute quad. It is half a mile north of Mt. Agassiz. (INF)

Arc Pass (over 12,880)   *Mount Whitney 15' and 7½'*
   A descriptive name, proposed by Chester Versteeg in 1936. (INF files.)
Added to maps by the USGS because it was in common use. (USGS.) (SNP,
INF)

Arch Rock   *Yosemite 15'*
   A natural tunnel on State Route 140 just north of the YNP entrance station.
Referred to in early accounts as "Tunnel Rock" and "Arched Rocks." (*YNN*
34, no. 1, Jan. 1955: 2.) (YNP)

Arch Rock (10,401)   *Kaiser Peak 15', Sharktooth Peak 7½'*
   Descriptive name: a large outcrop with a hole eroded through it. (SiNF)

Arctic Lake   *Mount Whitney 15' and 7½'*
   Proposed by Chester Versteeg in 1953. (SC papers in BL.) (SNP)

Ardeth Lake   *Tower Peak 15'*
Otto M. Brown, a YNP ranger from 1927 to 1946, named this lake for his wife. (Bingaman, *Guardians,* 103–4.) (YNP)

Armstrong Canyon   *Mt. Pinchot 15', Aberdeen 7½'*
It is possible the canyon was named for John S. Armstrong, who homesteaded 160 acres in sec. 27, T. 11 S., R. 34 E. in 1916. The homestead is about four miles east of the canyon's mouth. (INF)

Army Pass (over 12,000)   *Olancha 15'*
A route originally used by sheepmen. The trail was built in 1892, at a time when the US Army was patrolling Sequoia National Park, by black soldiers from Georgia—Troop K of the Fourth Cavalry. The name first appeared on the 1907 *Olancha* 30' map. (Farquhar: Versteeg, from Gen. M. F. Davis.) (SNP, INF)

Arndt Lake   *Tower Peak 15'*
Named by Lt. H. C. Benson in 1896 for First Sergeant Alvin Arndt, Troop I, Fourth Cavalry, US Army. (Farquhar: Benson.) In September 1893 Arndt led a detachment of troops from Slide Canyon to Tiltill Valley, and learned from sheepmen of a route from Matterhorn Canyon to Hetch Hetchy Valley. (*SCB* 1, no. 5, Jan. 1895: 168.) (YNP)

Arnold Meadow   *Shuteye Peak 15'*
James H. Arnold patented 160 acres in sec. 8, T. 6 S., R. 24 E. in 1892. (SiNF)

Arnot Peak (10,054), **Creek**   *Dardanelles Cone 15' and 7½'*
Nathaniel D. Arnot was a superior judge of Alpine County from 1879 to 1904. (Maule.) The name of the peak is on atlas sheet 56B of the Wheeler Survey, 1878–79. The creek first appears on the 1898 *Dardanelles* 30' map. (StNF, TNF)

Arrow Peak (3,950 m.–12,958)   *Mt. Pinchot 15' and 7½'*
Arrow Creek, Ridge   *Mt. Pinchot 15' and 7½', Marion Peak 15'*
Bolton Coit Brown named Arrow Peak in 1895 when he made the first ascent. He was wearing boots so worn that his feet "were almost literally on the ground," and he was by himself—but nevertheless he went up the northeast spur. "More than once the ridge narrowed to an actual edge which I had to straddle and hitch along. . . . A sharp rock cut the bare sole of my foot, but not deeply. . . . About midday I clambered up the last and summit rock . . . and swept my eyes around. It was perfect. . . . A sense of profound peace came over me. It was so still I heard only the ringing in my ears." (*SCB* 1, no. 8, May 1896: 307–8. Also a sketch map on p. 302 and a sketch of Arrow Peak on p. 306.) "Arrow Peak" and "Arrow Creek" first appeared on the 1907 *Mt. Whitney* 30' map; the USGS added "Arrow Ridge" on the *Mt. Pinchot* quad in 1953. (KCNP)

Arrowhead Lake   *Mt. Pinchot 15', Mt. Clarence King 7½'*
Named for its shape. The name was added to the 7½-minute quad because it

has been in common use for many years. Not named on the 15-minute quad; it is about 0.7 mile north of Fin Dome. (KCNP)

Arrowhead Spire   *Yosemite Valley 1:24,000*
   Probably named in the late 1930s by Sierra Club climbers, who at that time called it simply "Arrowhead." (*SCB* 25, no. 1, Feb. 1940: 55.) (YNP)

Artist Point, Creek   *Yosemite 15', Yosemite Valley 1:24,000*
   From this place, on June 20, 1855, the artist Thomas Ayres drew the first picture of the Yosemite Falls. Ayres, born in New Jersey, came to California in 1849, and accompanied James M. Hutchings on the first tourist trip to Yosemite Valley. This point "on account of its impressive comprehensiveness, and near proximity to Yo Semite, has been selected, by all the leading artists, as the best general view. This should receive the name of 'Artist Point' . . . ." (Hutchings, *Tourist's Guide for 1877*, 85.) Ayres was lost at sea en route from San Pedro to San Francisco in April 1858.
   Artist Point was mislocated on *Yosemite Valley* maps from 1907 through the edition of 1947; it was moved west one-fourth mile on the edition of 1958. (YNP)

Ash Mountain   *Kaweah 15'*
   Sequoia National Park headquarters. Named about 1926 by the park superintendent, Col. John R. White, for the Ash Peaks, which rise several thousand feet above the headquarters. (SNP files.) (SNP)

Ash Peaks; Ash Peaks Ridge   *Giant Forest 15'*
   "Named for the profusion of flowering ash trees growing on the north slopes." (Fry and White, 177.) But also, White states that the peaks were named by John W. Lovelace about 1860 because of the ash color of the mountains. (SNP files.) (SNP)

Aspen Valley   *Lake Eleanor 15'*
   Named for an abundance of quaking aspen. The namer is not known, but the name has existed since before 1897, when it first appeared on the USGS map. Jeremiah Hodgdon patented land here, and in 1879 built a two-story log cabin at the southeast end of the meadow. (Robert F. Uhte, "Yosemite's Pioneer Cabins," *SCB* 36, no. 5, May 1951: 51.) (YNP)

Aster Lake   *Triple Divide Peak 15'*
   Col. John R. White named this lake in the early 1920s for asters growing along the shore. (SNP files.) (SNP)

Atwell Mill, Grove, Creek   *Mineral King 15'*
   Site of a sawmill built by Collins and Redfield in 1879. In 1890, Isham Mullenix homesteaded 160 acres in secs. 11 and 12, T. 17 S., R. 30 E. A. J. Atwell bought the land from Mullenix. The property eventually wound up in the hands of a D. E. Skinner, who donated the land to the Department of the Interior. (Farquhar; GLO; SNP files.)
   In recognition of the gift, the grove was officially named "Skinner Grove Big Trees," and appeared that way on the 1934 and 1942 *Kaweah 30'* maps. But local people persisted in calling it "Atwell Grove," so in 1946 the BGN reversed

itself and approved the name of local use. The mill has long since disappeared. When it was operating, "the mill cut redwoods [i.e., sequoias] into posts, shingles, and flume boards. Many of the early homes and buildings of the county were built of lumber from this mill." (*Newsletter* 1, no. 2, Jan. 1969: 7.) (SNP)

Avalanche Creek   *Yosemite 15'*
The namer is not known, but may have been one of the members of the Whitney Survey who were in this vicinity in August and September of 1864. The name appears on the Wheeler Survey atlas sheet 56D, 1878–79, and the GLO plat of 1884. (YNP)

Avalanche Lake   *Kaiser Peak 15' and 7½'*
The lake is in a steep-sided glacial cirque, with knife-edge ridges from south to northwest. Probably named by the DFG in 1947. (DFG survey.) (SiNF)

Avalanche Peak (10,077), **Creek**   *Marion Peak 15'*
The peak was named by John Muir in 1891. (Muir, "A Rival of the Yosemite," *Century Magazine,* Nov. 1891, 79.) This name and that of Palmer Mountain, 1½ miles south, were accidentally transposed on the first three editions of the *Tehipite* 30' map; they were corrected on the edition of 1929. J. N. LeConte, on the map in *A Summer,* gives the name "Avalanche Cañon" to the presently unnamed stream flowing from directly below Avalanche Peak. The present USGS map makes Avalanche Creek the next stream to the east. (KCNP)

Avonelle Lake   *Tower Peak 15'*
Otto M. Brown, a YNP ranger from 1927 to 1946, named the lake for his daughter. (Bingaman, YNP files.) (YNP)

Aweetasal Lake   *Mt. Abbot 15', Mt. Hilgard 7½'*
Named in August 1951 by Elden H. Vestal of the DFG. He said the word refers to a type of Mono Indian back carrier for carrying babies. Two students of the Mono language said they did not know the word, and that the Mono language has no '1.' (Heyward Moore, *FPP* 26, no. 2, Summer 1984: 5.) (SiNF)

Babcock Lake (8,983)   *Tuolumne Meadows 15'*
Named by Lieutenant N. F. McClure in 1895 for John P. Babcock, chief deputy, California State Board of Fish Commissioners." (Farquhar: McClure.) (YNP)

Baboon Lakes   *Mt. Goddard 15', Mt. Thompson 7½'*
"My brother John stocked them. There was a bunch of CCC boys on the other side, and they hollered and waved about what way to go. They started in shedding their clothes, and John said they looked like a bunch of baboons going over the rocks." (Art Schober.) (INF)

Backbone Creek   *Kaweah 15', Mineral King 15'*
The Dillon Mill Road, for more than a mile, is on the crest of a sharp ridge between the North Fork of the Tule River and a small creek running parallel to the river. This stretch of road was known locally as "The Devil's Backbone;" hence the name of the creek. (SeNF)

Bacon Meadow   *Giant Forest 15'*
    For Fielding Bacon, a pioneer stockman (Farquhar: J. B. Agnew, Walter Fry.) The name appears on the first edition of the *Tehipite* 30' map, 1905. (SeNF)

Badaraco Camp   *Silver Lake 15', Caples Lake 7½'*
    An old family cow camp. (USGS.) Maggie O'Badaraco homesteaded 160 acres in secs. 20 and 29, T. 10 N., R. 18 E. in 1905. (ENF)

Bagley Valley   *Topaz Lake 15', Heenan Lake 7½', Wolf Creek 7½'*
    Probably named for an early settler. Called "Bagsley's Valley" by Joseph LeConte; he and his party camped here on August 17, 1870. (LeConte, *Ramblings,* 127.)

Bago, Mount (3,618 m.–11,868)   *Mt. Pinchot 15', Mt. Clarence King 7½'*
    The namer and the origin of the name are not known. Bolton Coit Brown and his wife Lucy climbed the peak in July 1896, as did J. N. LeConte and W. S. Gould. Brown described it as "the red peak south of the lake" (Charlotte Lake). On top, "a fine thunder-storm, growling over in the Mt. Williamson region, sent electricity at us. The invisible something passed with tingling prickles and a thin, squeaky, crackling sound through our outstretched fingertips; and Lucy's front hair streamed out towards the storm like the pictures in the high-school books on physics, and 'buzzed,' as she said." (*SCB* 2, no. 1, Jan. 1897: 20.) The name must have been applied soon thereafter, since it appeared on the 1907 *Mt. Whitney* 30' map. (KCNP)

Bakeoven Meadows, Pass   *Monache Mtn. 15'*
    Although on the same quadrangle, these two places are unrelated; they're about 15 miles apart. Gudde says the meadows' name derives from early-day sheepherders who built a mud and stone oven there for baking bread. (Gudde, *Place Names,* 19.) The Tulare County Historical Society says it was hunters, packers, and fishermen who built an oven. The same source says the pass was named for a bake oven made of rocks by early-day hunters, or possibly Indians. (*Newsletter* 1, no. 2. Jan. 1969: 7.) (Meadows, INF; Pass, SeNF)

Baker Creek   *Mt. Goddard 15', Big Pine 15', Mt. Thompson 7½',*
                                                        Coyote Flat 7½'
Baker Lake   *Big Pine 15', Coyote Flat 7½'*
    William A. Baker came to Owens Valley in 1850. He was at first a miner, and later he ran a sawmill with Tom Bell on Big Pine Creek. (INF archives.) In 1874 Baker patented 160 acres in sec. 13, T. 9 S., R. 33 E., about 1½ miles west of the town of Big Pine. (INF)

Baker Station   *Dardanelles Cone 15', Dardanelle 7½'*
    Greeneburry C. Baker, born in Missouri in 1845, came to California in 1864. In 1879 he built a station on the Sonora and Mono Road (present State Route 108); it is still known by his name. (Lang, H. O. *A History of Tuolumne County.* B. F. Alley: San Francisco, 1882, 323.) The 1879 GLO plat shows "Baker's House" in the NW¼ of sec. 35, T. 6 N., R. 20 E. Baker patented 160 acres in sections 34 and 35 on Dec. 20, 1890. (StNF)

Balch Park   *Camp Nelson 15'*
Allan C. Balch, a vice president of the San Joaquin Light and Power
Company, bought the former "Summer Home" of John J. Doyle—who had
owned it since 1885—for the purpose of donating it to Tulare County as a park.
When the land was given to the county in 1930, the county commissioners
named it "Balch Park."

Balloon Dome (6,879–6,881)   *Kaiser Peak 15', Balloon Dome 7½'*
"It rises to the height of 1800 feet above the river, and presents exactly the
appearance of the upper part of a sphere; or, as Professor Brewer says, 'of the
top of a gigantic balloon struggling to get up through the rock.' " (Whitney,
Geology, 401.) (SiNF)

Banner Peak (12,936–12,945)   *Devils Postpile 15', Mt. Ritter 7½'*
"Named by Willard D. Johnson, USGS topographer, in 1883, on account of
cloud-banners streaming from the summit." (Farquhar: J. N. LeConte.) (SiNF,
INF)

Barnard, Mount (4,264 m.–13,990)   *Mount Whitney 15',*
                                                 Mt. Williamson 7½'
Edward Emerson Barnard (1857–1923), a noted astronomer at the Lick
Observatory on Mount Hamilton and at Yerkes Observatory at the University
of Chicago. He discovered 16 comets and the fifth satellite of Jupiter.
The mountain was named by W. L., John, and William Hunter and
C. Mulholland, who made the first ascent on September 25, 1892. "This
summit we found to be a great block of granite, affording plenty of space for the
whole party to rest upon, but not much more than that. . . . After resting a little
while the party built a small monument [on] . . . this peak, which [we] decided to
call Mt. Barnard, in honor of the astonomer of Mt. Hamilton. . . . [We were] well
pleased that we had ascended a peak never before touched by human feet, and
bestowed upon it a name that will be remembered as long as the stars are studied
by human beings." (*SCB* 1, no. 3, Jan. 1894: 88–89.) (SNP, INF)

Barnes Mountain   *Huntington Lake 15', Dinkey Creek 7½'*
George W. Barnes patented 120 acres in sec. 20, T. 10 S., R. 25 E. in 1890,
and homesteaded 80 acres in secs. 28 and 33 in 1898. (SiNF)

Barney Lake   *Matterhorn Peak 15'*
"In 1918 . . . Mr. Andrew Smith, who was formerly Superintendent of
Mines at Bodie . . . accompanied our party to Barney Lake. He told us that
Barney Lake and also Peeler Lake . . . were both named after an old resident of
Bridgeport, Barney Peeler." (Letter, W. H. Spaulding to Farquhar, June 11,
1924, in *SCB* 12, no. 2, 1925: 126.) Barnabas Peeler patented 160 acres in sec.
9, T. 4 N., R. 24 E., on Nov. 20, 1880. (TNF)

Barney Riley Creek   *Topaz Lake 15', Heenan Lake 7½'*
What is now a jeep trail west of Little Cottonwood Canyon was originally a
horse trail leading to the Barney Riley homestead. (USGS.) (TNF)

Barrett, Lake   *Devils Postpile 15', Crystal Crag 7½'*
One of the Mammoth Lakes. Named for Lou Barrett, an early forester. (Schumacher, 51.) (INF)

Bartolas Country, Creek   *Kernville 15', Lamont Peak 15'*
Named for a Frenchman who herded sheep in this high meadow country. The name appears on the 1908 *Kernville* 30' map. (Crites, 268.) (SeNF)

Barton Peak (10,370), **Creek**   *Triple Divide Peak 15'*
For James Barton, an early-day cattleman in the area. The peak was named "Mt. Moraine" on the first three editions of the *Tehipite* 30' map; changed to "Barton Peak" on the 1929 edition at the suggestion of the Sierra Club. The creek was named after the peak. (Farquhar.) (KCNP)

Basket Dome (7,612)   *Hetch Hetchy Reservoir 15',*
Yosemite Valley 1:24,000
Galen Clark recited the legend of Tis-sa'-ack, who entered Yosemite Valley with her husband, carrying a great conical burden-basket. They hurried to the valley for water to slake their thirst. The woman was ahead, and when she reached Lake Ah-wei'-yah (Mirror Lake) she drank all the water before he arrived. He was angry, and beat her. She reviled him and threw her basket at him. And as they faced each other "they were turned into stone for their wickedness, and there they still remain. The upturned basket lies beside the husband where the woman threw it, and the woman's face is tear-stained with long dark lines trailing down. Half-Dome is the woman Tis-sa'-ack and North Dome is her husband, while beside the latter is a smaller dome which is still called Basket Dome to this day." (Clark, 87–90.) (YNP)

Battalion Pass   *Yosemite 15'*
The name was suggested by Chester Versteeg for a pass on the Chowchilla Mountain Road, about 3 miles southwest of Wawona, believed to be on the route taken by Major James Savage and the Mariposa Battalion in 1851. (YNP files.) (SiNF)

Baxter, Mount (4,004 m.–13,125)   *Mt. Pinchot 15',*
Kearsarge Peak 7½'
Baxter Lakes *Mt. Pinchot 15', Mt. Clarence King 7½', Kearsarge Peak 7½'*
Baxter Creek, Pass (over 12,320)   *Mt. Pinchot 15', Mt. Clarence King 7½'*
John Baxter was an Owens Valley rancher. J. N. LeConte and party stopped at Baxter's on their 1890 trip. Baxter "cordially invited us in, showed us the best place to camp, told us to help ourselves to fruit and honey, and did everything in his power to make us comfortable. We were somewhat astonished that a perfect stranger should take such an interest in us dirty 'tramps,' but Mr. Baxter said he had spent many a week in the mountains, and was thoroughly in sympathy with the *genus* camper." (LeConte, *A Summer,* 66.) The mountain was named by George R. Davis, USGS, who made the first ascent, in 1905. (LeConte, *Alpina,* 10.) (Mtn. and pass, KCNP, INF; creek and lakes, KCNP)

Bear Creek   *Mt. Abbot 15', Florence Lake 7½', Mt. Hilgard 7½'*
Bear Dome (9,945–9,947)   *Mt. Abbot 15', Florence Lake 7½'*
Bear Ridge   *Mt. Abbot 15', Florence Lake 7½', Graveyard Peak 7½'*
Bear Twin Lakes   *Mt. Abbot 15', Florence Lake 7½'*

Theodore S. Solomons said that the name "Bear Creek" was being used by sheepmen when he went there in 1894. At that time he gave the name "Bear Butte" to what was named "Bear Dome" by the USGS on the first *Mt. Goddard* 30' map, 1912. (Farquhar; *SCB* 1, no. 6, May 1895: 221–37.) "Bear Ridge" also appeared on the 1912 map. The lakes were first named on the 15-minute quad, probably for no better reason than that they are close together and of similar size, and aren't far from Bear Creek. (SiNF)

Bear Creek   *Huntington Lake 15', Dinkey Creek 7½',*
                                                  Nelson Mtn. 7½'
Bear Meadow, Mountain (9,526–9,512)   *Huntington Lake 15',*
                                                  Nelson Mtn. 7½'

The creek was named by Frank Dusy in the 1870s "because a miner had once been frightened by a bear." (Gustav Eisen: Eisen papers, CAS.) The creek is named on T. S. Solomons' map of 1896. The USGS apparently named the meadow and mountain; all three features are named on the first *Kaiser* 30' map, 1904. (SiNF)

Bear Creek Spire (over 13,720–13,713)   *Mt. Abbot 15', Mt. Hilgard 7½'*

Named by J. N. LeConte, James Hutchinson, and Duncan McDuffie in 1908, for the obvious reason that it is at the head of the Hilgard Branch of Bear Creek. (*SCB* 7, no. 1, Jan. 1909: 12, and map.) (SiNF, INF)

Bear Lake   *Tower Peak 15'*

While making a field survey, park rangers Gallison and Wallis saw a large bear at the lake. Because it was so "undomesticated"—unlike those of Yosemite Valley—they were favorably impressed, and named the lake in its honor. (YNP field survey, 1952.) (YNP)

Bear Paw Lake   *Mt. Abbot 15', Mt. Hilgard 7½'*

Named in 1952 by Elden H. Vestal of the DFG. (DFG survey.) At the headwaters of the Hilgard Branch and the East Fork of Bear Creek are more than 20 lakes. Thirteen of them have "bear" or bear-related names. All were apparently named by a DFG survey party in 1952, out of a need to identify the lakes by name rather than number. There is no sighting of a bear or a bear episode connected with any of these lakes.

"Bear Paw Lake" was "Bearpaw Lake" on the 15-minute quad. (SiNF)

Bearpaw Meadow   *Triple Divide Peak 15'*

"I'll tell you how Bearpaw Meadow was named. Jim Hamilton, for whom Hamilton Lakes were named, and Alex Anderson of Yokohl, used to pasture stock in that country. One of Anderson's men set a trap for a bear in the meadow, fastening the trap to a log. A bear was trapped by the paw. He dragged the log through the meadow until it caught between some rocks. The bear went over a little cliff, but the trap with the paw sticking up was just visible at the edge of the precipice as Anderson's man came to it. He named the place 'Bearpaw Meadow.' " (Robert Barton, *Los Tulares,* no. 40, June 1959.) (SNP)

Bearskin Meadow, Creek, Grove   *Tehipite Dome 15'*
The meadow was named first; the creek and grove derive from it. "Said to be named on account of a snow-patch that was the last to go in summer and which resembled a bearskin." (Farquhar: J. B. Agnew.) (SeNF)

Beartrap Lake   *Mt. Abbot 15', Mt. Hilgard 7½'*
Named by the DFG in 1952. (See **Bear Paw Lake.**) (SiNF)

Beartrap Meadow   *Giant Forest 15'*
The meadow "apparently was named by the sheepmen of the 1880s who used a large trap to catch a marauding bear when he went down to the creek for water." (*Newsletter* 1, no. 2, Jan. 1969: 9.) (SeNF)

Bearup Lake   *Tower Peak 15'*
"Named by Lieutenant N. F. McClure for a soldier in his detachment, 1894. Pronounced 'Beer-up.' " (Farquhar: McClure.) (YNP)

Beasore Meadows, Creek   *Shuteye Peak 15'*
George Powell, a pioneer prospector, said the correct spelling was "Beausore;" according to Sam Ellis this was pronounced "Bā' saw." Named for a stockman of the 1860s. (Farquhar: Versteeg.) Said to be named for the original settler, Tom Beasore, who lived until 1953. (Eccleston, 76.)
    Theodore S. Solomons spelled it "Basaw." (*Overland Monthly* 28, no. 164, Aug. 1896: 141.) The GLO plat of 1882 calls it "Basow's Meadows." (SiNF)

Beatitude, Mount   *Yosemite Valley 1:24,000*
Not on the map. The point marked "Old Inspiration Point" was originally known as "Mount Beatitude." (See **Inspiration Point** and **Old Inspiration Point.**)
    "There is a truism that 'Some things can be done as well as others.' In our opinion a full description is not one of them. A passage in the good book says, 'Eye hath not seen, neither hath ear heard, neither hath it entered into the heart of man to conceive what there is laid up in heaven for those who love and serve God.' Now . . . we simply wish to apply the language to those who have the good fortune to see Yo Semite from this stand-point." (Hutchings, *Scenes,* 1871, 144–45.) (YNP)

Beck Lakes (9,846 and 9,833)   *Devils Postpile 15', Mt. Ritter 7½'*
John Beck named the lakes for himself about 1882. He was one of the owners of the Minaret Mines, located on the south slope of Iron Mountain. (Farquhar: Versteeg.) Beck had a prospecting hole at the outlet of the lower Beck Lake sometime during the 1890s. (USGS, letter from Arch Mahan of Red's Meadow, Oct. 7, 1953.) (INF)

Beetlebug Lake (9,604)   *Kaiser Peak 15', Sharktooth Peak 7½'*
Probably named by Elden H. Vestal of the DFG, who surveyed the lake in 1953. (DFG survey.) (SiNF)

Belknap Creek; Belknap Camp Grove *Camp Nelson 15'*
Corrington G. Belknap patented 120 acres in sec. 35, T. 20 S., R. 31 E. in 1891. (SeNF)

Bench Lake *Mt. Pinchot 15' and 7½'*
Named by J. N. LeConte in 1902. (Farquhar: LeConte.) (KCNP)

Bench Lakes *Crystal Crag 7½'*
Probably named by the DFG. The names "Upper East Bench Lake" and "Lower East Bench Lake" were used by a survey party in 1961. (DFG survey.) The lakes are not named on the *Devils Postpile* 15' quad. The name applies to four lakes in the lower-right corner of the quad, just south of Lost Keys Lakes. (SiNF)

Bennett Creek *Kaweah 15'*
William F. Bennett was a stockman in the 1870s. (Farquhar: Walter Fry.) (SNP, SeNF)

Bennett Juniper *Dardanelles Cone 15', Dardanelle 7½'*
Said to be the largest and oldest specimen of the western juniper: over 40 feet in circumference, 85 feet high, several thousand years old. Discovered by Clarence Bennett in 1932. (*Historic Spots*, 565.) A lone juniper located near the center of sec. 5, T. 5 N., R. 20 E. (BGN Name Report.) (StNF)

Bennettville (site) *Tuolumne Meadows 15'*
Named for Thomas Bennett, Jr., president of the Great Sierra Consolidated Silver Mining Company. More than $350,000 was spent in building the town and developing the Great Sierra Mine, but not a penny's worth of gold, silver, or any other metal was taken out. Bennettville (also known as "Tioga") had a post office from March 1882 to November 1884. (Post Offices.) (INF)

Benson Lake *Tower Peak 15'*
Benson Pass (over 10,080) *Matterhorn Peak 15'*
Harry Coupland Benson (1857–1924), army officer; stationed in Sequoia National Park, 1891–92; acting superintendent of Yosemite National Park, 1905–08; in Yellowstone National Park, 1909–10. He was noted for his fanatical devotion to duty, and thus acquired the nickname "Batty" Benson. (Paden, 232.)
Benson developed many trails in Yosemite. The old "Hs" on trees throughout the park north of the Tuolumne River were cut by Benson's troops. (Bingaman, *Pathways*, 36.) The names were given in 1895. (Farquhar: Benson.) A biography and portrait of Benson are in *SCB* 12, no. 2, 1925: 175–79. (YNP)

Bernice Lake (10,217) *Tuolumne Meadows 15'*
Bernice Carle Lewis, wife of Washington B. Lewis, the first civilian superintendent of Yosemite National Park, 1916–28. (Farquhar files.) (YNP)

Beryl Lake (8,751) *Huntington Lake 15', Dogtooth Peak 7½'*
Possibly named by Scott M. Soule of the DFG, who surveyed the lake in 1946. (DFG survey.) (SiNF)

Betty Lake   *Huntington Lake 15', Nelson Mtn. 7½'*
Named in 1935 by Ted Anderson, former Dinkey packer, for his daughter.
(DFG survey.) (SiNF)

Beville Lake   *Triple Divide Peak 15'*
Named after a Visalia family that took outings in the mountains. (Farquhar
files: Versteeg from Geo. W. Stewart.) The name first sppears on the 1924 edition of the *Tehipite* 30' map. (KCNP)

Big Arroyo   *Triple Divide Peak 15', Kern Peak 15'*
In early days, Big Arroyo was called "Jenny Lind Cañon;" the stream in the
canyon was known as "Crabtree Creek." (Elliott, *Guide,* 41.)
"John Crabtree and Bill Corse had a mine on the east side of the Great
Western Divide which they named the Jenny Lind Mine; they called the creek
Jenny Lind Creek." (Farquhar: G. W. Stewart.) Crabtree and Corse obviously
were afflicted by memories of Jenny Lind, "the Swedish Nightingale" (1820–
87), an opera singer of international renown who had been in America from
1850 to 1852. (SNP)

Big Baldy (8,209); **Big Baldy Ridge, Grove**   *Giant Forest 15'*
Big Baldy's "summit is smooth and bare, and reflects the sun's rays.
Prominent from the valley floor throughout Tulare County." (*Newsletter* 1, no.
3, May 1969: 7.) An early name; it appeared on the 1905 *Tehipite* 30' map.
(KCNP)

Big Bear Lake   *Mt. Abbot 15', Mt. Hilgard 7½'*
Named in 1952 by Elden H. Vestal of the DFG. (DFG survey. See **Bear
Paw Lake.**) (SiNF)

Big Bird Lake (9,775)   *Triple Divide Peak 15'*
"Name given by James Clay, 1902; suggested by the tracks of a large bird
seen on the shore." (Farquhar: Clay.) The name appears as "Dollar Lake" on
early editions of the *Tehipite* 30' map. At the recommendation of the Sierra Club
it was changed to its present name on the edition of 1924, and was made official
by a BGN decision in 1962. (KCNP)

Big Chief Lake   *Mt. Abbot 15', Mt. Hilgard 7½'*
The largest of 10 lakes on West Pinnacles Creek. Named by Elden H. Vestal
of the DFG in August 1951. (Heyward Moore, *FPP* 26, no. 2, summer 1984: 6.)
(SiNF)

Big Five Lakes   *Mineral King 15'*
Named "The Five Lakes" by W. F. Dean in the 1890s. (Junep.) The name
was changed to "Big Five Lakes" beginning with the fourth edition of the
Kaweah 30' map, 1926, to accommodate the naming of nearby **Little Five
Lakes.** (SNP)

Big Horn Lake   *Tuolumne Meadows 15'*
"Because Mrs. Spuller discovered the core of a set of Sierra Bighorn sheep at
Finger Lake." (Spuller.) (INF)

Big Meadow   *Yosemite 15', Yosemite Valley 1:24,000*
Probably named by the Whitney Survey, since it is on the Hoffmann and Gardiner map of 1863–67 as "Big Meadows."
"As the name implies, these are extensive grassy flats that afford excellent pasturage for stock, and where much of the grain-hay used in Yo Semite is produced." (Hutchings, *In the Heart*, 290–91.) (YNP)

Big Meadows; Big Meadows Creek   *Giant Forest 15'*
". . . the ridge widened out into a plateau occupied by a large meadow; a number of cattle had been driven here, and the place was known to hunters as the 'Big Meadows.' " (Whitney, *Geology*, 370.) (SeNF)

Big Oak Flat Road   *Lake Eleanor 15', El Portal 15', Yosemite 15'*
The road reached the floor of Yosemite Valley on July 17, 1874, exactly one month after the Coulterville Road to the valley was opened. The name derives from the town of Big Oak Flat—which earlier was known as "Savage's Diggings," for Major Savage, commander of the Mariposa Batallion. (Paden, 124.)
"Nor must we pass unseen the sturdy branch-lopped and root-cut veteran trunk of a noble and enormous oak some eleven feet in diameter, still standing on our right; as it was from this once famous tree that 'Big Oak Flat,' the village through which we are passing, received its name." (Hutchings, *Scenes*, 1876, 95.)
"Big Oak Flat is a little mining village, on a little flat. The 'big oak' which gave name to the place has been undermined and killed. . . . It was nearly ten feet in diameter, and in the days of its glory must have been a grand tree." (Brewer, *Up and Down*, 401.)
The Big Oak Flat Road between Crane Flat and the valley was replaced by a modern road in 1940. The old road was used for downhill traffic only until October 1942, when the "zigzags" were destroyed by rockslides. (Paden, 299.)
The road was called the "Chinese and Yosemite Road" on the 1880 GLO plat, and "Groveland to Yosemite Road" on a 1906 GLO survey of the Yosemite National Park boundaries. (YNP, StNF)

Big Pete Meadow   *Mt. Goddard 15', North Palisade 7½'*
The name first appeared on the 15-minute quad, 1948. It has no significance, other than that the meadow is bigger than nearby "Little Pete Meadow." But *that* meadow was named for a person rather than because it is little. (KCNP)

Big Pine Creek; Big Pine Lakes   *Mt. Goddard 15', Mt. Thompson 7½',*
                        Big Pine 15', Split Mtn. 7½', Coyote Flat 7½'
A. W. Von Schmidt's township plat of 1856 showed present Big Pine Creek as "Pine Creek." In the early days there were many large pines along the creek from the present town to well up in the canyon. All were cut by the Bell sawmill. It is said that the town and creek were named for a group of unusually large pines, half a mile southwest of town, that was still standing at the turn of the century. (INF archives.) The Big Pine Lakes, numbered "First" through

"Seventh," probably were named by the DFG or the USGS as a matter of convenient identification. (INF)

Big Shot Lake   *Blackcap Mtn. 7½'*
Probably named by J. F. Bates of the DFG when he surveyed the lake in 1954. (DFG survey.) The name "Shot" probably refers to a shotglass, and was coined because of the lake's proximity to "Devils Punchbowl." (See also **Little Shot Lake** and **Jigger Lakes.**) The lake is not named on the *Blackcap Mtn.* 15' quad. It is the second small lake just east of Devils Punchbowl. (SiNF)

Big Spring   *Mineral King 15'*
"A natural spring several feet in diameter; used by early-day cattlemen." (*Newsletter* 1, no. 3, May 1969: 8.) (SNP)

Big Stump Grove   *Giant Forest 15'*
A grove of Big Trees that was cut down between 1880 and 1890. It contains the stump of the "Mark Twain Tree," and the stump of "Old Adam," which is 28 feet in diameter, was once used as a dance floor, and perhaps was the largest of all sequoias. (Fry and White, 103; Hall, *Sequoia,* 137.) (SNP)

Bigelow Peak (10,539), **Lake**   *Tower Peak 15'*
Major John Bigelow, Jr., Ninth Cavalry, US Army, acting superintendent of Yosemite National Park in 1904. (Farquhar.) The peak was named first; the name appears on the third edition (1912) of the *Dardanelles* 30' map. The lake was not named until the 1956 *Tower Peak* 15' quad. (YNP, StNF)

Bighorn Lake   *Mt. Abbot 15', Graveyard Peak 7½'*
Named in 1902 by Lincoln Hutchinson, J. S. Hutchinson, and C. A. Noble. "An exclamation of surprise burst from one of the party, and we found directly before us a band of 'big-horn' sheep. We had supposed the animal long since extinct in the Sierra, and at first we could scarcely believe our eyes. . . . We viewed them at leisure through our glasses, till suddenly they took fright and one after another set off with easy bounds over the boulders and snow. . . . Before us now lay a saddle in the ridge. . . . Two of the sheep . . . made for this saddle, and we followed closely in their footsteps. . . . there confronted us a wild array of rugged gorges and peaks glowing pink in the sinking sun, and deep down in the amphitheater below us lay an azure lake." (*SCB* 4, no. 3, Feb. 1903: 202–3.) A footnote added, "This we named Big Horn Lake." (SiNF)

Bighorn Lake   *Blackcap Mtn. 15' and 7½'*
Probably named by William A. Dill of the DFG, who surveyed the lake in 1948. (DFG survey.) (SiNF)

Bighorn Park   *Mount Whitney 15' and 7½'*
In the 1920s and early '30s various informal names were used: "Ibex Park," "Ibex Meadow," and "Outpost Camp." The present name was suggested in 1936 by Chester Versteeg. Sierra bighorn sheep were native to the area, but are no longer found there. (INF archives.) (INF)

Bighorn Plateau (11,407)   *Mount Whitney 15' and 7½', Mt. Kaweah 7½'*
"Named for the mountain sheep seen in the area." (*Newsletter* 1, no. 3, May

1969: 8.) The statement would be more accurate if it said "formerly seen." The name applies to an area and to a specific point, where there is a VABM—which makes one suspect that the name was given by the USGS. On earlier maps the high point was unnamed. The plateau was called "Sandy Plateau" on *Mt. Whitney* 30' maps, 1907 through 1927; changed to the present name on the edition of 1933. (SNP)

Biledo Meadow   *Yosemite 15'*
There are two cabins at Biledo Meadow. The one made of round timbers was built by Thomas Biledo in 1890. (The name was correctly spelled Biledeaux, according to a YNP ranger who knew him.) Biledo was a French-Canadian who came to the region in the 1880s, and was employed by the Mount Raymond Mining Company. (Robert F. Uhte, "Yosemite's Pioneer Cabins," *SCB* 36, no. 5, May 1951: 51.) (SiNF)

Bingaman Lake   *Mono Craters 15'*
John W. Bingaman was a YNP ranger from 1921 to 1956. "In 1930 I was a Patrol Ranger in Tuolumne Meadows. I decided to plant an unnamed lake in my district. I took two pack mules loaded with 6,000 rainbow-fry, making a successful plant. By so doing I established the right to call the lake Bingaman." (Bingaman's handwritten statement in YNP files.) (YNP)

Birch Mountain (4,146 m.–13,665), **Lake**   *Big Pine 15', Split Mtn. 7½'*
Namer unknown. The peak is identified in a Chester Versteeg photo in *SCB* 11, no. 4, 1923: opp. 422. A BGN decision in 1938, confirming the name, states: "The original Paiute name for the mountain is said to be paokrung and to mean 'mountain of stone.' " (INF)

Birchim Lake   *Mt. Tom 15', Mount Tom 7½'*
Possibly for James G. Birchim, who came to Round Valley in 1865. With his partners Joel Smith and A. A. Cashbaugh he built the Bishop Creek Flouring Mill. (INF archives.) Birchim patented 160 acres in secs. 5 and 8, T. 6 S., R. 31 E. in 1872, and homesteaded 160 acres in sec. 9 in 1877. (INF)

Bishop Creek   *Yosemite 15'*
Samuel Addison Bishop (1825–1893), First Sergeant in the Mariposa Battalion. The creek is named on the Hoffmann and Gardiner map, 1863–67; on the Wheeler Survey atlas sheet 56D, 1878–79, it appears as "Bishop's Creek." This is the same Bishop for whom the Owens Valley town and several geographic features are named. (YNP, SiNF)

Bishop Creek   *Mt. Goddard 15', Mt. Tom 15', Mt. Darwin 7½',*
                                             Mt. Thompson 7½', Tungsten Hills 7½'
Bishop Pass, Lake   *Mt. Goddard 15', North Palisade 7½'*
Bishop Park   *Mt. Goddard 15', Mt. Thompson 7½'*
Samuel A. Bishop came to California from Virginia in 1849; with the Mariposa Battalion in 1851; later at Fort Tejon with General Edward F. Beale; went to Owens Valley and settled on the creek that now bears his name, about three miles southwest of the town of Bishop. He left the area in 1864, became

one of the first supervisors of Kern County in 1866, and built the first San Jose streetcar line, in 1868. (Farquhar; Gudde, *Place Names*, 30; *Historic Spots*, 117.) (INF)

Black Bear Lake   *Mt. Abbot 15', Mt. Hilgard 7½'*
Named by Elden H. Vestal of the DFG in 1952. (See **Bear Paw Lake.**) (SiNF)

Black Divide   *Mt. Goddard 15' and 7½', North Palisade 7½'*
Named by George R. Davis, topographer for the USGS, when making the *Mt. Goddard* 30' map, 1907–09. (Farquhar: J. N. LeConte.) (KCNP)

Black Giant (13,330)   *Mt. Goddard 15' and 7½'*
"A few miles to the south rose a particularly inviting point, which certainly commands a peerless view. But time forbade an ascent this year [1904], so I named it the Black Giant and wondered how long it would stand as it has so far stood, an untrodden summit." (J. N. LeConte in *SCB* 5, no. 3, Jan. 1905: 236.) When making the *Mt. Goddard* 30' map in 1907–09, the USGS, apparently unaware of the name given by LeConte, called the peak "Mount Goode." In 1926, a BGN decision restored the name "Black Giant" and moved the name "Mount Goode" about five miles east-northeast to a peak on the Sierra crest. (Farquhar.) The first three editions of the *Mt. Goddard* 30' map contain the error; it is corrected beginning with the 1928 edition. (KCNP)

Black Mountain (4,051 m.–13,289)   *Mt. Pinchot 15',*
                                                       Mt. Clarence King 7½'
Named by the Wheeler Survey in the late 1870s. (*SCB* 4, no. 4, June 1903: 291; also LeConte, *Alpina*, 10.) (KCNP, INF)

Black Peak (9,773–9,771)   *Huntington Lake 15', Dogtooth Peak 7½'*
The name "Black Peak" appeared on the first *Kaiser* 30' map, in 1904, and remained that until 1982, when it was called "Potato Mtn" on the *Dogtooth Peak 7½'* map. "The name comes from the rock formation on top of the mountain; it looks like a pile of giant potatoes." (USGS name report.) However, a BGN decision in 1983 changed the name back to "Black Peak," so perhaps on a later edition of the *Dogtooth Peak* quad we will see a return to the early name. (SiNF)

Black Rock Pass (approx. 11,600)   *Mineral King 15'*
Judge W. B. Wallace said he went over this pass with a horse and pack stock in 1879, and believed he was the first to do so. It was once known as "Black Pass" and as "Cliff Pass." It was called "Black Rock Pass" on Lt. Milton F. Davis's map of 1896. The name derives from a band of black rock that is in strong contrast to the red and white formations nearby. (Farquhar.) (SNP)

Black Spring   *Yosemite 15', Yosemite Valley 1:24,000*
"These take their name from the color of the rich alluvial through which the delightfully refreshing waters of two full-flowing cold springs hurry down a deep-cut gully. . . . This, in appearance, is only one spring, while in reality it is formed of two, that boil out from beneath a large flat rock about a hundred yards distant, on sides opposite to each other." (Hutchings, *In the Heart*, 400.) (YNP)

Blackcap Mountain (11,560–11,559), **Basin**   *Blackcap Mtn. 15' and 7½'*
Probably named by the USGS during the 1907–09 survey for the *Mt. Goddard* 30' map; both names are on the first edition, 1912. (SiNF)

Blackie Lake   *Merced Peak 15'*
The DFG surveyors of this lake in 1946 reported that warden Herb Black said the lake was sometimes called "Blackie Lake," after himself. (DFG survey.) (SiNF)

Blackrock Mountain (9,606)   *Hockett Peak 15'*
Named by hunters for a large black boulder on the summit. (*Newsletter* 1, no. 3, May 1969: 9.) (INF, SeNF)

Blackrock Lake (10,444)   *Blackcap Mtn. 15', Mt. Henry 7½'*
Probably named by William A. Dill or Charles K. Fisher of the DFG when they surveyed the lake in 1947. (DFG survey.) (SiNF)

Blanc Lake   *Mount Tom 7½'*
Named in 1954 by Ralph Beck of the DFG. (Phil Pister. See **Alsace Lake.**) (SiNF)

Blayney Meadows   *Blackcap Mtn. 15', Ward Mountain 7½'*
Spelled "Blaney" on all maps up until publication of the *Ward Mountain* quad in 1982. For William Farris Blayney, who grazed sheep on the meadows from about 1872 to 1880. (BGN decision, 1970.)
    "The main headquarters at Blayney Meadows commanded the feeding grounds of the Paiute and French canyon, the upper San Joaquin and Evolution meadows; and at times the Goddard basin was also used." (Winchell, 158.) The original name was "Lost Valley." (Letter, Winchell to T. S. Solomons, March 30, 1896, in SC papers at BL.) Also known in early days as "Hidden Valley" or "Hidden Valley Meadows." (SiNF)

Bloods Toll Station; Bloods Creek   *Big Meadow 15', Tamarack 7½'*
Bloods Ridge, Meadow, Point (7,824)   *Tamarack 7½'*
Harvey S. Blood (1840–1910), a prominent citizen of Calaveras and Alpine counties, who settled in Grizzly Bear in the early 1860s. He owned and operated the main tollgate for the Big Tree–Carson Valley Turnpike, and collected tolls from 1864 until he died. (Wood, 44.)
    Blood patented 160 acres in 1880, and another 160 in 1889. He had one daughter, Reba, for whom Mount Reba is named. (StNF)

Bloody Canyon   *Mono Craters 15'*
    "After crossing the pass [Mono Pass], the way leads down Bloody Canyon—a terrible trail. You would all pronounce it utterly inaccessible to horses, yet pack trains come down, but the bones of several horses or mules and the stench of another told that all had not passed safely. . . . It was a bold man who first took a horse up there. The horses were so cut by sharp rocks that they named it 'Bloody Canyon,' and it has held the name—and it is appropriate—part of the way the rocks in the trail are literally sprinkled with blood from the animals." (Brewer, *Up and Down*, 415–16.)

Blossom Lakes   *Mineral King 15'*
Named in 1909 by R. B. Marshall, USGS, for Charles W. Blossom, a
Sequoia National Park ranger. (Farquhar: Marshall.) Blossom was one of only
four rangers on duty in 1906; Chief Ranger in 1916. (SNP)

Blue Canyon   *Tehipite Dome 15', Marion Peak 15',*
                                              Mt. Goddard 15' and 7½'
Blue Canyon Falls   *Marion Peak 15'*
Blue Canyon Peak (11,860–11,849)   *Mt. Goddard 15' and 7½'*
The canyon and falls were named by Frank Dusy and Gustav Eisen in the
late 1870s. (Elliott, *Guide,* 19; Eisen papers, CAS.)
The peak may have been named by J. N. LeConte in 1902. It appears in his
1903 list of peaks in the Sierra over 12,000 feet (*SCB* 4, no. 4, June 1903: 291.)
He estimated the altitude as 13,000 feet. His latitude is correct, but his longitude
indicates he applied the name to what is now "Finger Peak," which is just over a
mile farther west and is 12,404 feet. The USGS probably relocated the name
"Blue Canyon Peak" and named Finger Peak during the 1907–09 survey for the
Mt. Goddard 30' map; both names are in their present locations on the first edition, 1912. Blue Canyon acquires the name "Blue Canyon Creek" on the two
Mt. Goddard quads, an inconsistency that will doubtless be rectified on future
maps. (KCNP)

Blue Heaven Lake (11,821)   *Mt. Goddard 15', Mt. Darwin 7½'*
John Schober named it. "It was just about as high as you can get." (Art
Schober.) (INF)

Blue Lake (10,398)   *Mt. Goddard 15', Mt. Thompson 7½'*
Art Schober said that the lake was commonly known by this name before
1930. It was promoted as an official name by Chester Versteeg in 1936. The
name first appeared on the 15-minute quad, 1948. (INF archives.) (INF)

Upper Blue Lake (8,136)   *Markleeville 15', Carson Pass 7½'*
Lower Blue Lake (8,055); **Blue Creek**   *Markleeville 15',*
                                               Pacific Valley 7½'
The Blue Lakes "are used as storage reservoirs by the Amador Canal
Company. They have . . . been spoken of in connection with a scheme for
supplying San Francisco with water." (Wheeler Survey, *Report,* 1878, 142.)
(ENF)

Bohler Canyon   *Mono Craters 15'*
Joseph Bohler homesteaded 160 acres in sec. 33, T. 1 N., R. 26 E. in 1872,
and an additional 160 acres in secs. 27 and 34 in 1876. (INF)

Bolton Brown, Mount (4,112 m.–13,538)   *Big Pine 15', Split Mtn. 7½'*
Bolton Coit Brown, professor of drawing and painting at Stanford, 1891–
1902. Brown, often accompanied by his wife, Lucy (for whom "Lucys Foot
Pass" is named), made several remarkable exploring and mountaineering trips
in the Sierra Nevada between 1895 and 1899. He published half a dozen articles
in the *Sierra Club Bulletin,* accompanying them with a number of superb line
drawings.

The peak was named by Chester Versteeg and Rudolph Berls on August 14, 1922, when they made the first ascent. ". . . the true summit was a knife-edge jutting twelve yards to the east. Alternating on one side and then the other of the knife, the last few steps along a narrow ledge on which two people could not have passed, we stopped, not on, but beside, the summit-rock. It stood less than shoulder-high above us. It was impossible to stand on this splinter. We patted it affectionately. . . ." (Chester Versteeg in *SCB* 11, no 4, 1923: 426.) (KCNP, INF)

Bond Pass (approx. 9,700)   *Tower Peak 15'*
Frank Bond of the General Land Office; a member of the Yosemite National Park Boundary Commission in 1904; later chairman of the US Board on Geographic Names. (Farquhar: R. B. Marshall.) (YNP, StNF)

Boneyard Meadow   *Huntington Lake 15' and 7½'*
The meadow got its name from the drought of 1877. Down in the valley, nearly all the sheep died. Sheepmen rounded up a remaining few thousand head, drove them up to the meadow, and were hit by a heavy spring snowstorm that buried the feed. All the sheep died. (SiNF History Files.) The name appears on T. S. Solomons' 1896 map. (SiNF)

Bonita Lake   *Mt. Henry 7½'*
The name originates with the DFG; it derives from the scientific name for golden trout, *Salmo aguabonita*. (DFG survey.) On the *Blackcap Mtn.* 15' quad it is the first lake northeast of Upper Indian Lake. (SiNF)

Bonita Meadows, Creek, Flat   *Hockett Peak 15'*
Bonita is the Spanish word for "pretty." The names for the creek and meadows were on the first *Olancha* 30' map, 1907. (SeNF)

Boole Tree   *Tehipite Dome 15'*
The third largest known Sequoia, after the General Grant and General Sherman trees. Boole was the general manager of the Sanger Lumber Company when trees were being cut in this area, and the legend has it that he was responsible for saving the tree—the only sequoia that wasn't cut in the entire Converse Basin. Hank Johnston (*Redwoods*, p. 78) wrote that no one knows whether Boole had a role in saving the tree. (SeNF)

Boothe Lake   *Tuolumne Meadows 15'*
Named for Clyde Boothe, a YNP ranger from 1915 to 1927. (Bingaman, *Guardians*, 93–94.) Once the site of the Boothe Lake High Sierra Camp—established in 1923—which was later moved half a mile and renamed "Vogelsang." (YNP)

Boreal Plateau   *Kern Peak 15'*
A name suggested by Oliver Kehrlein because of the frigid, windswept character of the plateau. (François Matthes, SNP files. BGN decision in 1941.) (SNP)

Boron Springs   *Mt. Pinchot 15'*
The bad pronunciation of an informant or the inadequate hearing of a

surveyor has transformed a man's name into one of the elements. The land encompassing the springs was homesteaded in 1917 by John C. *Borum:* 156 acres in secs. 21 and 22, T. 13 S., R. 34 E. (INF)

Bottleneck Lake (11,122)   *Mt. Goddard 15', Mt. Darwin 7½'*
Named in the 1930s by John Schober for its shape. (Art Schober.) (INF)

Boundary Hill   *Hetch Hetchy Reservoir 15'*
A point on the boundary of the original Yosemite Grant. By the act of June 30, 1864, the federal government granted to the state of California as a state park the " 'Cleft' or 'Gorge' known as the Yo-Semite Valley, and . . . the 'Mariposa Big Trees Grove.' " The grant was made "upon the express condition that the premises shall be held for public use, resort, and recreation." The name "Boundary Hill" was given by Lt. Macomb of the Wheeler Survey. (YNP)

Bourland Mountain (7,691–7,692), **Meadow**   *Pinecrest 15',*
                                                    Cherry Lake North 7½'
Bourland Creek   *Pinecrest 15' and 7½', Cherry Lake North 7½'*
Named for John L. Bourland, sheriff of Tuolumne County, 1865–68. (StNF files.) (StNF)

Boyden Cave   *Tehipite Dome 15'*
"The cave was discovered by P. H. Boyden about five years ago [1907] and is at the point where the State road is expected to bridge the river. Mr. Boyden expects to light the cave with electricity, make ladders for the various chambers and get his pay by acting as guide." (*Inyo Register,* November 7, 1912.) (SeNF)

Bradley, Mount (4,043 m.–13,289)   *Mount Whitney 15',*
                                                    Mt. Williamson 7½'
Cornelius Beach Bradley (1843–1936) taught at Oakland High School, 1875–82; instructor and professor of rhetoric at the University of California, 1882–1911. Bradley was a charter member of the Sierra Club, and one of the 27 who signed the articles of incorporation on June 4, 1892. He was a director of the club until 1902, and was editor of the *Sierra Club Bulletin,* 1895–97. (Memorial in *SCB* 22, no. 1, Feb. 1937: 101–2)
The peak was named on July 5, 1898. "But unfortunately I was not on hand to save the other party from the serious indiscretion of naming their peak Mt. Bradley. I protest that I had done nothing to deserve such treatment at their hands. . . . there seems now no way to remedy the mischief, unless it be by making the ascent myself some time, and stealing the record!" (*SCB* 2, no. 5, Jan. 1899: 273–74.) (KCNP, INF)

Brainerd Lake   *Big Pine 15', Split Mtn. 7½'*
Lawson Brainerd was a White Mountain District ranger from 1924 to 1929. (INF archives.) The name was incorrectly spelled "Brainard" on the 15-minute quad. (INF)

Branigan Lake (also **Upper** and **Middle Branigan Lake)**   *Tower Peak 15'*
Branigan Lake was named in 1894 by Lt. N. F. McClure for a soldier of his

detachment. Branigan was later killed in the Philippines. (Farquhar: McClure. See also *SCB* 1, no. 5, Jan. 1895: 183.) The names of the upper and middle lakes were added to the *Tower Peak* 15' map, 1956. (YNP)

Brave Lake   *Mt. Abbot 15', Graveyard Peak 7½'*
The nearby Lake of the Lone Indian was named in 1902. When the *Mt. Abbot* 15' map was published in 1953 it acquired a number of Indian-type names: "Brave," "Warrior," and "Papoose." The situation became even worse on the *Graveyard Peak* quad, which also has "Chief" and "Squaw" lakes. It is possible that Brave Lake was named by William A. Dill of the DFG in 1945. (SiNF)

Breeze Creek   *Hetch Hetchy Reservoir 15', Tower Peak 15'*
Breeze Lake   *Merced Peak 15'*
Named in 1896 for William F. Breeze of San Francisco, who assisted his brother-in-law, Lt. H. C. Benson, in compiling Benson's map of Yosemite National Park. (Farquhar: Benson.) (YNP)

Brewer, Mount (4,136 m.–13,570)   *Mount Whitney 15',*
                                                 Mt. Brewer 7½'
Brewer Creek   *Triple Divide Peak 15', Mount Whitney 15',*
                                                 Mt. Brewer 7½'
Big Brewer Lake   *Triple Divide Peak 15'*
William Henry Brewer (1828–1910), the principal assistant and chief operative in the field to Whitney on the first California State Geological Survey. Brewer was interested in geography, geology, and botany—all the sciences underlying or connected with agriculture. He was professor of agriculture at the Sheffield Scientific School at Yale from 1864 to 1903.

"From the Sugar Loaf Rock (Sugarloaf) there is a magnificent view up the valley to the group of mountains forming the western crest of the Sierra, the culminating point of which was named Mount Brewer." (Whitney, *Geology*, 377–78.)

The first ascent was made by Brewer and Charles F. Hoffmann on July 2, 1864. "Temp. 35. Up at dawn to climb a high cone about five miles East, towards which we have been working for some time. H. and I went and were 8 hours in reaching it, a very hard climb. The peak much higher than we anticipated, being some 13,600 ft. Grand view, but more desolate than I have seen before. . . . Slid down a great snow slope. We were less than two minutes in coming down what it had taken us over three hours to surmount." (Brewer diary, July 2, 1864, in BL.)

Brewer, Hoffmann, and Gardiner made the second ascent two days later. The peak apparently was not climbed again until three Sierra Club members did it in 1895. In 1896 a woman with another Sierra Club party found on the summit the bottle containing Brewer's record of the second ascent. This was later removed to the Sierra Club's rooms in San Francisco, where it was destroyed by the earthquake and fire of 1906. (See *SCB* 1, no. 7, Jan. 1896: 288–89; *SCB* 2, no. 2, May 1897: 88; *SCB* 11, no. 3, 1922: 252.) (KCNP)

Bridalveil Fall, Creek, Meadow, Moraine   *Yosemite 15',*
Yosemite Valley 1:24,000

Hutchings claimed that he suggested the name on his first visit to Yosemite, in 1855. " 'Is it not as graceful, and as beautiful, as the veil of a bride?' to which Mr. Ayres rejoined, 'That is suggestive of a very pretty and most apposite name. I propose that we now baptize it, and call it, 'The Bridal Veil Fall,' as one that is both characteristic and euphonious.' " (Hutchings, *In the Heart,* 89.) Another who claimed the honor of naming the fall wrote: "We make bold to call it Bridal Veil; and those who may have the felicity to witness the stream floating in the embrace of the morning breeze, will acknowledge the resemblance, and perhaps pardon the liberty we have taken in attempting to apply so poetical a name to this Queen of the Valley." (Warren Baer, editor, *Mariposa Democrat,* Aug. 5, 1856.)

There were some who didn't like the name at all. ". . . in 1856 it was christened 'Falls of Louise' in honor of the first lady of our party that entered the valley. Thank Heaven, the cataract wouldn't stand this nonsense; and it seemed to me to be pleading with us to have the 'Bridal Veil' fully thrown aside, that it might be known forever by its Indian baptism, 'Pohono.' " (*Boston Transcript,* Jan. 26, 1861.) Other early names were "Queen of the Valley" and "Cascade of the Rainbow."

The Indians did indeed call the fall "Pohono;" the name was still in use in 1863 when the Whitney Survey was there. (Brewer, *Up and Down,* 404. See **Pohono Trail** for the differing explanations of the word's meaning.)

The names of the meadow and the moraine appear only on the 1:24,000 map. (YNP)

Bridgeport Valley   *Bodie 15', Fales Hot Springs 15', Matterhorn Peak 15'*

The first name for the valley was "Big Meadows," given sometime in the late 1850s when the area was being settled. It was referred to by that name by Joseph LeConte in 1870. (*Ramblings,* 118.) In 1863 a blacksmith shop was built just east of a footbridge across the East Walker River. Several other buildings were erected close by; due to the proximity of the bridge, the community was called "Bridgeport." It became the county seat of Mono County in 1864. (Cain, 29.)

Bright Dot Lake (10,535)   *Mt. Morrison 15', Convict Lake 7½'*

Bill Garner, a former owner of the Convict Lake Resort, named the lake in the 1930s because it is a bright blue spot—and after his wife, Dorothy Bright. (Phil Pister, DFG.) (INF)

Brightman Flat   *Dardanelles Cone 15', Dardanelle 7½'*

G. W. Brightman, an early settler. (Cain, 17.) (StNF)

Broder Meadows   *Monache Mtn. 15'*

John "Jack" Broder and his brother Scott came to the Owens Valley in 1860. They were cattle raisers and miners. (INF archives.) (SeNF)

Broderick, Mount (6,706)   *Yosemite 15', Yosemite Valley 1:24,000*

David Colbreth Broderick (1820–1859), US Senator from California, 1857–59. He was killed in a duel with David S. Terry, Chief Justice of the

California Supreme Court, as the result of political differences. (*Historic Spots*, 412.)

The name was originally applied to what is now called "Liberty Cap," which was given that name in 1865. The King and Gardiner map of 1865 calls it "Cap of Liberty or Mt. Broderick." (YNP)

Brown Bear Lake   *Mt. Abbot 15', Mt. Hilgard 7½'*
Named by the DFG in 1952 or 1953. (See **Bear Paw Lake.**) (SiNF)

Brown Bear Pass   *Tower Peak 15'*
Called by this name for many years by packers and local people. (Letter to USGS, May 25, 1959, from Vern Eaton, Stanislaus National Forest. (StNF)

Brown Lake   *Mt. Goddard 15', Mt. Thompson 7½'*
A man named Brown stocked the lake with fish. (Art Schober.) (INF)

Bruce, Mount (9,728)   *Merced Peak 15'*
Albert O. Bruce patented 160 acres in sec. 35, T. 4 S., R. 21 E. in 1889, and another 160 acres in sec. 35 in 1892, giving him the north half of the section—covering all of what is now North Wawona. The name "Mount Bruce" was proposed by the Park Service in 1976 to commemorate the Bruce family, who pioneered in the Wawona area in the 1850s. Approved by the BGN in 1976. It is a peak on Buena Vista Crest, six miles southwest of Merced Peak. The name is not on the present *Merced Peak* 15' quad, but will undoubtedly be on the *Sing Peak 7½'* quad when it is published. (YNP)

Bryant Creek   *Topaz Lake 15', Wolf Creek 7½'*
Andrew S. Bryant logged below this point in 1865. (Maule.) (TNF)

Bubbs Creek   *Marion Peak 15', Mt. Pinchot 15', Mount Whitney 15',*
                         Mt. Clarence King 7½', Mt. Brewer 7½'
"We kept in the cañon of the King's River to a point far west from where a large tributary flows in from the south. This tributary is called 'Bubbs Creek.' It was named for John Bubbs, who was one of our party." (Thomas Keough, "Over Kearsarge Pass in 1864," *SCB* 10, no. 3, Jan. 1918: 340.) The Whitney Survey party led by William H. Brewer met this group of prospectors on the trail between Big Meadows and Kings Canyon on July 18, 1864. (Brewer, *Up and Down*, 529.) (KCNP)

Buck Canyon, Creek   *Triple Divide Peak 15'*
"Some say it was named for Jim Budd, an Indian." (Farquhar: G. W. Stewart.) "For lack of another name, an early-day hunter named it after a buck deer he had just killed." (*Newsletter* 1, no. 4, June 1969: 3.) (SNP)

Buckeye Creek, Pass, Ridge, Hot Spring   *Matterhorn Peak 15'*
From the Buckeye Mill Company, owned and operated by E. Roberts during the 1860s. (Maule.) The creek is on the 1877 GLO plat. The buckeye tree is not native to this area. One might speculate that the name was given for or by a native of Ohio. (TNF)

Budd Creek, Lake   *Tuolumne Meadows 15'*
James H. Budd, governor of California, 1895–99. The creek was named

first; it appears on the first edition of the *Mt. Lyell* 30' map, 1901. The lake name was ratified by a BGN decision June 30, 1932. (YNP)

Buena Vista Peak (9,709), **Creek, Lake, Trail**   *Yosemite 15'*
Buena Vista Crest   *Merced Peak 15'*
A common name; Spanish for "beautiful view." The peak name is an early one: it appears on the Hoffmann and Gardiner map, 1863–67. The name "Buena Vista Pass" has also been approved by the BGN (June 30, 1932), but is not on the *Yosemite* 15' map—no doubt due to lack of space. The pass is crossed by a trail just east of Buena Vista Lake, in sec. 12, T. 4 S., R. 22 E. (YNP)

Buffin Meadow   *Bass Lake 15'*
Named for Edward Wheaton *Buffum*, an entrepreneur and businessman, who may have had a timber claim on this meadow. (SiNF history files.) (SiNF)

Bull Run Peak (9,495–9,493), **Lake** (8,333), **Creek**
               Dardanelles Cone 15', Spicer Meadow Res. 7½'
Probably named by the Wheeler Survey; the peak is named on atlas sheet 56D, 1878–79. The lake and creek are not named until the 15-minute quad, 1956. (StNF)

Bullet Lake   *Blackcap Mtn. 15' and 7½'*
Possibly named by Jack Criqui of the DFG when he surveyed it in 1948. (DFG survey.) (SiNF)

Bullfrog Lake   *Mt. Pinchot 15', Mt. Clarence King 7½'*
Called "Bryanthus Lake" by John Muir, a name that was used as late as 1902. (*SCB* 4, no. 3, Feb. 1903: 191.) However, J. N. LeConte referred to it as "Bullfrog Lake" in 1890, and made no mention of the earlier name. (*SCB* 1, no. 3, Jan. 1894: 100.) (KCNP)

Bunnell Cascade, Point (8,193)   *Merced Peak 15'*
Lafayette Houghton Bunnell (1824–1903) proposed the name of Yosemite Valley and also named many other features in and near the valley. Bunnell was born in Rochester, NY, served in the Mexican War, and came to California in 1849. As a member of the Mariposa Battalion, he was one of the first white men to enter Yosemite Valley, on March 27, 1851. Bunnell's book, *Discovery of the Yosemite, and the Indian War of 1851, which led to that event,* went through four editions between 1880 and 1911.

Bunnell Point was formerly called "Sugarbowl Dome;" it was renamed shortly before 1920. (Hall, *Yosemite,* 82.) Bunnell Cascade (mistakenly spelled with one 'l' on the USGS map), on the Merced River at the head of Lost Valley, also had earlier names: "Washburn Cascade," "Diamond Shower Fall," and "Little Grizzly Falls." The present name was approved by a BGN decision in 1932. (YNP)

Bunny Lake   *Mt. Morrison 15', Bloody Mtn. 7½'*
It is possible, though not confirmed, that the lake was named for Ivan Bunny, who was appointed as a Forest Ranger in the Inyo Forest Reserve in 1901. (INF archives.) (INF)

Burgson Lake   *Dardanelles Cone 15', Donnell Lake 7½'*
    Probably named for Ed Burgson, a cattleman during the 1940s. He was co-owner of the B & G (Burgson & Ghiorso) Cattle Company of Sonora. (StNF files.) (StNF)

Burnside Mine, Lake   *Markleeville 15', Carson Pass 7½'*
    "Legend" says the mine and lake were named for Ambrose Everett Burnside (1824–1881), a Union general in the Civil War. Burnside was later Governor of Rhode Island and a US Senator. (*Alpine Heritage*, 47.) The names appeared in a GLO surveyor's field notes in 1875. (TNF)

Burnt Camp Creek   *Kaweah 15'*
    "A brush fire burned out this drainage." (USGS, from Charlie Pawley, a Three Rivers rancher, 1957.) The local usage is "Burnt Creek." By a BGN decision it will be "Burnt Canyon Creek" when the *Dennison Peak 7½'* map is published. (SNP, SeNF)

Burnt Corral Meadows   *Hockett Peak 15'*
    A corral to protect sheep from wild animals burned down. (*Newsletter* 1, no. 4, June 1969: 4.) (SeNF)

Burst Rock   *Pinecrest 15'*
    A natural chamber formed by a huge boulder. It is on the old emigrant road, and the name was presumably given by emigrants. (*Historic Spots*, 566.) An alternative name is "Birth Rock," from the tale of a Mrs. Wilson, with an emigrant party, who gave birth at this place. (StNF)

Burton Camp   *Kernville 15'*
    Named after an old rancher who used the area during roundup. Called "Corral Meadow" on the *Kernville 30'* maps, 1908 to 1955. (USGS, 1956.) (SeNF)

Burton Meadow, Pass, Grove   *Tehipite Dome 15'*
    "Named for a stockman of an early day." (Fry and White, 102.) J. N. LeConte mentioned "Burton's Meadow" in the account of his 1890 trip. (LeConte, *A Summer*, 27.) (SeNF)

By-Day Creek   *Fales Hot Springs 15'*
    George Byron Day, known as "By" Day, was the first white man to winter in Bridgeport Valley. (Cain, 25–26.) Day homesteaded 160 acres in sec. 25, T. 5 N., R. 24 E., in 1879, and patented an additional 160 acres in sec. 26 in 1885. (TNF)

Cabin Lake   *Devils Postpile 15', Mt. Ritter 7½'*
    The site of a cabin built by David Nidever (Nydiver Lakes) in the early 1900s. (INF archives.) (INF)

Cabin Meadow, Creek   *Giant Forest 15'*
    The meadow was named for a cabin left by an early sheepherder. (*Newsletter* 1, no. 4, June 1969: 5.) It first appeared on the 1905 *Tehipite 30'* map; the creek name was added in 1956. (SNP)

Cactus Point (3,738)   *Giant Forest 15'*
   Named by the Park Service for the number of Spanish dagger plants (*Yucca gloriosa*) on the mountain. (SNP files.) (SNP)

Cahoon Meadow, Creek, Rock Lookout (9,278)   *Mineral King 15'*
Cahoon Mountain (4,229)   *Kaweah 15'*
   George W. Cahoon lived on the South Fork of the Kaweah River in the late 1800s, and had a summer home at the meadow that bears his name. (Farquhar: G. W. Stewart.) Cahoon homesteaded 160 acres in sec. 16, T. 18 S., R. 29 E.— just southwest of Cahoon Mountain—in 1885. (Mtn., SeNF; others, SNP)

California Creek   *Bass Lake 15'*
   The name probably derives from the California Lumber Company, which built a mill on this creek in 1873–74. (Johnston, *Thunder,* 14.) (SiNF)

California Falls   *Tuolumne Meadows 15'*
   Named in July 1892. ". . . then follow the river closely to the head of a cascade of unrivaled beauty and grandeur. We named it the California Cascade." (R. M. Price, "Through the Tuolumne Cañon," *SCB* 1, no. 6, May 1895: 203.) (YNP)

Caltech Peak (4,216 m.–13,832)   *Mount Whitney 15', Mt. Brewer 7½'*
   Named for the California Institute of Technology; approved by a BGN decision in 1962. (SNP)

Camiaca Peak (11,739)   *Matterhorn Peak 15'*
   In the Yosemite National Park files there is a copy of a handwritten note from Doug Hubbard about an Indian who gave him a piece of root to chew; it tasted like ginseng. The Indian said that when he was young he gathered large quantities of the root and took them to the Sioux country to trade for buffalo robes. "He told me his name was Cloudy Camiaca. . . . later, when mapping a part of Yosemite National Park I applied it to a rather fine peak there. I thought I was playing quite a joke on Californians and at the same time giving Camiaca a final trip." (YNP, TNF)

Camp Curry   *Yosemite 15', Yosemite Valley 1:24,000*
   David A. Curry (1860–1917) and Jennie Foster Curry (1861–1948) set up seven tents in Yosemite Valley in 1899, the beginning of Camp Curry and the present Yosemite Park and Curry Company. (Farquhar; *YNN* 34, no. 1, Jan. 1955: 4.) (YNP)

Camp Seven (site)   *Tehipite Dome 15'*
   The site of a lumber camp of the Hume-Bennett Lumber Company (name changed to Sanger Lumber Company in 1917), constructed in 1917 in the Windy Gulch Grove of sequoias. (Johnston, *Redwoods,* 124.) (SeNF)

Canebrake Creek   *Lamont Peak 15', Onyx 15' and 7½', Walker Pass 7½'*
   In 1853 Robert S. Williamson, in charge of the Pacific Railroad Survey, found Indians collecting a kind of bulrush, or cane, along the banks of this creek. "As the creek had no name that I knew of, I endeavored to ascertain its Indian name, and found it to be Chay-o-poo-ya-päh—the accent strong on the last

syllable. I understood it to mean the creek of the bulrushes." (Williamson, *Report,* 15.) The present name—meaning "a thicket of canes"—was applied by the USGS on the first *Kernville* 30' map, 1908.

Campfire Lake   *Kaiser Peak 15' and 7½'*
Possibly named in 1947 by Don A. La Faunce of the DFG. (DFG survey.) (SiNF)

Cape Horn   *Blackcap Mtn. 15', Courtright Reservoir 7½'*
Possibly named by the USGS during the 1907–09 survey for the *Mt. Goddard* 30' map; it is on the first edition, 1912, and is also on a 1910 Sierra National Forest map. It is a narrow, sharp, jutting ridge. A cartographer with imagination may have likened its shape to Cape Horn at the tip of South America. (SiNF)

Caples Lake (7,798–7,797), **Creek**   *Silver Lake 15' and 7½',*
                                                        Tragedy Spring 7½'
James "Doc" Caples passed this way headed west in 1849. In the 1850s he returned to what was at first called "Lake Valley" by the early emigrants (later called "Twin Lakes"), and constructed a station that became a regular stopping place on the Carson Valley and Big Trees road—present-day State Route 88, the Carson Pass route. The present enlarged Caples Lake was formed by damming Caples Creek. Other early names were "Clear Lake" and "Summit Lake." An 1877 GLO Survey called the creek "Alpine Creek." (ENF)

Cardinal Mountain (4,083 m.–13,397)   *Mt. Pinchot 15' and 7½'*
Cardinal Lake   *Mt. Pinchot 15' and 7½', Big Pine 15', Split Mtn. 7½'*
George R. Davis of the USGS named the mountain because of the brilliant coloring of its summit—like the red cap of a cardinal. The lake was named from the mountain. (Farquhar: J. N. LeConte.) Both names appeared on the first edition of the *Mt. Whitney* 30' map in 1907. (KCNP)

Carillon, Mount (13,552)   *Mount Whitney 15' and 7½'*
The name was proposed by Chester Versteeg for the peak's bell-tower shape; approved by the BGN in 1938. (INF archives.) However, another reason has been cited for the origin of the name. "From the winds which whistle across the crest and through its shattered summit rocks producing the music of a carillon tower." (Los Angeles *Times,* March 30, 1938.) (SNP, INF)

Carol Col (11,762)   *Mount Tom 7½'*
Named for Carol Kassler Ransford (1928–1974). In 1973 she led a group of hikers over a previously unnamed ridge on the northwest rim of Humphreys Basin. Although the name does not appear on the 7½-minute quad, published in 1982, it was approved by the BGN in 1978. It is 0.2 mile east-southeast of Roget Lake. (SiNF)

Carroll Creek   *Olancha 15', Lone Pine 15', Mt. Langley 7½'*
For A. W. de la Cour Carroll, an early Sierra Club member. Carroll was a member of the fourth party to climb Mt. Williamson, and named Mt. LeConte in

1895. (*SCB* 1, no. 3, Jan. 1894: 90–2; *SCB* 1, no. 8, May 1896: 325–26.) (INF)

Carson River, Pass, Canyon, Range, Spur (8,290–8,297)   *Silver Lake 15', Markleeville 15', Sonora Pass 15', Freel Peak 15', Topaz Lake 15', and eight of the newer 7½' maps.*
Christopher (Kit) Carson (1809–1868), a mountain man, scout, soldier, and Indian agent. He was with John C. Frémont on Frémont's second exploring expedition; the party crossed the Sierra at Carson Pass in February 1844. Frémont named the river for Carson; the other "Carson" names derive from that. "Carson River" appears for the first time on the Preuss map of 1848. "Carson Pass" and "Carson Cañon" are on Britton and Rey's map of California by George H. Goddard, 1857.
In the 19th century the Carson Pass route was known as the "Amador and Carson Valley Road." The Carson Range was at one time called the "Rose Mountain Range;" it was changed to its present name by a BGN decision in 1939. (TNF, ENF)

Carson Peak (3,325 m.–10,909)   *Devils Postpile 15', Mammoth Mtn. 7½'*
"For the first owner of the Silver Lake Resort." (Smith, 24.) (INF)

Cartago Creek   *Olancha 15'*
The former town of Cartago was created as a steamer landing on the southwest shore of Owens Lake to handle shipments of silver bullion from Cerro Gordo. John Baptiste Daneri, native of Sardinia and a Lone Pine merchant, built the landing, a large warehouse, and a store, in 1872. For six months the place didn't have a name, and was referred to as "Lakeville" and "Danerisburg." On November 1, 1872, Daneri named it "Cartago," perhaps— as Lingenfelter suggested—in the hope that he was creating "the Carthage of the West." (Richard E. Lingenfelter, "The Desert Steamers," *Journal of the West* 1, no. 2, Oct. 1962.)
The creek was called "Carthage Creek" on all editions of the *Olancha 30'* map, 1907–47. It appeared as "Cartago Creek" on the 15-minute quad, 1956, a change that was ratified by a BGN decision in 1961. (INF)

Cartridge Creek   *Marion Peak 15', Mt. Pinchot 15' and 7½'*
Cartridge Pass (over 11,680)   *Mt. Pinchot 15' and 7½'*
The creek was named by Frank Lewis, an early stockman and hunter, in the 1870s. "While hunting there with a young friend, Harrison Hill, I wounded a bear and told him to finish it. He became excited and threw all the shells out of his Winchester without firing a shot." (Farquhar: letter from Frank Lewis, Feb. 12, 1926.) Bolton C. Brown called the pass "Red Pass" in 1895. (*SCB* 1, no. 8, May 1896: 304–5.) This was the route followed by the John Muir Trail until a trail was built over Mather Pass in 1938. "Cartridge Creek" appears on the first edition of the *Mt. Whitney 30'* map, 1907; the pass shows up on the fourth edition, 1919. (KCNP)

Cary Peak (8,727–8,726), **Canyon**   *Freel Peak 15', Woodfords 7½'*
William and John Cary (or Carey) were early settlers in Carson Valley. In

1853 John built a sawmill at a place that became known as "Cary's Mills." The name was changed to "Woodfords" in 1869. (Maule; *Historic Spots,* 26, which says the mill was built about 1851.) George H. Goddard (*Report,* 1855) reported that he stopped at Cary's and had a good supper there. "Cary's Peak" and "Cary's" appear on separate maps of Alpine County about 1870. (TNF)

Casa Diablo Hot Springs   *Mt. Morrison 15', Old Mammoth 7½'*
The namer is not known; the name already existed in 1890. "We stopped at the deserted Casa Diablo Hot Springs, to examine the establishment. There was a hotel, several cottages, and bath houses all deserted and gone to ruin. This was built during the prodigious excitement subsequent to the discovery of the Mammoth Mine just west of here, and shared in the collapse of that great speculation." (LeConte, *A Summer,* 99–100.) (INF)

Casa Vieja Meadows   *Hockett Peak 15'*
"In 1903, John Lacy, then running cattle in the Monache country, told me the name was given for an old house or cabin in that locality." (Douglas Robinson, INF archives.) (INF)

Cascade Cliffs   *Yosemite Valley 1:24,000*
"A huge massive granite formation on the south side of Little Yosemite Valley, about two miles east of Nevada Fall. Water cascades down these cliffs throughout much of the year." (*YNN* 34, no. 1, Jan. 1955: 4.) Not named on the *Merced Peak* 15' map, although it has been on the valley map since the first edition, 1907. (YNP)

Cascade Lake   *Tuolumne Meadows 15'*
Named by Everett Spuller in 1932 "because of the cascade coming down from the glacierette from North Peak." (Spuller.) (INF)

Cascade Valley   *Mt. Morrison 15', Bloody Mtn. 7½'*
A name given by George R. Davis, USGS. (Farquhar.) In 1908 it was called "Peninsula Meadow" by J. N. LeConte and J. S. Hutchinson, because of a peninsula jutting into the stream. (*SCB* 7, no. 1, Jan. 1909: 7.) (SiNF)

The Cascades   *Yosemite 15', Yosemite Valley 1:24,000*
Cascade Creek   *Hetch Hetchy Reservoir 15', Yosemite 15',*
        Yosemite Valley 1:24,000
"Nearly three miles below the valley, in the cañon, are two beautiful cascade falls of over seven hundred feet each. I named these falls the Cascades on a first exploration [in 1851], the name being suggested by their formation and twin-like appearance." (Bunnell, *Report,* 12–13.)
John Muir crossed Cascade Creek in 1869. "Never was a stream more fittingly named, for as far as I have traced it above and below our camp it is one continuous bouncing, dancing, white bloom of cascades." (Muir, *First Summer,* 140.) (YNP)

Case Mountain (6,818); **Case Mountain Grove**   *Kaweah 15'*
Bill Case had a cabin at the head of Salt Creek. He was famous for driving a

mixed team: a horse, a mule, a burro, and a steer. (Farquhar: Guy Hopping, Walter Fry.)

Cassidy Meadows   *Kaiser Peak 15', Balloon Dome 7½'*
   Named for an early sheepman. (Farquhar: Versteeg, from Ellis.) The name was James Cassidy. (SiNF history files.) Winchell spelled it "Cassaidy" (p. 157). The name appears on the 1904 *Kaiser* 30' map. "Cassidy Bridge" (a footbridge across the San Joaquin River) is new on the *Balloon Dome* quad. (SiNF)

Castilleja Lake   *Mount Whitney 15', Mt. Brewer 7½'*
   Named by Bolton C. and Lucy Brown in 1896. "This we named Castilleja Lake, the castilleja blossoms being especially perfect and brilliant upon its shores." (*SCB* 2, no. 1, Jan. 1897: 21.) *Castilleja chromosa,* Indian paintbrush. This name has never been on USGS maps. It's the small lake at the junction of the routes to Harrison Pass and Lucys Foot Pass, 0.7 mile east-northeast of the north end of Lake Reflection. (KCNP)

Castle Domes   *Mt. Pinchot 15' and 7½'*
   Probably named by the USGS during the 1905 survey for the *Mt. Whitney* 30' map; the name is on the first edition, 1907. (KCNP)

Castle Peak (10,677)   *Tehipite Dome 15'*
   Probably named by the USGS during the 1903 survey for the *Tehipite* 30' map; it is on the first edition, 1905. (SiNF)

Castle Point (8,041–8,045)   *Silver Lake 15', Caples Lake 7½'*
   George H. Goddard (*Report,* 1855) has "Castle Peak" in his list of places along the route, but does not say that he named it or that it was an existing name. In 1853 Goddard gave the name "Castle Peak" to a mountain many miles to the southeast. (See **Tower Peak.**) This "Castle Peak" was changed to "Castle Point" by the Wheeler Survey on atlas sheet 56B, 1876–77, probably to avoid the duplication of names. (ENF)

Castle Rock (over 9,600)   *Pinecrest 15'*
   Named by the Wheeler Survey before 1878. ". . . the name 'Castle Rocks' has been given to some peaks north of the Relief Trail at the head of the Stanislaus." (Wheeler Survey record found atop Dunderberg Peak in 1947, in *SCB* 33, no. 3, March 1948: 123.) (StNF)

Castle Rock (7,740)   *Hockett Peak 15'*
   Named "because the rock formation resembled a castle." (*Newsletter* 1, no. 5, July 1969: 72.) The name is on the first *Olancha* 30' map, 1907. (SeNF)

Castle Rocks (9,180), **Creek**   *Mineral King 15'*
   "Named by Professor Dean, who had a homestead near there." (Junep.) "Strongly resemble medieval castles on the Rhine." (Tobin.) The creek got its name from the rocks. (SNP)

Cataract Creek   *Mt. Goddard 15', North Palisade 7½'*
   "The outlook was across the great valley of Palisade Creek and directly up the rugged gorge by which we had descended from Amphitheater Lake. Down

the middle tumbled the foaming stream, a long line of silver, lost here and there amongst the talus-piles. Cataract Creek, we called it, and marveled at its wonderful setting." (J. N. LeConte, "The Ascent of the North Palisades," *SCB* 5, no. 1, Jan. 1904: 10–11.) (KCNP)

Cathedral Peak (10,940), **Lakes, Pass, Fork** (of Echo Creek)
Tuolumne Meadows 15'
Cathedral Range　　　　　*Tuolumne Meadows 15', Merced Peak 15'*
Cathedral Creek　　　*Tuolumne Meadows 15', Hetch Hetchy Reservoir 15'*
The peak was named by the California Geological Survey in 1863. "From a high ridge, crossed just before reaching this lake [Tenaya], we had a fine view of a very prominent exceedingly grand landmark through all the region, and to which the name of Cathedral Peak has been given. . . . the majesty of its form and its dimensions are such, that any work of human hands would sink into insignificance if placed beside it." (Whitney, *Geology,* 425.)
First ascent by John Muir, September 7, 1869. "This I may say is the first time I have been at church in California, led here at last, every door graciously opened for the poor lonely worshiper." (Muir, *First Summer,* 336.)
The names of the other Cathedral features derive from the peak. The pass and one lake—the larger one—had been named by the time of the first *Mt. Lyell* 30' map, 1901. (YNP)

Cathedral Rocks, Spires　　　*Yosemite 15', Yosemite Valley 1:24,000*
James M. Hutchings named Cathedral Spires in September 1862; the Rocks were apparently named at about the same time, since both names are on King and Gardiner's 1865 "Map of the Yosemite Valley."
"The Cathedral Rocks and Spires, known as Poo-see-na-chuc-ka, meaning 'Mouse-proof Rocks,' from a fancied resemblance in shape to their acorn magazines or *caches.*" (Bunnell, *Discovery,* 1911, 217.)
An earlier name for the rocks was "The Three Graces." (Hutchings, *In the Heart,* 400.) (YNP)

Cecil Lake　　　　　　　*Mt. Morrison 15', Bloody Mtn. 7½'*
Possibly named in 1945 by William A. Dill of the DFG, but for whom is not known. (DFG survey.) (SiNF)

Cedar Creek　　　　　　　　　　　　　　　*Giant Forest 15'*
A name used by the first settlers in the area. There are many cedars growing in the creek's upper basin. (USGS, from Caryl Homer, rancher descendant of a pioneer family.) (SNP)

Cedar Grove　　　　　　　　　　　　　　　*Marion Peak 15'*
Incense cedars are abundant in the area. In 1897 Hugh Robinson built a small hotel here, but he had no permit and was forced out by the government the following year. The name "Cedar Grove" was in use as early as 1902. (*SCB* 4, no. 4, June 1903: 317.) John Muir referred to the area as "Deer Park" on his 1891 trip. (*Century Magazine,* Nov. 1891.) The name "Cedar Grove Hotel" was on the *Tehipite* 30' maps from 1905 to 1924; "Hotel" was deleted beginning with the edition of 1929. (KCNP)

Cedric Wright, Mount (3,761 m.–12,372)   *Mt. Pinchot 15' and 7½'*
  George Cedric Wright (1899–1959), "internationally known photographer whose photography has made a significant contribution to the appreciation of the natural scene." (BGN decision, 1961.) The mountain is not named on the first edition of the *Mt. Pinchot* 15' quad. It is about a mile north of Woods Lake, which is on the Sawmill Pass trail. (KCNP)

Center Mountain (11,273)   *Matterhorn Peak 15'*
  Probably named by the USGS during the 1905–09 survey for the *Bridgeport* 30' map; it is on the first edition, 1911. (YNP, TNF)

Center Peak (12,760), **Basin; Center Basin Crags**   *Mount Whitney 15',*
                                                        Mt. Williamson 7½'
  Cornelius Beach Bradley and Robert M. Price named the peak on July 5, 1898, when Bradley made the first ascent. (*SCB* 2, no. 5, Jan. 1899: 272.) Both the peak and the basin were named on the 1907 *Mt. Whitney* 30' map. The USGS added "Center Basin Crags" to the *Mount Whitney* 15' quad because it was in common use by climbers. (KCNP; crags also in INF)

Chagoopa Falls   *Kern Peak 15'*
Chagoopa Creek, Plateau   *Kern Peak 15', Mount Whitney 15',*
                                                        Mt. Kaweah 7½'
  The falls was named in 1881 by W. B. Wallace, J. W. A. Wright, and F. H. Wales. "There are five waterfalls on the sides [of Kern Canyon] from 1,500 to 3,000 feet high, the water of which drops three or four hundred feet at a plunge.... We named the highest of these Shä-goo-päh Falls, after an old Pi Ute chief." (*MWCJ* 1, no. 1 May 1902: 9–10.) The name is said by Elliott (*Guide,* pp. 38–39) to be the Indian name for Mount Williamson. Kroeber (p. 38) says it is almost certainly a Mono word, but the meaning is unknown.
  The plateau was named by William R. Dudley and party in July 1897. "We have it mapped as the Chagoopah Plateau, as it is traversed by the creek forming the Chagoopah Falls." (*SCB* 2, no. 3, Jan. 1898: 187.) The creek name was ratified by a BGN decision in 1928. The falls was called "Cañon Falls" on a Sequoia National Park map in 1906. Although the falls was named first, it was the last to get on the USGS maps. The creek and plateau were on the 1907 *Olancha* 30' map; the falls made the fourth edition, 1927. (SNP)

Chain Lakes   *Tehipite Dome 15'*
  Probably named by the DFG during the 1940s; possibly in 1948 by Scott M. Soule. (DFG survey.) (SiNF)

Chalfant Lakes   *Mt. Abbot 15', Mt. Hilgard 7½'*
  Pleasant Arthur Chalfant (1831–1901), newspaper editor. He established the *Inyo Independent* in 1870; sold that paper and started the *Inyo Register* in 1885. His son, Willie Arthur Chalfant, continued as editor of the paper, and was the author of several books of regional lore and history. It is not certain which Chalfant the lakes are named for. (INF)

Chamberlain Lake (10,459)   *Mt. Abbot 15', Florence Lake 7½'*
  Joel Oliver Chamberlain (1896–1977). Chamberlain ran a service station in

Fresno for more than 20 years. He hunted in the Hooper Creek basin, and knew the country well. In 1947 he guided a USFS survey party to the lake. By way of thanks, Neil Perkins and Harvey Sauter of the Forest Service named the lake for him. (Heyward Moore, *FPP* 25, no. 5, Spring 1984: 9–10.) (SiNF)

Chamberlains Camp   *Blackcap Mtn. 15', Courtright Reservoir 7½'*
"The present cabin [1961] was built by Carl Chamberlain in 1945; he ran cattle on the 'Post Corral Allotment' at that time." (SiNF history files.) (SiNF).

Chamberlin, Mount (4,014 m.–13,169)   *Mount Whitney 15' and 7½'*
Thomas Crowder Chamberlin (1843–1928), glaciologist, and the ranking geologist in America during his time. He researched glacial phenomena and studied the evolution of climates through geologic periods. The name was suggested by the Sierra Club; approved by the BGN, November 1940. (SNP)

Chapel Lake   *Mt. Goddard 15' and 7½'*
Named in 1948 by William A. Dill of the DFG because of its proximity to Cathedral Lake. (DFG survey.) (SiNF)

Charity Valley; Charity Valley Creek   *Markleeville 15', Carson Pass 7½'*
Mormons named Hope Valley in 1848. Faith and Charity valleys were named by surveyors in 1855. "From Indian Valley we went northward . . . and entered a small valley *which we called Charity Valley.*" (Goddard, *Report.*)
"And now abideth faith, hope, charity, these three." (I Corinthians 13:13.) (TNF)

Charlotte Lake (3,165 m.–10,370), **Creek, Dome** (3,253 m.–10,690)
                                  Mt. Pinchot 15',Mt. Clarence King 7½'
The name appears on Hoffmann's map, 1873, but the origin is unknown. The lake was known as "Rhoda Lake" at one time; that name was used by J. N. LeConte in 1890. (*A Summer,* 56, 58–59.) It had been given by a party from Independence in honor of Mrs. Charles Houle, who frequently camped at the lake in the 1880s. (Farquhar files.) Called "Charlotta Lake" by Bolton C. Brown in 1896. (*SCB* 2, no. 1, Jan. 1897: 19–20.) The USGS added the dome's name to the 7½-minute quad because it had been in common use for many years. The dome is just west of Charlotte Creek and 1.2 miles south of Gardiner Pass. (KCNP)

Charybdis (13,096–13,091)   *Mt. Goddard 15' and 7½'*
In 1895 Theodore S. Solomons and Ernest C. Bonner pioneered a route from Mt. Goddard to Simpson Meadow, passing between two peaks they named "Scylla" and "Charybdis." (See **Scylla.**)
". . . and Charybdis underneath swallows down the black water. Three times a day she spouts it out, three times a day she swallows it down: she is a terror—don't you be there when she swallows! No one could save you from destruction. . . ." (Homer, 130.)
Called "Charybdis Peak" on the first three editions of the *Mt. Goddard* 30' map; changed to "Charybdis" in 1928. (KCNP)

Chasm Lake (11,011–10,990)   *Mt. Goddard 15' and 7½'*
The name was proposed by Lewis Clark of the Sierra Club. (Letter from David Brower to C. A. Ecklund, USGS, March 7, 1951.) (KCNP)

Chepo Saddle   *Bass Lake 15'*
Jim Chepo, "a Mono Indian," was allotted 80 acres in secs. 5 and 6, T. 7 S.,
R. 22 E. in 1920. (SiNF)

Cherry Lake, Creek, Ridge   *Lake Eleanor 15', Pinecrest 15',*
                                        Cherry Lake North 7½'
The origin of the name is not known, but it is an old one: "Cherry Valley" is
on the Wheeler atlas sheet 56D, 1878–79. The lake is artificial; it was formed
by damming Cherry Creek. (StNF)

Chevaux Lake   *Mt. Hilgard 7½'*
Named in 1954 by Ralph Beck of the DFG. (See **Alsace Lake.**) (SiNF)

Chief Lake   *Graveyard Peak 7½'*
Called "Warrior Lake" on the *Mt. Abbot* 15' map. That name was moved to
another lake. (BGN decision, 1969. See **Brave Lake.**) (SiNF)

Chilkoot Lake   *Shuteye Peak 15'*
Chilkoot Creek   *Bass Lake 15', Shuteye Peak 15'*
   "Probably named at the time of the Klondike gold rush for the famous
Chilkoot Pass." (Farquhar files: letter, Versteeg from T. S. Solomons.) Chilkoot
Lake appears on the 1904 *Kaiser* 30' map. The creek was called "Willow
Creek" on the 1904 edition; changed to "Chilkoot Creek" in 1923. (SiNF)

Chilnualna Creek, Fall, Lakes   *Yosemite 15'*
   A name of uncertain meaning and unknown origin. Said to mean "leaping
water." (YNP files.) The creek was named first; it was spelled "Chilnoialny" on
the Hoffmann and Gardiner map, 1863–67, and "Chilnoalna" by a GLO
surveyor in 1883. The creek and the fall—with the present spelling—were on the
first *Yosemite* 30' map, 1897. The name for the lakes was approved by the BGN
in 1932. (YNP)

Chimney Lake (9,484)   *Blackcap Mtn. 15', Courtright Reservoir 7½'*
   Named in 1945 by Rae Crabtree, Coolidge Meadow packer, "because of a
monument resembling a chimney." (DFG survey.) (SiNF)

China Garden   *Fales Hot Springs 15', Chris Flat 7½'*
   "Back in the 1800s, any place where Chinamen grew vegetables to sell to
mining camps was known as 'China Garden.' " (USGS.) This one was named
"Chinaman Flat" on *Bridgeport* 30' maps from 1911 to 1951. (TNF)

Chinquapin   *Yosemite 15'*
Chinquapin Falls   *El Portal 15'*
   For the bush chinquapin, *Castanopsis sempervirens.* (There is no longer a
ranger station at the road junction, as shown on the *Yosemite* 15' quad.) Called
"Chinquapin Flat" by Hutchings. (*In the Heart*, p. 474.) The name is on the
McClure map of 1895 and the *Yosemite* 30' map, 1897. On the 1884 GLO plat
it is called "Glacier Point Station." (YNP)

Chiquito Creek, Lake, Pass   *Merced Peak 15'*
Chiquito Creek, Ridge   *Shuteye Peak 15'*
   Chiquito is a Spanish diminutive. The creek was originally called "Chiquito

Joaquin," meaning the "Little Joaquin"—a branch of the San Joaquin River. The name appears on Hoffmann and Gardiner's map of 1863–67. Gardiner referred to "Chiquita Joaquin" and "Chiquita Ridge." (Gardiner's journal, July 26, 1866; copy in Farquhar papers, BL.) Theodore S. Solomons also used "Chiquita Joaquin" on his 1896 map. All the present "Chiquito" names are on the *Mt. Lyell* 30' map, 1901, and the *Kaiser* 30' map, 1904. (SiNF; pass, SiNF, YNP)

Chittenden Lake   *Merced Peak 15'*
William A. Dill and Scott M. Soule of the DFG reported in 1946 that this lake is named after a Fresno family. A galvanized iron sign on a tree near the outlet read: "Chittenden Lake. Doris & Ruby. Mary & Ken. Corynne & Bob. July 5, 1930. El. 9,800." (SiNF)

Chittenden Peak (9,685)   *Tower Peak 15'*
Hiram Martin Chittenden (1858–1917), a military engineer and historian; graduated from West Point in 1884. He worked on road construction in Yellowstone National Park, 1891–93. In 1904 he was a member of the boundary commission for Yosemite National Park. He is best known for his definitive work, *The American Fur Trade of the Far West* (1902). On his maps of 1895 and 1896, Lt. McClure called the peak "Jack Main Mt.," a name derived from "Jack Main Canyon," immediately to the west. (YNP)

Chocolate Peak (11,682–11,658), **Lakes**   *Mt. Goddard 15',*
                                                                Mt. Thompson 7½'
The peak probably was named for its color by the USGS during the 1907–09 survey for the *Mt. Goddard* 30' map; it is on the first edition, 1912. The lakes were first named on the 15-minute quad. (INF)

Chris Flat   *Fales Hot Springs 15', Chris Flat 7½'*
A meadow in the West Walker River Canyon where Christopher Telge had a small dairy in the late 1870s. (Maule.) (TNF)

Church Dome   *Kernville 15'*
A descriptive name, given by early-day hunters. (*Newsletter* 1, no. 5, July 1969: 74.) The name is on the first *Kernville* 30' map, 1908. (SeNF)

Cienega Mirth   *Big Pine 15', Coyote Flat 7½'*
" 'Cienega' is Spanish and 'Mirth' is Scotch for a swampy place. According to an old-timer, a party camped there had such a good time they named it Camp Mirth." (Schumacher, 90.) (INF)

Circle S Ranch   *Mt. Goddard 15'*
The place originally belonged to Art Schober's father. When he died, his younger brother inherited it. He later sold it to a party named Shreve. The 'S' in the name is for Shreve. (Art Schober.) The USGS has omitted the name on the *Mt. Thompson* 7½' quad because it is a commercial enterprise. (INF)

Cirque Lake, Creek   *Mt. Abbot 15', Florence Lake 7½'*
The lake was named in 1948 by Scott M. Soule and Jack Criqui of the DFG

because "of the very pronounced cirque in which it is located." (DFG survey.) (SiNF)

Cirque Crest   *Marion Peak 15', Mt. Pinchot 15' and 7½'*
   Probably named by the USGS during the 1903 survey for the *Tehipite 30'* map; it is on the first edition, 1905. (KCNP)

Cirque Mountain (10,714)   *Matterhorn Peak 15'*
   Probably named by the USGS during the 1905–09 survey for the *Bridgeport 30'* map; it is on the first edition, 1911. (TNF)

Cirque Peak (12,900), **Lake**   *Olancha 15'*
   Cirque Peak was climbed by J. N. LeConte and two companions in 1890; they were not the first, since they found a monument on the summit. It is possible, though not certain, that they named the peak. "On the northern slope of our mountain was a vast cirque, the most perfect I had ever seen." (LeConte, *A Summer,* 72.) Cirque Peak appeared on the 1907 *Olancha 30'* map, and the lake on the *Olancha 15'* quad in 1956. (INF)

The Citadel (11,738–11,744)   *Mt. Goddard 15', North Palisade 7½'*
   The name was proposed by the Sierra Club in 1941. (SC papers in BL.) (KCNP)

Clarence King, Mount (3,934 m.–12,905)   *Mt. Pinchot 15',*
                                                              Mt. Clarence King 7½'
   Clarence King (1842–1901), a member of the Whitney Survey from 1863 to 1866. The peak was named by the members of the Brewer party in 1864. King headed the United States Geological Exploration of the Fortieth Parallel, 1867–78, and became the first chief of the US Geological Survey, 1879–81. The written work for which he is best known is *Mountaineering in the Sierra Nevada,* 1872.
   The first ascent was made by Bolton C. Brown in 1896. "It is a true spire of rock, an uptossed corner at the meeting of three great mountain walls. . . . The top of the summit-block slopes northwest, is about fifteen feet across, and as smooth as a cobblestone. If you fall off one side, you will be killed in the vicinity; if you fall off any of the other sides, you will be pulverized in the remote nadir beneath." (*SCB* 2, no. 2, May 1897: 96–97.) (KCNP)

Clark Fork (of the Middle Fork of the Stanislaus River)
Dardanelles Cone 15' and 7½', Sonora Pass 15' and 7½', Dardanelle 7½'
   In 1862 the state legislature authorized a commission to locate and construct a wagon road from Sonora to Aurora. They decided on a route up a branch of the Middle Fork, which they named after a member of the commission: Clark, the commissioner from Tuolumne County. (StNF)

Clark, Mount (11,522); **Clark Range, Canyon, Fork** (of Illilouette Creek)
                                                              Merced Peak 15'
   Galen Clark (1814–1910), the first guardian of Yosemite State Park (1864), and discoverer of the Mariposa Grove. When in his forties he feared that he was going to die of a lung ailment. He went to the mountains for the sake of his health,

built a cabin in the spring of 1857 at what became "Clark's Station" (now Wawona), and lived another 43 years.

The mountain was once called "Gothic Peak," and later, the "Obelisk," a name given by the Whitney Survey. The name "Mt. Clark" appears on the Hoffmann and Gardiner map, 1863–67.

"Mr. King, who, with Mr. Gardner, made the ascent of the peak [1866], says that its summit is so slender, that when on top of it they seemed to be suspended in air." (Whitney, *The Yosemite Guide-Book,* 1870, 109.) (YNP)

Clark Point *Yosemite Valley 1:24,000*
On the south side of Merced Canyon, near Vernal Fall. The Yosemite Valley commissioners named the point in 1891 for Galen Clark. (*YNN* 34, no 1, Jan. 1955: 4.) The name did not appear on the map until the ninth edition, 1970. (YNP)

Clavey Meadow, River *Pinecrest 15' and 7½', Cherry Lake North 7½'*
Jane A. Clavey patented 160 acres in sec. 21, T. 3 N., R. 18 E., in 1897. The river was called "Big Cañon Creek" in the GLO surveyor's field notes in 1880. (StNF)

Claw Lake *Mt. Abbot 15', Mt. Hilgard 7½'*
Named by the DFG in 1952. (See **Bear Paw Lake.**) (SiNF)

Cleaver, The *Matterhorn Peak 15'*
Oliver Kehrlein and Henry Beers named this long "cleaver," or sharp arête, when they made the first ascent, July 3, 1933. (Farquhar files; also *SCB* 19, no. 3, June 1934: 31.) (TNF)

Clicks Creek *Camp Nelson 15'*
Named after Mark (or Martin) Click, a pioneer sheepman in 1877. (*Newsletter* 1, no. 6, Oct. 1969: 103.) (SeNF)

Cliff Creek *Mineral King 15', Triple Divide Peak 15'*
The creek received its name from "Cliff Pass," an early name for "Black Rock Pass." (*Newsletter* 1, no. 6, Oct. 1969: 103.) (SNP)

Cliff Lake (9,438) *Huntington Lake 15', Dogtooth Peak 7½'*
The lake has a sheer rock cliff and talus on the southwest side. It was probably named by William A. Dill and Scott M. Soule of the DFG in 1950. (DFG survey.) (SiNF)

Cloud Canyon *Triple Divide Peak 15'*
"I named it 'The Cloud Mine' because the clouds hung so low overhead. At the same time I named the creek Cloud Creek and put the name in my notebook. I often referred to my mine as being up in the clouds." (Letter from Judge William B. Wallace, in *SCB* 12, no. 1, 1924: 48.) For a period there was confusion between this canyon and Deadman Canyon, several miles to the west. On the first *Tehipite* 30' map, 1905, Cloud Canyon was mistakenly called "Cloudy Canyon." On the 1912 edition, Cloud Canyon was called "Deadman Canyon," and Deadman was called "Copper Canyon." By the 1924 edition the names were restored to their present places. (KCNP)

Cloudripper (13,525–13,501)   *Mt. Thompson 7½'*
The name first appeared in *The Climbers Guide,* and was added to the map
by the USGS because it was in common use. On the *Mt. Goddard* 15' quad it is
1.1 miles east by south from Chocolate Peak, marked "13501." (INF)

Clouds Rest (9,926)   *Tuolumne Meadows 15', Yosemite Valley 1:24,000*
"Cloud's Rest . . . was so named by a squad from C Company, who had
passed up the middle branch [the Merced River], and were turned back by seeing
the clouds gather on that peak for a snowstorm that followed that night, the
second of our first entrance into the valley." (Bunnell, *Report,* 11; see also
Bunnell, *Discovery,* 1880, 11.) That makes the date of naming March 28, 1851.
Clouds Rest was mistakenly called "Tanaya Peak" on a GLO 1885 plat,
surveyed in 1883. (YNP)

Clough Cave   *Kaweah 15'*
Discovered by William O. Clough (1851–1917), a miner and prospector, on
April 6, 1885. (*Nature,* No. 4, Jan. 20, 1925.) Clough died on the Franklin Pass
trail in the fall of 1917 while trying to reach the lake to shut off the water from the
power company's flume for the winter. (Farquhar: Guy Hopping) (SNP)

Clover Creek   *Mineral King 15'*
Wild clover along its banks made excellent pasture for early sheepmen.
(*Newsletter* 1, no. 6, Oct. 1969: 103) (SNP)

Clyde Meadow   *Mount Whitney 15' and 7½'*
Named in 1931 by Francis P. Farquhar for Norman Clyde, who discovered
this "most beautiful camp-ground I had yet seen in the Sierra." (Robert L. M.
Underhill in *SCB* 17, no. 1, Feb. 1932: 54.) (INF)

Clyde Spires (12,955)   *Mt. Darwin 7½'*
The two spires were first climbed on July 22, 1933, by a group of Sierra Club
members who named them for their leader, Norman Clyde. (*SCB* 19, no. 3, June
1934: 94.) (KCNP, INF)

Coats Meadow   *Mt. Goddard 15', Mt. Thompson 7½'*
William L. Coats homesteaded 160 acres in sec. 22, T. 8 S., R. 31 E. in
1896. His former homestead is still private land—an inholding within Inyo National Forest.

Cockscomb (10,719–10,720)   *Sharktooth Peak 7½'*
This descriptive name is now applied to what was called "Sharktooth Peak"
on the *Kaiser Peak* 15' map. That name has been moved about 1.6 miles northeast to the peak it should have been on all along. (BGN decision, 1969.) (SiNF)

Cockscomb (over 11,040)   *Tuolumne Meadows 15'*
François E. Matthes, USGS, named this peak in 1919. "The writer does not
claim to be a connoisseur in poultry; nevertheless, he believes that the likeness
to a lobate cockscomb is fairly close." (*SCB* 11, no. 1, Jan 1920: 26.) Called
"Cockscomb Crest" and "Cockscomb Peak" before being given the present
name. (YNP)

Coffeepot Canyon *Kaweah 15', Mineral King 15'*
"Oldtimers say a hunting party found an old coffeepot at a camp ground in this canyon, and used the utensil as a sort of mail box for travelers. (Junep.) (SNP)

Colby Mountain (9,631) *Hetch Hetchy Reservoir 15'*
Colby Meadow *Mt. Goddard 15', Mt. Darwin 7½'*
Colby Pass (about 12,000), **Lake** (10,595) *Triple Divide Peak 15'*
William Edward Colby (1875–1964), a member of the Board of Directors of the Sierra Club for 49 years, 47 of them as Secretary and two as President. One of the most influential conservationists of the first half of the 20th century; instrumental in enlarging Sequoia and creating Kings Canyon and Olympic national parks; first chairman of the California State Park Commission, 1927–36. (See "Remembering Will Colby" in *SCB* 50, no. 10, Dec. 1965: 69–78.)

The mountain was named by R. B. Marshall, USGS. (Farquhar: Marshall.) The name appeared on the *Yosemite 30'* map in 1911.

The meadow was named in 1915 by members of the USFS who were building a segment of the John Muir Trail. (Farquhar.)

The pass was named by a Sierra Club party on July 13, 1912, because Colby had suggested it as a shorter and easier route from the Kings River to the Kern. (*SCB* 9, no. 1, Jan. 1913: 2.)

Colby Lake was first known as "Hutchinson Lake," probably for James S. Hutchinson, who was with the first party to take pack stock across Colby Pass, in 1920. (Farquhar files; also *SCB* 11, no. 2, Jan. 1921: 128–29.) The name "Colby Lake" was proposed by the Sierra Club in 1927. (*SCB* 13, no. 1, Feb. 1928: 85–86.) (Mountain, YNP; meadow, KCNP; pass, KCNP, SNP; lake, KCNP.)

College Lake, Rock (9,055–9,076) *Kaiser Peak 15' and 7½'*
The lake probably was named in 1947 by Charles K. Fisher of the DFG. (DFG survey.) It is not known who named College Rock, nor when, except that it was before the 15-minute quad was issued in 1953. (SiNF)

Colony Mill, Meadow, Peak (6,132) *Giant Forest 15'*
The Kaweah Co-operative Commonwealth Colony was established in 1886. The colony had claims on timberland in the Giant Forest area, and intended to be economically self-sufficient by cutting and marketing lumber on a socialistic basis. The colony was building a road to Giant Forest. It reached Colony Mill by 1890, in which year Sequoia National Park was established. That put an end to the colony's plans for Giant Forest. The colony collapsed the following year amid charges of fraud and dishonesty, and with dissension among the members. (*The Kaweah Commonwealth,* Nov. 1889; *Out West,* Sept. 1902; Robert V. Hine. *California's Utopian Colonies.* San Marino: The Huntington Library, 1953.) The peak was named last, the result of a BGN decision in 1928. (SNP)

Colosseum Mountain (3,794.9 m.–12,473) *Mt. Pinchot 15', Aberdeen 7½'*
Probably named by the USGS during the 1905 survey for the *Mt. Whitney*

30' map. It appears on the first edition, 1907, but is not listed in J. N. LeConte's "Elevations," 1903. (*SCB* 4, no. 4, June 1903: 285–91.) (KCNP, INF)

Colt Lake   *Blackcap Mtn. 15' and 7½'*
    Named in 1948 by William A. Dill of the DFG because it is shaped like a colt's head and is close to Horsehead Lake. (DFG survey.) (SiNF)

Columbia Finger (over 10,320)   *Tuolumne Meadows 15'*
Columbia Rock (BM 5,031)   *Yosemite 15', Yosemite Valley 1:24,000*
    "Columbia" has been used since the founding of the country as a poetic and patriotic name for the United States of America. (For perhaps the earliest known use of the name, see: George R. Stewart, *Names on the Land,* first Sentry edition, p. 171.) It is not known who named either of these features. "Columbia Finger" dates to at least 1915. (*SCB* 9, no. 4, Jan. 1915: photo opp. 292.) "Columbia Rock," a viewpoint on the Yosemite Falls trail, first appeared on the 1907 *Yosemite Valley* map. (YNP)

Columbine Lake   *Mineral King 15'*
    Joseph Palmer (see **Palmer Mountain**) named the lake for the quantities of columbine growing around it. (Farquhar: W. F. Dean.) The name is on the first *Kaweah* 30' map, 1904. (SNP)

Columbine Peak (12,662–12,652)   *Mt. Goddard 15', North Palisade 7½'*
    A descriptive name, proposed by the Sierra Club sometime before 1939. Columbines grow almost to the summit. (Letter, David Brower to C. A. Ecklund, USGS, Mar. 7, 1951.) (KCNP)

Comb Spur, Creek   *Marion Peak 15'*
    The spur probably was named by the USGS during the 1903 survey for the *Tehipite* 30' map; the name is on the first edition, 1905. The formation is a row of peaks reminiscent of the teeth of a comb. The creek was first named on the 15-minute quad. (KCNP)

Confusion, Lake   *Blackcap Mtn. 7½'*
    Named by the USGS because there was confusion over which way it drained and whether it belonged in Kings Canyon National Park or Sierra National Forest. On the *Mt. Goddard* 30' maps the lake doesn't appear at all. On the *Blackcap Mtn.* 15' map it is unnamed, and is shown to be just west of the LeConte Divide, in the national forest. On the new 7½' map it is in the national park, just east of the divide, and drains both directions. (KCNP)

Conifer Ridge   *Mineral King 15'*
    A ridge covered with a stand of conifers. The name was suggested by H. Y. Alles. (Tobin.) (SNP)

Conness, Mount (12,590); **Conness Creek, Lakes, Glacier**
                                        Tuolumne Meadows 15'
    John Conness (1821–1909), a native of Ireland, came to the US in 1836; member of the California legislature, 1853–54, 1860–61; US senator, 1863–69; lived in Massachusetts from 1869 until his death.
    The peak was named in 1863 by the Whitney Survey—for good reason.

"Mount Conness bears the name of a distinguished citizen of California, now a United States Senator, who deserves, more than any other person, the credit of carrying the bill organizing the Geological Survey of California, through the Legislature." (Whitney, *Yosemite Guide-Book,* 1870, footnote 100.) Conness also introduced the bill in the Senate that granted Yosemite Valley and the Mariposa Grove to the state.

"Conness Peak" and the creek are on the Wheeler Survey atlas sheet 56D, 1878–79; the lakes and glacier appeared on the *Tuolumne Meadows* 15' map, 1956. (Mount, YNP, INF; creek, YNP; lakes and glacier, INF)

Consultation Lake (3,560 m.–over 11,760)   *Mount Whitney 15' and 7½'*
According to a BGN decision (1937–38), the lake was named about 1904 when the men who laid out the first trail to the summit of Mt. Whitney from the east consulted here as to which direction the trail should take. However, it seems to have been named by A. W. de la Cour Carroll and party on August 28, 1895—with no reason given *why* they named it thus. (*SCB* 1, no. 7, Jan. 1896: 291.) (INF)

Contact Pass (over 11,760)   *Big Pine 15', Split Mtn. 7½'*
The pass received its name from the contact between two different types of granite. (*SCB* 24, no. 3, June 1939: 48.) (INF)

Converse Basin, Creek, Mountain (7,208)   *Tehipite Dome 15'*
Charles P. Converse came to California in 1849; opened a general store at Coarsegold in 1851; ran a ferry across the San Joaquin River at the present town of Friant until 1869; built the first jail in Fresno County, and was the first person confined in it. (Farquhar; also Winchell, 71–72, 86.)
On election day in September 1876, a drunk inside a saloon threw a cobble at Converse, narrowly missing him. Converse fired in return, but also missed. A friend of the drunk hit Converse from behind, knocking him to his knees. Converse shot that man dead; the Grand Jury freed him on the ground that he acted in self-defense. After this episode, Converse said he became "more uneasy, irresolute and unsettled." He moved into the mountains south of the Kings River, and claimed (although he never secured title to) "a large amphi-theater of forest and chaparral encircled by mountain ridges." This became known as "Converse Basin," an area later denuded of its timber, including Big Trees, in the Millwood operations. (Vandor, vol. 1, 137–39.) For the complete story of lumbering in the Converse region see Johnston, *Redwoods,* with an excellent biographical sketch of Converse on pp. 55–58. (SeNF)

Convict Lake (7,621–7,580), **Creek**   *Mt. Morrison 15', Convict Lake 7½'*
Twenty-nine convicts escaped from prison at Carson City, Nevada, on September 17, 1871. Six of them headed south, and murdered a mail rider from Aurora. Posses from Aurora and Benton caught up to the convicts near "Monte Diablo Creek"—now Convict Creek. Robert Morrison (for whom Mt. Morrison is named), a Benton merchant and leader of the posse, was killed in the encounter. The convicts escaped, but three of them were captured a few days

later. Two of those were lynched while being returned to the jail at Carson City. (Chalfant, *Inyo*, 251–55.)

A Mrs. A. A. Forbes, of Bishop, said that the Indian name for Convict Lake was "Wit-sa-nap." The legend is in *SCB* 9, no. 1, Jan. 1913: 55. (INF)

Conway Summit   *Bodie 15′*
John Andrew Conway settled near here in 1880. (Smith, 33.)

Cony Crags (10,867 and 10,539)   *Merced Peak 15′*
Named for the abundant "conies" (*Ochotona princeps muiri*), sometimes called "pikas" or "rock-rabbits," living in talus around the crags. (BGN, 1963.) (YNP)

Cooper Peak (9,603), **Meadow, Pocket**   *Pinecrest 15′*
W. F. Cooper ran cattle in the area from 1861 until 1900; a tree at the meadow is inscribed with Cooper's name and the date 1861. The cabin and barn at Cooper Meadow (the barn was the original cabin) were built in 1875 and 1865, respectively. They are eligible for the National Register of Historic Places. (StNF files.) The peak and the meadow are named on the first *Dardanelles* 30′ map, 1898. (StNF)

Copper Creek   *Marion Peak 15′*
The existence of a copper deposit was known prior to 1868, when E. C. Winchell and two others visited the Kings River Canyon. "Another stream emerges from a glen east of the Pyramid [North Dome], to which, because of its proximity to the copper mine alluded to in the early part of this sketch, we applied the name 'Malachite Creek.' " (San Francisco *Daily Morning Call*, Sept. 12, 1872; also in *SCB* 12, no. 3, 1926: 247. Malachite is copper carbonate.) The name "Copper Creek" was in use in 1890, when two men were working the small mine. (LeConte, *A Summer.*) (KCNP)

Cora Lakes   *Merced Peak 15′*
Cora Creek   *Merced Peak 15′, Devils Postpile 15′, Cattle Mtn. 7½′*
R. B. Marshall of the USGS named the lakes for Mrs. Cora Cressey Crow. (Farquhar: Marshall.) The name appeared on the third edition of the *Mt. Lyell* 30′ map, 1910. The creek was first named on the 15-minute maps. (SiNF)

Corbett Lake (9,070)   *Mt. Abbot 15′, Mt. Givens 7½′*
According to J. E. (Shorty) Cunningham, a packer (1947), the lake was named "several years ago" for "Young Corbett," a Fresno prizefighter. (DFG survey.) (SiNF)

Corcoran, Mount (over 13,760)   *Lone Pine 15′, Mt. Langley 7½′*
William Wilson Corcoran (1798–1888), banker and philanthropist, patron of art. In the Corcoran Gallery of Art in Washington there is a painting by Albert Bierstadt entitled "Mount Corcoran in the Sierra Nevada," dated 1878. Wheeler, in *Geographical Report*, 1889, p. 99, says "This peak has since been called Mount Corcoran by the artist, Mr. Albert Bierstadt." He was referring to Mt. Langley, originally called "Sheep Mountain." In 1891 the BGN gave a decision in favor of "Corcoran" for what is now Langley. In 1905, R. B. Marshall of

the USGS, not knowing of the Corcoran decision, gave the name "Mount Langley" to the old "Sheep Mountain." On the seventh edition of the *Mt. Whitney* 30′ map (1933), "Corcoran Mtn" appeared in place of "Mount Langley." After many years of protest, the BGN in 1968 reversed itself, restored "Mount Langley" to its rightful place, and stuck the name "Mount Corcoran" on a peak 1.2 miles northwest of Langley. (Farquhar, *History*, 186.) (SNP, INF)

Coronet Lake   *Mt. Abbot 15′, Mt. Hilgard 7½′*
Probably named by the DFG in 1953; perhaps it struck the surveyors as a crownlike ornament in its isolated setting. (SiNF)

Corral Meadow (77 Corral)   *Devils Postpile 15′, Cattle Mtn. 7½′*
In the 1870s a stock trail was built from Soldier Meadow directly across the canyon of the North Fork of the San Joaquin River to a corral in this meadow— constructed in 1877. The name " '77' Corral" was on the *Mt. Lyell* 30′ maps, was omitted from the 15-minute map, and has been restored on the *Cattle Mtn.* 7½′ map. (SiNF)

Cotter, Mount (3,875 m.–12,721)   *Mt. Pinchot 15′, Mt. Clarence King 7½′*
Richard Cotter was a packer with the California Geological Survey in 1864. He and Clarence King made the first ascent of Mt. Tyndall, and named Mt. Whitney from the summit of Tyndall. (Photo of the field party of 1864 in Farquhar, *History,* 135.) The name was suggested by a Sierra Club party in 1935. (*SCB* 21, no. 1, Feb. 1936: 93.) Approved by the BGN, 1937–38. Bolton C. Brown called the mountain "Precipice Peak" in 1899. (*SCB* 3, no. 2, May 1900: 136–38.)

Cottonwood Creek   *Lake Eleanor 15′, Hetch Hetchy Reservoir 15′*
This name is on the Hoffmann and Gardiner map, 1863–67, and therefore may have been named by the California Geological Survey. It is used by Hoffmann in a letter to Whitney, Sept. 10, 1873. (BL.) (YNP)

Cottonwood Creek, Pass (over 11,120); **Little Cottonwood Creek**
Olancha 15′
Cottonwood Lakes   *Olancha 15′, Mt. Langley 7½′*
These are old names. Undoubtedly the creeks were named first. They already had their names, derived from cottonwood trees along the lower reaches, in 1890. (LeConte, *A Summer,* 70–71.) Cottonwood Pass was once known locally as "Chicken Spring Pass." (*SCB* 11, no. 3, 1922: 285.) (INF)

Coulterville Road   *El Portal 15′, Yosemite 15′, Yosemite Valley 1:24,000*
George W. Coulter opened a store in 1849 in the place that was later to bear his name. He was one of the first commissioners appointed to manage the Yosemite Park grant, 1864. The Coulterville Road and the Big Oak Flat Road were in competition to reach Yosemite Valley; the former won out, reaching the valley floor on June 17, 1874, one month before the competitor. Thus the first wheeled vehicles entered Yosemite Valley over this road, even though the Big Oak Flat Road eventually got the lion's share of the traffic. The best account of the building of the two roads is in Paden and Schlichtmann. (YNP, StNF)

Council Lake   *Mt. Abbot 15', Mt. Hilgard 7½'*
Named by Elden H. Vestal of the DFG "after the tribal or other council held by Indians and, also, to signify a meeting or convergence of waters in the basin." (Heyward Moore, *FPP* 26, no. 2, summer 1984: 5.) (SiNF)

Courtright Reservoir, Dam (8,184)   *Blackcap Mtn. 15',*
                                            Courtright Reservoir 7½'
H. H. Courtright (1887–1956); in the electrical supply business in Fresno; president of the San Joaquin Light and Power Corp.; general manager of the Pacific Gas and Electric Company. The reservoir was formed by a rockfill dam across Helms Creek, completed in 1958. Before it was flooded, part of the area was named "Sand Meadows." (SiNF)

Coy Creek, Flat   *Camp Nelson 15'*
Milton M. Coy patented 160 acres in secs. 3 and 10, T. 21 S., R. 31 E. in 1891. (SeNF)

Crabtree   *Patterson Mtn. 15'*
John F. Crabtree homesteaded 157 acres in sec. 36, T. 12 S., R. 26 E. in 1911. (SeNF)

Crabtree Campsite   *Pinecrest 15' and 7½'*
O. S. Crabtree, who lived in Knights Ferry, patented 160 acres in sec. 29, T. 4 N., R. 19 E. in 1898 under the Swamp & Overflow Act. The patent was later declared invalid by the state because it was not swamp and overflow land. (StNF files.) The location is named "Crabtree Camp" on the 15-minute quad. (StNF)

Crabtree Lake   *Blackcap Mtn. 15' and 7½'*
Named for Rae Crabtree, the Coolidge Meadow packer, in 1945. (DFG survey.) (SiNF)

Crabtree Meadow, Creek, Lakes, Pass   *Mount Whitney 15' and 7½'*
For W. N. Crabtree, who ran cattle in the meadow before the turn of the century. (Farquhar: J. R. White, 1930.) The meadow and creek were named on the first *Mt. Whitney* 30' map, 1907. The name "Crabtree Pass" was added to the 7½-minute quad by the USGS because it has been in common use for many years. The pass is the saddle between the headwaters of Crabtree and Rock creeks, just southwest of Mount McAdie. (SNP)

Crag Peak (9,455), **Creek**   *Monache Mtn. 15'*
The peak probably was named by the USGS during the 1905 survey for the *Olancha* 30' map; it is on the first edition, 1907. The creek was first named on the 15-minute quad, 1956. (SeNF)

Craig Peak (11,090)   *Tower Peak 15'*
Named by R. B. Marshall for John White Craig, US Army. (Farquhar: Marshall.) (YNP)

Crane Flat, Creek; North Crane Creek   *Lake Eleanor 15', El Portal 15'*
"This name was suggested by the shrill and startling cry of some sand-hill

cranes we surprised as they were resting on this elevated table." (Bunnell, *Discovery,* 1880, 316.) "It is often visited by blue cranes to rest and feed on their long journeys." (Muir, *First Summer,* 122.)

A differing opinion says that Crane Flat was named after a man named Crean. (Baron de Hubner, *A Ramble Around the World,* 1875, 177.) (YNP)

Crane Valley   *Bass Lake 15'*

Crane Valley is no longer on the maps; it is under the waters of Bass Lake. It was originally named on April 18, 1851, by members of the Mariposa Battalion. "As we entered the valley selected for our camping place, a flock of sand-hill cranes rose from it with their usual persistent yells; and from this incident their name was affixed to the valley, and is the name by which it is now known." (Bunnell, *Discovery,* 1911, 111. Also see Eccleston, 74.) (SiNF)

Crater Crest (11,394)   *Matterhorn Peak 15'*

Several craters on a mile-long ridge. Probably named by the USGS during the 1905–09 survey for the *Bridgeport* 30' map; the name is on the first edition, 1911. (TNF)

Crater Lake   *Kaiser Peak 15', Huntington Lake 15', Dogtooth Peak 7½',*
                                                          Mt. Givens 7½'

A descriptive name. The lake lies in a small pocket on the shelf of a ridge, and probably was named in 1946 by William A. Dill and Scott M. Soule of the DFG. (DFG survey.) (SiNF)

Crater Mountain (3,924 m.–12,874)   *Mt. Pinchot 15' and 7½'*

The peak was almost certainly named by the USGS in 1905 during the survey for the first *Mt. Whitney* 30' map, 1907. A benchmark was placed on the peak. As further evidence, it was not listed in J. N. LeConte's "Elevations." (KCNP)

Crazy Lake (over 11,040)   *Mt. Abbot 15', Florence Lake 7½'*

Named in 1948 by a DFG survey party. The lake is in a bleak area. Scott M. Soule, a biologist, commented in his report that "anyone visiting this lake is crazy." (Heyward Moore, *FPP* 25, no. 5, spring 1984: 10.) (SiNF)

Crescent Lake, Creek   *Yosemite 15'*

The lake name is an old one; it appears on the Hoffmann and Gardiner map, 1863–67. McClure's map, 1895, shows it as "Duncan Crescent Lake," evidently referring to a noted bear hunter. "A mile brought us to Crescent Lake . . . still partly covered with melting ice. At the northern end of the lake we came upon a forlorn little cabin, half-buried in a snow-drift. . . . Bones of deer and of other game were littered about the room, one end of which was cumbered with the wreck of a huge chimney of rock. . . . It was once the summer home of Jim Duncan, a man whose fame as a hunter still lingers in the memory of old Sierra back-woodsmen." (Chase, 160.) (YNP)

Crescent Meadow, Creek   *Triple Divide Peak 15'*

The meadow was named before 1900. It was described by John Muir as the most beautiful meadow in the Sierra. (Tobin. See *SCB* 12, no. 3, 1926: photo opp. 308.) (SNP)

Crocker, Mount (12,458–12,457)   *Mt. Abbot 15' and 7½'*
    Charles Crocker (1822–1888), one of the "Big Four" who financed and built the Central Pacific Railroad. Named by R. B. Marshall, USGS, during the survey for the *Mt. Goddard* 30' map, 1907–09. (Farquhar: Marshall.) (INF, SiNF)

Crocker Point (7,090)   *Yosemite 15', Yosemite Valley 1:24,000*
    Probably named for Charles Crocker of the Central Pacific Railroad. (*YNN* 34, no. 1, Jan. 1955: 5.) The name first appeared on the *Yosemite Valley* map of 1907. (YNP)

Crocker Ridge   *Lake Eleanor 15'*
    Henry Robinson Crocker (1827–1904), the proprietor of "Crocker's Station," later called "Crocker's Sierra Resort," fifteen buildings constructed between 1880 and 1887 on the Big Oak Flat Road. The resort lasted until about 1920. (Farquhar; also Paden, 207–12.) Crocker homesteaded 160 acres in sec. 33, T. 1 S., R. 19 E. in 1883. (StNF)

Crown Rock (9,342), **Creek, Valley, Ridge**   *Tehipite Dome 15'*
    The rock was named "Crown Mountain" by Frank Dusy about 1870 for its crownlike rocky cap. The other features were named from the mountain. (Farquhar: L. A. Winchell.) T. S. Solomons' 1896 map shows "Crown Mountain" about where unnamed peak "7906" is, 1.5 miles northwest of Kettle Dome. The creek and valley were named on LeConte's 1893 map, and the ridge appeared on the first *Tehipite* 30' map, 1905. (SiNF; creek partly in KCNP)

Crystal Cave; Cave Creek   *Giant Forest 15'*
    The cave was discovered in 1918 by A. L. Medley and C. M. Webster, and was named by Walter Fry for its crystalline formations. (*Nature,* Jan. 20, 1925.) The cave was named on the fourth *Tehipite* 30' map, 1929, and the creek appeared on the 15-minute quad. (SNP)

Crystal Crag (10,377–10,364), **Lake**   *Devils Postpile 15',*
                                                     Crystal Crag 7½'
    The crag is a "wedge" or "island" of granite past which two arms of a glacier flowed. (Smith, 19.) The lake is the highest of the Mammoth Lakes; it was named on the GLO plat in 1879. (INF)

Crystal Creek   *Tehipite Dome 15', Marion Peak 15'*
    Probably named by L. A. Winchell or T. S. Solomons. The name "Crystal Veil Falls" is on Solomons' map drawn in 1897. (*SCB* 12, no. 2, 1925: 127.) (KCNP)

Cunningham Lake (9,110)   *Kaiser Peak 15', Mt. Givens 7½'*
    Vaud Cunningham, a former Huntington Lake packer, probably named the lake for himself in the 1940s. (DFG survey.) (SiNF)

Cyclamen Lake   *Mineral King 15'*
A name suggested by J. A. Peak (Tobin), for the many cyclamens growing
on its shores (Junep). BGN decision, 1928. (SNP)

Cyrus Canyon   *Isabella 15', Lake Isabella North 7½', Weldon 7½'*
Joseph Cyrus homesteaded 120 acres in sec. 34, T. 25 S., R. 33 E. in 1886.
(SeNF)

Dade, Mount (over 13,600)   *Mt. Abbot 15' and 7½'*
A peak probably named by the USGS during the survey in 1907–09 for the
first *Mt. Goddard* 30' map, 1912. It is not listed in J. N. LeConte's "Elevations." The first ascent was on August 19, 1911, by Liston and McKeen of
Fresno. On a piece of the *Ladies Home Journal* they left at the summit, they
described themselves as "locators of this valuable peak." (*SCB* 16, no. 1, Feb.
1931: 103.) (INF, SiNF)

Dale Lake (10,330–10,326)   *Blackcap Mtn. 15', Mt. Henry 7½'*
The lake was named for John Dale, Dinkey Creek packer, by DFG
personnel when the lake was first planted with fish, in 1936. (DFG survey.)
(SiNF)

Dana, Mount (13,053); **Dana Plateau, Lake**   *Mono Craters 15'*
Dana Meadows, Fork (of the Tuolumne River)   *Tuolumne Meadows 15',*
                                                        Mono Craters 15'
Named in 1863 by the Whitney Survey for James Dwight Dana (1813–
1895), professor of natural history and geology at Yale, 1849–90. Dana is con-
sidered the foremost geologist of his time; he provided the first comprehensive
summary of North American geology.
In 1889, J. N. LeConte copied from a record he found on the summit: "State
Geological Survey, June 28, 1863. J. D. Whitney, W. H. Brewer, Charles F.
Hoffmann, ascended this mountain June 28th and again the 29th. We give the
name of Mount Dana to it in honor of J. D. Dana, the most eminent American
geologist. Approximate height 13,126 feet." (*SCB* 11, no. 3, 1922: 247.) Only
Brewer and Hoffmann climbed the mountain on the 28th; Whitney was not
feeling well. He and Brewer went up on the 29th. (Brewer, *Up and Down*, 408–
9.) The ascent on the 28th was the first recorded one. "Up very early, and with
Hoffmann started for Mt. Dana. Icy, over rocks and snow, and made the summit
in 4 hours. So up by 10 A.M. and staid nearly 4 hours." (Brewer's diary, June
28, 1863, in BL.) (YNP, INF)

Dangberg Camp   *Freel Peak 15' and 7½'*
Since this is called a "camp," and is located at one end of a large, open
grassland (Hope Valley), one feels certain that it was—or is—a summer cow
camp. Two men named Dangberg patented land about four miles south of the
camp early in this century: Clarence O. Dangberg, 160 acres in secs. 2 and 11,
T. 10 N., R. 18 E. in 1903; George F. Dangberg, 160 acres in sec. 3, T. 10 N., R.
19 E. in 1906. (TNF)

Dardanelles, The (8,834–8,875)   *Dardanelles Cone 15',*
                                                 Spicer Meadow Res. 7½'
Dardanelles Cone (9,524)   *Dardanelles Cone 15' and 7½'*
Dardanelles Creek   *Dardanelles Cone 15', Spicer Meadow Res. 7½',*
                                                 Donnell Lake 7½'
   The namers of these features are not known. The name "Dardanells" is on
George H. Goddard's "Map of Sonora Pass," 1853. "Dardanelles Cone" and
"Dardanelles Creek" are on the Wheeler Survey atlas sheet 56B, 1876–77;
"The Dardanelles" first appears on the *Dardanelles* 30' map, 1898.
Undoubtedly named because of a resemblance to the rock formations along The
Dardanelles, the strait between the Aegean Sea and the Sea of Marmara
separating Asian and European Turkey (the Hellespont of ancient times). In
Tuolumne County the name has also been applied to a resort on State Route
108—"Dardanelle." (StNF)

Dark Canyon   *Kernville 15', Hockett Peak 15'*
   Steep, sheltered walls keep it in shadow much of the time. (*Newsletter* 1, no.
7, Feb. 1970: 131.) (SeNF)

Darwin, Mount (13,831–13,830); **Darwin Glacier, Canyon, Bench**
      Mt. Goddard 15', Mt. Darwin 7½' ("Darwin Bench" on 7½' only)
   Charles Robert Darwin (1809–1882), English naturalist, author of *Origin
of Species,* a major exponent of the theory of evolution.
   The peak was named in 1895 by Theodore S. Solomons and E. C. Bonner.
"Immediately upon our right towered a long, thin ridge of reddish buff granite,
fully two miles in length, whose crest rose into several peaks, the whole upper
surface of the wall being crowned with fantastically shaped pinnacles . . . which
we called Mt. Darwin." (Solomons in *Appalachia* 8, no. 1, 1896: 47.)
   The first ascent was made by E. C. Andrews of the Geological Survey of
New South Wales and Willard D. Johnson, USGS, on August 12, 1908. "I
begged [Johnson] to allow me to take our record in the small baking-powder
tin . . . and place it on the actual summit. . . . I made use of a monstrous icicle
one foot in diameter to assist me in climbing the broken masonry of the
outstanding peak. I had just placed the record in position on the summit, and was
looking around for a few loose rocks with which to secure it—and I commenced
the fearful descent to the chimney for this purpose—when it dawned on me that
the descent was more perilous than the ascent. . . . I thereupon reached upward
for the tin, placing it in my pocket, knowing full well that I would never have the
courage to make the ascent of the chimney the second time." (Letter, Andrews
to Farquhar, Sept. 26, 1923, in *SCB* 12, no. 1, 1924: 88–90.) (KCNP, INF)

Daulton Creek, Station   *Shuteye Peak 15'*
   H. C. Daulton was an early stockman in the lower Kaiser Creek basin.
(Winchell, 157.) (SiNF)

Davis Lake (11,058–11,084)   *Mt. Goddard 15', Mt. Darwin 7½'*
   George Robert Davis (1877–1922), topographic engineer with the USGS,
worked on more than 30 quadrangles including the *Mt. Whitney* and *Mt.*

Goddard 30′ sheets. The name was recommended in 1925 by the Sierra Club. Obituary and portrait in *SCB* 12, no. 2, 1925: 180. (KCNP)

Davis Lake (10,484)   *Blackcap Mtn. 15′, Mt. Henry 7½′*
Named for Bill Davis, a sheepman, according to John Dale, a former Dinkey Creek packer. (DFG survey.) (SiNF)

Davis, Mount (3,750 m.–12,311)   *Devils Postpile 15′, Mt. Ritter 7½′*
Lieutenant Milton Fennimore Davis (1864–1938), with the first troops assigned to guard the newly created Yosemite National Park, in 1891, at which time he made the first ascent of the mountain. The name was applied by Lt. N. F. McClure in 1894.

"I ascended the peak on Aug. 31, 1891. I took two days for the trip. Slept out without blankets at timber-line, making a fire of the last tree. I was accompanied most of the way by a Methodist preacher, Dr. E. W. Beers, of Anamosa, Iowa. The trip nearly killed him." (Letter, Davis to Versteeg, in Farquhar files.) "Beers gave out and did not cross the last gorge and make the last 2,000 feet." (*SCB* 12, no. 3, 1926: 305.) (SiNF, INF)

Day Needle (over 14,000)   *Mount Whitney 15′ and 7½′*
William Cathcart Day (1857–1905) of Johns Hopkins University, later professor of chemistry at Swarthmore College. Day was with Langley's scientific expedition to the summit of Mount Whitney in 1881. The name is not on USGS or USFS maps, yet it was named at the same time and in the same way as "Keeler Needle," which *is* on the maps. "Day" is the pinnacle immediately south of "Keeler." (SNP, INF)

Deadman Canyon   *Triple Divide Peak 15′*
A sheepherder's grave at the lower end of the canyon gave rise to a number of stories. "A sheepherder named Alfred Moniere who died and was buried there in 1887." (*Newsletter* 1, no. 7, Feb. 1970: 131.)

The sheepman was murdered in 1877. (Hall, *Sequoia*, p. 118.)

"Only a poor Portugese sheep-herder lies buried there, but no Pharaoh nor king of ancient or modern times has mausoleum half so magnificent." (*MWCJ* 1, no. 3, May 1904: 108.)

"We passed the grave of a Basque sheep-herder, inclosed within a primitive fence of logs, with its French inscription on the carved headboard, beginning '*Ici repose* Jean le Basque,' or whatever his name may have been . . . ." (*SCB* 6, no. 3, June 1907: 158.)

On the 1912 edition of the *Tehipite* 30′ map, this canyon was called "Copper Canyon," for the small copper mine that had formerly existed at the head of the canyon. (See **Cloud Canyon.**) (KCNP)

Deadman Pass, Creek   *Devils Postpile 15′, Mammoth Mtn. 7½′*
In about 1868 the headless body of a man was found near the creek. It was presumed to be Robert Hume, a miner from Carson City, who had been killed by his partner. The beginnings of this tale are in the story of the "Lost Cement Mines" in Mark Twain's *Roughing It*. The fullest details are in W. A. Chalfant's

Gold, Guns & Ghost Towns. The name has been extended to "Deadman Summit" on US 395. (INF)

Dechambeau Creek   *Bodie 15'*
    The Dechambeau family were early settlers at Mono Lake. (Cain, 87.) Louis W. Dechambeau homesteaded 80 acres in sec. 24, T. 2 N., R. 25 E. in 1901. (INF)

Deer Flat   *El Portal 15'*
    "The first encampment reached after leaving Bull Creek was 'Deer Flat,' so named by us from having startled a small drove as we went into camp here. One of the deer was shot, and afforded an addition to our camp supplies." (Bunnell, *Discovery,* 1911, 321.) (StNF)

Deerhorn Mountain (4,048 m.–13,265)   *Mount Whitney 15',*
                                                                    Mt. Brewer 7½'
    Named in 1895 by J. N. LeConte because of the resemblance of its double summit to two horns. (Farquhar: LeConte.) (KCNP)

Delaney Creek   *Tuolumne Meadows 15'*
    John Muir made his first sortie into the Sierra Nevada, from the foothills to Tuolumne Meadows, as a shepherd in the employ of Pat Delaney, in 1869. "Mr. Delaney has hardly had time to ask me how I enjoyed my trip, though he has facilitated and encouraged my plans all summer, and declares I'll be famous some day, a kind guess that seems strange and incredible to a wandering wilderness-lover with never a thought or dream of fame while humbly trying to trace and learn and enjoy Nature's lessons." (Muir, *First Summer,* 342.) (YNP)

Den Lake   *Mt. Abbot 15', Mt. Hilgard 7½'*
    Named by the DFG in 1952. (See **Bear Paw Lake.**) (SiNF)

Dennison Ridge, Mountain (8,650)   *Mineral King 15'*
    The ridge was named first, after a pioneer who built a trail in the 1860s connecting the foothills with the High Sierra. The name was apparently transferred to the mountain at the time of the first park boundary survey, 1899–1900. (SNP files, John R. White, 1928.) "Dennison was a mountaineer; killed near the old North Fork waterpower sawmill by accidentally tripping the wire on a set-gun he had rigged up for a bear." (Otter, 29.) (SNP)

Depressed Lake (10,870)   *Mt. Abbot 15', Florence Lake 7½'*
    The lake is set in a sharp-walled depression near the top of a ridge, and has no outlet. It was named in 1948 by Scott M. Soule and Jack Criqui of the DFG. (DFG survey.) (SiNF)

Desolation Lake (11,375–11,381)   *Mt. Tom 15', Mount Tom 7½'*
    Named by J. N. LeConte in 1898. (Farquhar: LeConte.) A smaller lake, downstream, was given the name "Lower Desolation Lake" (11,157) with the publication of the *Mt. Tom* 15' quad in 1949. (SiNF)

Detachment Meadow   *Merced Peak 15'*
    The precise origin of the name is not known, but it dates to the time when the

US Army was patrolling Yosemite National Park, in the 1890s. The name appears on the first edition of the *Mt. Lyell* 30' map, 1901. (SiNF)

Devils Bathtub (9,167)   *Mt. Abbot 15', Graveyard Peak 7½'*
Named because of its shape by George R. Davis, USGS, about 1907. (Farquhar: Davis.) (SiNF)

Devils Crags (highest, over 12,400)   *Mt. Goddard 15', North Palisade 7½'*
Named by J. N. LeConte sometime before 1903, since the name is in LeConte's list of peaks in the Sierra Nevada over 12,000 feet. (*SCB* 4, no. 4, June 1903: 285–91.) (KCNP)

Devils Postpile   *Devils Postpile 15', Mammoth Mtn. 7½',*
                                                     Crystal Crag 7½'
"Some miles farther down the river, near the place of crossing of the Mammoth trail, there is a splendid specimen of columnar basalt, which was photographed many years ago by Mr. J. M. Hutchings while crossing the mountains. In every scenic freak the sheepherder recognizes the handiwork of his Satanic majesty. The formation is therefore known to local fame as the Devil's Woodpile." (Theodore S. Solomons in *SCB* 1, no. 3, Jan. 1894: 74.)

President Taft proclaimed the "Devil Postpile National Monument" on July 6, 1911. (*SCB* 8, no. 3, Jan. 1912: 170–73, 226–27.) The feature was identified as "Devil Postpile" on the *Mt. Lyell* 30' maps from 1901 through the edition of 1944; it was changed to "Devils Postpile National Monument" on the final edition, in 1948. (INF)

Devils Punchbowl (10,098)   *Blackcap Mtn. 15' and 7½', Mt. Henry 7½'*
Possibly named by the USGS during the 1907–09 survey for the first edition of the *Mt. Goddard* 30' map, 1912. (SiNF)

Devils Table (7,236–7,222)   *Kaiser Peak 15', Mt. Givens 7½'*
Origin unknown; first appeared on the *Kaiser Peak* 15' map, 1953. The formation was called "Jericho Mesa" by A. L. Jordan and H. H. Bliss in 1917. (*SCB* 10, no. 3, Jan. 1918: 292.) (SiNF)

Devils Washbowl   *Mt. Goddard 15', North Palisade 7½'*
Might have been named in the 1930s by Halladay, a packer, when two or three mules he had roped together slipped into a whirlpool in the Middle Fork of the Kings River and were drowned. (Art Schober.) (KCNP)

Dewey Point (7,385)   *Yosemite 15', Yosemite Valley 1:24,000*
Admiral George Dewey commanded the American fleet in the one-sided victory over the Spanish fleet in the Battle of Manila Bay, May 1, 1898. He was the great American hero of his time; many suggested him for president. In a public interview on April 4, 1900, he said he would be "only too willing to serve. . . . Since studying this subject I am convinced that the office of President is not such a very difficult one to fill." Neither party brought up his name at its convention. (DAB) The name appeared on the first edition of the *Yosemite Valley* map, 1907. (YNP)

Diamond Mesa   *Mount Whitney 15', Mt. Williamson 7½'*
"So named by early sheepmen because of its diamond shape." (Junep.)
Referred to in 1898 by C. B. Bradley as a "high quadrate mesa." (*SCB* 2, no. 5,
Jan. 1899: 274.) (SNP)

Diamond Peak (4,001 m.–13,126)   *Mt. Pinchot 15',*
                                            Mt. Clarence King 7½'
Named by the USGS during the 1905 survey for the *Mt. Whitney* 30' map.
(LeConte, *Alpina,* 10.) (KCNP)

Diamond-X Lake   *Blackcap Mtn. 15', Mt. Henry 7½'*
William A. Dill of the 1947 DFG survey party named the lake on July 28 of
that year after the Diamond-X pack train owned by John Dale of Dinkey Creek.
(DFG survey.) (SiNF)

Diaz Creek, Lake   *Lone Pine 15', Mt. Langley 7½'*
The brothers Rafael and Eleuterio Diaz had a cattle ranch on the creek in the
1860s. (Farquhar: Versteeg.) Each brother patented 160 acres in secs. 2 and 3,
T. 16 S., R. 36 E. on April 20, 1874. Rafael homesteaded 160 acres in secs. 4
and 9 in 1886. Eleuterio's widow, Augustia, homesteaded 160 acres in secs. 9
and 10 in 1892. Abraham Diaz homesteaded 160 acres in sec. 10 in 1898. Thus
the brothers and their descendants owned adjoining lands totaling 1¼ square
miles around Diaz Lake and where Diaz Creek comes out of the hills. (INF)

Dillon Mill (site), Canyon; Dillonwood Grove   *Mineral King 15'*
Nathan P. Dillon established a sawmill at the site in the late 1870s.
(*Newsletter* 1, no. 7, Feb. 1970: 133.) Dillon patented 80 acres in the NW¼ of
sec. 10, T. 19 S., R. 30 E. in 1885; 160 acres in secs. 3 and 4 in 1887; and 160
acres in secs. 17 and 20 in 1896. George Dillon patented 160 acres in sec. 3 in
1887. The 1882 GLO plat shows "Dillon's Sawmill" in the NW¼ of sec. 10.
The present *Mineral King* quad shows the site of the mill almost a mile north of
there, in sec. 3. (SeNF)

Dingley Creek   *Tuolumne Meadows 15'*
Named by the Wheeler Survey. (Letter, Col. Benson to Versteeg, in
Farquhar files.) (YNP)

Dingleberry Lake (10,489)   *Mt. Goddard 15', Mt. Darwin 7½'*
John Schober named it. He was in the sheep business at the time, and
christened the lake for the dingleberries on the hind ends of his sheep. (Art
Schober.) (INF)

Dinkey Creek   *Huntington Lake 15', Dinkey Creek 7½', Nelson Mtn. 7½'*
Dinkey Meadow, Mountain (6,723–6,697), **Dome** (7,701–7,697)
                    Huntington Lake 15', Dinkey Creek 7½'
First and **Second Dinkey Lake**   *Huntington Lake 15', Dogtooth Peak 7½'*
Four hunters had a dog named Dinkey who was injured in a fight with a
grizzly bear at the creek in August 1863. (Farquhar: L. A. Winchell; also see
Elliott, *History,* 232.) The creek was named on T. S. Solomons' map of 1896,
"Dinkey Lake" on the first *Kaiser* 30' map, 1904, and the other "Dinkey"
names on the 15-minute quad, 1953. (SiNF)

Disappearing Creek   *Mt. Goddard 15' and 7½'*
   Named by Theodore S. Solomons in 1895 when he and E. C. Bonner came
down the Enchanted Gorge (which he also named) on their way from Mt.
Goddard to Simpson Meadow. (Farquhar: Solomons.) (KCNP)

Disappointment Lake (10,342)   *Blackcap Mtn. 15', Mt. Henry 7½'*
   Rae Crabtree, the Coolidge Meadow packer, reported in 1945 that the lake
was named by some tourists who had poor fishing there. (DFG survey.) (SiNF)

Disappointment Peak (4,242 m.–13,917)   *Big Pine 15', Split Mtn. 7½'*
   Named by J. Milton Davies, A. L. Jordan, and H. H. Bliss when they made
the first ascent on July 20, 1919. In a can they left a note reading: "The
undersigned made a first ascent of this peak this day and were disappointed not
to find it the highest point of the Middle Palisade. We hereby christen this
summit "Peak Disappointment." (*SCB* 11, no. 3, 1922: 266.) (KCNP, INF)

Disaster Peak (10,047)   *Sonora Pass 15', Disaster Peak 7½'*
Disaster Creek   *Dardanelles Cone 15' and 7½'*
   September 6, 1877: "We had finished a very successful day's work, and
were completing our labors by putting up the usual monument. . . . Mr. Cowles
[the topographer] loosened a heavy mass, which, slipping from its bearings,
precipitated him some 15 feet upon the jagged rocks below, passing over his legs
as it rolled on. Mr. Vail and myself, on hastening to his assistance, were
inexpressibly shocked to find that both legs had been broken." (Lt. M. M.
Macomb, Wheeler Survey, *Report,* 1878, 143.) Macomb named the peak; the
creek name was added, probably by the USGS, with publication of the
Dardanelles 30' map in 1898. (StNF, TNF)

Discovery Pinnacle (4,192 m.–over 13,760)
                                    Mount Whitney 15' and 7½'
   The name was suggested by Chester Versteeg in 1953. (SC papers in BL.)
Added to maps by the USGS because it was in common use. (SNP, INF)

Diving Board   *Yosemite 15', Yosemite Valley 1:24,000*
   "Never have I seen such a frightful precipice in all my experience. The edge
which my hands grasped was not more than a few inches thick, and below there
was nothing, absolutely nothing, but air down for 3,500 feet. Even the upper part
of the cliff could not be seen, for evidently the rock upon which we were lying
overhung the abyss. . . . To anyone who wants the experience of looking over a
first-class precipice, without being caged in by gas-pipe railings, I can
recommend this place above all others." (J. N. LeConte in *SCB* 9, no. 3, Jan.
1914: 134.) LeConte and James S. Hutchinson made this first ascent on July 26,
1912. (YNP)

Dog Lake   *Tuolumne Meadows 15'*
   In 1898 Robert B. Marshall of the USGS named this lake because he found
an abandoned sheepdog with a litter of puppies here. (Farquhar: Marshall.)
(YNP)

Doghead Peak (11,102)   *Matterhorn Peak 15'*
   A descriptive name; origin unknown. Quite possibly named by the USGS,

since it first appears on the first edition of the *Bridgeport* 30' map, 1911. The first mention in print is by Harold C. Bradley in *SCB* 8, no. 2, June 1911: 136–37. (YNP)

Dollar Lake   *Mt. Pinchot 15', Mt. Clarence King 7½'*
    Named for its shape—round, like a silver dollar. The name was added to the 7½-minute quad by the USGS beause it was in common use. Not named on the 15-minute quad; it is on the John Muir Trail, about 1.3 miles north by east from Fin Dome. (KCNP)

Dome Rock (7,221)   *Camp Nelson 15'*
    An old name; it appears on the 1881 GLO plat. (SeNF)

Donkey Lake   *Mt. Goddard 15', Mt. Thompson 7½'*
    Named in the 1930s by packer Art Schober. "We had burros in a pasture up there." (INF)

Donohue Pass, Peak (12,023)   *Mono Craters 15'*
    The pass and peak were named in 1895 by Lt. N. F. McClure for Sergeant Donohue, Troop K, 4th Cavalry, when Donohue made the first ascent of the peak. (Farquhar: McClure; also letter, Brig. Gen. M. F. Davis to Chester Versteeg, Farquhar files.) (YNP, INF)

Dore Cliff, Pass   *Tuolumne Meadows 15'*
    Paul Gustave Doré (1832–1883), a noted French artist and illustrator, who had great popular success for many years, especially in America and England. Named by Israel C. Russell, USGS, about 1882. ". . . a scarp of grander proportions than those below crosses the trough and forms a wall of rock more than a thousand feet high. This rocky wall, together with the cliffs forming the eastern side of the gorge as far as Lake Cañon, has been named, in honor of the great French artist, the Doré Cliffs." (Russell, *Quaternary,* 332–33.) (INF)

Doris Lake (6,823)   *Kaiser Peak 15', Mt. Givens 7½'*
    Ruby Rouch and her daughter Alva planted the lake with fish in 1928, and named it after Alva's daughter Doris. (DFG survey.) (SiNF)

Dorothy Lake; Dorothy Lake Pass   *Tower Peak 15'*
    R. B. Marshall of the USGS named the lake for Dorothy Forsyth, daughter of Major William W. Forsyth, acting superintendent of Yosemite National Park, 1909–12. (Farquhar: Marshall.) The lake was called "Jack Main's Lake" by Lt. N. F. McClure in 1894. (*SCB* 1, no. 5, Jan. 1895: 181.) The name "Dorothy Lake" first appears on the third edition of the *Dardanelles* 30' map, 1912. "Dorothy Lake Pass" was added to the *Tower Peak* 15' quad, 1956. (Lake, YNP; pass, YNP, TNF)

Dorst Creek   *Giant Forest 15'*
    Joseph Haddox Dorst (1852–1916), captain of the Fourth Cavalry, US Army, the first acting superintendent of Sequoia and General Grant national parks, 1891–92. (Farquhar.) (SNP)

Dougherty Peak (12,244)**, Creek, Meadow**   *Marion Peak 15'*
    All three features were named before 1903 for Bill and Bob Dougherty,

pioneer sheepmen, who grazed their herds in Granite Basin, and in Simpson Meadow on the Middle Fork of the Kings River. (Winchell, 158.) (KCNP)

Douglas Creek   *Dardanelles Cone 15', Dardanelle 7½'*
The 1879 GLO plat and surveyor's field notes locate "Douglas House" in the northeast quarter of sec. 28, T. 6 N., R. 20 E. Francis *Douglass* patented 160 acres in sec. 28 in 1891. (StNF)

Dragon Peak (12,995)   *Mt. Pinchot 15', Mt. Clarence King 7½',*
                                            Kearsarge Peak 7½'
Dragon Lake   *Mt. Pinchot 15', Mt. Clarence King 7½'*
The peak was named because its outline as seen from Rae Lakes resembles a dragon; the lake was named from the peak. (Farquhar.) Both names appear on the fifth edition of the *Mt. Whitney* 30' map, 1921. (KCNP, INF)

Dry Meadows   *Hockett Peak 15'*
Named by Harry Quinn, an early sheepman, because the meadow dried up in the spring when he brought his herd to pasture. (*Newsletter* 1, no. 9, Dec. 1970: 190.) (INF)

Duck Lake   *Tehipite Dome 15'*
Named by Rae Crabtree and Bill White (probably in the 1940s) because they saw a duck on it. (DFG survey.) (SiNF)

Dumbbell Lakes (lower, 11,108; upper, 11,410)   *Mt. Goddard 15',*
                                            North Palisade 7½'
"First it was over hard-frozen snowfields, and then over huge granite fragments to the margin of a lonely lake. This, from its shape, we called Dumbbell Lake." (J. N. LeConte in *SCB* 5, no. 1, Jan. 1904: 7.) LeConte referred to the lower lake. USGS surveyors probably applied the name to both lakes, since "Dumbbell Lakes" is on the first *Mt. Goddard* 30' map, 1912. (KCNP)

Dumonts Meadows   *Topaz Lake 15', Wolf Creek 7½'*
For a French-Canadian woodcutter, one of many who supplied the Comstock mines. (Gudde: Maule.) "Dumont's Meadow" is on the Wheeler atlas sheet 56B, 1876–77. (TNF)

Dunderberg Peak (12,374), **Creek**   *Matterhorn Peak 15'*
"Locally called Castle Peak, but which we named [in 1878] Dunderberg, after the mines of that name upon its northerly slope, desiring to avoid duplicating the name which we had already given to the castellated volcanic mass north of the Central Pacific Railroad near Summit Station." (Wheeler Survey, Lt. Macomb *Report,* 1879, 2233.) Called "Castle Peak" on Goddard's map, 1857. (Duplication and switching of names involved three peaks; see **Tower Peak** and **Mount Warren.**) On June 20, 1947, Birge M. and Malcolm Clark found a tin cannister on the peak that contained the Wheeler Survey record from 1878. (*SCB* 33, no. 3, March 1948: 123.)

Gudde states that the mine was probably named after the Union man-of-war *Dunderberg,* launched in 1865, which had probably been named after Dunderberg Mountain in New York state. (Gudde, *Place Names,* 95.)

Dunderberg Creek extends onto the *Bodie* 15' quad, where there is also the site of Dunderberg Mill. A. F. Bryant and George K. Porter, under the Mining Act of 1870, bought the lots on which the mill was situated, in January 1874. (GLO.) (TNF)

Durrwood Creek, Camp   *Hockett Peak 15'*
For Billy Durrwood, an early resident of South Fork Valley and the Kernville area. (SeNF files.) It is likely that Durrwood Meadows on the *Kernville* 15' quad was named for the same person. (SeNF)

Dusy Branch, Basin   *Mt. Goddard 15', North Palisade 7½'*
Dusy Meadows, Creek   *Blackcap Mtn. 15', Ward Mountain 7½'*
Frank Dusy (1836–1898), born in Canada, came to California in 1858 and to Fresno County in 1864. He was a sheepman who took his stock into the mountains in the region of the North and Middle Forks of the Kings River. He discovered Tehipite Valley in 1869, and explored the Middle Fork as far as the Palisades in 1877. (Elliott, *History,* 213.)

Dusy took the first photographs of Tehipite in 1879, carrying a bulky portrait camera, studio tripod, wet plates, and chemicals. L. A. Winchell, in 1879, gave Dusy's name to the branch of the Middle Fork north of the Palisades. (Farquhar: Winchell; see also Winchell, 157, 159.) Portrait of Dusy in *SCB* 11, no. 4, 1923: opp. 383.

The lakes in what is now Dusy Basin were called "Dusy Lakes" on the *Mt. Goddard* 30' maps from 1923 through the final edition in 1951. (Basin and branch, KCNP; meadows and creek, SiNF)

Dutch Johns Meadow   *Mt. Tom 15', Tungsten Hills 7½'*
Johann Albars homesteaded 22½ acres in the northwest corner of sec. 3, T. 8 S., R. 31 E. in 1915. (INF)

Eagle Peak (11,845), **Creek**   *Matterhorn Peak 15'*
Probably named by the USGS during surveying for the *Bridgeport* 30' map, 1905–09, since it has a benchmark and was used as a triangulation point. Both names are on the first edition of the map, 1911. The creek was called "Mill Creek" on the 1877 GLO plat and in the field notes because where it flowed into Buckeye Creek was "Hemerville's sawmill," at the center of sec. 5, T. 4 N., R. 24 E. (TNF)

Eagle Peak (10,318)   *Huntington Lake 15', Nelson Mtn. 7½'*
Probably named by USGS surveyors in 1901–02; the name is on the first edition of the *Kaiser* 30' map, 1904. (SiNF)

Eagle Peak (9,370–9,385), **Creek, Meadow**   *Dardanelles Cone 15',*
                                                        Dardanelle 7½'
Origin unknown, but possibly named by the Wheeler Survey; the peak and the creek are named on atlas sheet 56D, 1878–79. The meadow is named on the first *Dardanelles* 30' map, 1898. (StNF)

Eagle Peak (7,779), **Creek**   *Yosemite 15', Yosemite Valley 1:24,000*
Eagle Peak Creek, Meadows   *Hetch Hetchy Reservoir 15',*
                                                Yosemite Valley 1:24,000

Eagle Tower   *Yosemite Valley 1:24,000*
Eagle Peak is the highest of the Three Brothers. It was called "Eagle Point"
by Joseph LeConte in 1870. (*Ramblings,* 70.) It also had that name on the
Wheeler atlas sheet 56D, 1878–79.
One source states that Eagle Peak was named in 1870. " . . . the lady whom I
married a year later [1871] was in that excursion to Eagle Peak. She was the first
white woman ever there, and she suggested the name 'Eagle Peak' to Mr. Muir at
the time, and he kept his promise to her that it should thereafter be so known.
Before that it was simply the highest of the 'Three Brothers.' " (Letter, Nelson F.
Evans, The Prudential Insurance Company of America, to Mrs. Helen Muir
Funk, Dec. 28, 1914; a condolence letter, four days after Muir died.)
"This was so named from its being such a favorite resort of this famous bird
of prey. . . . I once had the pleasure of conducting the Rev. J. P. Newman, D.D.,
and Rev. Sutherland, D.D. (each, then, of Washington, D.C.), to its wondrous
summit, when, after a long, and evidently constrained silence the former
suddenly ejaculated, 'Glory! Hal-le-lu-jah—Glory! Hal-le-lu-jah!' (the doctor
was a Methodist, you know) then turning around, the tears literally streaming
down his cheeks, he thus expressed himself: 'Well, Mr. H., if I had crossed the
continent of America on purpose to look upon *this one view,* I should have
returned home, sir, perfectly satisfied.' " (Hutchings, *In the Heart,* 479.)
"Eagle Tower" appeared on Lt. N. F. McClure's map of 1896, "Eagle
Creek" on the *Yosemite Valley* map in 1927, "Eagle Peak Creek" and
"Meadows" on the 15-minute maps in 1956. (YNP)

Eagle Scout Peak (12,040), **Creek**   *Triple Divide Peak 15'*
An expedition of Boy Scouts from the San Joaquin Valley was
commemorated by giving the name "Eagle Scout Peak" to a mountain on the
Great Western Divide. Francis P. Farquhar of the Sierra Club led three of the
scouts on a first ascent of the peak on July 15, 1926. (*SCB* 12, no. 4, 1927: 420.)
The names first appeared on the fourth edition of the *Tehipite* 30' map, 1929.
Before 1929, the creek was named "North Fork of Middle Fork of Kaweah
River." (SNP)

Eagle Peaks (9,645), **Spur**   *Tehipite Dome 15'*
Possibly named by the USGS in 1903 during surveying for the *Tehipite* 30'
map; on the first edition, 1905. (SeNF)

East Lake (2,886 m.–9,445)   *Mount Whitney 15', Mt. Brewer 7½'*
East Creek   *Mount Whitney 15', Mt. Pinchot 15', Mt. Brewer 7½',*
                                              Mt. Clarence King 7½'
The lake was named by a State Hydrographic Survey party in 1881 or 1882
for Thomas Benton East, a hunter, trapper, and cattleman of Eshom Valley,
Tulare County. (Farquhar: Versteeg, from Ellis and Fry.) The features were
called "Brewer Lake" and "Brewer Creek" on Davis's map of 1896. Bolton C.
Brown in 1896 called the creek "South Cañon," meaning the south fork of
Bubbs Creek. (*SCB* 2, no. 1, Jan. 1897: 20.) The name probably was extended
to the creek by the USGS during the 1905 survey for the *Mt. Whitney* 30' map;
it is on the first edition, 1907. (KCNP)

Ebbetts Pass (8,732–8,731), **Peak**   *Markleeville 15', Ebbetts Pass 7½'*
"The pass we called Ebbets' Pass, in memory of Major Ebbets, who went over it in the spring of 1851." (Goddard, *Report,* 90.) It is uncertain whether Ebbetts first saw the pass named for him in 1850 or 1851. The naming took place as the result of the 1853 surveying expedition. Ebbetts was killed in the explosion of the steamer *Secretary* in San Francisco Bay in 1854. (*Alta California,* April 16, 1854.) The pass was named on Goddard's map of 1857, but the Whitney Survey omitted it from their maps because it was not in use locally. The name was restored by the USGS with the publication of the *Markleeville 30'* map, 1893. (StNF)

Echo Lake (11,602)   *Mt. Goddard 15', Mt. Darwin 7½'*
"I named that. I had a rifle at the time and was hunting deer. I shot across the darned lake, and things just seemed to vibrate." (Art Schober.) Named in the 1930s or 1940s. (INF)

Echo Peaks (over 11,040), **Lake**   *Tuolumne Meadows 15'*
Echo Creek   *Tuolumne Meadows 15', Merced Peak 15'*
Echo Valley   *Merced Peak 15'*
Echo Peak and Echo Creek probably were named by the Wheeler Survey; both are on atlas sheet 56D, 1878–79. The peak remained singular until the fifth edition of the *Mt. Lyell 30'* map, 1922. The lake name first appeared on the *Tuolumne Meadows 15'* quad, 1956, and the valley name on the *Merced Peak 15'* quad, 1953. (YNP)

Edison, Lake Thomas A. (spillway, 7,643)   *Mt. Abbot 15', Kaiser Peak 15', Graveyard Peak 7½', Sharktooth Peak 7½', Mt. Givens 7½'*
The lake was named in the early 1950s when Mono Creek was dammed, flooding Vermilion Valley. That name was given the valley in September 1894 by Theodore S. Solomons and Leigh Bierce. "The middle portion of the creek flows through an extensive flat covered by a growth of tamarack and other trees, which give it a park-like appearance. This flat is at least five miles long by a mile in average width. From the color of its soil, we christened it Vermilion Valley." (*SCB* 1, no. 6, May 1895: 227.) Solomons said that sheepmen called it "the Park." (*Overland Monthly* 27, no. 161, May 1896: 486.) (SiNF)

Edna Lake   *Merced Peak 15'*
Named by R. B. Marshall, USGS, for Edna Bowman, later Mrs. Charles J. Kuhn. (Farquhar: Marshall.) (YNP)

Edyth Lake   *Pinecrest 15', Tower Peak 15'*
Major William W. Forsyth named the lake in 1910 for Edyth Nance, daughter of Colonel John T. Nance. (Farquhar.) The name was on the *Dardanelles 30'* maps as "Edith Lake" from 1912 through 1947; the spelling was officially changed to "Edyth" by a BGN decision in 1932. (YNP)

Ehrnbeck Peak (11,240)   *Tower Peak 15'*
Lt. Arthur R. Ehrnbeck, US Army, made a report in 1909 on a comprehen-

sive road and trail project for Yosemite National Park. (Farquhar; see *Appendix A, Rept. of the Acting Supt. of YNP, 1909.*) (YNP, TNF)

Eisen, Mount (12,160)   *Mineral King 15'*

Gustavus Augustus Eisen (1847–1940), a scientist-conservationist, member of the California Academy of Sciences for 66 years and of the Sierra Club for 48 years, one of the important advocates for establishing Sequoia and General Grant national parks in 1890. Gustav Eisen was born in Sweden. He came to California in 1873, and was with Frank Dusy on a number of journeys into the Kings River region of the Sierra Nevada between 1874 and 1880. The name for the mountain was requested by the Academy of Sciences in December 1940, and approved by the BGN in September 1941. Eisen's ashes are interred on the north side of the mountain. (Eisen papers, CAS.) (SNP)

El Capitan (7,569); **El Capitan Gully, Meadow**   *Yosemite 15',*
Yosemite Valley 1:24,000

The name was given by the Mariposa Battalion in 1851. "The native Indian name . . . is *To-tó-kon oo-lah,* from *To-tó-kon,* the Sandhill Crane, a chief of the First People. (C. Hart Merriam in *SCB* 10, no. 2, Jan. 1917: 206.)

"The famous cliff, El Capitan, the Captain, is a Spanish interpretation of the Indian name To-tock-ah-noo-lah, meaning the 'Rock Chief.' " (Bunnell, *Report,* 1889–90, 9.) "Upon one occasion I asked [Tenaya], 'Why do you call the cliff Tote-ack-ah-noo-la?' The Indian's reply was, 'Because he looks like one. . . . Come with me and see.' . . . As the Indian reached a point a little above and some distance out from the cliff, he triumphantly pointed to the perfect image of a man's head and face, with side whiskers, and with an expression of the sturdy English type, and asked, 'Does he not look like Tote-ack-ah-noo-la?' The 'Rock Chief,' or 'Captain,' was again Sandino's [the interpreter's] interpretation of the word while viewing the likeness." (Bunnell, *Discovery,* 1911, 214–15.)

There is also a legend type of explanation that is repeated throughout Yosemite literature. Galen Clark says that Tul-tok-a-nú-la is from the measuring worm (tul-tok-a-na) which crawled up the face of the rock to rescue two small boys who were beyond being saved by any other creatures of the valley. (Clark, 92–95.)

According to one source, the original English name was "Crane Mountain," not for the reason given above but for the sandhill cranes that entered the valley by flying over the top of El Capitan. (*YNN* 34, no. 1, Jan. 1955: 6.) And finally, Hutchings' *California Magazine* 1, no. 1, July 1856: 3, called it "Giant's Tower." (YNP)

Elba Lake   *Mount Tom 7½'*

Named by Ralph Beck of the DFG in 1954. (Phil Pister. See **Alsace Lake.**) (SiNF)

Elbow Hill (over 9,200)   *Tuolumne Meadows 15'*

A descriptive name, probably applied by the Wheeler Survey. It is in the sketchbook of J. Calvert Spiller, topographical assistant with Lt. Macomb, and is on atlas sheet 56D, 1878–79. (YNP)

Eleanor, Lake (Reservoir)   *Lake Eleanor 15'*
Eleanor Creek   *Pinecrest 15', Lake Eleanor 15'*
The lake was named in the 1860s by the Whitney Survey for Eleanor Goddard Whitney (1856–1882), daughter of Josiah Dwight Whitney, state geologist and director of the first California Geological Survey. The name is on the Hoffmann and Gardiner map, 1863–67. The name of the creek first appears on the Wheeler Survey atlas sheet 56D, 1878–79.
   The small natural lake occupied the center part of sec. 35 and a small part at the upper left of sec. 36 in T. 2 N., R. 19 E. The dam that converted it into a reservoir for San Francisco was built in 1917–18; it raised the lake level thirty-five feet. (YNP)

Electra Peak (12,442)   *Merced Peak 15'*
Probably named by the USGS in 1898–99 during the survey for the *Mt. Lyell* 30' map, published in 1901; the USGS determined the altitude by triangulation, as reported by J. N. LeConte, "Elevations." (YNP, SiNF)

Elephants Back (9,585–9,603)   *Markleeville 15', Carson Pass 7½'*
A rather fanciful descriptive name for a long, ridge-like mountain. (See photo and sketch in *SCB* 44, no. 7, Oct. 1959: 60.) George H. Goddard (*Report, 1855*) called it "the Elephant" in his list of places along the route. A map of Alpine County, made about 1870, has it as "Elephant Mountain." The Wheeler Survey atlas sheet 56B, 1876–77, calls it "Elephant's Back." (ENF, TNF)

Elevenmile Creek   *Yosemite 15'*
Named for a stage station on the old Wawona Road, eleven miles from Wawona. Shown as "Eleven Mile Sta." on the Wheeler atlas sheet 56D, 1878–79. (YNP)

Elizabeth Lake (9,508)   *Tuolumne Meadows 15'*
R. B. Marshall of the USGS named the lake in 1909 for Elizabeth Crow Simmons, a niece. (Farquhar: Marshall.) (YNP)

Elizabeth Pass (over 11,360)   *Triple Divide Peak 15'*
Stewart Edward White and his wife, Elizabeth, crossed from the head of Deadman Canyon to the Middle Fork of the Kaweah River in 1905; they named the pass for Mrs. White. (White, *The Pass,* 1906, 157–58.) The account of their trip was first published in *Outing Magazine,* March, April, May 1906.
   The pass was once known as "Turtle Pass." (Fry and White, 178.) There is a rock about four feet long, at the east end of the pass, that looks remarkably like a turtle. (Farquhar files.) (SNP)

Ellery Lake (9,489)   *Mono Craters 15'*
For Nathaniel Ellery, the State Engineer in charge of constructing the road from Mono Lake to Tioga Pass in 1909. (Farquhar; see also *SCB* 7, no. 3, Jan. 1910: 195–96.) The original name was "Rinedollar Lake," for a man of that name who had a mine nearby. (USGS.) (INF)

Ellis Meadow   *Triple Divide Peak 15'*
Sam L. N. Ellis, an early head ranger for the USFS in the Kings River region, and one-time supervisor of Tulare County. (Farquhar: Fry.) (KCNP)

El Portal *El Portal 15'*
Spanish for "The Gateway." It was named in 1907 by officials of the Yosemite Valley Railroad. The railroad company had hoped to build the line into the valley itself, but could not get the right-of-way from the federal government. It settled for building a wagon road from El Portal to the valley. (Johnston, *Railroads*, 15.) The GLO plat of 1884 shows "Wharton's Ranch" where El Portal now is. (StNF)

Emerald Lake *Mt. Morrison 15', Bloody Mtn. 7½'*
Origin unknown. The names "Emerald Lake" and "Way Lake" were inadvertently transposed on the *Mt. Morrison* 15' quad; they are correctly shown on the newer map. (USGS.) (INF)

Emerald Lake *Triple Divide Peak 15'*
Named in 1925 by Supt. John R. White of Sequoia National Park. (Farquhar.) (SNP)

Emerald Lakes *Mt. Goddard 15', Mt. Darwin 7½'*
Named in the 1930s by John Schober for their intensely blue color. (Art Schober.) (INF)

Emerald Peak (12,546–12,543) *Blackcap Mtn. 15', Mt. Henry 7½'*
Named by Theodore S. Solomons and Ernest C. Bonner in July 1895. ". . . a massive rock which rears its head at the angle formed by the cañon and gorge. This rock, which we have called Emerald Point, is of a bright green color. . . ." (Solomons in *Appalachia* 8, no. 1, 1896: 46.) (KCNP)

Emerald Pool *Yosemite 15', Yosemite Valley 1:24,000*
Named in 1856. "The descent between the Nevada and the Vernal Falls is about three hundred feet, and in its rapid flow into the 'Emerald Pool' it is broken into countless liquid diamonds." (Bunnell, *Report*, 1889–90, 12.)
It was first called "Frances Pool," for Mrs. Jane Frances Neal, the first white woman to visit Nevada Fall. (Mariposa *Democrat*, Aug. 5, 1856.) (YNP)

Emeric Lake, Creek *Tuolumne Meadows 15'*
Named in 1896 by Lt. N. F. McClure for Henry F. Emeric, president of the California Board of Fish Commissioners. (Farquhar.) (YNP)

Emerson, Mount (13,118); **Emerson Lake** (11,219–11,196)
Mt. Goddard 15', Mt. Darwin 7½'
"I have named a grand *wide-winged* mountain on the head of the Joaquin Mount Emerson. Its head is high above its fellows and wings are white with ice and snow." (John Muir, letter to Mrs. Carr, September 1873, in Badè, vol. 1, 389.) Ralph Waldo Emerson (1803–1882), essayist, poet, lecturer, and philosopher, visited Yosemite Valley in 1871 and went to the Mariposa Grove with Muir.
Muir made a mistake in location; he was putting Emerson's name on Mt. Humphreys, which had already been named by the Whitney Survey. The present Mount Emerson was probably designated by the USGS in 1907–09 during the survey for the *Mt. Goddard* 30' map, first published in 1912. The *Mt. Goddard* 15' map (1948) shows "Mt. Emerson" as the eastern of two peaks,

with an altitude of 13,225. The *Mt. Darwin* 7½' quad shows that peak as being 13,204, but puts "Mt. Emerson" on the western peak of 13,118.

Emerson Lake was originally called "Tobe Lake," after Tobe Way, the packer who first stocked it. (Art Schober.) (INF)

Emma, Mount (10,525); **Emma Lake**   *Fales Hot Springs 15'*
Probably named for Emma Mack, whose parents lived at Hardy Station at the junction of US 395 and State Route 108. This was the presumption of Sen. Maurice Mack of Nevada, her brother. (Maule. See also **Anna Lake**.) (TNF)

Enchanted Gorge   *Mt. Goddard 15' and 7½'*
The name was given in July 1895 by Theodore S. Solomons to the gorge on Disappearing Creek, with its head between Scylla and Charybdis. He named the other three features at the same time. (*Appalachia* 8, no. 1, 1896: 55.) "The Enchanted Gorge, so named because of the many remarkable features it possesses, and the weirdness of its scenery. . . ." (MS of Solomons, 1896, in Farquhar Papers, BL.) (KCNP)

Epidote Peak (over 10,880)   *Matterhorn Peak 15'*
Probably named by the USGS during the 1904–09 survey for the *Bridgeport* 30' map; it appears on the first edition, 1911. Epidote is a silicate of iron, calcium, and aluminum, often greenish in color. (TNF)

Ericsson, Mount (13,608); **Ericsson Crags**   *Mount Whitney 15',*
Mt. Brewer 7½'
The peak was named in 1896 by Bolton C. and Lucy Brown. "As it seemed that we were the first to make this ascent, we built a monument and left a record, naming it, in honor of Capt. John Ericsson, and in recognition of its extremely craggy character, *Crag Ericsson*." (*SCB* 2, no. 2, May 1897: 92.)

John Ericsson (1803–1889), born in Sweden, came to the US in 1839. An engineer and inventor, best known for designing and building the ironclad *Monitor*, which fought the *Merrimac* at the Battle of Hampton Roads, March 9, 1862.

The mountain has always been called "Mt. Ericsson" on maps. "Ericsson Crags" was added to the *Mount Whitney* 15' map because of its use by climbers and its appearance on other maps. (KCNP, SNP)

Erin Lake (11,645)   *Mount Whitney 15' and 7½'*
So named because its shape resembles that of Ireland. Suggested by Chester Versteeg. (SC papers in BL.) BGN decision 1937–38. (SNP)

Eshom Valley, Creek, Point   *Giant Forest 15'*
John Perry Eshom, a native of North Carolina, came to California in 1849. He mined in Mariposa County, and later homesteaded in Eshom Valley. He sometimes took dried fruit from his ranch across the mountains to sell in Virginia City, Nevada. (*Los Tulares*, no. 30, March 1957: 3.) (SeNF)

Eureka Valley   *Dardanelles Cone 15', Dardanelle 7½'*
Eureka, Greek for "I have found it," is supposed to be what Archimedes exclaimed when he discovered a method of detecting the amount of alloy mixed

with gold in the crown of the king of Syracuse. The word is the motto of California. Eureka Valley may have been named by the Wheeler Survey; it is on atlas sheet 56D, 1878–79. (StNF)

Evans Grove, Creek *Tehipite Dome 15'*
"Named after John Evans, who lived near the grove for years and protected it from fires." (Fry and White, 114.) (SeNF)

Evelyn Lake *Mineral King 15'*
Evelyn Clough, sister of William O. Clough, discoverer of Clough Cave. She first married George Cahoon (see **Cahoon Meadow,** etc.), and later was Mrs. Busby, Mrs. Mentier, and Mrs. Long. (Farquhar: Ansel F. Hall; also Fry and White, 178.) (SNP)

Evelyn Lake (10,328) *Tuolumne Meadows 15'*
Named for a daughter of Major William W. Forsyth, acting superintendent of Yosemite National Park, 1909–12. (Farquhar: R. B. Marshall.) The name first appeared on the third edition of the *Mt. Lyell* 30' map, 1910. (YNP)

Evolution Lake (10,852–10,850), **Creek, Valley, Basin** *Mt. Goddard 15',*
Mt. Darwin 7½'
Evolution Creek, Meadow, Valley *Blackcap Mtn. 15', Mt. Henry 7½'*
In July 1895 Theodore S. Solomons named six peaks at the headwaters of the San Joaquin River for the foremost exponents of the theory of evolution: Mounts Darwin, Fiske, Haeckel, Huxley, Spencer, and Wallace. At the same time he named Evolution Lake. The peaks are often referred to as the "Evolution Group," although that is not an official name. (*Appalachia* 8, no. 1, Jan. 1896: 48–50.) Evolution Creek was named by J. N. LeConte in 1904, replacing the former unwieldy name of "The Middle Branch of the South Fork of the San Joaquin River." (*SCB* 5, no. 3, Jan. 1905: 229.) The "Evolution" names for the valley, basin, and meadow were added by the USGS to the third edition of the *Mt. Goddard* 30' map, 1923. (KCNP)

Ewe Lake *Mt. Goddard 15' and 7½'*
Named in 1948 by William A. Dill of the DFG because of its proximity to Bighorn Lake. (DFG survey.) (SiNF)

Excelsior Mountain (12,446) *Matterhorn Peak 15'*
Probably named by the USGS during surveying for the *Bridgeport* 30' map, 1905–09. It is on the first edition of the map (1911), but is not in J. N. LeConte's "Elevations." (YNP, INF)

Fairview Dome (9,731) *Tuolumne Meadows 15'*
Possibly named by the Wheeler Survey; the name is on atlas sheet 56D, 1878–79. Lt. N. F. McClure's map of 1895 calls it "Soda Springs Buttes," but notes that it is also called "Fairview Dome." John Muir wrote, ". . . a majestic dome which long ago I named the *Glacier Monument.*" (Muir, *Parks,* 87.) In another book Muir said he named it "Tuolumne Glacier Monument." (Muir, *The Yosemite,* 178.) In 1905 the present name was in use, but it was sometimes called "Tuolumne Monument." (*SCB* 5, no. 3, Jan. 1905: 219.) (YNP)

Faith Valley   *Markleeville 15', Carson Pass 7½'*
Named by government surveyors in 1855 to correspond with "Hope Valley"
and "Charity Valley." (Goddard, *Report.*) (TNF)

Fales Hot Springs   *Fales Hot Springs 15'*
Samuel ("Sam") Fales, born in Michigan in 1829, came to Sacramento in
the 1860s and to Antelope Valley, Mono County, in 1868. He developed the hot
springs in 1877, and lived there until his death in 1932. Frémont, in the
Memoirs of his second expedition, related that his party saw these hot springs
on January 27, 1844. (Maule, *Western Folklore* 7, no. 2, April 1948: 174–75.)
Fales patented 160 acres of the land surrounding the springs, in 1882. (GLO.)
    "During the day (July 15, 1863) we passed a very large and copious hot
spring; the water is boiling, and a stream large enough for a small mill runs
away." (Brewer, *Up and Down,* 422.)
    Apparently someone developed the springs before Fales, but couldn't make
a go of it. Joseph LeConte passed by in 1870. "Everything suitable for a
watering-place is found here—hot baths, vapor baths, accommodations for
visitors, etc.,—although in somewhat rude style. . . . it is now entirely
abandoned." (LeConte, *Ramblings,* 122.) (TNF)

Fallen Moon, Lake of the   *Marion Peak 15'*
The lake was named in 1921 by Frank Ernest Hill, who wrote a romantic,
gushing poem about it. (*SCB* 11, no. 4, 1923: 374.) (KCNP)

Fantail Lake   *Tuolumne Meadows 15'*
Named by Everett Spuller, in 1932, because of its shape. (Spuller.) (INF)

Farewell Gap, Canyon   *Mineral King 15'*
Named about 1872 by miners, probably because one gets a last glimpse to
the north from this pass when headed south from Mineral King. (Farquhar:
Wallace.) (SNP, SeNF)

Farrington Siphon   *Mono Craters 15'*
Archibald Farrington, Jr., patented 320 acres in secs. 26, 27, 34, and 35, T.
1 N., R. 26 E. in 1909, and another 280 acres in secs. 31 and 32 in 1917.
(INF)

Fay Creek   *Kernville 15', Isabella 15', Weldon 7½'*
Almeron Fay homesteaded 160 acres in sec. 22, T. 25 S., R. 34 E. in 1884.
(SeNF)

Feather Lake   *Mt. Abbot 15', Graveyard Peak 7½'*
This lake was supposed to have been named "Vermilion Lake," but that
name was mistakenly placed where it is now when the 15-minute quad was
published in 1953. The present Feather Lake was given that name because of its
position relative to Arrowhead Lake. (BGN decision, 1965; DFG survey.) The
lake is not named on the 15-minute quad; it is 0.7 mile northwest of Vermilion
Lake. (SiNF)

Ferguson Creek, Meadow   *Triple Divide Peak 15'*
S. L. N. Ellis named the creek for Andrew D. Ferguson in the early 1920s.
(Farquhar.) He raised cattle and horses, was a grain buyer, was in the oil

business, and was later a county game warden. In 1916 he was appointed field agent for the DFG. (Vandor, vol. 1, 1085–86.) Ferguson was the founder of the summer colony of Wilsonia.

The creek was called "Bog Creek" on the first three editions of the *Tehipite* 30' map; changed to "Ferguson Creek" on the 1929 edition. The meadow was called "Long Meadow" on the first four editions; changed to "Ferguson Meadow" on the 1939 edition. (KCNP)

Fernandez Pass (10,175), **Creek, Lakes**   *Merced Peak 15'*
First Sergeant Joseph Fernandez, Troop K, Fourth Cavalry, US Army, was with Lt. Harry C. Benson in the exploration of the headwaters of the Merced River, 1895–97. He was also in Yosemite National Park later, when Benson was the acting superintendent. Benson named the pass. (Farquhar: Benson.) The creek and lakes were first named on the *Merced Peak 15'* map, 1953. (Pass, YNP, SiNF; creek and lakes, SiNF)

Filly Lake   *Blackcap Mtn. 15' and 7½'*
Named in 1948 by William A. Dill of the DFG because it is close to Horsehead Lake. (DFG survey.) (SiNF)

Fin Dome (3,558 m.–11,693)   *Mt. Pinchot 15',*
                                                                Mt. Clarence King 7½'
Named by Bolton C. Brown in 1899. On a sketch map he depicted the features between Rae Lakes and Sixty Lake Basin (neither of those yet named at the time) as a south-facing monster: "The Sea Serpent." Of the names of the serpent's parts, "The Fin" is the only one that stuck. What Brown called "The Head" is the feature with an unchecked elevation of 11,942 feet. "The Tail" was the long ridge running north from Fin Dome. (*SCB* 3, no. 2, May 1900: 136, 138, 142, 146.) (KCNP)

Finger Lake   *Tuolumne Meadows 15'*
Everett Spuller named it in 1932 for its shape. (Spuller.) (INF)

Finger Peak (12,404)   *Mt. Goddard 15' and 7½'*
Probably named by the USGS in the 1907–09 survey for the *Mt. Goddard* 30' map. It is on the first edition of that map (1912), but is not in J. N. LeConte's "Elevations." (KCNP)

Finger Peaks (highest, over 11,440)   *Matterhorn Peak 15'*
Probably named by the USGS during the 1905–09 survey for the *Bridgeport* 30' map; it appears on the first edition, 1911. (YNP)

Finger Rock (9,606)   *Tehipite Dome 15'*
Possibly named by the USGS during the 1903 survey for the *Tehipite* 30' map; it appears on the first edition, 1905. (SiNF)

Finger Rock (9,145)   *Monache Mtn. 15'*
Possibly named by the USGS during the 1905 survey for the *Olancha* 30' map; it appears on the first edition, 1907. (SeNF)

Fingerbowl Lake   *Huntington Lake 15', Dogtooth Peak 7½'*
Earlier known as "Lake Elsie" and "Little Deep Lake." It is in a cirque

located in a steep amphitheater, and possibly was named by Scott M. Soule and
Sidney Shute of the DFG. (DFG survey.) (SiNF)

Fireplace Bluffs, Creek   *Yosemite 15', Yosemite Valley 1:24,000*
"Fireplace Bluffs" is a descriptive name; the namer is unknown. It appears
on the first edition of the *Yosemite Valley* map, 1907. The name for the creek
was added on the fourth edition, 1927. (YNP)

Fish Creek   *Devils Postpile 15', Crystal Crag 7½', Mt. Morrison 15',*
        Bloody Mtn. 7½', Mt. Abbot 15' and 7½', Graveyard Peak 7½'
Fish Valley   *Devils Postpile 15', Crystal Crag 7½'*
"Apropos of the sheepmen, I afterward learned that such of the fraternity as
had visited the cañon were less strongly impressed by its scenic features than by
the abundance of trout; hence they gave the stream the name Fish Creek,
ignoring the cañon completely, except (possibly) to recognize it as forming the
banks of the creek." (Theodore S. Solomons in *SCB* 1, no. 3, Jan. 1894: 79.)
(SiNF)

Fish Creek; Fish Creek Meadow   *Monache Mtn. 15'*
These are old names, origin unknown. The creek was named on the 1873
GLO plat; the name for the meadow was in use in 1889. (Boyd, *A Climb.*)
(SeNF)

Fisher Lakes   *Tower Peak 15'*
The name was approved by a BGN decision in 1965, but the decision didn't
say for what or whom the name was given. It probably is for Charles K. Fisher,
who surveyed the lakes for the DFG in 1952. (DFG survey.) Not named on
early editions of the 15-minute quad. It is a group of five small lakes just north of
Lertora Lake. (StNF)

Fishgut Lakes (11,010)   *Mt. Goddard 15', Mt. Darwin 7½'*
John Schober named them sometime after he stocked them during the
1930s. When he visited the lakes again, he found a visible collection of fish guts
that successful fishermen had thrown back into one of the lakes. (Art Schober.)
(INF)

Fiske, Mount (13,503–13,524)   *Mt. Goddard 15', Mt. Darwin 7½'*
"A mile south of Mt. Wallace, Mt. Fiske (named after the distinguished
American historian and writer on the Evolution philosophy) rears a dark granite
pyramid into the clear sky." (Theodore S. Solomons in *Appalachia* 8, no. 1,
Jan. 1896: 48.) One of the "Evolution Group" named by Solomons in 1895.
John Fiske (1842–1901), through his writings, helped to spread a knowledge of
Darwin and Spencer in the United States.
    On the first two editions of the *Mt. Goddard* 30' map (1912 and 1918)
"Mount Fiske" was incorrectly placed at the point where the Goddard Divide
intersects the main crest of the Sierra. It was put on the proper peak on the third
edition, 1923. On the *Mt. Darwin* 7½' quad, "Mt Fiske Glacier" has been
added—just north of the peak. (KCNP)

Fissures, The   *Yosemite 15', Yosemite Valley 1:24,000*
An old, descriptive name for a feature on the Pohono Trail just east of Taft
Point. "A cleft or split in the rock . . . one thousand feet deep, five feet wide at
the top and front, and grows gradually narrower as it extends downward and
backward into the mountain." (Bancroft's *Tourist Guide,* 1871, 31.) The name
was confirmed by the BGN in 1932, but it did not appear on any map until the
Yosemite 15' quad in 1956. (YNP)

Flat Note Lake   *Mt. Abbot 15', Mt. Hilgard 7½'*
See **Medley Lake.** (SiNF)

Flatiron Butte (over 11,360)   *Matterhorn Peak 15'*
Flatiron Ridge   *Matterhorn Peak 15', Fales Hot Springs 15'*
Possibly named by the USGS during the 1905–09 survey for the *Bridgeport*
30' map; both names are on the first edition, 1911. (TNF)

Fleming Mountain (10,796), **Creek, Lake**   *Blackcap Mtn. 15',*
                                                                    Mt. Henry 7½'
Probably named by the USGS during the 1907–09 survey for the *Mt.
Goddard* 30' map; the mountain and the creek are on the first edition, 1912. The
lake first appeared on the *Blackcap Mtn.* 15' quad, 1953. (SiNF)

Fletcher Creek   *Tuolumne Meadows 15', Merced Peak 15'*
Upper Fletcher Lake; Fletcher Peak (11,408)   *Tuolumne Meadows 15'*
The creek and lake were named in 1895 by Lt. N. F. McClure for Arthur G.
Fletcher, of the State Board of Fish Commissioners, who was instrumental in
stocking the streams in Yosemite National Park. (Farquhar: McClure.) The
creek and "Fletcher Lake" were on the first edition of the *Mt. Lyell* 30' map,
1901. The peak was first named on the ninth edition, 1948. It had formerly been
called "Baker Peak," after a cook at the Boothe Lake High Sierra Camp. (BGN,
1932.)
      There is no reason to have an "Upper" lake unless there is a "Lower" one;
there is not one here. The present "Townsley Lake" (which see) was once called
"Upper Fletcher Lake." The BGN decision of 1932 gave the name "Fletcher
Lake" to the lake in sec. 34, T. 1 S., R. 24 E.—but that one is "Townsley Lake"
on the map. The present "Upper Fletcher Lake" is in sec. 33. (YNP)

Flora Lake   *Pinecrest 15'*
Named for Miss Flora Coleman of Mannsboro, Virginia, a cousin of R. B.
Marshall of the USGS. (Farquhar files.) (YNP)

Florence Lake   *Mt. Abbot 15', Blackcap Mtn. 15', Ward Mountain 7½',*
                                                       Florence Lake 7½'
Florence Rock (7,704)   *Florence Lake 7½'*
Theodore S. Solomons, Walter A. Starr, and Allen L. Chickering named the
lake on July 18, 1896. "Going down the other side we saw before us Lost Valley,
or Blaney Meadows, and came to a beautiful lake with water-lilies galore, which
we named Florence Lake after Starr's sister." (Solomons in *SCB* 20, no. 1, Feb.
1935: 62.) Contrary to Farquhar and Gudde, Solomons said they did *not* camp

at the lake, but at the lower end of Blaney (now Blayney) Meadows. He made a similar notation in his copy of Farquhar's *Place Names,* in Farquhar Papers, BL.

The lake was enlarged by a dam in the 1920s, and is a Southern California Edison reservoir. (SiNF)

Florence, Mount (12,561)   *Merced Peak 15'*
Florence Creek, Lake   *Tuolumne Meadows 15', Merced Peak 15'*
The peak was named for Florence Hutchings, daughter of James Mason Hutchings. "Florence Hutchings, and her brother, whose short legs were projected to larboard and starboard from the saddle . . . led off the cavalcade. Let us give the girl, for her own and her father's sake, some graceful mountain height, and let it be called Mt. Florence." (Taylor, 237–38.) Florence was the first white child born in Yosemite Valley, August 23, 1864, and she died there on September 26, 1881. (See Sargent, *Pioneers,* 34–37.)

"Florence Mt" and the creek are named on the first *Mt. Lyell* 30' map, 1901; the peak was changed to "Mt Florence" on the fifth edition, 1922. The lake was first named on the 15-minute quads in the 1950s. (YNP)

Florence Peak (12,432)   *Mineral King 15'*
Probably named by the USGS during the 1902 survey for the *Kaweah* 30' map. It is on the first edition of the map (1904), but is not in J. N. LeConte's "Elevations," 1903. (SNP, SeNF)

Foerster Peak (12,058), **Creek**   *Merced Peak 15'*
Lewis Foerster (1868–1936), a corporal in Troop K, Fourth Cavalry, on duty in Yosemite National Park in 1895 under the command of Lt. McClure. "In the policing of these wonderful recreation grounds, his service was outstanding, and it was in recognition of his achievements and because of his close association with the particular region, that I gave his name to a prominent peak on the park boundary and placed it on the map that I was then preparing." (McClure, in a memorial to Foerster; in *SCB* 22, no. 1, Feb. 1937: 102–3.) (YNP, SiNF)

Folger Peak (over 9,680)   *Dardanelles Cone 15' and 7½'*
In 1866 Robert M. Folger was the proprietor of the *Alpine Chronicle,* the first California newspaper published east of the Sierra, at Markleeville. His brother, Andrew C. Folger, had just been appointed the first postmaster of that town. The peak is 14 miles south of the town, and "was no doubt named for one of the brothers." (Maule, *Western Folklore* 6, no. 4, Oct. 1947: 376.) (StNF)

Foolish Lake (over 10,880)   *Mt. Abbot 15', Florence Lake 7½'*
Named in 1948 by a DFG survey party. Scott M. Soule, biologist, who named Crazy Lake, continued in the same vein with this lake, stating that "it would be foolish for anyone ever to revisit it." (Heyward Moore, *FPP* 25, no. 5, Spring 1984: 10.) (SiNF)

Foresta   *El Portal 15', Yosemite 15'*
In 1913 A. B. Davis bought 200 acres, called himself the Foresta Land Company, and built a summer resort. The place was designed to appeal to people of culture, and seemed to promise "seminar discussions under the

peacefully thought-provoking surroundings of Yosemite National Park." It was a sort of summer Chautauqua, known as the "Foresta Summer Assembly." But it didn't pay off. Davis abandoned it in 1915 and returned to his home in New York. Three years later the main hotel building burned under mysterious circumstances. Foresta is now a subdivision, with a scattering of summer cottages. (*YNN* 34, no. 3, March 1955: 43–45.) (YNP)

Forester Pass (over 4,000 m.–over 13,120)   *Mount Whitney 15',*
                                                          Mt. Williamson 7½'
Named on August 18, 1929, by Frank Cunningham, then supervisor of Sequoia National Forest, for the foresters (of whom he was one) who had discovered the pass. (Jesse W. Nelson, SeNF files.) The John Muir Trail was completed across the pass in 1931, thus eliminating the former route via Shepherd and Junction passes, the only part of the trail that went east of the Sierra crest. The name was approved by the BGN in 1938. (KCNP, SNP)

Forgotten Canyon   *Kern Peak 15'*
So called because it is out of the way and "forgotten" by most travelers. (SNP files.) It first appeared on the fourth edition of the *Olancha* 30' map, 1927. (SNP)

Forsyth Peak (11,180)   *Tower Peak 15'*
William Woods Forsyth (1856–1933), US Army, acting superintendent of Yosemite National Park, 1909–1912. Robert B. Marshall, topographer on the *Mt. Lyell* 30' map, was a close friend of Forsyth. He named this peak and a "Forsyth Pass" (on McClure's map of 1896, but no other) on the Forsyth Trail between Clouds Rest and Tenaya Lake, and also named individual features for each of Forsyth's four daughters and two sons-in-law. (Farquhar, *History,* 216.) (YNP)

Foster Ridge   *Huntington Lake 15' and 7½'*
John Foster, born in England, was an early Fresno County sheepman. His summer camp was near the mountain ridge that bears his name. He died in the mountains in July 1882. The name appears on the first *Kaiser* 30' map, 1904. (SiNF history files; Vandor, vol. 2, 2135.) (SiNF)

Four Gables (over 12,720)   *Mt. Tom 15', Mount Tom 7½'*
Probably named by the USGS during the 1907–09 survey for the *Mt. Goddard* 30' map. It is on the first edition, 1912, and is not in J. N. LeConte's "Elevations." (SiNF, INF)

Four-Mile Trail   *Yosemite Valley 1:24,000*
In 1871 James McCauley (who about four years later built the "Mountain House" at Glacier Point) hired John Conway to build a trail from the valley to Glacier Point. Conway had superintended construction of the "Zigzag" on the Big Oak Flat Road. (Paden, 285.) "At the entrance of the trail we found a small toll-house, kept by a far-seeing Irishman, named Macaulay, who built the trail. It cost $3,000 and it took eleven months of steady, hard labor to build it." (Jackson, 127.) The toll was one dollar. Later rebuilding of the trail lengthened it to about five miles. On the map it is labeled the "Glacier Pt-Fourmile Trail." (YNP)

Fox Meadow   *Giant Forest 15'*
John Fox was for many years a hunter, packer, and guide in the Kings River region. He built several cabins in the Kings River Canyon, and a suspension bridge across the river. (Farquhar.) In 1890 J. N. LeConte met Fox, as did Bolton C. Brown in 1896. "But Fox can afford to be flippant about bears; he used to be a professional hunter of them, and long ago he, with his partner, killed two hundred and thirty-six grizzlies in the Rocky Mountains. But at last a grizzly got his partner, and Fox exchanged the Rockies for an abode in the Sierra. He has been there seventeen years now; says he likes it better than he does anything else, and proposes to 'stay with it.' " (Brown in *SCB* 2, no. 2, May 1897: 91.) (SeNF)

Franklin Lakes, Pass, Creek   *Mineral King 15'*
The lakes were named in the 1870s by James Crabtree for his "Lady Franklin" mine. (Farquhar: W. B. Wallace.) Lady Franklin was the widow of Sir John Franklin, English explorer, who died in the Arctic in 1847. For more than a decade Lady Franklin organized and financed a series of expeditions in an endeavor to learn his fate. Her actions created great sympathy and admiration, and after she visited the United States in the early 1860s there seems to have been a spate of naming things for her—including "Lady Franklin Rock" in Yosemite Valley.
The two lakes were called "Silver Lakes" on the first two editions of the *Kaweah* 30' map; changed to "Franklin Lakes" on the 1921 edition. "Franklin Pass" appeared in 1942. "Franklin Creek" appeared on the *Mineral King* 15' map, 1956, but was not verified by the BGN until 1968. It was formerly "East Fork Kaweah River." (SNP)

Fraser Lakes   *Tower Peak 15'*
The name was approved by a BGN decision in 1965. The decision didn't state for whom the lakes were named, but probably for J. C. Fraser of the DFG. (DFG survey.) Not named on early editions of the 15-minute quad. It is a group of four small lakes about 0.3 mile south of the center of Emigrant Lake. (StNF)

Fredericksburg Canyon   *Freel Peak 15', Woodfords 7½'*
Maule suggests that the town of Fredericksburg, started in 1864, may have been named for Frederick Frevert, who operated a sawmill nearby. Gudde offers the idea that the strong Southern sentiment in this region may have caused the town to be named after the Confederate victory at Fredericksburg, Virginia, in December 1862. As a third possibility, there was a Friedrich Bruns (who later anglicized his name to "Frederick") who patented 158 acres in the SE¼ of the SE¼ of sec. 12, T. 11 N., R. 19 E., and the N½ of the SW¼ of sec. 7, T. 11 N., R. 20 E. in 1877. The second part of that description encompasses the present crossroads of Fredericksburg. (TNF)

Freel Peak (10,881)   *Freel Peak 15' and 7½'*
The highest point in the Lake Tahoe region, named in 1874 for James Washington Freel by the US Coast Survey, which used the peak for triangula-

tion. According to Maule, Freel was an early squatter on land adjacent to the peak. (ENF, TNF)

French Canyon   *Mt. Abbot 15', Mt. Tom 15', Mt. Hilgard 7½',*
Mount Tom 7½'

French Lake (11,265–11,259)   *Mt. Tom 15', Mount Tom 7½'*

The name "French Canyon" was unknown to J. N. LeConte in 1898 and J. S. Hutchinson in 1904. (*SCB* 2, no. 5, Jan. 1899: 249–62; and *SCB* 5, no. 3, Jan. 1904: 153–75.) It first appears on LeConte's map based on a 1908 trip. (*SCB* 7, no. 1, Jan. 1909: 22.) It is also on the first edition of the *Mt. Goddard* 30' map, 1912. Thus, I assume that it was named either by LeConte or by the USGS during its survey, 1907–09. French Lake was not named until the *Mt. Tom* 15' map, 1949. (SiNF)

Fresno Dome (7,540)   *Bass Lake 15'*

The name appeared on the *Mariposa* 30' map, 1912, as a replacement for the original name, "Wamelo Rock." That name probably was given by the Whitney Survey; it is on Hoffmann's map of 1873. There is no explanation of its meaning.

"I caught sight of a lofty granite dome, called Wa-mello by the Indians, looming into the free sky far above the forest. . . ." (John Muir, writing from "Fresno Grove of Big Trees," in the San Francisco *Daily Evening Bulletin,* September 21, 1875.) The name "Fresno Grove" no longer exists. (See **Nelder Grove.**) (SiNF)

Frying Pan Lake   *Merced Peak 15'*

Charles K. Fisher of the DFG reported in 1948 that the name was given in 1940 by John Handley, formerly of the DFG's Madera hatchery. No reason was given for the name, but it is probably for the lake's shape, which is almost perfectly round. (DFG survey.) (SiNF)

Frys Point (4,594)   *Giant Forest 15'*

Walter Fry (1859–1941), born in Illinois, came to California in 1887. He worked for a lumber company for a while, but then balked at cutting down any more of the Big Trees. He entered government service in 1901, worked his way up, was superintendent of Sequoia and General Grant national parks, 1914–20, and US Commissioner for those two parks from 1920 until his death in 1941. (Farquhar.) Memorial in *SCB* 27, no. 4, Aug. 1942: 113–14. (SNP)

Fuller Meadow, Buttes (6,408)   *Shuteye Peak 15'*

Frank F. Fuller homesteaded 160 acres in sec. 35, T. 6 S., R. 24 E. in 1900. (SiNF)

Funston Meadow, Creek, Lake (10,840); **Upper Funston Meadow**
Kern Peak 15'

James Funston grazed sheep in the meadow from about 1870 until his death in 1899. He had patented 400 acres, which he willed to Harry Quinn, who in turn sold it to Stephen T. Mather in 1922. Mather placed it in trust, and it became part of Sequoia National Park when the park was enlarged in 1926.

(Farquhar: letter from Versteeg, Dec. 9, 1925, with information from S. L. N. Ellis.)

There is also an "Upper Funston Meadow," where Funston Creek flows into the Kern River. The present "Sky Parlor Meadow" was called "Upper Funston Meadow" on the first three editions of the *Olancha* 30′ map, 1907–22. The present Funston Meadow was originally called "Lower Funston Meadow." "Funston Camp"—in the lower meadow—disappeared with the publication of the 1927 edition of the map. The lake was first named on the 15-minute quad, 1956. (SNP)

Gabb, Mount (13,741–13,711) *Mt. Abbot 15′ and 7½′*
William More Gabb (1839–1878) joined the Whitney Survey in 1862. "Gabb, our paleontologist, young, grassy green, but decidedly smart and well posted in his department—he will develop well with the hard knocks of camp." (Brewer, *Up and Down,* 261.)

The peak was named by a Whitney Survey party led by Brewer, in 1864, as they went west down Mono Creek, which at that time was called the "Middle Fork of the San Joaquin." It is not certain that the present named peak is the one the survey party named. It was described as "another patch of slate . . . these form rather prominent knobs, one of which was called Mount Gabb." (Whitney, *Geology,* 397.) The present Mt. Gabb has no slate on it.

"The paleontologist was a distinctly loquacious person. One can imagine, then, the laughter of these lean, brown men when Dr. Cooper, the serious, the unbending, announced that he had discovered a new species of the old brachiopod genus, *Lingula;* and that in honor of his friend William More Gabb he had bestowed upon it the name of *Lingula gabii.*" (Brewster, 239.)

The first ascent of the peak was in June 1917 by A. L. Jordan and H. H. Bliss. "Finding no evidence that the peak had been climbed before, we made out a statement, placed it in a 'dehydro' can, and left it in a cairn on the summit." (*SCB* 10, no. 3, Jan. 1918: 292.)

Portrait of Gabb in *SCB* 12, no. 2, 1925: opp. p. 126. (SiNF)

Gabbot Pass (over 12,240) *Mt. Abbot 7½′*
Named because it is on the divide between Mounts Gabb and Abbot. It was apparently placed on the map by the USGS because it was in common use; the name is in *The Climber's Guide,* p. 126. (SiNF)

Gabbott Meadow *Dardanelles Cone 15′, Spicer Meadow Res. 7½′*
Named for the Gabbott family, who ran a string of cattle in the area. The name is spelled "Gabbot" on the 15-minute map. (BGN.) (StNF)

Gabbro Peak (over 10,960) *Matterhorn Peak 15′*
Gabbro is a granular, igneous rock. This peak's name is the sort of name only a geologist would give. The peak was probably named by the USGS during the 1905–09 survey for the *Bridgeport* 30′ map; it is named on the first edition, 1911. (TNF)

Gable Lakes, Creek   *Mt. Tom 15', Mount Tom 7½'*
These features were first named on the 15-minute map (1949), and undoubtedly derive from "Four Gables," just to the south. (INF)

Gale Peak (10,693), **Lake**   *Merced Peak 15'*
Captain George Henry Goodwin Gale (1858–1920), Fourth Cavalry, US Army; acting superintendent of Yosemite National Park in 1894, and of Sequoia and General Grant national parks, 1896–97. The peak was named by Lt. N. F. McClure in 1894. (Farquhar: McClure.) The lake was named for the peak in 1946 by a DFG survey party under William A. Dill. (DFG survey.) (Peak, YNP, SiNF; lake, SiNF)

Gallats Lake (over 10,000)   *Mount Whitney 15', Mt. Kaweah 7½'*
The origin is not known, but it was probably named for a sheepherder. William R. Dudley, on his "Sketch-Map of the Kaweah Group of Mountains," calls it "Gallat's Corral and Lake." (*SCB* 2, no. 3, Jan. 1898: plate XXV.) (SNP)

Gallison Lake (over 10,400)   *Tuolumne Meadows 15'*
Arthur L. Gallison, a YNP ranger from 1916 to 1953, planted fish in the lake in 1916. The name was proposed by rangers Bingaman and Eastman. (Bingaman, *Guardians*, 93.) (YNP)

Gardiner, Mount (3,934 m.–12,907);
Gardiner Pass (3,429 m.–over 11,200), **Basin, Lakes**
                           Mt. Pinchot 15', Mt. Clarence King 7½'
Gardiner Creek *Marion Peak 15', Mt. Pinchot 15', Mt. Clarence King 7½'*
"Two peaks lying just in front of it [the crest] are especially fine . . . the northern being a little the highest. This we named Mount King, and the southern one Mount Gardner." (Whitney, *Geology*, 392.)
James Terry Gardiner (1842–1912), a member of the Whitney Survey, 1864–67; member of the Geological Survey of the 40th Parallel (King Survey), 1867–72; member of the Geological Survey of the Territories (Hayden Survey), 1872–75. James's father spelled the name without the "i" and so did James until his second marriage, 1881, when he restored the "i", which had been in the old family name. (Farquhar files.)
The mountain and the creek were spelled "Gardner" on maps until the sixth edition of the *Mt. Whitney* 30' sheet, 1927. The other "Gardiner" features were added to the 15-minute maps, 1953.
Biographical sketch in Brewer, *Up and Down*, pp. 468–69; portraits on cover of *Up and Down* (same in Farquhar, *History*, 135), and in *Up and Down* following p. 168. (KCNP)

Gardisky Lake (over 10,480)   *Tuolumne Meadows 15', Mono Craters 15'*
Al Gardisky built a small cabin east of Tioga Pass in 1919 and a log-cabin store in 1920 on the site of the present Tioga Pass Resort, which he later enlarged into a lodge. Named in 1932 by Mrs. Everett Spuller. (Spuller.) (INF)

Garfield Grove, Creek   *Mineral King 15'*
Named by R. B. Marshall, USGS, for James Abram Garfield (1831–1881), 20th president of the United States. (Farquhar: Marshall.) The grove was

probably named in 1916, when Marshall was superintendent of national parks, Dept. of the Interior. The name appeared on the third edition of the *Kaweah* 30' map, 1921. The creek was first named on the *Mineral King* 15' quad. (SNP)

Garnet Lake (2,950 m.–9,678)   *Devils Postpile 15', Mt. Ritter 7½'*
   Origin unknown. On Solomons' map of 1896, it is called "Badger Lake," while the name "Garnet Lake" is applied to what is now "Shadow Lake." (INF)

Gayley, Mount (4,118 m.–13,510)   *Big Pine 15', Split Mtn. 7½'*
                                             Mt. Goddard 15', North Palisade 7½'
   In honor of Prof. Charles Mills Gayley of the English Department, University of California, Berkeley. The name was proposed by the Sierra Club sometime before 1939. (Letter, David Brower to C. A. Ecklund, USGS, March 7, 1951, in Farquhar files.) Although the name appears on four maps, the summit is on the *Big Pine* 15' and the *Split Mtn.* 7½' quads. (INF)

Gaylor Lakes, Peak (11,004)   *Tuolumne Meadows 15'*
   Andrew J. Gaylor, born in Texas in 1856; a packer with the US Cavalry in his youth; Yosemite National Park ranger, 1907–21. He died of a heart attack at the Merced Lake ranger station while on patrol, 1921. (Bingaman, *Guardians*, 13, 85.) The name was first given to the lakes. It was later extended to the peak, as suggested by David Brower, and verified by Walter A. Starr, Sr. as being in common use. (USGS.) (Lakes, YNP; peak, YNP, INF)

Gem Lake, Pass   *Mono Craters 15', Devils Postpile 15', Mt. Ritter 7½'*
   Originally named "Gem-o'-the-Mountains" by Theodore C. Agnew, an early miner. (See **Agnew Meadow**, etc. Farquhar: N. F. McClure.) The USGS shortened the name, and also applied it to the pass, during the 1898–99 survey for the *Mt. Lyell* 30' map. The lake has been dammed, and is a reservoir for Southern California Edison. (INF)

Gemini (over 12,880–12,866)   *Mt. Abbot 15', Mt. Hilgard 7½'*
   A twin-peaked mountain, named for Gemini, a constellation containing the bright stars Castor and Pollux. The name was suggested by Chester Versteeg, Oliver Kehrlein, and Toni Ganero of the Sierra Club in 1953; approved by the BGN, May 1957. (SC papers in BL) (SiNF)

Gendarme Peak (13,252–13,241)   *Mt. Goddard 15', Mt. Thompson 7½'*
   The name first appeared in *The Climber's Guide*. It was made official by a BGN decision in 1969. Not named on early editions of the 15-minute quad. It is one mile north of Mt. Agassiz, marked "13241." (INF)

General Grant Grove   *Giant Forest 15', Tehipite Dome 15'*
   The "General Grant Tree" was discovered by Joseph Hardin Thomas in 1862. (Fry and White, 99.) It was named in August 1867 by Mrs. Lucretia P. Baker, member of a pioneer family of Visalia, for Ulysses Simpson Grant, commander-in-chief of the US Army, 1864–69, and 18th president of the US, 1869–77. The name of the tree was later extended to the grove, which earlier had called the "Visalia Big Tree Grove." (LeConte, *A Summer*, 24.) A

four-square-mile area was established as "General Grant National Park" in 1890. It is now known as the "Grant Grove" portion of Kings Canyon National Park. (KCNP)

General Sherman Tree; Sherman Creek   *Giant Forest 15'*
General William Tecumseh Sherman (1820–1891), Union general in the Civil War, commander-in-chief of the US Army, 1869–84. The tree was discovered and named by James Wolverton on August 7, 1879. (Fry and White, 182.) The tree was also called the "Karl Marx Tree," undoubtedly so named by members of the Kaweah Colony, whom George W. Stewart referred to as "a colony of Socialists." (Visalia *Delta,* Aug. 28, 1890.) (SNP)

Genevra, Mount (3,979 m.–13,055)   *Mount Whitney 15',*
                                                          Mt. Brewer 7½'
Named in 1899 for Mrs. Genevra Magee, by Helen M. Gompertz, J. N. LeConte, and others, who were with Mrs. Magee on the summit of Mount Brewer. (Farquhar: Helen M. LeConte.) (KCNP, SNP)

George Creek   *Mount Whitney 15', Lone Pine 15',*
                                     Mt. Williamson 7½', Manzanar 7½'
"The chief Indian headquarters of the southern part of the valley was at Chief George's rancheria on the creek which still bears his name." (Chalfant, *Inyo,* 186.) Chief George was a leader of the Piute Indians in the Owens Valley fighting in 1863. According to Schumacher (p. 33), Chief George acquired his name in 1860 when he guided Dr. Samuel Gregg George on a prospecting trip and took the name for his own. (INF)

George, Lake (9,008)   *Devils Postpile 15', Crystal Crag 7½'*
Named for George Calvert of Pine City, a short-lived mining camp during the Mammoth gold rush in the late 1870s. (Smith, 19; Gudde, *Gold Camps,* 267. See also **Mary, Lake.**) The name appears on the 1879 GLO plat. (INF)

Gianelli Cabin   *Pinecrest 15' and 7½'*
A man named Gianelli built a cabin here in 1905. (USGS.) A GLO plat in 1926 called it "Diamond's Cabin." Marked as only a "Site" on the newer map. (StNF)

Giant Forest   *Giant Forest 15'*
Hale D. Tharp was the first white man to visit Giant Forest, in 1858. (Farquhar: Fry.) "This part of the Sequoia belt seemed to me the finest, and I then [1875] named it 'the Giant Forest.' " (Muir, *Parks,* 300.) But according to Walter Fry, who knew the early pioneers, a Civil War veteran named Palmer was the first to use the name "Giant Forest." (White, 30–31.) (SNP)

Gibbs, Mount (12,764); **Gibbs Canyon, Lake**   *Mono Craters 15'*
"Started for the summit [of Mt. Dana] but took the next peak s. of Mt. Dana, fearing O. [Frederick Law Olmsted] could not reach the other. This I managed to get his horse up, so that he rode to the top, where we lunched. He named the peak Mt. Gibbs." (Brewer diary, August 31, 1864, in BL.)

Oliver Wolcott Gibbs (1822–1908), professor of science at Harvard, 1863–87, a lifelong friend of J. D. Whitney. Brewer and Olmsted made the first ascent. Olmsted was the chairman of the first Board of Commissioners to manage the Yosemite Grant, 1864.

Gibbs Canyon was named by Israel C. Russell in the early 1880s. (Russell, *Quaternary*, 336.) Gibbs Lake was first named on the *Mono Craters* 15' map, 1953. (Mountain, YNP, INF; canyon and lake, INF)

Gibson, Mount (over 8,320)   *Hetch Hetchy Reservoir 15'*
Origin unknown, but probably named by the USGS during the 1893–94 survey for the *Yosemite* 30' map. It is on the first edition, 1897, yet is not on Lt. McClure's map of 1895 or of 1896. (YNP)

Gilbert Lake   *Mt. Pinchot 15', Kearsarge Peak 7½'*
Gilbert was an Independence pioneer who tried to secure the water rights to the lake for an irrigation project. (Schumacher, 87–88.) (INF)

Gilbert, Mount (13,106–13,103)   *Mt. Goddard 15', Mt. Thompson 7½'*
Grove Karl Gilbert (1843–1918), geologist, with the Wheeler and Powell surveys, author of important monographs on Lake Bonneville and the Henry Mountains. (Farquhar: R. B. Marshall.) The peak probably was named by Marshall; it is on the first edition of the *Mt. Goddard* 30' map, 1912. Portrait and biographical sketch in *SCB* 10, no. 4, Jan. 1919: 391–99.) (KCNP, INF)

Gillett Mountain (8,361)   *Pinecrest 15'*
Named in 1909 by R. B. Marshall, USGS, for James Norris Gillett; member of Congress, 1903–07; governor of California, 1907–11. (Farquhar: Marshall.) (StNF)

Gilman Lake   *Matterhorn Peak 15'*
Robert Gilman Brown, vice-president and general manager of the Standard Consolidated Mining Co. of Bodie. The lake was named in 1905 by an engineer of that company who was mapping the Green Creek basin. (Farquhar.) (TNF)

Gin Flat   *Lake Eleanor 15'*
"As related to me by Mr. John B. Curtin, construction of the Big Oak Flat Road was primarily done by Chinese labor. Various camps along the route were supplied by Chinese merchants from Jamestown. Delivering one consignment . . . a barrel of Chinese gin . . . dropped and burst wide open. That locality is still known as *Gin Flat*." (Letter, May 25, 1961, J. H. Wegner to Douglass Hubbard, in YNP files.) For a somewhat different version, see Paden, p. 229. The name first appears on Lt. McClure's map, 1896. (YNP)

Giraud Peak (12,608–12,585)   *Mt. Goddard 15', North Palisade 7½'*
Probably named for Pierre Giraud, Inyo County sheepman, known as "Little Pete." (Farquhar; see **Little Pete Meadow.**) Erroneously spelled "Giroud" on all editions of the *Mt. Goddard* 30' map. (KCNP)

Glacier Canyon   *Mono Craters 15'*
Named by Israel C. Russell in the 1880s. (Russell, *Quaternary*, 324.) (INF)

Glacier Creek *Mt. Goddard 15', North Palisade 7½'*
J. N. LeConte and party named this "Glacier Brook" in July 1903. (*SCB* 5, no. 1, Jan. 1904: 9.) (KCNP)

Glacier Divide *Blackcap Mtn. 15', Mt. Goddard 15', Mt. Henry 7½', Mt. Darwin 7½'*
Probably named by the USGS during the 1907–09 survey for the *Mt. Goddard* 30' map; the name is on the first edition, 1912. It is aptly named: there are more than a dozen glaciers on the north side of the divide, which forms the boundary between Kings Canyon National Park and Sierra National Forest. (KCNP, SiNF)

Glacier Monument (11,165), **Creek** *Marion Peak 15'*
"At the head of the valley, in a position corresponding to that of the Half Dome in Yosemite, looms the great Glacier Monument, the broadest, loftiest, and most sublimely beautiful of all these wonderful rocks." (John Muir, the namer, in *Century Magazine* 43, no. 1, Nov. 1891.) (KCNP)

Glacier Point (7,214) *Yosemite 15', Yosemite Valley 1:24,000*
The precise origin of the name is not known. Bunnell wrote: "The name of 'Glacier Point' is said to be Pa-til-le-ma, a translation of which I am unable to give." (Bunnell, *Discovery,* 1880, 213.) Clarence King wrote, concerning his activities with the Whitney Survey in 1864, from atop Sentinel Dome: "A little way to the east, and about a thousand feet below the brink of the Glacier Point . . ." (King, 151.) But that still doesn't say who named it, or when. However, the name *is* on the King and Gardiner map of 1865. One might note that it is a different *sort* of name than all the others in and around Yosemite Valley up to that time. It is scientific/geologic; all the others are romantic, quasi-Indian, fanciful, patriotic, or for a presumed Great Man. That sort of circumstantial evidence seems to point to someone on the Whitney Survey as the namer. (YNP)

Glacier Lake (over 11,600), **Ridge** *Triple Divide Peak 15'*
". . . we found the source of the Roaring River in a beautiful circular lake fed by a well-formed glacier. . . . From this point the open upper valley of the river stretches straight away northwardly." (William R. Dudley in *SCB* 2, no. 3, Jan. 1898: 186–87; also see sketch map, plate XXV.) This took place in July 1896. The ridge name probably derives from the lake. Both names were on the first edition of the *Tehipite* 30' map, 1905. (KCNP)

Glen Aulin *Tuolumne Meadows 15'*
James McCormick, later the secretary of the US Geographic Board, said that R. B. Marshall of the USGS asked him to suggest a name for a beautiful little valley. "I at once suggested Glen Aulin, 'beautiful valley or glen,' and wrote it for him in this way, that it might be correctly pronounced—the '*au*' as in *author.* The correct Gaelic (Irish) orthography is *Gleann Alainn.*" (Letter, McCormick to Farquhar, Feb. 11, 1926.) The name appeared on the fourth edition of the *Mt. Lyell* 30' map, 1914. (YNP)

Glen Pass (11,978)   *Mt. Pinchot 15', Mt. Clarence King 7½'*
Glen H. Crow, USFS ranger, an assistant with the USGS during the 1905 survey for the *Mt. Whitney* 30' map. Crow was a brother-in-law of R. B. Marshall of the USGS. (Farquhar: Mrs. R. B. Marshall.) The name was incorrectly spelled "Glenn" on the first five editions of the map, 1907 through 1921; it was corrected beginning with the edition of 1927. The pass was called "Blue Flower Pass" by Bolton C. Brown in 1899. (*SCB* 3, no. 2, May 1900: 135–49.) (KCNP)

Goat Mountain (12,207), **Crest**   *Marion Peak 15'*
Said to have been named for mountain sheep, mistakenly called goats, that were once seen there. (Farquhar: J. N. LeConte.) The name was already in use in 1896, when LeConte and his party made the first recorded ascent. (*SCB* 2, no. 2, May 1897: 79.) Goat Mountain may have been the then-unnamed peak climbed by Gardiner and Hoffmann on July 22, 1864. (Brewer, *Up and Down*, 531.) (KCNP)

Goddard, Mount (13,568); **Goddard Divide, Creek**
                                        Mt. Goddard 15' and 7½'
North Goddard Creek; Goddard Canyon   *Blackcap Mtn. 15',*
                                        Mt. Henry 7½'
The peak was named in 1864 by Brewer's party of the Whitney Survey. "Thirty-two miles north-northwest is a very high mountain, called Mount Goddard, in honor of a Civil Engineer who has done much to advance our knowledge of the geography of California, and who is the author of 'Britton & Rey's Map.' " (Whitney, *Geology,* 382.) George Henry Goddard (1817–1906), born in England, came to California in 1850; surveyor with the Ebbetts exploring expedition in 1853, and with Sherman Day in 1855.
The first ascent came 15 years later. "In the fall of 1879, the author and a companion climbed Mt. Goddard, scaling the wall at the north-western front, to the eaves of a long slope of broken and jagged rock, which ended at the western end of the twin apexes marking the mountain's summit. . . . A monument . . . was built of the slabs of slate-like fragments strewn about. A record dated September 23, 1879, was signed by the author and L. W. Davis, and deposited in an empty baking powder can, which was buried in the center of the monument." (Winchell, 160–61.)
Goddard Creek was perhaps named by Theodore S. Solomons and E. C. Bonner in July 1895. ". . . we continued the descent of the gorge to its confluence with Goddard Creek, which from Mt. Goddard we had identified as heading in a number of lakes on the southeastern base of the mountain." (*Appalachia* 8, no. 1, 1896: 56.) Goddard Divide and North Goddard Creek were probably named by the USGS during the 1907–09 survey for the *Mt. Goddard* 30' map. All the "Goddard" features are named on the first edition, 1912, except for Goddard Canyon, which shows up on the third edition, 1923. The divide is also on the *Mt. Darwin* 7½' quad, as is North Goddard Creek. Goddard Creek is also on the *Marion Peak* 15' quad. (KCNP)

Goethe, Mount (13,264); **Goethe Glacier, Lake, Cirque**

Mt. Goddard 15', Mt. Darwin 7½'

Johann Wolfgang von Goethe (1749–1832), greatest of German poets. In 1949, the 200th anniversary of Goethe's birth, Erwin G. Gudde suggested the name for the hitherto unnamed highest peak of the Glacier Divide, and for the glacier on its north side. David Brower also suggested applying the name to the lake (11,531–11,528) and the cirque. All the names were approved by the BGN that same year. "Goethe Cirque" was omitted from the *Mt. Goddard* 15' map because of lack of space. (Mtn., KCNP, SiNF; others, SiNF)

Golden Bear Lake (3,405 m.–11,175)

Mount Whitney 15', Mt. Williamson 7½'

The name was proposed by Chester Versteeg in 1953, presumably to honor the University of California at Berkeley. (SC papers in BL.) The name was added to the map by the USGS because it was in common use. (KCNP)

Golden Trout Creek   *Kern Peak 15'*

The creek was first called "Whitney Creek" because its source is near the peak (Mt. Langley) climbed by Clarence King in 1871, thinking it was Mt. Whitney. The error was discovered in 1873, but the name remained for many years. (See J. N. LeConte, *A Summer*, 77.) In 1881 it was renamed "Volcano Creek" for the lava formations along part of its route. (*MWCJ* 1, no. 1, May 1902: 2.) That name didn't stick. The USGS, in the 1905 survey for the *Olancha* 30' map, applied the name "Golden Trout Creek," retaining "Volcano" for the falls only. (Farquhar: R. B. Marshall.) (INF)

Gomez Meadow   *Olancha 15'*

Espitacio Gomez patented 160 acres in sec. 1, T. 19 S., R. 36 E. in 1874. This land is just south of Cartago, on present-day US 395; the meadow is about six miles west of there, on the crest at the head of Cartago Creek. (INF)

Goodale Mountain (3,893 m.–12,790), **Creek**

Mt. Pinchot 15' and 7½'

Thomas Jefferson Goodale (1830–1894), a native of Connecticut, came to California in 1849 or 1850, and to the Owens Valley in the late 1860s. He was briefly a newspaper editor, publishing the *Inyo Lancet* in 1871. His brother, Ezra M. Goodale, homesteaded 160 acres in secs. 22, 23 and 27, T. 11 S., R. 24 E. in 1881. The homestead included land watered by Goodale Creek before it was diverted into the Los Angeles Aqueduct. (*Inyo*, 148–49; GLO.) (INF)

Goodale Pass (10,997)   *Mt. Abbot 15', Graveyard Peak 7½'*

Probably named for Augustus ("Gus") Goodale, son of Thomas J. Goodale, at one time a USFS ranger. (Farquhar.) The route over the pass was pioneered by Lincoln Hutchinson and party in July 1902. (*SCB* 4, no. 3, Feb. 1903: 196–97.) (SiNF)

Goode, Mount (13,085–13,092)   *Mt. Goddard 15', North Palisade 7½'*

Richard Urquhart Goode (1858–1903), a topographer and geographer with the USGS. In the 1907–09 survey for the *Mt. Goddard* 30' map, the USGS

84 PLACE NAMES OF THE SIERRA NEVADA

placed Goode's name on a peak that was already named: Black Giant. The name "Mt. Goode" was where "Black Giant" now is on the first three editions of the map. The appropriate correction was made by a BGN decision in 1926, and beginning with the fourth edition (1928) "Black Giant" replaced "Mt Goode," while the latter was applied to a previously unnamed peak on the main crest of the Sierra. (Farquhar.) (KCNP, INF)

Gordon Lake (9,888–9,882)   *Mt. Abbot 15', Florence Lake 7½'*
Named for Gordon Bartholomew, an employee of Southern California Edison. He was the damkeeper at Florence Lake, 1938–53, and a snow surveyor during the winter. (Heyward Moore, *FPP* 25, no. 5, Spring 1984: 10.) (SiNF)

Gorge of Despair   *Tehipite Dome 15', Marion Peak 15'*
Named in 1879 by Lilbourne A. Winchell. (Farquhar, conversation with Winchell, 1921, in Farquhar Papers, BL.) First appearance on Theodore S. Solomons' 1897 *Map of Tehipite Valley.* (*SCB* 12, no. 2, 1925: opp. 127.) (KCNP)

Gould, Mount (3,964 m.–13,005)

Mt. Pinchot 15', Mt. Clarence King 7½'
The first ascent was made July 20, 1890, by J. N. LeConte, Hubert Dyer, Fred S. Phelby, and Cornelius B. Lakenan. They named it "University Peak," for the University of California at Berkeley. (Dyer in *Appalachia* 6, no. 4, 1892: 285.) ". . . we climbed rapidly for an hour toward a high peak, reaching its top at last about 11 a.m. (This peak I afterwards called Mt. Gould.) The actual summit, however, was about 100 feet beyond, and consisted of a perfect obelisk of blocks piled up about 80 feet high, and rose some 20 feet above the point on which we stood. From the base upward it decreased regularly in size to about 12 inches at the top which was perfectly flat. After resting awhile, I succeeded in climbing to the very summit, and stood on that rather ticklish point some minutes, till the sun came out for Bert to take my photograph." (LeConte, *A Summer,* 63.)

The switch in names was made in 1896, when LeConte and party made the first ascent of a higher peak to the south, which they called "University Peak." The former peak of that name they called "Mt. Gould" for Wilson S. Gould, a member of the party. (Farquhar: LeConte.) (KCNP, INF)

Grace Meadow   *Tower Peak 15'*
For Grace Sovulewski, daughter of Gabriel Sovulewski, who came to Yosemite National Park in 1895 as quartermaster sergeant with the US Army. He returned as a civilian employee in 1906, and during the following thirty years was largely responsible for the development and maintenance of the park's trail system. Grace married Frank B. Ewing, a park ranger from 1916 to 1950. (Bingaman, *Pathways,* 44–45.) "Grace Meadow" appeared on the third edition of the *Dardanelles* 30' map, 1912. (YNP)

Graham Meadow, Mountain (over 6,080)   *Bass Lake 15'*
The meadow was named for one of two Grahams, who probably were related. Thomas A. Graham patented 160 acres in the SE¼ of sec. 13, T. 7 S.,

R. 22 E. in August 1889. Hugh Graham patented 80 adjacent acres in sec. 24 in December 1889. "Graham Mountain," three miles north of the meadow, may have been named by or for the same people. (SiNF)

Grand Canyon of the Tuolumne River   *Hetch Hetchy Reservoir 15'*
   The nine miles of the river from Muir Gorge to the Hetch Hetchy Reservoir. It is not known who originated the name. John Muir called it the "Great Tuolumne Canyon" in *Overland Monthly,* August 1873. It was called "The Grand Cañon of the Tuolumne" by R. M. Price when he and another man went down through it in July 1892. (*SCB* 1, no. 1, Jan. 1893: 9–16.) The name has been on the maps since the first *Yosemite* 30' sheet, 1897. (YNP)

Grand Dike   *Tehipite Dome 15', Marion Peak 15'*
   In 1864 the Whitney Survey gave the name "Dyke Ridge" to what is now Monarch Divide. (Whitney, *Geology,* 370.) Grand Dike is at the east end of that divide, and was probably named by the USGS during the 1903 survey for the *Tehipite* 30' map; it is on the first edition, 1905. (SeNF)

Grand Mountain (9,491)   *Hetch Hetchy Reservoir 15'*
   "Grand Mt. stands right at the mouth of Cathedral Cañon (I mean the cañon omitted on the map) that is on the lower side of it. Grand Mt. certainly is a Grand Mt., bare granite nearly to the summit." (Letter, Charles F. Hoffmann to J. D. Whitney, Sept. 10, 1873, in BL.) In this letter Hoffmann said that Grand Mountain was named by John Muir. Theodore S. Solomons called the mountain "Tuolumne Castle" in 1896. (*Appalachia* 8, no. 2, 1896: 173.) (YNP)

Grand Sentinel (8,504)   *Marion Peak 15'*
   This formation was perhaps named by John Muir; it appears on Muir's map of 1891. (*Century Magazine* 43, no. 1, Nov. 1891.) (KCNP)

Granite Basin, Pass (10,673), **Creek, Lake**   *Marion Peak 15'*
   Brewer's field party of the Whitney Survey visited Granite Basin in 1864, but although describing it as having "granite masses" and "embracing basins of bare rock," they didn't actually use the name "Granite Basin." In 1868, E. C. Winchell applied a different name to the creek. ". . . a furious torrent darts out of a steep gully on the north side, with deafening roar, and gave us trouble in crossing, for which we repaid it with the title, 'Thunder Creek.' " (San Francisco *Daily Morning Call,* Sept. 12, 1872; also in *SCB* 12, no. 3, 1926: 247.)
   The name "Granite Basin" was in use when J. N. LeConte made his first trip into the Kings River region, 1890. He referred to Granite Pass (or perhaps the general area of the pass) as the "Great Divide." On his map, he called Granite Creek "Kellogg Creek," and showed a "Mt. Kellogg" at its headwaters— doubtless for Vernon L. Kellogg, professor of entomology at Stanford. John Muir used those same names on his 1891 map in *Century Magazine.* The basin, pass, and creek had their present names on the first edition of the *Tehipite* 30' map, 1905. "Granite Lake" appeared on the 15-minute quad, 1953. (KCNP)

Granite Dome (10,322)   *Tower Peak 15'*
   Probably named by the Wheeler Survey; it is on atlas sheet 56D, 1878–79. (StNF)

Granite Gorge   *Tehipite Dome 15'*
Possibly named by the USGS during the 1903 survey for the *Tehipite 30'*
map; it appears on the first edition, 1905. (SiNF)

Granite Knob (9,050)   *Monache Mtn. 15'*
Possibly named by the USGS during the 1905 survey for the *Olancha 30'*
map; it is on the first edition, 1907. (SeNF)

Granite Lake (over 11,480)   *Mt. Goddard 15', Mt. Darwin 7½'*
Named by Art Schober in the 1930s because it lies in a basin surrounded
entirely by granite. (Art Schober.) (INF)

Granite Park   *Mt. Abbot 15', Mt. Hilgard 7½'*
Possibly named by the USGS during the 1907–09 survey for the *Mt.
Goddard 30'* map; it appears on the first edition, 1912. (INF)

Grant Lake (7,130)   *Mono Craters 15'*
A letter from Col. Benson to Chester Versteeg (Farquhar files) states that the
lake was named by the California Geological Survey about 1875. This is
obviously incorrect, since the Survey was disbanded in 1873. On the 1857 GLO
plat, surveyed in 1856 by A. W. Von Schmidt, the much smaller natural lake is
named "Gull Lake." This same name was used on plats in 1879 and 1885.
"Grant Lake" is on the first edition of the *Mt. Lyell* 30' map, 1901. (INF)

Grant Lakes   *Hetch Hetchy Reservoir 15'*
Origin unknown. They are shown, but not named, in Whitney's *Yosemite
Guide-Book,* pocket edition, 1871. The name appears on the first edition of the
Yosemite 30' map, 1897. (YNP)

Grasshopper Flat, Creek   *Kern Peak 15'*
From the numerous grasshoppers found in the early days; a favorite baiting
ground for fishermen. (*Newsletter* 1, no. 10, March 1971: 253.) (SeNF)

Grassy Lake   *Mt. Abbot 15', Graveyard Peak 7½'*
There is an extensive meadow at the upper end of the lake, which probably
was named by William A. Dill of the DFG in 1943. (DFG survey.) (SiNF)

Graveyard Meadow, Peak (11,494), **Lakes;**
Upper Graveyard Meadow   *Mt. Abbot 15', Graveyard Peak 7½'*
"Some Portugese sheepmen operated like a gypsy outfit, refusing to
recognize the agreed-upon boundaries of the various sheep ranges. The other
sheepherders tried to drive them out, but without success. They [the Portugese]
were shot in the back while cooking their supper in camp." (Leo Porterfield,
taped interview, INF archives.) Only "Graveyard Meadows" was on the *Mt.
Goddard* 30' map, 1912. The peak, lakes, and meadows were on the 15-minute
map. On the *Graveyard Peak* quad the meadows become singular. (SiNF)

Gray Peak (11,574), **Creek**   *Merced Peak 15'*
The peak was probably named by the Wheeler Survey, since it appears on
atlas sheet 56D, 1878–79. The creek was named from the peak, and is on the
first edition of the *Mt. Lyell* 30' map, 1901. (YNP)

Grayling Lake   *Merced Peak 15'*
Named when grayling were first planted in the lake, in 1930. (YNP files.)
(YNP)

Grays Meadow   *Mt. Pinchot 15', Kearsarge Peak 7½'*
James M. Hutchings and party crossed the mountains from Independence to
the Kings River Canyon in the fall of 1875, and gave a condensed listing of
where they had been. "To Todd's place, later called Gray's Meadows, 7 miles
from Independence." (*Inyo Independent,* Oct. 23, 1875, in Cragen, 174.) A
Mr. Gray and G. Washington Todd were owners of the Kearsarge Mines.
(Cragen, 175.) If that is the correct story of the origin of "Grays Meadow,"
Gray had to wait a long time; the name first appeared on the *Mt. Whitney* 30'
map with the fifth edition, 1921. (INF)

Great Cliffs (10,196–10,218)   *Mt. Goddard 15', North Palisade 7½'*
Probably named by J. N. LeConte in 1903. The name is not on Bolton C.
Brown's map of 1895, but is on LeConte's map of 1904, which was made four to
six years before the USGS survey. (Map in *SCB* 5, no. 1, Jan. 1904: 18.)
(KCNP)

Great Sierra Mine   *Tuolumne Meadows 15'*
One cabin and a couple of shafts are all that remain of the endeavors of the
Great Sierra Consolidated Silver Company in the 1880s. (See **Bennettville.**)
(YNP)

Great Western Divide   *Mt. Whitney 15', Triple Divide Peak 15',*
                           Mineral King 15', Kern Peak 15', Mt. Brewer 7½'
Called the western ridge by the Whitney Survey. (Whitney, *Geology,* 382.)
William R. Dudley used the phrase "the great Western Divide of the Sierra" in
1896. (*SCB* 1, no. 7, Jan. 1896: 254.) It is first shown as "Great Western
Divide" on J. N. LeConte's 1896 map. (*SCB* 2, no. 2, May 1897: 128–29.)
Gudde says that LeConte claims to have named the divide in 1896. (Gudde,
Place Names, 127.) (KCNP, SNP, SeNF)

Green Creek, Lake   *Matterhorn Peak 15'*
Green Creek is an old name; it is on the Wheeler Survey atlas sheet 56D,
1878–79, and in a GLO surveyor's field notes in 1882. Although a connection
cannot be proved, there was a man named Green who came to Bridgeport Valley
in the early 1860s and built a log house on the east side of the valley. (Cain, 25–
26.) Green Creek flows into the East Walker River in the southern part of the
valley. "Green Lake" appeared on the first *Bridgeport* 30' map, 1911. (TNF)

Green Treble Lake   *Tuolumne Meadows 15'*
Apparently a misnomer. According to Everett L. Spuller, in 1932 he named
the large lake "Treble" because there were three lakes in the group. The one
adjacent to it he called "Green Lake," after a forest ranger of that name who was
at the Lee Vining ranger station for many years. On the map, these two names
apply only to the larger lake; the smaller one has no name. (Spuller.) (INF)

Greenstone Lake   *Tuolumne Meadows 15'*
Named in 1932 for its green-colored rocks. (Spuller.) (INF)

Gregorys Monument (over 13,920)   *Mount Whitney 15', Mt. Brewer 7½'*
Warren Gregory explored the region of the Kings-Kern Divide in 1894.
(*SCB* 1, no. 6, May 1895: 214–20.) The name was given by Bolton C. Brown in
1896. (*SCB* 2, no. 1, Jan. 1897: 21–26, plate VI.) (KCNP)

Grey Butte (11,365)   *Matterhorn Peak 15'*
Possibly named by the USGS during the 1905–09 survey for the *Bridgeport*
30' map, 1911. It is not on the McClure map of 1896. (YNP)

Grinnell Lake (10,804); **Little Grinnell Lake**   *Mt. Abbot 15' and 7½'*
Grinnell Lake was named in 1940 by Leon A. Talbot, at the suggestion of
Elden H. Vestal—both of the DFG. The "Little" lake was named in 1943 by
William A. Dill of the DFG. (*SCB* 36, no. 4, April 1951: 11.) Joseph Grinnell
was professor of zoology at the University of California, 1908–39. (SiNF)

Grizzly Creek, Lakes   *Marion Peak 15'*
The creek already had its name in 1896; it may have been named by John
Fox, a pioneer and bear hunter. (See **Fox Meadow.**) (*SCB* 2, no. 1, Jan. 1897:
44.) The lakes first appear on the *Marion Peak 15'* map, 1953. (SeNF)

Grizzly Peak (over 10,320), **Meadow, Lake**   *Tower Peak 15'*
The peak may possibly have been named during the 1891–96 survey for the
Dardanelles 30' map; it is on the first edition, 1898. The meadow and lake first
appear on the *Tower Peak 15'* map, 1956. (StNF, TNF)

Grizzly Peak (6,219)   *Yosemite 15', Yosemite Valley 1:24,000*
Origin unknown. It may have been because the shape looked like the hump
of a grizzly bear, or because it was a "grizzly" (difficult) climb. (*YNN* 34, no. 1,
Jan. 1955: 7.) Hutchings quotes a letter from Charles A. Bailey, who made the
first ascent about 1885. (Hutchings, *In the Heart,* 454–55.) It was called
"Grizzly Point" on all the *Yosemite* 30' maps until 1951, but was already
"Grizzly Peak" on the first *Yosemite Valley* map, 1907. (YNP)

Grouse Creek   *Yosemite 15'*
"Grouse" is one of the more overused geographic names in the Sierra. This
one may have been named by the Whitney Survey. It is on the Hoffmann and
Gardiner map, 1863–67. (YNP)

Grouse Lake   *Yosemite 15'*
"One day, after a long tramp (in September 1857) I stopped to rest by the
side of a small lake about eight miles from the present site of Wawona, and I then
named it Grouse Lake on account of the great number of grouse found there."
(Clark, 95.) (YNP)

Grouse Meadow   *Mt. Goddard 15', North Palisade 7½'*
Named by Lil A. Winchell in 1879. (Farquhar: Winchell.) The name has
been "Grouse Meadows" on all maps prior to publication of the *North Palisade*
7½' quad, 1982. (KCNP)

Grover Anton Spring   *Mt. Pinchot 15', Aberdeen 7½'*
Grover W. Anton homesteaded 160 acres in secs. 20 and 29, T. 12 S., R. 34
E. in 1919. (INF)

Grover Hot Springs   *Markleeville 15' and 7½'*
John Hawkins (see **Hawkins Peak**) was an early owner of the hot springs.
Alvin M. Grover bought a half interest in the property in 1878, and later
acquired it all. (*Alpine Heritage,* 54.) John C. Frémont's second exploring
expedition to the West camped at the hot springs on February 3, 1844. The
name appears as "Grovers Springs" on all the editions of the *Markleeville* 30'
map (1891–1905), as "Grovers Hot Springs" on the 15-minute quad, and as
"Grover Hot Springs" on the 7½' quad. The area is now a state park.

Gruff Lake   *Mt. Abbot 15', Mt. Hilgard 7½'*
Named by the DFG in 1952. (See **Bear Paw Lake.**) (SiNF)

Guitar Lake   *Mount Whitney 15' and 7½'*
Said to have been named for its shape by Clarence King in the 1870s.
(*MWCJ* 1, no. 1, May 1902: 4.) The name was added to the 7½-minute quad by
the USGS because it has been in common use for many years. Not named on the
15-minute quad; it is just south of the John Muir Trail between Crabtree Meadow
and Trail Crest. (SNP)

Gull Lake (7,598)   *Mono Craters 15'*
So called by Israel C. Russell in the 1880s. (Russell, *Quaternary,* 343.)
Named "Granite Lake" on the 1879 and 1885 GLO plats. (INF)

Gunsight   *Yosemite 15', Yosemite Valley 1:24,000*
Named by Yosemite National Park rangers. One looks up the lower
Cathedral Rocks gully and sees the Leaning Tower centered in the sights. (*SCB*
25, no. 1, Feb. 1940: 118–19.) First appeared on the *Yosemite* 15' map, 1956.
(YNP)

Guyot, Mount (3,749 m.–12,300); **Guyot Creek, Flat**
                                         Mount Whitney 15' and 7½'
"Immediately west of us was a bare granite cone or pyramid, with great snow
masses [September 3, 1881] on its northern and eastern slopes. This the party
agreed, at [Captain J. W. A.] Wright's request, to call Mount Guyot, in honor of
the distinguished Swiss geologist and geographer, whose lectures for two years
at Princeton, New Jersey, are among the pleasantest recollections of his college
days. The pass was also named Guyot Pass." (Elliott, *Guide,* 49.)
Arnold Henri Guyot (1807–1884), born in Switzerland, came to America in
1848, professor of physical geography and geology at Princeton, 1854–84. "Mt
Guyot" and "Guyot Creek" are on the first edition of the *Mt. Whitney* 30' map,
1907. Guyot Flat was called "Sand Flat" on the first six editions of the map,
1907–27; changed to its present name in 1933. Guyot Pass has never been
named on the maps. (SNP)

Haeckel, Mount (13,418–13,435)   *Mt. Goddard 15', Mt. Darwin 7½'*
One of the "Evolution Group," named in 1895 by Theodore S. Solomons for
Ernst Heinrich Haeckel (1834–1919), professor of zoology at the Univer-

sity of Jena. (*Appalachia* 8, no. 1, 1896: 48.) Haeckel was the first German biologist to give wholehearted support to the theory of evolution. (KCNP, INF)

Haiwee Creek, Pass   *Monache Mtn. 15'*
The first mention of the name is by the California-Nevada Boundary Survey of 1861. (Sacramento *Daily Union,* August 10, 1861.) *Haiwee* is the Indian word for "dove." The land once known as "Haiwee Meadows" is now covered by the Haiwee Reservoir. (Chalfant, *Inyo,* 219.) "Haiwee Creek" is on the first edition of the *Olancha* 30' map, 1907. The pass was first named on the 15-minute quad, 1956. (INF)

Hale, Mount (4,113 m.–over 13,440)   *Mount Whitney 15' and 7½'*
George Ellery Hale (1868–1938), astrophysicist; organized the Kentwood, Yerkes, and Mount Wilson observatories; director of Mount Wilson Observatory, 1904–23; internationally renowned for research in solar physics and stellar evolution. The name was suggested by the Sierra Club. (SC papers in BL. BGN decision, 1940.) (SNP)

Half Dome (8,842)   *Yosemite 15', Yosemite Valley 1:24,000*
"The names 'North Dome,' 'South Dome,' and 'Half Dome' were given by us during our long stay in the valley from their localities and peculiar configuration. Some changes have been made since they were adopted. The peak called by us the 'South Dome' has since been given the name of 'Sentinel Dome,' and the 'Half Dome,' Tis-as-ack, represented as meaning the 'Cleft Rock,' is now called by many the 'South Dome.' The 'Half Dome' was figuratively spoken of as 'The Sentinel' by our mission Indians, because of its overlooking the valley." (Bunnell, *Discovery,* 1880, 212.) Although Half Dome was briefly called "South Dome" (because it was across from North Dome), the name "Half Dome" was soon firmly established; it was on the King and Gardiner map of 1865. There were, of course, the inevitable attempts at interpreting Indian names or legends.
"Tissaack, South Dome in Yosemite, is . . . the name of a woman who according to tradition was transformed into the mountain." (Kroeber, 62.)
"Tis-se-yak, South Dome. This is the name of a woman who figures in a legend. . . . The Indian woman cuts her hair straight across the forehead, and allows the sides to drop along her cheeks, presenting a square face, which the Indians account the acme of female beauty, and they think they discover this square face in the vast front of South Dome." (Powers, 364.)
"Until the fall of 1875 the storm-beaten summit of this magnificent landmark was a *terra incognita,* as it had never been trodden by human feet. . . . This honor was reserved for a brave young Scotchman, a native of Montrose, named George G. Anderson, who by dint of pluck, skill, unswerving perseverance, and personal daring, climbed to its summit, and was the first that ever successfully scaled it. This was accomplished at 3 o'clock P.M. of October 12, 1875." (Hutchings, *In the Heart,* 456–57.)
Some early suggested names (doubtless we would think any of them appropriate had it always been there) were "Goddess of Liberty," "Mt. Abraham Lincoln," and "Spirit of the Valley." (YNP)

Hall Mountain (8,628–8,625), **Meadow**   *Huntington Lake 15',*
                                                     Nelson Mtn. 7½'
Hall was an early sheepman and cattle rancher who settled in the meadow about 1870. (Winchell, 158.) The meadow was called "House Meadow" on the *Kaiser* 30' map, 1904–50. Both "Hall" names first appeared on the 15-minute quad. (SiNF)

Halstead Meadow, Creek   *Giant Forest 15'*
Sam Halstead pastured horses in the meadow from 1872 to 1890. (Farquhar: Fry.) "Named after John Halstead, cattleman." (White, 178.) The meadow is named on the first *Tehipite* 30' map, 1905. The creek was named "Suwanee River" on the first three editions of the map; changed to "Halstead Creek" on the 1929 edition. (SNP)

Hamilton Lakes, Creek   *Triple Divide Peak 15'*
James Hamilton, born in Wisconsin in 1865, moved to California in 1909. (Vandor, vol. 2, 1979–80.) He at one time owned Redwood Meadow and Wet Meadow. The lakes were named for him because he stocked them with fish, which he carried on his back from Big Arroyo. (White, 178.) The names appeared on the fourth edition of the *Tehipite* 30' map, 1929. On the first three editions, Hamilton Creek was named "Deer Creek." The name "Hamilton Lakes" originally applied to the largest lake and the two lakes upstream from it. By a 1968 BGN decision the name now applies to only the two lower lakes. The upper lake, just north of Eagle Scout Peak, is now named "Precipice Lake." The crescent-shaped lake below the largest lake is nameless. (SNP)

Hangmans Bridge   *Markleeville 15' and 7½'*
According to local legend, a man accused of a murder in Alpine County was being transferred to Mono County because it was assumed he could not get a fair trial in Alpine. Alpine County was short of money, and it seemed to some that the extra expense would have forced the county to disorganize. The prisoner was lynched and hanged from a bridge a mile south of Markleeville—perhaps to preserve the financial integrity of the county. (*Alpine Heritage,* 47.)

Hanna Mountain (11,486)   *Matterhorn Peak 15'*
Thomas R. Hanna made the preliminary survey of the Hetch Hetchy project, in 1905, and was owner of the May Lundy Mine from 1920 to 1940. (Gudde, from Maule.) If Gudde is correct, it is one of the great ironies of the time. Hanna was the son-in-law of John Muir, the foremost opponent of the damming of Hetch Hetchy Valley. The name "Hanna Mtn" appears on the first *Bridgeport* 30' map, 1911. (TNF)

Happy Gap   *Tehipite Dome 15'*
". . . the lightly timbered saddle of the main divide, called by our guide 'Happy Gap.' " (*SCB* 2, no. 1, Jan. 1897: 45.) The guide was John Fox. (See **Fox Meadow.**) "Happy Gap" is a pass on a route—no longer used—between the South Fork of the Kings River and Tehipite Valley. "Those who succeed in getting a pack-train to this point at once perceive the appropriateness of the name." (Farquhar: LeConte.) (SiNF, SeNF)

Happy Isles *Yosemite 15', Yosemite Valley 1:24,000*
"I have named them the *Happy Isles,* for no one can visit them without for the while forgetting the grinding strife of *his* world and being happy." (Letter, W. E. Dennison, Guardian of Yosemite Valley, Oct. 25, 1885, in YNP files.) Earlier called "Island Rapids" by James M. Hutchings. (*YNN* 34, no. 1, Jan. 1955: 8.) (YNP)

Harden Lake *Hetch Hetchy Reservoir 15'*
Apparently named by the Whitney Survey for James ("Johnny") Hardin who had a ranch and sawmill, and later a small stopping place on the Big Oak Flat Road, at what is still named "Harden Flat," on state route 120. (Paden, 202–4.) The names "Hardins Ranch" and "Hardins Lake" are on Hoffmann and Gardiner's map of 1863–67. The BGN designated the lake as "Helen Lake" in 1932, but reversed that decision in favor of "Harden Lake" once more, in 1937. (YNP)

Harriet Lake *Merced Peak 15'*
Probably named by R. B. Marshall, USGS. It appears on the maps at the same time as other lakes named by Marshall for women (Edna, Evelyn, Marie). First appearance on the third edition of the *Mt. Lyell* 30' map, 1910. One might speculate that it was named for Harriet Monroe, a long-time Sierra Club member who was on a number of the club's outings, including the one to Yosemite National Park in 1909. (Memorial in *SCB* 22, no. 1, Feb. 1937: 101.) (YNP)

Harrington, Mount (11,005) *Marion Peak 15'*
". . . the trail then climbs a ridge, crossing it just below a lofty and striking granite dome, which Mr. Fox calls Mt. Harrington."(*SCB* 2, no. 1, Jan. 1897: 45.) There is no mention of who Harrington was. (SiNF, SeNF)

Harris Ranch *Bass Lake 15'*
James M. Harris patented 160 acres in secs. 25 and 26, T. 5 S., R. 20 E. in 1881, and homesteaded 160 more acres in sec. 25 in 1886. (SiNF)

Harrison Pass (about 12,800) *Mount Whitney 15', Mt. Brewer 7½'*
"The trip of this summer [1895] has brought out the further fact that the pass has long been known and used by sheep-herders under the name of Harrison's Pass." (*SCB* 1, no. 7, Jan. 1896: 290.) The year before, the pass was called "Madary's Pass," for M. R. Madary of Fresno, who came up to the pass from the south in 1892 but did not cross it. (*SCB* 1, no. 6, May 1895: 187–98.)
"Ben Harrrison herded sheep in the upper Kern in the '80s. He was part Cherokee Indian. He built a monument on the pass. It was probably used by sheepmen in 1875 or 1876." (Farquhar: Versteeg, from Robert M. Woods, an early sheep-owner.)
"According to my notion, it will hardly be a popular pass until a windlass and cable are put at its head." (Bolton C. Brown in *SCB* 2, no. 2, May 1897: 93.) (KCNP, SNP)

Harry Birch Springs *Mt. Pinchot 15', Aberdeen 7½'*
The name is an error in spelling. Harry *Burt* homesteaded 160 acres in sec.

17, T. 12 S., R. 34 E. in 1919. The springs are about ¼ mile west of the homestead's property line. (INF)

Hart Meadow, Tree; Hartland   *Giant Forest 15'*
   William H. Hart patented 80 acres in sec. 24, T. 14 S., R. 28 E. (location of the "Hart Tree") in 1888. Michael Hart patented 40 acres in sec. 14 ("Hart Meadow") in 1890. "Hartland" (a community) was named for William Hart, who operated a small sawmill near the town of Badger. (*Newsletter* 2, no. 1, July 1971: 13.) (Mdw. and tree, KCNP; town, SeNF)

Harvey Lake   *Mt. Abbot 15', Florence Lake 7½'*
   Named by the DFG in 1947 for Harvey Sauter of the High Sierra Pack Station. (Heyward Moore, *FPP* 25, no. 5, Spring 1984: 10–11.) (SiNF)

Haskell Meadow   *Shuteye Peak 15'*
   For Bill and John Haskell, early sheepmen. (Farquhar: Versteeg, Ellis.) (SiNF)

Hawkins Peak (new, 10,024–10,023)   *Markleeville 15' and 7½'*
   John Hawkins squatted on a ranch east of the peak in 1858. (Maule; also *Alpine Heritage,* p. 54, which says the year was 1854.) Hawkins also owned the hot-springs property three miles west of Markleeville. In 1878 he sold a half interest to Alvin Grover, who later acquired it all. (See **Grover Hot Spring.**) Leander Hawkins, a brother of John, was one of the party of college men with Joseph LeConte in the summer of 1870. (LeConte, *Ramblings,* 130–31.) Hawkins Creek, running west from the peak, is first named on the *Carson Pass* 7½' quad, 1979.) (TNF)

Haystack Peak (10,015)   *Tower Peak 15'*
   Probably named by the Wheeler Survey; it is on atlas sheet 56D, 1878–79. (YNP)

Hazel Green Creek, Ranch   *Lake Eleanor 15'*
   "The next camp named [after 'Deer Flat'] was 'Hazel Green,' from the number of hazel bushes growing near a beautiful little meadow." (Bunnell, *Discovery,* 1911, 321.) (Creek in YNP; ranch in StNF)

Heather Lake   *Mt. Henry 7½'*
   Named for the large amount of heather around the lake; added to the map because it was in common use. (USGS.) (SiNF)

Heather Lake   *Triple Divide Peak 15'*
   Named in 1925 by Supt. John R. White of Sequoia National Park, "because of the prevailing flowers." (Letter, White to Scoyen, 1950, SNP files.) Appeared on the fourth edition of the *Tehipite* 30' map, 1929. (SNP)

Heenan Lake (7,084), **Creek**   *Topaz Lake 15', Heenan Lake 7½'*
   Heenan was a miner in the Leviathan Mine, north of the lake; he was killed in the 1860s by a blast at the mine. (Maule.) The lake is named on the first edition of the *Markleeville* 30' map, 1891. It was enlarged about 1914 by the erection of a 37-foot-high dam. (USGS.) The creek was named officially by a BGN decision in 1957.

Helen, Lake   *Matterhorn Peak 15'*
Named in 1932 by Al Gardisky for a "lady friend." (Spuller.) (INF)

Helen Lake (11,617–11,595)   *Mt. Goddard 15' and 7½'*
R. B. Marshall named the lake for Helen Muir Funk, one of John Muir's two daughters, during the 1907–09 survey for the *Mt. Goddard* 30' map. (Farquhar: Marshall.) (KCNP)

Helen, Lake   *Tower Peak 15'*
R. B. Marshall named this one in 1909 for Helen Keyes, daughter of Colonel Forsyth and wife of Lt. Edward A. Keyes. (Farquhar: Marshall.) The name appeared on the third edition of the *Dardanelles* 30' map, 1912. (TNF)

Helen Lake   *Mono Craters 15'*
R. B. Marshall, USGS, named the lake in 1909 for Helen Coburn Smith, daughter of George Otis Smith, director of the USGS, 1907–31. (Farquhar: Marshall.) The name appeared on the third edition of the *Mt. Lyell* 30' map, 1910. (YNP)

Helen of Troy, Lake (3,816 m.–12,515)   *Mount Whitney 15',*
                                                Mt. Williamson 7½'
Proposed by Chester Versteeg in 1953. (SC papers in BL.) (INF)

Hell Diver Lakes   *Mt. Goddard 15', Mt. Darwin 7½'*
John Schober named them. "Hell divers"—little coots that dive for fish. (Art Schober.) (INF)

Hell For Sure Pass (over 11,320), **Lake** (10,762)   *Mt. Goddard 15',*
                                                    Mt. Henry 7½'
The name was first used in print by J. N. LeConte; he crossed the pass in 1904 on what had been called the "Baird" trail. (*SCB* 5, no. 3, Jan. 1905: 237.) The lake was first named on the *Mt. Goddard* 15' map, 1953. (pass, KCNP, SiNF; lake, SiNF)

Helms Meadow, Creek   *Huntington Lake 15', Blackcap Mtn. 15',*
                              Dogtooth Peak 7½', Ward Mountain 7½'
William Helm, born in Ontario, Canada, in 1837, came to California in 1859 and "settled near Big Dry Creek, about seven miles northeast of the site of the present town of Fresno." (Winchell, 104.) Helm and Frank Dusy were partners in sheep-raising in the late 1860s and early '70s. (Farquhar: L. A. Winchell; see also Vandor, vol. 2, 1547–48.) (SiNF)

Hengst Peak (11,127)   *Mineral King 15'*
Albert Alfred Hengst (1868–1944), a Three Rivers business and civic leader, conservationist, and pioneer trail builder, who in 1905 began transplanting golden trout from east-slope streams and lakes. (BGN decision, 1980.) The peak is about 1¼ miles west-northwest of White Chief Peak. It is not named on the present USGS topo map, but is on the Sequoia National Forest map. (SNP, SeNF)

Henness Ridge, Branch   *Yosemite 15', El Portal 15'*
James A. Hennessy, a native of Ireland; the name was misspelled

"Henness" by the Wheeler Survey. Hennessy grew vegetables at what is now El Portal for early Yosemite visitors. (*Yosemite Road Guide,* 74.) The GLO plat of 1884, secs. 17 and 18, T. 3 S., R. 20 E., shows "House, Barn, Hennessey's Ranch," about ½ mile east of what is named "Rancheria Flat" on present maps. (StNF)

Henry, Mount (12,196)   *Blackcap Mtn. 15', Mt. Henry 7½'*
    Named by J. N. LeConte (probably in 1904) for Joseph Henry (1797–1878), the foremost American physicist of his time; professor of natural philosophy at Princeton, 1832–78; first secretary of the newly-created Smithsonian Institution, 1846–78; second president of the National Academy of Sciences, 1868–78; largely responsible for creation of the US Weather Bureau. (Farquhar: LeConte; also EB.) (KCNP, SiNF)

Henry Peak (9,354–9,352)   *Dardanelles Cone 15',*
                                                Spicer Meadow Res. 7½'
    Probably named by the Wheeler Survey; it first appears on atlas sheet 56D, 1878–79. Called "Henry's Peak" in a GLO surveyor's field notes in 1879. (StNF)

Hermit, The (12,328–12,360)   *Mt. Goddard 15', Mt. Darwin 7½'*
    "A colossal, sugarloaf-shaped buttress of fractured granite stood sharply up, the advance Guard of the host of peaks presently to be described, yet so conspicuously separated from them as to suggest the name The Hermit." (Theodore S. Solomons in *Appalachia* 8, no. 1, 1896: 46.) (KCNP)

Hermit Valley   *Markleeville 15', Pacific Valley 7½'*
    Named "Mokelumne Valley" by Murphy's exploring party of 1855. The present name was bestowed by Lady Franklin, who visited the spot in 1862. (Wood, 51.) That name was in use when the Whitney Survey party was in the area in 1863. (Brewer, *Up and Down,* 431, 434.) Other earlier names were "Holden's" and "Ritchie's Station." (Whitney, *Geology,* 445.) (StNF)

Hester Lake (11,255–11,246)   *Mt. Goddard 15', North Palisade 7½'*
    Robert M. Hester was the co-pilot of a B-24 bomber that was lost in a Sierra snowstorm in December 1943. His father, Clinton Hester of Los Angeles, unsuccessfully searched for the plane in the Kings Canyon area for fourteen summers. He died in 1959. In July 1960 the wreckage of the plane was found in the lake by an NPS ranger and two USGS geologists. The lake is named in commemoration of father and son. (BGN decision, 1960.) Not named on early editions of the *Mt. Goddard* 15' quad. It is three-fourths of a mile southwest of Langille Peak. (KCNP)

Hetch Hetchy Reservoir   *Lake Eleanor 15', Hetch Hetchy Reservoir 15'*
Hetch Hetchy Dome (6,165)   *Lake Eleanor 15'*
    "Named from a Central Miwok word denoting a kind of grass or plant with edible seeds abounding in the valley." (Kroeber, 42.)
    "Hetch Hetchy is the name of a species of grass that the Tuolumne Indians used for food, and which grows on the meadow at the lower end of the valley.

The grain, when ripe, was gathered and beaten out and pounded into meal in mortars." (Sanchez, 230–31.)

"Hatchatchie Valley (erroneously spelled Hetch Hetchy)." (Powers, 357.)

". . . in the Indian language used by Tenaya, Hetchy means 'tree.' At the end of the valley where the trail from the ridge comes in . . . there are twin yellow pine trees, and the Indians, therefore, called the valley 'Hetchy Hetchy,' or 'The Valley of the Two Trees.' " (Versteeg from J. V. Wolff, supervisor of Stanislaus National Forest, 1920s; in Farquhar files.)

Either Joseph or Nate Screech, or both, was the first white man to enter Hetch Hetchy Valley, in 1850. (Paden, 188–92; also Farquhar.) "Hetch Hetchy Valley" and "Hetch Hetchy Fall" are on the Hoffmann and Gardiner map, 1863–67. The valley was called "Hatch Hatche Meadows" on the 1880 GLO plat and in the surveyor's field notes. On July 5, 1883, Joseph Screech patented 160 acres—the SE¼ of sec. 9—in T. 1 N., R. 20 E. On the same day, Nate Screech patented 160 acres in sec. 10.

Hetch Hetchy Dome was not named on the maps until the eighth edition of the *Yosemite* 30' sheet, 1951. It had been described, but not named, many years earlier by John Muir. "On the opposite [north] side of the valley facing Kolana there is a counterpart of the El Capitan of Yosemite rising sheer and plain to a height of 1,800 feet." (*SCB* 6, no. 4, Jan. 1908: 212.)

Whatever the name "Hetch Hetchy" means—grass, seeds, trees—it is no longer relevant; everything is covered by water. O'Shaughnessy Dam was built between 1919 and 1923, and was raised another 85 feet during the years 1935–38. (YNP)

Hidden Lake   *Mineral King 15'*
A small lake off-trail with steep, rocky banks. (*Newsletter* 2, no. 1, July 1971: 28.) BGN decision, 1928. Appeared on the fifth *Kaweah* 30' map, 1934. (SNP)

Hidden Lake   *Tuolumne Meadows 15'*
A small lake that cannot be seen from the trail. (Confirmed by BGN, 1932.) It is on the first *Mt. Lyell* 30' map, 1901. (YNP)

High Sierra Trail   *Triple Divide Peak 15', Mount Whitney 15',*
                                       Kern Peak 15', Mt. Kaweah 7½'
A trail built in the early 1930s from Crescent Meadow (in Giant Forest) to the John Muir Trail at Wallace Creek. (SNP)

Highland Lakes (8,613 and 8,584)   *Dardanelles Cone 15' and 7½'*
Highland Creek   *Spicer Meadow Res. 7½', Dardanelles Cone 15' and 7½'*
"In the immediate vicinity of the lakes [Highland Lakes] a number of prospect-holes attest the presence of a mining-camp, which bore the name of Highland City, although there is not now a vestige of a house remaining." (Wheeler Survey, *Report* of Lt. Macomb, 1878, 142.) "Highland Creek" was mentioned in a GLO surveyor's field notes in 1879. (StNF)

Highland Peak (10,935–10,934)   *Markleeville 15', Ebbetts Pass 7½'*
". . . we occupied the important points in the neighboring mass of

mountains, that nearest the town [Silver Mountain City] being known as Silver Mountain. We named the loftiest point . . . Highland Peak." (Wheeler Survey, *Report* of Lt. Macomb, 1878, 142.) (TNF)

Hilgard, Mount (13,361); **Hilgard Branch, Lake**   *Mt. Abbot 15',*
Mt. Hilgard 7½'
"Mount Hilgard from the west is a striking mass, strongly suggesting Castle Peak in Tuolumne County. It was thus named at the suggestion of an admiring former pupil of Professor Hilgard, Mr. Ernest C. Bonner, who accompanied me on one of my outings (in 1895)." (Theodore S. Solomons, manuscript, 1896, 66, in BL.) Eugene Woldemar Hilgard (1833–1916), a native of Bavaria; professor of agriculture at the University of California, 1875–1903. (Farquhar.) The lake was not named until the 15-minute map, 1953. (SiNF)

Hilton Creek   *Mt. Morrison 15', Convict Lake 7½', Mt. Abbot 7½'*
Hilton Creek Lakes   *Mt. Abbot 15' and 7½'*
Richard Hilton, a blacksmith from Michigan, owned a hotel—the Inyo House—in Independence. He traded the hotel for a ranch in Round Valley in 1869 or 1870. Later he had a "milk ranch" in Long Valley, and supplied butter to Mammoth and other mining camps from the 1870s to about 1900. (INF archives.) In 1891 Hilton patented 440 acres in secs. 23 and 24, T. 4 S., R. 29 E.—land that is now under the waters of Lake Crowley. (INF)

Hiram Peak (9,795–9,760), **Meadow, Canyon**
Dardanelles Cone 15' and 7½'
Named for Hiram Tyre, who grazed cattle in the region in the early days. (StNF files.) (StNF)

Hitchcock, Mount (4,019 m.–13,184); **Hitchcock Lakes**
Mount Whitney 15' and 7½'
On September 7, 1881, the Rev. F. H. Wales of Tulare climbed Mount Young, where he built a monument and left a record of its name, "and the name of another handsome peak just south of it, which, from his suggestion, was named Mount Hitchcock, for Professor Charles Hitchcock, of Dartmouth, where Mr. Wales spent his college days." (Elliott, *Guide,* 49–50.)
Charles Henry Hitchcock (1836–1919), professor of geology at Dartmouth, 1868–1908, conducted the first high mountain observatory in the US, on Mount Washington, NH, winter of 1870–71. (Farquhar.) The mountain was first named on the second edition of the *Mt. Whitney* 30' map, 1910. The lakes were called "Twin Lakes" on the map from 1907 to 1927; changed to the present name on the seventh edition, 1933. (SNP)

Hite Cove   *El Portal 15'*
John R. Hite, frontiersman, explorer, miner, and "squawman," discovered a rich mine here in 1861. (Bingaman, *Pathways,* 20.) The name is on the Hoffmann and Gardiner map, 1863–67, as "Hite's Cove." (SiNF)

Hobler Lake   *Blackcap Mtn. 15', Ward Mountain 7½'*
The lake is named for Sig Hobler, a cattleman, according to John Dale, a former Dinkey packer. (DFG survey.) (SiNF)

Hockett Meadows, Lakes   *Mineral King 15'*
Hockett Peak (8,551), **Meadows; Hockett Peak Creek**   *Hockett Peak 15'*
John Benjamin Hockett (1828–1898), born in Arkansas, pioneered in Tulare County in 1849. He is noted for building (1862–64) the "Hockett Trail," from the South Fork of the Kaweah River across the mountains to Lone Pine. (Farquhar: Versteeg. See also *MWCJ*, no. 2, 1903: 67; *SCB* 1, no. 1, Jan. 1893: 1–4; and *SCB* 1, no. 3, Jan. 1894: 101–3.)

"Hockett Meadows" on the South Fork of the Kaweah was named in 1869 by Ira Blossom. (SNP files.) The name is on the first edition of the *Kaweah 30'* map, 1904; the lakes were added in 1921.

It is my supposition that the other "Hockett" features were named for the same man. "Hockett Peak" is on the first *Olancha 30'* map, 1907. The meadows and creek are not named until the 15-minute map, 1956. (First meadows and the lakes, SNP; others, SeNF)

Hodgdon Ranch   *Lake Eleanor 15'*
On the Old Big Oak Flat Road, 1.3 miles inside the Yosemite National Park boundary. Jeremiah Hodgdon of Vermont settled here in 1865. It served as the headquarters for his summer cattle camp. (Paden, 214–16.)

He also fed and housed travelers to Yosemite Valley, in a crude sort of way. "Three, four, five in a room; some on floors, without even a blanket. . . . Food? Yes. Junks of beef floating in bowls of fat, junks of ham ditto, beans ditto, potatoes as hard as bullets, corn-bread steaming with saleratus, doughnuts ditto, hot biscuits ditto; the whole set out in indescribable confusion and dirt, in a narrow, unventilated room, dimly lit by two reeking kerosene lamps. . . . Not in the wildest and most poverty-stricken little town in Italy could such discomfort be encountered." (Jackson, 95–96.) (YNP)

Hoffman Meadow, Creek   *Kaiser Peak 15', Balloon Dome 7½'*
Possibly named for Milton D. *Huffman*, an early sheepman and a Fresno County supervisor from 1909 to 1917. (Vandor, vol. 1, 1061–62.) (SiNF)

Hoffmann, Mount (10,850); **Hoffmann Creek**
     Hetch Hetchy Reservoir 15'
"Climbed a peak over 10,000 feet high which we called Mt. Hoffmann, and had one of the sublimest views I have ever had of the Sierra." (Brewer diary, June 24, 1863, in BL.)

Charles Frederick Hoffmann (1838–1913), born in Germany, came to California in 1858. He was topographer and geographer with the Whitney Survey throughout its entire existence, 1860–74. Portraits in *SCB* 11, no. 4, 1923: plate CXI; and *SCB* 12, no. 2, 1925: plate XLIV. (YNP)

Hogan Mountain   *Bass Lake 15'*
Samuel L. Hogan patented 160 acres in sec. 32, T. 5 S., R. 21 E. in 1877. This area is now named "Sonny Meadow." On the 1875 GLO plat it was "Hogan's Meadow." (SiNF)

Hogback Peak (11,077)   *Marion Peak 15'*
Possibly named by the USGS during the 1903 survey for the *Tehipite 30'* map; it is on the first edition, 1905. (KCNP, SiNF)

Hoist Ridge   *Patterson Mtn. 15', Tehipite Dome 15'*
    In 1892–93 the Kings River Lumber Company built a narrow-gauge rail line into this area, and a steep incline up to the ridge. Logs cut in the valleys below were hoisted up to the ridge by donkey steam engines, then lowered down the incline to the railroad. The donkey engines were replaced by a permanent hoist in 1894. (Johnston, *Redwoods,* 43–44, *et seq.*) (SeNF)

Hole Ranch   *Shuteye Peak 15'*
    This name might be an error. In 1887 William H. *Hall* patented 160 acres in sec. 30, T. 7 S., R. 23 E., a quarter-section including what is now called "Hole Ranch." (SiNF)

Holster Lake   *Blackcap Mtn. 15' and 7½'*
    Possibly named in 1948 by Charles K. Fisher of the DFG. (DFG survey.) (SiNF)

Homers Nose (over 9,040); **Homers Nose Grove**   *Mineral King 15'*
    John Orth, a surveyor for the General Land Office, named "Homers Nose" in 1872 because of its resemblance to the nose of his guide, John Homer. Homer was a pioneer of the Kaweah region. (Farquhar files: Versteeg from Homer family.) (SNP)

Honeymoon Lake   *Mt. Tom 15', Mount Tom 7½'*
    Named by Art Schober. "A bunch of us were going to take our honeymoons up there—but we never did." (Art Schober.) (INF)

Hoopah Lake   *Mt. Abbot 15', Mt. Hilgard 7½'*
    Named in August 1951 by Elden H. Vestal of the DFG. Vestal wrote that the word means "a type of woven carrier for water, used by Indians." This interpretation is disputed by students of the Mono language. (Heyward Moore, *FPP* 26, no. 2, Summer 1984: 6.) (SiNF)

Hooper, Mount (12,349); **Hooper Creek, Lake** (10,599)   *Mt. Abbot 15',*
                                                            Florence Lake 7½'
    Major William Burchell Hooper (1836–1903), a native of Virginia; at one time owned the Occidental Hotel in San Francisco. The mountain and the creek were named by R. B. Marshall, USGS, probably during the 1907–09 survey for the *Mt. Goddard* 30' map; both names are on the first edition, 1912. (Farquhar: Marshall.) Hooper Lake was named in 1948 by Scott M. Soule and Jack Criqui of the DFG, "because it is at the headwaters of Hooper Creek and directly under Mount Hooper." (Heyward Moore, *FPP* 25, no. 5, Spring 1984: 11.) (SiNF)

Hoover Lakes, Creek   *Merced Peak 15'*
    Three lakes north of Buena Vista Crest, and the creek flowing from them, were named for Herbert C. Hoover by Forest S. Townsley, probably in the late 1920s. Townsley was at that time the Chief Ranger in Yosemite National Park, and a friend of Hoover. (YNP files.) (YNP)

Hoover Lakes   *Matterhorn Peak 15'*
    Theodore Jesse Hoover, a brother of former President Hoover, professor of mining and metallurgy at Stanford, 1919–41. In 1904–05 Hoover was the

manager of the Standard Consolidated Mining Co. of Bodie. An engineer of the company gave the name in 1905. (Farquhar: T. J. Hoover.) (TNF)

Hope Valley   *Markleeville 15', Carson Pass 7½', Freel Peak 15' and 7½'*
   July 29, 1848. "Moved across about one mile and a half and camped at the head of what we called Hope Valley, as we began to have hope." (Gudde, *Bigler*, 117–18.) Henry W. Bigler and other members of the disbanded Mormon Battalion, en route back to Great Salt Lake. (TNF)

Hopkins, Mount (12,304–12,302); **Hopkins Creek, Pass**
Upper Hopkins Lakes (11,082); **Lower Hopkins Lake** (10,354)
                                           Mt. Abbot 15' and 7½'
   The mountain was named by R. B. Marshall, USGS, during the 1907–09 survey, for Mark Hopkins (1813–1878), one of the organizers of the Central Pacific Railroad. (Farquhar: Marshall.) The creek was named at the same time. The lakes were first named on the 15-minute quad. The name "Hopkins Pass"— directly north of Upper Hopkins Lakes—has been omitted on the 7½-minute quad. (SiNF)

Horse Corral Meadow, Creek   *Giant Forest 15', Triple Divide Peak 15'*
   In 1868 E. C. Winchell called the meadow "Crescent Lawn, a spacious meadow encircled on the southeast by a grand arc of granite mountains thinly clad with pines." (San Francisco *Daily Morning Call*, Sept. 11, 1872; also in *SCB* 12, no. 3, 1926: 241.)
   Jasper H. Harrell drove his horses into the mountains in the summer of 1877, after a dry winter, to save them from starvation. He built a corral, and gave the meadow its present name at that time. (Farquhar: Agnew.) (SeNF)

Horsehead Lake   *Blackcap Mtn. 15' and 7½'*
   Named in 1948 by William A. Dill and Jack Criqui of the DFG because its outline resembles the shape of a horse's head. (DFG survey.) (SiNF)

Horseshoe Bend; Horseshoe Bend Grove   *Tehipite Dome 15'*
   A descriptive name: the Kings River makes a horseshoe-shaped bend to the north. Possibly named by the USGS during the 1903 survey for the *Tehipite 30'* map; it is on the first edition, 1905. "Horseshoe Bend Grove" was added to the 15-minute quad, 1952. (SeNF)

Horsethief Canyon   *Freel Peak 15' and 7½', Woodfords 7½'*
   There is a tale that travelers going up West Carson Canyon, west of Woodfords, were frequently robbed of their horses. The thieves fattened the horses in meadows at the head of the canyon, then went northeast down to the Nevada side and sold the horses to other travelers. (*Alpine Heritage*, 47.) (TNF)

Horton Lake, Creek; Upper Horton Lakes   *Mt. Tom 15', Mount Tom 7½'*
   William Horton, of Jackson, Michigan, came to Round Valley in 1864—one of the earlier settlers. (INF files.) He homesteaded 160 acres in sec. 28, T. 6 S., R. 31 E. in 1874, and added another 80 acres in 1884. The upper lakes were first named on the 15-minute quad, 1949. (INF)

Hospital Rock *Giant Forest 15'*

A huge boulder overhanging in such a way as to form a spacious room. According to Hale Tharp it was the main camp of the Potwisha Indians, and their seat of government. (Farquhar.)

In 1873 Alfred Everton was accidentally shot in a bear trap he had set. George Cahoon carried Everton to the rock, and left him there while he went for assistance. Thereafter it was known as "Hospital Rock." (*Nature,* no. 5, Feb. 17, 1925.) (SNP)

Hossack Meadow, Creek *Camp Nelson 15'*

Named for John Hossack, a pioneer stockman. (Fry and White, 107.) (SeNF)

Hotel Creek *Marion Peak 15'*

Hugh Robinson built a log hotel in Cedar Grove in 1897; it was illegal, since he hadn't filed on the property. The government forced him to abandon it the following year. It was torn down in 1931. (See **Cedar Grove.**) The creek was called "Fox Creek" by J. N. LeConte in 1890. (LeConte, *A Summer.*) (KCNP)

Hume; Hume Lake (5,201) *Tehipite Dome 15'*

Thomas Hume was a wealthy Michigan lumberman. He headed a combine that bought out the Sanger Lumber Company in 1905 and moved the operations to Long Meadow on Tenmile Creek. Hume Dam was built across the creek in 1908; the lake began filling in 1909. (For the details of Hume's life and business activities, see Johnston, *Redwoods;* also Johnston, *Whistles.*) Hume is now a summer community and recreation area. (SeNF)

Hummingbird Lake *Tuolumne Meadows 15'*

Named in 1932 by Al Gardisky because at one time he saw many hummingbirds there. (Spuller.) (INF)

Hummingbird Lake *Blackcap Mtn. 7½'*

Ted Anderson, a packer, and Elden H. Vestal of the DFG named the lake in 1955, partly from its shape and partly because they saw a Calliope hummingbird there. (DFG survey.) On the *Blackcap Mtn.* 15' quad the lake is unnamed; it is 1.5 miles south by west from Portal Lake. (SiNF)

Humphreys, Mount (13,986); **Humphreys Lakes** *Mt. Tom 15',*
Mount Tom 7½'

Humphreys Basin *Mt.Tom 15', Mt. Goddard 15', Mount Tom 7½',*
Mt. Darwin 7½'

Andrew Atkinson Humphreys (1810–1883), soldier and engineer, the grandson of Joshua Humphreys, who designed the "Constitution" and other frigates of the War of 1812. Humphreys distinguished himself in the Civil War. After the war he was chief engineer of the US Army until he retired in 1879. The mountain was named by the Whitney Survey; it appears on Hoffmann's map of central California, 1873.

James S. Hutchinson, Jr. and Edward C. Hutchinson made the first ascent on July 18, 1904. "The summit of Humphreys is not more than eight feet square. . . . It is one mass of cracked and broken blocks, thrown loosely together in such a way as to warn one to move cautiously lest the whole top should break off and fall into the great abyss to the eastward. . . . Probably no one had ever stood where we then were, unless perhaps during the early Jurassic period, before the mountain was fully sculptured. Then the mariners of that age (if there were any) might have sailed upon the waters of the Pacific close to the base of the mountain, and, there landing, have climbed up its then gently sloping sides." (*SCB* 5, no. 3, Jan. 1905: 171–72.)

Humphreys Lakes were first named on the *Mt. Tom* 15' quad, 1949. (Peak, SiNF, INF; basin and lakes, SiNF)

Hunewill Peak (over 11,680), **Hills, Lake, Ranch**   *Matterhorn Peak 15'*
N. B. Hunewill built two sawmills on Buckeye Creek in the 1860s. He was one of the earliest settlers in the Bridgeport region; he homesteaded 160 acres in secs. 13 and 14, T. 4 N., R. 24 E. in 1876. The "Hunewill Ranch" is now the Circle H Guest Ranch. (GLO; Cain, 28, 34.)

The name of the peak was misspelled "Hennerville" on all the editions of the *Bridgeport* 30' map, 1911 through 1951. That mistake apparently was due to a GLO surveyor in 1877. "Mr. Hennerville's Saw mill sits directly in the center of sec. 5, and is run by water from Mill Creek." (Field notes, GLO.) "Mill Creek" was the name for what is now Eagle Creek. Strangely, "Hunewill Hills" was spelled correctly all along. The 1877 GLO plat spelled the name "Hemerville's sawmill." The lake was first named (correctly) on the 15-minute quad. (TNF)

Hungry Packer Lake (11,071)   *Mt. Goddard 15', Mt. Darwin 7½'*
John Schober named it about 1934. He and his companions, when stocking this lake and Midnight Lake, had expected to return the same day. They got caught by nightfall, and had to spend the night without blankets or food. (Art Schober.) (INF)

Huntington, Mount (12,394–12,405)   *Mt. Abbot 15' and 7½'*
Named by R. B. Marshall, USGS, for Collis Potter Huntington (1821–1900), one of the organizers of the Central Pacific Railroad. (Farquhar: Marshall.) Almost certainly named during the 1907–09 survey for the *Mt. Goddard* 30' map. It is on the first edition, 1912, but is not on J. N. LeConte's list of peaks in the Sierra over 12,000 feet, compiled in 1903. (*SCB* 4, no. 4, June 1903: 285–91.) The *second* ascent was by David Brower, Norman Clyde, and Hervey Voge, July 14, 1934, who found they had been preceded by a Basque. ". . . perhaps the only sheepherder who ever climbed a peak and left a notation of his act of indiscretion." (Brower in *SCB* 20, no. 1, 1935: 75.) (SiNF, INF)

Huntoon Valley, Creek, Camp   *Fales Hot Springs 15'*
The brothers Sidney and Almond Huntoon were early arrivals (in the 1850s) in Bridgeport Valley. (Cain, 25–26.) Sidney patented 600 acres in secs. 26, 27, and 35, T. 6 N., R. 24 E. in 1886. Huntoon Valley (through which US 395 runs) was apparently the route followed by Joseph LeConte and party in 1870. He called it "Tamarack Valley." (LeConte, *Ramblings,* 120.) (TNF)

Hurd Peak (12,237–12,219), **Lake**   *Mt. Goddard 15', Mt. Thompson 7½'*
"Its name is derived from the late Mr. H. C. Hurd, an engineer who, while

making certain explorations of this region, climbed it in 1906. So far as known, this was the first ascent." (Walter L. Huber in *SCB* 10, no. 4, Jan. 1919: 440.) The peak's name appeared on the third edition of the *Mt. Goddard* 30' map, 1923. The lake's name appears on the 15-minute quad, 1948. (INF)

Hutching Creek   *Merced Peak 15'*
On the first eight editions of the *Mt. Lyell* 30' map this stream was called "North Fork of Lyell Fork" of the Merced River. On the final edition, in 1948, it was changed to "Hutching Creek," which is how it appears on the 15-minute quad. It was named for Florence Hutchings, daughter of James Mason Hutchings. The BGN in 1978 decided that it should be "Hutchings," and that it is for James, not his daughter. (YNP)

Hutchings, Mount (10,785)   *Marion Peak 15'*
James Mason Hutchings (1818–1902), born in England, came to California in 1849, with the first tourist party to visit Yosemite Valley, 1855. Hutchings made a living by running a hotel in the valley, but his reputation came from being the foremost booster and promoter of the glories of Yosemite. He published *Hutchings' California Magazine,* and wrote two memorable books: *Scenes of Wonder and Curiosity in California,* and *In the Heart of the Sierras.*
It is odd that the only significant feature named for Hutchings is a peak overlooking Kings Canyon. In the fall of 1875 Hutchings crossed the Sierra from Independence to Kings Canyon; the peak may have been named then. It first appears on John Muir's map accompanying his article in *Century Magazine,* November 1891. (KCNP)

Hutchinson Meadow   *Mt. Abbot 15', Mt. Hilgard 7½'*
The name was proposed in 1922 by Chester Versteeg to honor James S. and Edward C. Hutchinson, who made the first ascent of Mount Humphreys. (Farquhar files.) James was an explorer and climber in the Sierra for many years. The name appeared on the third edition of the *Mt. Goddard* 30' map, 1923. (SiNF)

Hutton, Mount (11,990–11,998)   *Mt. Henry 7½'*
Named for James Hutton (1726–1797), Scottish geologist who established the modern science of geology.
The name was suggested by Albert C. Gerould of Philadelphia. "The idea for the name came from the Fentons' *Giants of Geology* where they point out that Hutton was the first man to understand the whole cycle of geology from erosion and sedimentation to mountain erection. I always get a little tired of the way Prof. Whitney named everything after himself and his friends." (Letter, Gerould to Farquhar, June 5, 1973.) Approved by BGN decision, 1973. The name also appears on the *Blacktop Mtn.* 7½' quad, indicating the south side of the mountain but not its summit. The mountain is not named on the *Blacktop Mtn.* 15' quad. It is the summit marked 11998, about 1½ miles due south of Hell For Sure Pass. (SiNF)

Huxley, Mount (13,086–13,117)   *Mt. Goddard 15', Mt. Darwin 7½'*
One of the "Evolution Group" of peaks named by Theodore S. Solomons in

July 1895. Thomas Henry Huxley (1825–1895), English biologist, a supporter of the doctrine of evolution.

"There are Mt. Spencer and Mt. Huxley, between which there exists a wonderful similarity, not only in the analogy of their positions, but in the peculiar resemblance they bear to each other in size and shape, in the sharpness of their summits, in the snow-gorges that flute their sides, and in the smoothness and purity of the cream-colored granite out of which the peaks are sculptured." (Solomons in *Appalachia* 8, no. 1, 1896: 49.) (KCNP)

Hyatt Lake   *Pinecrest 15'*
    Named in 1909 by R. B. Marshall for Edward Hyatt, Jr., who was with a USGS field party that year. Hyatt was the California state engineer, 1927–50. (Farquhar: Marshall; and files.) (StNF)

Ian Campbell, Mount (10,616)   *Mt. Givens 7½'*
    Named for Dr. Ian Campbell (1899–1978), Chief of the California Division of Mines and Geology, state geologist, and first chairman of the California Advisory Committee on Geographic Names. Campbell did geologic investigations on the peak and the surrounding area. (BGN decision, 1982.) The peak is not named on the *Kaiser* 15' quad. It is in the lower right corner, 2¼ miles east-southeast of Mt. Givens. (SiNF)

Iceberg, The (8,350); **Iceberg Meadow**   *Sonora Pass 15',*
                                                             Disaster Peak 7½'
    Probably named by the USGS; both names appeared on the third edition of the *Dardanelles* 30' map, 1912. (StNF)

Iceberg Lake (2,979 m.–9,773)   *Devils Postpile 15', Mt. Ritter 7½'*
    The lake is fed by a small glacier and a permanent snowfield, and often has ice floating in it until late summer. The namer is not known, but the name was in use at least as early as 1923. (*SCB* 12, no. 1, 1924: 30.) It first appeared on the 15-minute quad, 1953. (INF)

Iceberg Peak (9,781–9,720)   *Dardanelles Cone 15' and 7½'*
    Probably named by the USGS during the 1891–96 survey for the *Dardanelles* 30' map; it is on the first edition, 1898. (StNF)

Iceland Lake   *Tower Peak 15'*
    Formerly one of the "Lewis Lakes;" changed to its present name by a BGN decision in 1965. (StNF)

Ickes, Mount (3,942 m.–12,968)   *Mt. Pinchot 15' and 7½'*
    Named in 1964 for Harold L. Ickes, Secretary of the Interior from 1933 to 1946. "In naming this rugged mountain in his memory, we recall that it was his iron will which successfully prevailed in the struggle to save Kings Canyon from the plunderers of the land. He, more than any other person, was instrumental in saving this magnificent park area for posterity." (Secretary of the Interior Stewart L. Udall, Feb. 6, 1964.) Not named on the first edition of the 15-minute quad; it is 1½ miles west by south from Pinchot Pass, marked 12968. (KCNP)

Illilouette Fall, Creek, Ridge, Gorge   *Yosemite 15',*
Yosemite Valley 1:24,000

"*Tululowehäck*. The cañon of the South Fork of the Merced, called the Illilouette in the California Geological Report, that being the spelling given by Messrs. King and Gardner,—a good illustration of how difficult it is to catch the exact pronunciation of these names. Mr. Hutchings spells it Tooluluwack." (Whitney, *Yosemite Guide-Book,* 1870, 17.)

"This cañon is called by Professor J. D. Whitney the 'Illilouette,' a supposed Indian name; but I have never questioned a single Indian that knew anything whatever of such a word; while every one, without exception, knows this cañon either by Too-lool-a-we-ack or Too-lool-we-ack; the meaning of which, as nearly as their ideas can be comprehended and interpreted, is the place beyond which was the great rendezvous of the Yo Semite Indians for hunting deer." (Hutchings, *In the Heart,* 440.)

"I think it advisable to call this the Glacier Fall, and, therefore, give it that name. . . . The name of 'Illeuette' is not Indian, and is, therefore, meaningless and absurd." (Bunnell, *Discovery,* 1880, 203.)

Everyone had trouble with the name. On the 1884 GLO plat it is spelled "Illionette" and "Illioneth." The creek was still called "Tu-lu-la-wi-ak or South Cañon" as late as the Wheeler Survey map of the valley, 1883. The gorge was first named on the fourth edition of the USGS map of the valley, 1927. (YNP)

Inconsolable Range   *Mt. Goddard 15', Mt. Thompson 7½',*
North Palisade 7½'

Inconsolable Lake   *Mt. Thompson 7½'*

The range may have been named by the USGS during the 1907–09 survey for the *Mt. Goddard* 30' map; it is on the first edition, 1912. The lake was first named on the 7½-minute quad. On the *Mt. Goddard* 15' quad it is 0.3 mile northeast of Bull Lake. (INF)

Independence Peak (3,579 m.–11,744), **Creek**   *Mt. Pinchot 15',*
Kearsarge Peak 7½'

"Camp Independence" was established and named by Lt.-Colonel George Spafford Evans, of the Second Cavalry, on Independence Day, July 4, 1862. (Letter cited in Cragen, p. 25.) The creek was called "Little Pine Creek" from the time of the first settler (Charles Putnam, in 1861) until the fourth edition of the *Mt. Whitney* 30' map, 1919, when it received its present name. The peak was named on the first edition of that map, 1907, possibly by the USGS during the survey in 1905. (INF)

Indian Canyon; Indian Canyon Creek   *Yosemite Valley 1:24,000,*
Hetch Hetchy Reservoir 15'

"It was up this cañon that the Indian prisoners escaped in 1851 . . . from which circumstance originated the name; and it was down this that the avenging Monos crept, when they substantially exterminated the Yo Semite tribe in 1853." (Hutchings, *In the Heart,* 375.)

This ravine became known to us as 'Indian Cañon,' though called by the

Indians 'Le-Hamite,' 'the arrow-wood.' It was also known to them by the name of 'Scho-tal-lo-wi,' meaning the way to *Fall Creek.*' " (Bunnell, *Discovery,* 1880, 169.)

Powers said the Indians used a generic word for canyon—Ma'-ta—and held up both hands to indicate perpendicular walls. (Powers, 364.)

"Indian Cañon" is on King and Gardiner's map, 1865. The creek was at first called "Indian Creek;" the name was changed by a BGN decision in 1932 to avoid confusion with another Indian Creek, which flows into the Merced River near El Portal. (YNP)

Indian Cave   *Yosemite Valley 1:24,000*
Formed by huge boulders piled on top of one another; said to have been occupied by the Yosemite Indians as a winter shelter. Ansel Hall said the Indians named the cave "Hol'-low,' " but sometimes called it "Lah-koo'-hah," which meant "Come out!" (Hall, *Yosemite,* 22.) It has been on the valley map since the first edition, 1907. On the *Yosemite* 15' quad it is simply marked "Cave." (YNP)

Indian Creek   *Yosemite 15', El Portal 15'*
A common name but an old one. The creek crosses the Wawona Road near Chinquapin and joins the Merced River above El Portal. It was named by early travelers, the Mariposa Battalion, or the Whitney Survey. It is on the Hoffmann and Gardiner map, 1863–67. (YNP, StNF)

Indian Creek, Basin; Indian Basin Grove   *Tehipite Dome 15'*
Indians gathered at Indian Basin to sell their wares to lumbermen when the area was heavily logged in the 1890s. (Fry and White, 113.) (SeNF)

Indian Head (8,965)   *Kern Peak 15'*
Possibly named by the USGS during the 1905 survey for the *Olancha* 30' map; it is on the first edition, 1907. (INF)

Indian Rock (8,522), **Ridge**   *Hetch Hetchy Reservoir 15',*
                                            Yosemite Valley 1:24,000
Both these names probably derived from nearby Indian Canyon. Indian Rock is one of the points on the boundary of the original grant of Yosemite Valley in 1864. The name appears on the Wheeler Survey map of the valley, 1883. "Indian Ridge" is on the first *Yosemite* 30' map, 1897. (YNP)

Infant Buttes (10,290–10,137)   *Mt. Abbot 15', Florence Lake 7½'*
Named by Theodore S. Solomons, probably in 1895. (Farquhar: Solomons.) (SiNF)

Ink Rocks (over 11,040)   *Matterhorn Peak 15'*
Possibly named by the USGS during the 1905–09 survey for the *Bridgeport* 30' map; the name is on the first edition, 1911. (TNF)

Inspiration Point   *Yosemite 15', Yosemite Valley 1:24,000*
A viewpoint on the old Wawona Road, less than a thousand feet above the east end of the Wawona Tunnel. The original "Inspiration Point" is no longer marked on the maps. What is called "Old Inspiration Point" was actually "Mount Beatitude." (See the entries for those two names.) (YNP)

Ionian Basin *Mt. Goddard 15' and 7½'*
The name was proposed by Lewis Clark of the Sierra Club, who thought it fitting because of the basin's proximity to Scylla and Charybdis. (Letter, David Brower to C. A. Ecklund, USGS, March 7, 1951.) (KCNP)

Ireland Lake (10,735), **Creek,** *Tuolumne Meadows 15'*
Named by Lt. Harry C. Benson for Dr. Merritte Weber Ireland of the US Army Medical Corps, who was on duty in Yosemite National Park in 1897. Ireland was later surgeon general of the army for 13 years. (Farquhar: Benson.) (YNP)

Iridescent Lake (3,629 m.–11,924) *Mount Whitney 15' and 7½'*
"So named because of the varied colors of its wavelets in the morning sun." (SNP files.) The name appeared on the eighth edition of the *Mt. Whitney* 30' map, 1937.) (SNP)

Iron Mountain (3,318.2 m.–11,149), **Creek, Lake** *Devils Postpile 15',*
Cattle Mtn. 7½'
The mountain was probably named by the Wheeler Survey; it is on atlas sheet 56D, 1878–79. Iron Creek is named on the first edition of the *Mt. Lyell* 30' map, 1901. Iron Lake is first named on the 15-minute quad. (SiNF, INF)

Iron Mountain (9,166), **Lakes** *Shuteye Peak 15'*
Iron Creek *Yosemite 15', Bass Lake 15'*
The mountain probably was named by the Whitney Survey; it is on the Hoffmann and Gardiner map, 1863–67. The creek is first named on the *Yosemite* 30' map, 1897, and the lakes appear on the 15-minute quad. (SiNF)

Iron Spring *Yosemite 15', Yosemite Valley 1:24,000*
The red stains from this spring can be seen from Glacier Point. It was called "Chalybeate Spring" on the Wheeler Survey map of Yosemite Valley, 1883. ("Chalybeate" means water impregnated with the salts of iron.)
"I once visited this spring in company with the eminent English chemist, Dr. F. R. Lees, of Leeds, and he pronounced it the finest and most valuable chalybeate spring he had ever seen." (Hutchings, *In the Heart.* 391.) (YNP)

Irvine, Mount (13,770) *Mount Whitney 15' and 7½'*
Norman Clyde made the first ascent in June 1925, and named the peak for Andrew Irvine, who was lost on the British Mount Everest expedition in June 1924. (*SCB* 12, no. 3, 1926: 306. For biographical information on Irvine, see *SCB* 12, no. 2, 1925: 182–83; also *The Fight for Everest*, 1924. See also **Mallory, Mount.**) Mount Irvine was first named on the sixth edition of the *Mt. Whitney* 30' map, 1927. (INF)

Irwin Bright Lake *Hetch Hetchy Reservoir 15'*
Robert Bright stated that this lake was named for his deceased son Irwin, who planted 37 rainbow trout in the lake. (USGS.) A BGN decision in 1932 spelled the first name "Irving;" this was corrected to "Irwin" by a 1960 decision. The lake had formerly been known as "Lily Lake" and "Saddle Horse Lake." (BGN.) (YNP)

Isabella Tunnel   *Ebbetts Pass 7½'*
The tunnel—never completed—was driven to intersect the IXL and Exchequer mines near the head of IXL Canyon, to serve as a drain. It is about 2,000 feet long. (USGS, letter from Carl C. Munck, April 30, 1979.) This property was developed by the Isabel (or Isabella) Mining Company of London, England, in the 1870s. (Clark, *Mines,* 29.) (TNF)

Isberg Pass, Peak (10,996), **Lakes**   *Merced Peak 15'*
Lt. N. F. McClure named the pass in 1895 for the native Norwegian in his command who discovered it while they were exploring for a route from the Merced River to the Minarets region. The peak was named from the pass. Both names are on the first *Mt. Lyell* 30' map, 1901. The lakes were first named on the 15-minute quad, 1953. (YNP, SiNF; lakes in SiNF only)

Island Pass (over 10,170)   *Devils Postpile 15', Mt. Ritter 7½'*
Probably named by the USGS during the 1898–99 survey for the *Mt. Lyell* 30' map; it is on the first edition, 1901. The first use of the name in print is by J. N. LeConte in 1908. (*SCB* 7, no. 1, Jan. 1909: photo opp. 6.) (INF)

Isosceles Peak (12,321)   *Mt. Goddard 15', North Palisade 7½'*
Lewis and Nathan Clark named the peak about 1939 for its appearance when seen from Dusy Basin. (Lewis Clark.) (KCNP)

Italy, Lake (11,202); **Italy Pass**   *Mt. Abbot 15', Mt. Hilgard 7½'*
The lake was named by the USGS during the 1907–09 survey for the *Mt. Goddard* 30' map, because of a vague resemblance to the shape of Italy, which became apparent when it was drawn on the map. (Farquhar: Marshall.) The pass name derives from the lake, and first appears on the 15-minute quad. (SiNF; pass also INF)

Iva Bell Hot Springs   *Devils Postpile 15', Crystal Crag 7½'*
Called "Fish Creek Hot Springs" on the 15-minute quad, and incorrectly located, the springs are on the north side of Sharktooth Creek. (USGS Name Report, 1980.) Iva Bell Clark was born unexpectedly at the springs in July 1936, surprising both parents; Mrs. Clark had thought she had a tumor. (Smith, 56.) (SiNF)

Izaak Walton, Mount (12,077–12,099); **Izaak Walton Lake**
                                        Mt. Abbot 15', Graveyard Peak 7½'
The peak was named by Francis P. Farquhar in 1919 for Izaak Walton (1593–1683), "to whom all fisherman and lovers of good literature are indebted for *The Compleat Angler,* first published in 1653." (Farquhar; also *SCB* 11, no. 1, 1920: 46.) The name appeared on the fourth edition of the *Mt. Goddard* 30' map, 1928. The lake was first named on the 15-minute quad. (SiNF)

Jack Flat Camp   *Mineral King 15'*
Called "Jack Ass Flats" on the Dillon Road survey notes, 1877. Probably named for Nate Dillon's mules, which hauled the empty lumber cars uphill to the mill. (Otter, 156. See **Dillon Mill.**) (SeNF)

Jack Main Canyon   *Tower Peak 15'*

"Some years ago I was discussing a trip I had made through Jack Main Canyon with Mr. C. H. Burt. . . . He told me that as a boy he had often herded sheep through Jack Main Canyon and volunteered the information that the canyon was named after an old sheep-herder who ranged sheep in that region whose name was Jack Means. Mr. Burt said that the name of the canyon as it appeared on the maps was incorrect; that all the early sheep and cattle men in that region called the canyon 'Jack Means Canyon,' and that the present name of the canyon was a corruption of that name." (Letter, W. H. Spaulding to Farquhar, in *SCB* 12, no. 2, 1925: 126.) The name first appears on Lt. McClure's map of 1895. (YNP)

Jackass Meadow, Creek, Butte (7,238), **Rock** (7,112)   *Shuteye Peak 15'*
Jackass Meadow, Creek, Lakes   *Merced Peak 15'*

". . . it bears the mellifluous title of 'Jackass Dome.' This dome is perhaps over 10,000 feet high, and lends its majestic name to an extensive meadow. Through it meanders a wide and quiet stream . . . and to this creek the same aristocratic title has been assigned." (J. W. A. Wright, San Francisco *Post*, July 26, 1869, 3.)

"Many meadows were passed, into which large numbers of cattle had been driven. One of these is known as Neal's Ranch, or Jackass Meadows." (Whitney, *The Yosemite Guide-Book*, 138.) Wright's "Jackass Dome" may be the rock tower called "Balls" since the first edition of the *Mt. Lyell* 30' map, 1901. The creek and meadow are named on the 1882 GLO plat of T. 5 S., R. 24 E. All the features except the lakes were named on the first editions of the *Kaiser* and *Mt. Lyell* 30' maps. The USGS probably named the butte and rock during the 1901–02 survey. "Little Jackass Meadow," on the Wheeler Survey atlas sheet 56D (1878–79) and the *Mt. Lyell* 30' maps from 1901 to 1914, was changed to "Soldier Meadow" on the fifth edition, 1922. (SiNF)

Jackass Meadows, Dike   *Mt. Abbot 15', Florence Lake 7½'*

"The picturesque sheep-bridge, constructed of slender tamarack trunks, which spans the river here, is called Jackass Bridge, and the succession of flats just below are correspondingly the Jackass Meadows." (Theodore S. Solomons in *Appalachia* 8, no. 1, 1896: 42.) Lil A. Winchell said that the meadows were earlier called "Injun Flats," an "old (and still being used at that time) camping ground for the trans-Sierra natives in their migrations." (Letter, Winchell to Solomons, April 1896, in SC papers, BL.)

The meadows was "Meadow" on the *Mt. Goddard* 30' and *Mt. Abbot* 15' maps. Jackass Dike ("Dyke" on the 30-minute maps) was probably named by the USGS during the 1907–09 survey. (SiNF)

Jawbone Creek, Falls, Pass (6,292)   *Pinecrest 15', Cherry Lake North 7½'*

In the late 1860s a Frenchman named Jarbau had a cabin at the confluence of what are now named Jawbone and Skunk creeks. Oldtimers called the northerly creek "Jarbau Creek," a name that was gradually transformed into "Jawbone." (StNF files.) (StNF)

Jawbone Lake   *Mt. Abbot 15', Mt. Hilgard 7½'*
Named by Elden H. Vestal in August 1951 because its shape resembles an animal's jawbone. (Heyward Moore, *FPP* 26, no. 2, Summer 1984: 5.) (SiNF)

Jeff Davis Peak (9,065–8,990)   *Markleeville 15', Carson Pass 7½'*
The peak was called "Sentinel Rock" on the Wheeler Survey atlas sheet 56B, 1876–77. The present name appears on the first *Markleeville 30'* map, 1891. Gudde suggests it may have been in local use long before, since many of the inhabitants of nearby Summit City (abandoned in the late 1860s) were Confederate sympathizers. (Gudde, *Place Names*, 156.) The creek was first named on the 15-minute quad. (TNF)

Jenkins, Mount (7,921)   *Owens Peak 7½'*
Named for James Charles Jenkins (1952–1979), a noted authority on the flora, fauna, and history of the southern Sierra Nevada, and the author of several guidebooks. (BGN decision, 1984.) Inasmuch as this is a new name, it is not on present maps. The peak is 1.3 miles north by west from Morris Peak, and 2.1 miles south by east from Owens Peak.

Jennie Lake   *Giant Forest 15'*
S. L. N. Ellis named the lake for his wife, Jennie, in 1897. (Farquhar: Versteeg, from Ellis.) (SeNF)

Jenny Creek   *Mineral King 15'*
Probably named for Nate Dillon's mules. (Otter, 156. See **Jack Flat Camp** and **Dillon Mill**.) (SeNF)

Jepson, Mount (4,081.3 m.–13,390)   *Big Pine 15', Split Mtn. 7½'*
Willis Linn Jepson (1867–1946), professor of botany at the University of California, 1899–1937; charter member of the Sierra Club; helped found the Save-the-Redwoods League; founded the California Botanical Society. (See *SCB* 32, no. 5, May 1947: 104–7.)
An earlier unofficial name was "Pine Marten Peak." It is not named on the *Big Pine 15'* quad, but the altitude is given. It is on the Sierra crest, one mile south-southeast of Mt. Gayley. (KCNP, INF)

Jewelry Lake   *Pinecrest 15'*
About 1915 Joe Ratto and Tom Costa stopped at this lake, which was then unnamed, to fish. Costa was a "conservative spender," and had brought only three jeweled spinners for fishing. He quickly lost two of them to fish who continued to swim around with the spinners in their mouths. He made a cast or two with the last spinner, but when a large trout was about to strike, Costa jerked it out of reach because he would rather keep the spinner than catch a fish. Thereafter, they called the lake "Jewelry Lake." (StNF files, from Joe Ratto.) (StNF)

Jigger Lakes   *Mt. Henry 7½'*
Probably named by the DFG when the lakes were surveyed in 1954; they were at first named "Big Jigger" and "Little Jigger." (DFG survey. See **Big Shot Lake**.) The lakes are not named on the *Blackcap Mtn.* 15' quad. They are the two lakes just west of Devils Punchbowl. (SiNF)

Jigsaw Pass (12,622)   *Mt. Goddard 15', North Palisade 7½'*
The name was proposed by the Sierra Club in 1934. (Letter, David Brower
to C. A. Ecklund, USGS, March 7, 1951.) (INF)

Jim Quinn Spring   *Silver Lake 15', Tragedy Spring 7½'*
James Quinn homesteaded 160 acres in sec. 6, T. 9 N., R. 16 E. and sec. 31,
T. 10 N., R. 16 E. in 1891. (ENF)

JO Pass (9,410)   *Triple Divide Peak 15'*
"About August, 1889, I crossed the pass with pack stock. Sheepmen and
saddle stock had crossed before. Probably first used by sheepmen in 1875. I
gave the name to the pass from initials cut on tree some years before by John
Wesley Warren. He started to cut his name, 'John,' but cut only the first two
letters." (Farquhar: Ellis, as told to Versteeg.) (SNP, SeNF)

Jobs Peak (10,633), **Canyon**   *Freel Peak 15', Woodfords 7½'*
Jobs Sister (10,823)   *Freel Peak 15' and 7½'*
Moses Job settled in Carson Valley, Nevada, about 1854, and operated a
store. (Maule.) The general name "Job's Group of Mountains" (which included
Freel Peak at the time) was used in the State Surveyor General's *Report* of
1855, p. 141. The names first appeared in their present form on the Wheeler
Survey atlas sheet 56B, 1876–77. The canyon was first named on the 15-minute
quad. (Jobs Sister, ENF, TNF; others, TNF)

Joe Devel Peak (4,062 m.–13,325)   *Mount Whitney 15' and 7½'*
Joseph Devel was a member of the Wheeler Survey party that made the first
ascent of the peak, on September 20, 1875. The name was given by Owen L.
Williams of the Sierra Club on July 7, 1937, when he found the records of the
Wheeler party, and of later climbers, on the summit. (*SCB* 23, no. 2, April
1938: 108–9.) (SNP)

John Muir Trail
"The idea of a crest-parallel trail through the High Sierra came to me one day
while herding my uncle's cattle in an immense unfenced alfalfa field near
Fresno. It was in 1884 and I was fourteen." (Theodore S. Solomons in *SCB* 25,
no. 1, Feb. 1940: 28.)
"Sleeping that night [in 1895] at the base of Mt. Huxley, warmed by our fire
of gnarled juniper, I dreamed of my task fully done. A well-marked trail led from
the distant Yosemite past the long lake, up the snow-basin, and over the divide to
the King's River. I hope my dream was prophetic. The way, at all events, is
clear. Only the trail waits to be built." (Solomons in *Appalachia* 8, no. 1, 1896:
49.) The "long lake" and the "divide" were Wanda Lake and Muir Pass, which
were not named until about 1907.
Solomons did the earliest explorations for what later became the John Muir
Trail. (*SCB* 1, no. 6, May 1895: 221–37.) J. N. LeConte continued the search
for the best route. (*SCB* 7, no. 1, Jan. 1909: 1–22, and sketch map.) In 1915 the
California legislature, in response to a Sierra Club proposal, made an initial
appropriation of $10,000 for construction of the trail, which was to be named
for John Muir, who had died in December 1914. A good survey of the trail's

construction is by Walter L. Huber in *SCB* 15, no. 1, Feb. 1930: 37–46. The John Muir Trail as it exists today was completed when the sections were built over Forester Pass in 1931 and Mather Pass in 1938.

John Muir Trail Cabin   *Mt. Henry 7½'*
A historic cabin used by construction crews building the John Muir Trail. (SiNF)

Johnson Meadows, Creek   *Shuteye Peak 15'*
Ole Johnson patented 160 acres in sec. 6, T. 6. S., R. 24 E. in 1892. (SiNF)

Johnson, Mount (12,871–12,868)   *Mt. Goddard 15', Mt. Thompson 7½'*
In 1917 R. B. Marshall named a peak northeast of Parker Pass in memory of Willard D. Johnson of the USGS. (This is now named "Mt. Lewis," on the *Mono Craters* 15' quad.) But there was already a "Johnson Peak" nine miles to the west, so the name "Mount Johnson" was transferred to a peak on the Sierra crest close to mountains named for other notable members of the Geological Survey: Powell, Thompson, Gilbert, and Goode.

Johnson (1861–1917) was a topographer with the USGS from 1882 to 1913. He was mainly concerned with mapping and glacial studies in the Sierra Nevada and in Colorado, and made the first ascents of Banner Peak, 1893, and Mount Darwin, 1908. (KCNP, INF)

Johnson Peak (11,070)   *Tuolumne Meadows 15'*
Named in the 1890s by R. B. Marshall, USGS, for a survey-party teamster who was useful as a guide because he had been with Professor Davidson's party at Mount Conness in 1890. (Farquhar: Marshall.) (YNP)

Johnston Lake, Meadow   *Devils Postpile 15', Mammoth Mtn. 7½'*
Named for a promoter of the old Minaret Mine, which was operated from 1928 to 1930. (Smith, 59–60.) (INF)

Jones Canyon   *Topaz Lake 15', Wolf Creek 7½'*
Jones and his partner named Smith were in the lumber business. (Maule.) (TNF)

Jordan, Mount (13,344)   *Mount Whitney 15', Mt. Brewer 7½'*
David Starr Jordan (1851–1931), scientist and educator, a charter member of the Sierra Club, and president and chancellor of Stanford University from 1891 to 1916. The name was suggested by the Sierra Club in 1925, and ratified by the BGN in 1926. In 1899, while on an exploring and climbing trip, Jordan proposed the name "Crag Reflection" for a portion of the peak that now bears his name. (*SCB* 3, no. 1, Jan. 1900: 109–11.) In 1895 Bolton C. Brown gave the name "Mt. Jordan" to the highest peak in the Palisades, but that name lost out to J. N. LeConte's renaming of the peak "North Palisade." (*SCB* 5, no. 1, Jan. 1904: 3–4.)

There is a memorial article and portrait of Jordan in *SCB* 17, no. 1, Feb. 1932: 43–48.) (KCNP, SNP)

Jordan Peak (9,115)   *Camp Nelson 15'*
John J. Jordan built a trail across the Sierra from Yokohl Valley to Owens

Valley in 1861. In 1862 he drowned while trying to cross the Kern River on a raft. (Otter, 31–33, 156.) (SeNF)

Josephine Lake (10,430)   *Triple Divide Peak 15'*
Named by S. L. N. Ellis for Josephine Perkins (Farquhar: Jim Barton.) (KCNP)

Julius Caesar, Mount (over 13,200–13,196)   *Mt. Abbot 15', Mt. Hilgard 7½'*
Alfred H. and Myrtle Prater, who in 1928 made the first ascent, chose the name because of the peak's proximity to Lake Italy. (Letter, Hervey Voge to USGS, August 23, 1955; also *SCB* 19, no. 3, June 1934: 97.) The peak was not named on a map until the 15-minute quad, 1953. (SiNF, INF)

Jumble Lake   *Mt. Abbot 15', Mt. Hilgard 7½'*
Named by the DFG in 1952. It was at first called "Jumble Moraine Lake" because of the large moraine of enormous jumbled boulders separating it from Lake Italy. (DFG survey.) (SiNF)

Junction Bluffs   *Devils Postpile 15', Cattle Mtn. 7½', Crystal Crag 7½'*
Possibly named by the USGS during the 1898–99 survey for the *Mt. Lyell* 30' map; the name is on the first edition, 1901. The bluffs overlook the junction of Fish Creek and the Middle Fork of the San Joaquin River. (SiNF)

Junction Butte (2,005 m.–6,564)   *Devils Postpile 15', Cattle Mtn. 7½'*
Possibly named by the USGS during the 1898–99 survey for the *Mt. Lyell* 30' map; the name is on the first edition, 1901. The butte overlooks the junction of the North and Middle forks of the San Joaquin River. (SiNF)

Junction Meadow   *Mount Whitney 15', Mt. Kaweah 7½'*
Embraces the junctions of the Kern River with the Kern-Kaweah River and with Wallace Creek; named in 1881 by W. B. Wallace. (Farquhar: G. W. Stewart.) (SNP)

Junction Meadow   *Mt. Pinchot 15', Mt. Clarence King 7½'*
At the junction of East Creek and Bubbs Creek. It may have been named by J. N. LeConte, who first used the name in print. (*SCB* 8, no. 4, June 1912: photo opp. 274.) (KCNP)

Junction Peak (13,888), **Pass** (over 13,200)   *Mount Whitney 15',*
Mt. Williamson 7½'
The peak was named by J. N. LeConte in 1896. (Farquhar: LeConte.) It is at the junction of the Kings-Kern Divide with the main Sierra crest. Junction Pass takes its name from the peak; it was opened in 1915 by construction of the John Muir Trail. The name first appears on the sixth edition of the *Mt. Whitney* 30' map, 1927. (KCNP, SNP, INF)

Junction Ridge   *Tehipite Dome 15'*
Possibly named by the USGS during the 1903 survey for the *Tehipite* 30' map; it is on the first edition, 1905. The west end of the ridge is above the junction of the Middle and South forks of the Kings River. (SiNF, SeNF)

June Lake (7,616)   *Mono Craters 15'*
The name appears in Israel C. Russell's report, and is shown on the
accompanying map by Willard D. Johnson. (Russell, *Quaternary,* 343.) It was
called "Silver Lake" on the 1879 and 1885 GLO plats. (INF)

June Mountain (10,116–10,135)   *Mammoth Mtn. 7½'*
The name undoubtedly derives from "June Lake." A ski lift reaches the
summit. It was not named on the *Devils Postpile* 15' quad. (INF)

Kaiser Peak (10,310–10,320), **Ridge, Creek**   *Kaiser Peak 15' and 7½'*
Kaiser Pass (9,184–9,175), **Ridge; Kaiser Pass Meadow, Kaiser Peak**
Meadow   *Kaiser Peak 15', Mt. Givens 7½'*
Kaiser Creek, Ridge   *Shuteye Peak 15'*
It is odd that such a widespread name, including also "Kaiser Wilderness,"
has no definitely known origin. "Kaiser or Keyser: both are used locally. The
name is very old, and its rightful spelling unknown. I remember hearing the old
miners speak of Kaiser Gulch (a placer district) way back in 1862, the year of
the big flood; but I know nothing as to the name." (Letter, Lil A. Winchell to
T. S. Solomons, April 1896, in SC Papers in BL.) "Kaiser Gulch" appears on
Hoffman's map of Central California, 1873. Bancroft's map of 1882 has
"Kaiser Creek." "Kaiser Peak," "Kaiser Peak Meadows," "Kaiser Pass,"
"Kaiser Creek Diggings" (now the location of a Forest Service station), and
"West Fork Kaiser Creek" all appeared on the first *Kaiser* 30' map, 1904, and
were probably added by the USGS. The present "Kaiser Ridge" was "Kaiser
Crest" on the 30-minute map from 1904 through 1939, then was unnamed until
1953. The "Kaiser Ridge" on the *Shuteye Peak* quad is a different formation
altogether. (SiNF)

Kanawyers (site)   *Marion Peak 15'*
Napoleon ("Poly") Peter Kanawyer (1849–1908). Kanawyer first came to
the Kings River Canyon in 1884. In 1887 he relocated a small copper mine; later
he brought his family each summer; built a new trail from Millwood into the
canyon; and established a small camp where he catered to the Sierra Club and
other hikers. (*SCB* 26, no. 1, Feb. 1941: 37.)
Viola A. Kanawyer patented the "Buckhorn Lode" mining claim in secs. 11
and 14, T. 13 S., R. 31 E. in 1915, and the "Dome" and "Unice" lodes in secs.
11, 12, and 14 in 1917. These patents were bought by the government in 1938.
(GLO.) There is a photograph of Kanawyer's cabin with both Kanawyers,
Joseph LeConte, and others, taken in 1900, in *SCB* 29, no. 5, Oct. 1944: no. 16.
(KCNP)

Karls Lake   *Pinecrest 15'*
Named for Karl Defiebre, who owned a hotel at the town of Pinecrest before
the Second World War. (StNF files.) (StNF)

Kavanaugh Ridge   *Matterhorn Peak 15'*
Stephen Kavanaugh was employed to tunnel into a gold vein high on the
ridge about 1900. He also located the Chemung Mine in the Bodie Hills (on the
Bridgeport 15' quad), which he named after his home town in Illinois. (Gudde:

Maule.) In 1900 Kavanaugh homesteaded 160 acres on secs. 23 and 26, T. 3 N., R. 25 E. The homestead was on Virginia Creek, northwest of Conway Summit, on the *Bodie* 15' quad. (TNF)

Kaweah, Mount (4,206.8 m.–13,802); **Kaweah Basin**
Mount Whitney 15', Mt. Kaweah 7½'
Black Kaweah; Red Kaweah; Kaweah Gap   *Triple Divide Peak 15'*
Kaweah Peaks Ridge   *Triple Divide Peak 15', Mount Whitney 15',*
Mt. Kaweah 7½'

The name "Kaweah" derives from the Kaweah River. "Kaweah Peak" was the first use of the word in the high Sierra; it is on the Wheeler Survey atlas sheet 65, but is located too far west. In 1881 J. W. A. Wright, F. H. Wales, and W. B. Wallace climbed this highest peak of the group and named it "Mount Kaweah." They named the other major peaks of the group, from west to east, "Mount Abert," "Mount Henry," and "Mount LeConte." (Elliott, *Guide*, 47–49, 59.) Those names didn't catch on; they are now "Black Kaweah," "Red Kaweah," and "Gray Kaweah"—the latter not an official name.

The *Mt. Whitney* 30' map, 1907, had "Kaweah Basin" and "Kaweah Peaks." The latter became simply "Mt. Kaweah" on the sixth edition, 1927. The *Tehipite* 30' map, 1905, had "Kaweah Peaks," which was changed to "Black Kaweah" and "Red Kaweah" on the fourth edition, 1929. "Kaweah Peaks Ridge" and Kaweah Gap" showed up on the fifth edition, 1939. The gap was named in 1926 by John R. White, then superintendent of Sequoia and General Grant national parks. (SNP)

Kaweah River

"*Kaweah* River is named after a Yokuts tribe called Kawai, or probably more exactly, Gā'wia. They lived on or near the river where it emerges from the foothills into the plains. The name has no known connection with the almost identically pronounced southern California term Cahuilla." (Kroeber, 114.)

The river was discovered by the Gabriel Moraga expedition in 1806, and named *San Gabriel*. (Arch. MSB, vol. 4, Muñoz, Oct. 20, 1806.) As late as 1850 (Derby's map) it was shown as "River Frances or San Gabriel," but thereafter the present name was used.

"The next stream we came to was the Pi-pi-yu-na, or Kah-wée-ya, and very commonly known as the Four Creeks." (Williamson, *Report,* 13.)

There are many variations of spelling, pronunciation, and presumed meaning for the name. "Kaweah was originally 'Kah-wah,' accented on the last syllable, and some Indians say it means 'I squat here,' or 'Here I rest,' " (W. B. Wallace in *MWCJ* 1, no. 1, May 1902: 9.) "Name does not mean 'Here I rest,' but 'Ka' is Indian name for crow and 'wia' Indian name for water, name meaning 'crow-water.' 'Ka' came from sound of crow's noise. There were buzzards and crows by the thousands around the site of Visalia and along the river clear up to the foothills." (Versteeg from Walter Fry, in Farquhar files.) Early American settlers referred to the river as "Cow-eer." (Fry.) In early accounts the spelling "Cawia" is sometimes seen. There are four forks of the Kaweah River: North, Middle, East, and South. (SNP, SeNF)

Kearsarge Pass, Lakes, Pinnacles   *Mt. Pinchot 15',*
                                                   Mt. Clarence King 7½'
Kearsarge Peak (3,846 m.–12,598)   *Mt. Pinchot 15',*
                                                   Kearsarge Peak 7½'
Thomas Keough wrote that he and his party built the trail up the east side of
Kearsarge Pass in the summer of 1864. "We called the pass 'Little Pine Pass,'
after Little Pine Creek, which heads near the pass." ("Little Pine Creek" was an
early name for Independence Creek.) The rest of our party, who left us soon
after we climbed up over Little Pine Pass, found a gold mine near the pass on
their way home which they called the 'Cliff Mine.' . . . it was through this
discovery that the pass came to be known as 'Kearsarge Pass.' . . . Our
crowd . . . were all Union men, and when the news came that the Kearsarge had
sunk the Alabama, our boys named the district where the Cliff Mine was the
'Kearsarge District' to taunt the Rebels. The little town which grew up at the
mine was called 'Kearsarge City,' and the pass came to be called the 'Kearsarge
Pass,' and the mountain just to the north of the pass 'Kearsarge Mountain.' "
(*SCB* 10, no. 3, Jan. 1918: 340, 342. See **Alabama Hills.**)
    The USS *Kearsarge* was named for Kearsarge Peak in Merrimack County,
New Hampshire. Thus, four geographic features of the Sierra Nevada have
derived their names from an Appalachian peak via a warship and a mine.
(*Appalachia* 8, no. 4, Dec. 1915: 377; also vol. 1, no. 1, 1876: 152–65, on the
origin and/or correctness of "Kearsarge" or "Pigwacket.")
    "Kearsarge City" was created in 1865 and destroyed by an avalanche in the
spring of 1866. The mountain just north of the pass is Mount Gould; Kearsarge
Peak, on whose slopes several mines were located, is almost two miles east-
northeast of the pass. The lakes were called "University Lakes" on a 1906
Sequoia National Park map. All the features had their present names on the first
Mt. Whitney 30' map, 1907. (Pass, KCNP, INF; peak, INF; lakes and
pinnacles, KCNP.)

Keeler Needle (over 14,000)   *Mount Whitney 15' and 7½'*
    James Edward Keeler (1857–1899), an assistant to Samuel P. Langley on
the latter's scientific expedition to the summit of Mount Whitney in 1881.
Keeler was director of the Allegheny Observatory, 1891–98, and director of the
Lick Observatory, 1898–99. (EB. See **Day Needle.**) (SNP, INF)

Keith, Mount (4,259.7 m.–13,977) *Mount Whitney 15', Mt. Williamson 7½'*
    William Keith (1838–1911), charter member of the Sierra Club, noted
California landscape painter. (*SCB* 8, no. 2, June 1911: 130.)
    The peak was named by the LeConte party from the summit of University
Peak, July 12, 1896. (*SCB* 2, no. 2, May 1897: 84.) (KCNP, INF)

Kellers Ranch   *Patterson Mtn. 15'*
    Samuel B. Keller homesteaded 61.5 acres in sec. 21, T. 12 S., R. 26 E. in
1916. (SeNF)

Kelty Meadow   *Bass Lake 15'*
    A misspelled name. Frank *Keltie* homesteaded 160 acres in secs. 2 and 3, T.
6 S., R. 22 E. in 1886. (SiNF)

Kendrick Peak (10,390), **Creek**   *Tower Peak 15'*
Colonel Forsyth named the peak in 1912 for Henry Lane Kendrick (1811–1891), professor of chemistry at the US Military Academy from 1857 to 1880. (Farquhar: H. C. Benson.) The name appeared on the third edition of the *Dardanelles* 30' map, 1912. The creek, which is also on the *Pinecrest* 15' quad, was called "East Fork Eleanor Creek" on the *Dardanelles* 30' maps from 1898 through 1924; it was changed to the present name on the fifth edition, 1939. (YNP)

Kennedy Lake (7,801), **Creek, Meadow**   *Sonora Pass 15' and 7½'*
Kennedy Peak (10,718), **Creek, Canyon**   *Tower Peak 15'*
Kennedy Canyon   *Sonora Pass 15', Pickel Meadow 7½'*
All these features apparently are named for two brothers. Andrew L. Kennedy patented a strip of land encompassing Kennedy Lake in 1886. (Gudde, *Place Names*, 163.) In 1896, Lincoln Hutchinson noted that J. F. Kennedy of Knight's Ferry claimed two or three thousand acres of land in the vicinity of the creek, meadow, and lake. (*SCB* 2, no. 5, Jan. 1899: 280.)
The 1883 GLO plat and surveyor's field notes identify "Kennedy's Lower Camp" in sec. 2 and "Kennedy's Meadow West" in secs. 2 and 11, T. 5 N., R. 20 E. The lake is also named, as is "Kennedy Bros. Upper Camp," at the lake. Hutchinson referred to the low divide between the head of Kennedy Creek and Kennedy Canyon as "Kennedy Pass," but that name has never been on USGS maps. (Canyon, TNF; others, StNF)

Kennedy Mountain (11,433), **Canyon, Pass, Creek**
E Kennedy Lake; W Kennedy Lake   *Marion Peak 15'*
The peak and canyon may have been named for a USGS employee during the 1903 survey for the *Tehipite* 30' map; both names are on the first edition, 1905. The other "Kennedy" names were added when the 15-minute quad was published in 1953. (KCNP)

Kern River   *Kernville 15', Hockett Peak 15', Kern Peak 15',*
                    Mount Whitney 15', Mt. Kaweah 7½', Mt. Brewer 7½'
Kern Peak (11,510), **Canyon, Hot Spring, Lake; Little Kern Lake**
                                                         Kern Peak 15'
Kern Canyon, Point, Ridge   *Mount Whitney 15', Mt. Kaweah 7½'*
Kern Flat   *Hockett Peak 15'*
Edward Meyer Kern (1823–1863), artist and draftsman, topographer with John C. Frémont's third expedition to the West. The river was named by Frémont. He had split the expedition into two parties; Kern was with the Walker-Talbot detachment, which crossed Walker Pass in December 1845 and camped on the river. "From these circumstances the pass in which Walker and Kern were encamped was called Walker's Pass; and, as no name was known to Colonel Frémont for the stream which flowed from it, he named it Kern River. The stream was, and is now, known to the native Californians as the Po-sun-co-la, a name doubtless derived from the Indians. When I was at the ordinary crossing place of the river, and preparing a small raft to cross, three Californians

118

rode up to the opposite bank, and asked, in Spanish, if this was the Po-sun-co-la." (Williamson, *Report,* 17.)

Thus are false conclusions drawn. "Po-sun-co-la" actually was given in August 1806 by Padre Zalvidea. "The river we called *La Porciuncula,* from the Saint's day of Los Angeles Pueblo, the 2d of August, as it was discovered by us on that day, and our chaplain, the Rev. Father Jose Maria Zalvides [Zalvidea] . . . celebrated solemn high mass with the best material and assistance we poor sinners of soldiers could give him." (A reminiscent account by an old soldier, son of Raymundo Carillo, San Francisco *Daily Evening Bulletin,* June 5, 1865.)

The river was first called *Rio de San Felipe* by Garcés when he came upon it on May 1, 1776, a river "whose waters, crystalline, bountiful, and palatable, flowed on a course from the east through a straitened channel." (Garcés, vol. 1, 281.)

Kern Lake and Little Kern Lake were created by a landslide in the winter of 1867–68. (W. F. Dean, *MWCJ* 1, no. 1, May 1902: 14.) All the "Kern" names, including "Little Kern River" and "South Fork Kern River," were on the first editions of the *Olancha* and *Mt. Whitney* 30' maps, 1907, except "Kern Hot Spring," which appeared in 1927. (SNP, INF, SeNF)

Kern-Kaweah River   *Triple Divide Peak 15', Mount Whitney 15',*
Mt. Kaweah 7½'

"In the month of July, 1897, our party of four—Prof. W. R. Dudley (special botanist of the Stanford University), Messrs. Otis Wright and Harry Dudley (students at Stanford), and I—camped at the junction of the three branches of the Kern, and here we crossed the East and Middle Forks and began our climb up the west branch of the Kern, or Kern-Kaweah, as we afterward named it." (W. F. Dean in *MWCJ* 1, no. 1, May 1902: 13; see also *SCB* 2, no. 3, Jan. 1898: 188.)

This branch of the Kern was named "Cone Creek" in 1881 by J. W. A. Wright for a US Army Officer; it appears on Wright's map in Elliott, *Guide.* (Farquhar: W. B. Wallace. See also *SCB* 12, no. 1, 1924: 47.) The name "Kern-Kaweah River" appears on the first editions of the *Tehipite* and *Mt. Whitney* 30' maps, but is inexplicably omitted on the last two editions (1937 and 1939) of the *Mt. Whitney* sheet. (SNP)

Kerrick Canyon   *Tower Peak 15'*
Kerrick Meadow   *Matterhorn Peak 15'*
James D. Kerrick took sheep into the mountains about 1880. The canyon was named first, by the Wheeler Survey. (Letter, Col. Benson to Versteeg.) Versteeg said that John Lembert gave the name to Lt. McClure in 1894. (Farquhar files.) The name is on McClure's map of Yosemite National Park, 1895. The meadow is named on the first *Bridgeport* 30' map, 1911. (YNP)

Kettle Dome (9,466), **Ridge**   *Tehipite Dome 15'*
Frank Dusy named the dome in the 1870s, calling it "Kettle Rock." (Farquhar from Winchell, Oct. 18, 1921, in Farquhar papers, BL.) It had that name on Davis's map of 1896, but was changed—probably by the USGS—to

"Kettle Dome" on the first *Tehipite* 30' map, 1905. "Kettle Ridge" also appeared on that map. (KCNP, SiNF)

Kettle Peak (10,041)   *Triple Divide Peak 15'*
"From this camp, and the next (No. 169) two miles farther up the divide, an examination was made of an interesting and characteristic feature in the topography of this granitic region, and to which the name of 'The Kettle' was given. This is a rocky amphitheatre at the head of a stream [Sugarloaf Creek] which flows back directly northeast from its source towards the axis of the chain, for a distance of twelve miles, and then turns and enters King's River, a peculiar and almost unique course for a stream in the Sierra Nevada." (Whitney, *Geology,* 374.)
"Just east of that camp [June 26, 1864] we climbed a steep hill, and came suddenly to a precipice. Beyond was a great basin, or valley, the head of which is an immense rocky amphitheater. . . . There is a little lake in this basin, about 1,600 feet below the brink of the cliffs." (Brewer, *Up and Down,* 522.) (KCNP, SNP)

Kettle Peak (11,010)   *Matterhorn Peak 15'*
Probably named by the USGS during the 1905–09 survey for the *Bridgeport* 30' map; it is on the first edition, 1911. (TNF)

Kettle Ridge   *Blackcap Mtn. 15' and 7½', Mt. Goddard 15' and 7½'*
Probably named by the USGS during the 1907–09 survey for the *Mt. Goddard* 30' map; it is on the first edition, 1912. (KCNP, SiNF)

Keyes Peak (10,670)   *Tower Peak 15'*
Colonel Forsyth named the peak in 1912 for his son-in-law, Lt. Edward A. Keyes. (Farquhar: Benson.) (YNP)

Keyhole, The (over 12,500)   *Mt. Goddard 15', Mt. Darwin 7½'*
A name applied by Sierra Club climbers, probably in the 1930s or 1940s, for a notch in the Glacier Divide. It was added to the map by the USGS because it was in common use. First described in print in *The Climber's Guide to the High Sierra,* 1954. This might be the "Snow-Tongue Pass" used by J. S. Hutchinson and party in 1904. (*SCB* 5, no. 3, Jan. 1905: 160.) (KCNP, SiNF)

Kibbie Lake   *Pinecrest 15'*
Kibbie Creek   *Lake Eleanor 15', Pinecrest 15'*
Kibbie Ridge   *Lake Eleanor 15', Pinecrest 15', Cherry Lake North 7½'*
The name has always been misspelled on maps and in print. Horace G. *Kibbe* planted trout in Lakes Eleanor and Vernon in 1877, and lived at Lake Eleanor for many years. (Versteeg, from Benson and McClure, in Farquhar files; also Bingaman, *Pathways,* 34.)
"Lake Eleanor was stocked in early days by a cattleman named Kibbie, who packed the fish from Cherry Creek to the lake, carrying them in coal-oil cans." (Walter A. Starr in *SCB* 20, no. 1, Feb. 1935: 58.) Kibbie homesteaded 175 acres in secs. 34 and 35, T. 2 N., R. 19 E. in 1883—land that is now under the waters of Lake Eleanor Reservoir. (Lake and creek, YNP; ridge, YNP, StNF)

Kings River, Canyon   Canyon on *Marion Peak 15'*

"We found, after having traveled five leagues, the *Rio de los Santos Reyes,* which had been discovered in the previous year, 1805." (Arch. MSB, vol. 4, Muñoz, Oct. 14, 1806.)

"It was the custom of the Spanish explorers to select names for places along their route from the church calendar. Thus, when they gave the name *Rio de los Santos Reyes,* or 'River of the Holy Kings,' it might be inferred that they were at that river on the 6th of January, the day of Epiphany, sacred to the memory of the three kings or magi who brought gifts to the infant Jesus." (Farquhar, "Spanish Discovery of the Sierra Nevada," *SCB* 13, no. 1, Feb. 1928: 58.)

Frémont, who reached the river on April 8, 1844, called it both "River of the Lake" (*Expedition,* 363) and "Lake Fork" (*Memoir,* 18.) The latter name was used by Preuss on his two maps. After he learned the Spanish name, Frémont called it "*Rio Reyes* of Tulare lake." (*Memoir,* 30.) This became anglicized into "Kings River," although some Americans fell into the bad habit of writing it "King's River," which is how it appeared on the Wheeler Survey atlas sheet 56D, 1878–79. The USGS used "King River" on the first edition of the *Tehipite* 30' map, but corrected it to "Kings" on the second edition, 1912. "Kings Canyon National Park" was created in 1940. The names "Kings River Canyon" and "the canyon of Kings River" were in use from the time of the Whitney Survey's explorations in 1864, but the name "Kings Canyon" did not get on USGS maps until the *Marion Peak* 15' quad, 1953. There are three forks of the river: North, Middle, and South. (River, KCNP, SeNF, SiNF; canyon, KCNP)

Kings-Kaweah Divide   *Triple Divide Peak 15', Giant Forest 15'*

The name was approved by the BGN in 1983. It is not on the 15-minute maps, but probably will be on the 7½-minute maps when they are published. The divide extends west-northwest from Triple Divide Peak, along the boundary between Kings Canyon and Sequoia national parks, to peak 9551 just west of Jennie Lake, and from there to Shell Mountain. (KCNP, SNP, SeNF)

Kings-Kern Divide   *Mount Whitney 15', Mt. Brewer 7½'*

The first use of the name in print is by Warren Gregory. (*SCB* 1, no. 6, May 1895: 214–20.) It is on the first edition of the *Mt. Whitney* 30' map, 1907, and was ratified by a BGN decision in 1928. (KCNP, SNP)

Upper and **Lower Kinney Lake; Kinney Creek, Reservoir**
                              Markleeville 15', Ebbetts Pass 7½'

David Kinney, a pioneer of Alpine County. (Maule.) A native of Iowa, a farmer at Silver Mountain in 1873. (Gudde, *Place Names,* 166.) (TNF)

Kirkwood; Kirkwood Lake, Creek, Meadows   *Silver Lake 15',*
                                          Caples Lake 7½'

Zack Kirkwood built a log stage station and inn here in 1864. (*Historic Spots,* 29.) Cornelius B. Bradley and two companions passed by in the summer of 1895. "Kirkwood's is a postoffice and dairy ranch, furnishing good rough accommodation, if one is fortunate enough to escape quarters in the 'corral.'" (*SCB* 1, no. 8, May 1896: 321.) (ENF)

oseph N. LeConte, the first ascent of Mount Gould, 1890. "I stood on that rather ticklish point some minutes, till the sun came out for Bert to take my photograph."

The lines must be straight and true: devotion to duty drives a surveyor up a tree.

Francis P. Farquhar, climber and conservationist, author of *Place Names of the High Sierra*, atop Mount Whitney in 1930.

William H. Brewer of the Whitney Survey, about 1864. "I have counted up my traveling in the state—15,105 miles. Surely a long trail!"

Lafayette Houghton Bunnell, namer of Yosemite Valley. A member of the Mariposa Battalion, discoverers of the valley in March 1851.

Lt. Montgomery Meigs Macomb, in charge of the Wheeler Survey field parties in the Sierra, 1876–78.

The University Excursion Party of 1870. Standing: Charles Phelps, Jack Bolton, Jim Perkins, Prof. Joseph LeConte, Frank Soulé, Dell Linderman, George Cobb. Seated: Charles Stone, Leander Hawkins, Everett B. Pomroy. "Our party is dissolved. But its memory still lives; its spirit is immortal."

Frank Dusy, in 1873. Sheepman, explorer, photographer; discovered Tehipite Valley in 1869.

Col. Harry Coupland Benson, superintendent of Yosemite National Park, 1905–08; mapmaker, trail builder, nemesis of sheepmen.

Edward Meyer Kern, taken from a daguerreotype.
Kern was an artist and draftsman, and topographer
with Frémont's third expedition to the West, 1845-
46.

Lilbourne A. Winchell, in 1884. Pioneer explorer
of the Middle Fork of the Kings River; made the
first ascent of Mount Goddard, 1879.

Theodore S. Solomons, explorer, mapmaker, and photographer in the Sierra in the 1890s. He established the route for the northern half of the John Muir Trail.

George R. Davis of the US Geological Survey; topographer of the *Mt. Goddard* and *Mt. Whitney* 30′ quadrangles.

Members of the California Geological Survey, 1863: Chester Averill, William M. Gabb, William Ashburner, Josiah Dwight Whitney, Charles F. Hoffmann, Clarence King, William H. Brewer.

The intrepid explorers at journey's end, 1904. Robert Pike, Ed Hutchinson, J. N. LeConte, Jim Hutchinson.

Kirman Lake (7,176)   *Fales Hot Springs 15'*
For Richard Kirman, Sr., an early cattleman. (Maule.) Kirman was a banker in Reno, and a large landowner in this area around 1870. (USGS, from Mono County records.) The name of the lake was misspelled "Carmen" on all the editions of the *Bridgeport* 30' map. (TNF)

Knapsack Pass (over 11,680–11,673)   *Mt. Goddard 15',*
North Palisade 7½'
The pass was discovered by A. L. Jordan in 1917. (*SCB* 10, no. 3, Jan. 1918: 294.) The name was suggested by Chester Versteeg in 1935. (Farquhar files.) (KCNP)

Knight Camp   *Dogtooth Peak 7½'*
This was named "Qualls Camp" on the *Huntington Lake* 15' quad, and will be again on future editions of the *Dogtooth Peak* 7½' quad. The present name is from Walter Knight, the last cattleman to use the camp. (See **Qualls Camp.**) (SiNF)

Knob Lake   *Mt. Tom 15', Mount Tom 7½'*
There is a knoblike rock tower on the southwest shore of the lake, which possibly was named by Elden H. Vestal of the DFG in 1950. (DFG survey.) (SiNF)

Koip Peak (12,979), **Crest** (12,668)   *Mono Craters 15'*
Named by Willard D. Johnson, USGS, about 1883. (Farquhar: J. N. LeConte.) "Koip Peak, between Mono and Tuolumne counties, is probably, like near-by Kuna Peak, named from a Mono Indian word. *Koipa* is 'mountain sheep' in the closely related Northern Paiute dialect." (Kroeber, 45.) (Peak, INF; crest, INF, YNP)

Kolana Rock (over 5,760)   *Lake Eleanor 15'*
"Standing boldly out from the south wall is a strikingly picturesque rock called 'Kolana' by the Indians, the outermost of a group 2,300 feet high corresponding with the Cathedral Rocks of Yosemite both in relative position and in form." (John Muir in *SCB* 6, no. 4, Jan. 1908: 212.) The name appeared on the fifth edition of the *Yosemite* 30' map, 1911. (YNP)

K P Pinnacle   *Yosemite Valley 1:24,000*
A Sierra Club name, probably derived from Henry Knoll and Jack Pionteki, who in 1941 made the first ascent. (USGS.) (YNP)

Kuna Peak (over 12,880)   *Mono Craters 15'*
Kuna Creek, Crest, Lake   *Tuolumne Meadows 15', Mono Craters 15'*
Kuna Peak was named by Willard D. Johnson, USGS, about 1883. (Farquhar: J. N. LeConte.) "Kuna Peak . . . is probably named from the Shoshonean word *Kuna,* usually meaning 'fire' but appearing in the Mono dialect of the vicinity with the signification of 'fire-wood.' " (Kroeber, 45.) (Peak, INF; others, YNP)

L Lake   *Mt. Tom 15', Mount Tom 7½'*
Probably named in 1951, for its shape, by Ralph Beck of the DFG. (DFG survey.) (SiNF)

La Tete Lake   *Mount Tom 7½'*
Named in 1954 by Ralph Beck of the DFG. (Phil Pister. See **Alsace Lake**.)
(SiNF)

Ladder Lake (10,498–10,491)   *Mt. Goddard 15', North Palisade 7½'*
Named in the early thirties by one Halladay, a South Fork packer, because
the route to it was so steep it was like climbing a ladder. (Art Schober.) (KCNP)

Ladeux Meadow   *Silver Lake 15', Mokelumne Peak 7½'*
A misspelling. Frank *Le Doux* homesteaded 160 acres in secs. 22 and 23, T.
9 N., R. 17 E. in 1903. (ENF)

Lake Basin   *Marion Peak 15', Mt Pinchot 15' and 7½'*
A name applied by J. N. LeConte in July 1902, when he used it descrip-
tively rather than as a formal name. (*SCB* 4, no. 4, June 1903: 259–60.) A year
later he called it "Cartridge Creek Lake Basin," and on his map named it simply
"The Lake Basin." (*SCB* 5, no. 1, Jan. 1904: 5, map.) (KCNP)

Lake Canyon   *Tuolumne Meadows 15', Bodie 15'*
The name undoubtedly dates from the Tioga-Bennettville mining excitement
of 1878; it is on the 1881 GLO plat. It was up this canyon that heavy machinery
was hauled to the Great Sierra Mine during the winter of 1881–82. (INF)

Lamarck, Mount (13,417); **Lamarck Creek, Col** (over 12,880); **Upper
Lamarck Lake** (10,918); **Lower Lamarck Lake** (10,662)
                                    Mt. Goddard 15', Mt. Darwin 7½'
Jean Baptiste Pierre Antoine de Monet de Lamarck (1744–1829), a French
pre-Darwinian evolutionist who espoused the theory that characteristics
developed by use or habit or environmental change may be inherited. The peak
was named to agree with the six peaks of the "Evolution Group" named by
Theodore S. Solomons in 1895. The name was almost certainly applied by the
USGS during the 1907–09 survey for the *Mt. Goddard* 30' map. It is on the first
edition, 1912, but is not in J. N. LeConte's "Elevations." The creek also is
named on the 1912 map.
    Art and John Schober named the col "Schober's Pass" in 1939; it was Art
who scouted out the pass and built a trail to it. (Art Schober.) David Brower
suggested the name "Lamarck Col," which was in use as early as 1942. (*SCB*
27, no. 4, Aug. 1942: 89.) (KCNP, INF; lakes and creek, INF)

Langille Peak (12,018–11,991)   *Mt. Goddard 15', North Palisade 7½'*
Harold Douglas Langille (1874–1954), a forest inspector for the General
Land Office who made a tour of inspection of the Sierra Forest Reserve in 1904.
The name (pronounced "Lan'-jil") was given by Charles H. Shinn, head ranger
of the forest reserve. (KCNP)

Langley, Mount (4,275 m.–14,042)   *Lone Pine 15', Mt. Langley 7½'*
Samuel Pierpont Langley (1834–1906), physicist, astronomer, and avia-
tion pioneer; director of the Allegheny Observatory, 1867–87; secretary of the
Smithsonian Institution, 1887–1906. Langley led an expedition to the summit
of Mount Whitney in 1881 to conduct experiments in solar heat.

Clarence King made the first ascent of the mountain (which was then called "Sheep Mountain") in 1871, thinking he was making the first ascent of Mount Whitney. In 1905 the name was changed to "Mount Langley." (*SCB* 7, no. 3, Jan. 1910: 141.) It was so named on the first six editions of the *Mt. Whitney* 30' map, 1907–27. Due to a long-running series of errors, mis-identification, and political decisions, the peak was called "Corcoran Mtn" for two editions of the map. It has been "Mount Langley" again since 1937. (See **Corcoran, Mount.**)

"It will be found that apparently the only reason for naming this 'Mt. Corcoran' was to enable a painter named Bierstadt to sell a picture of the mountain, or an alleged picture of the mountain, to the wealthy art patron in Washington, Mr. Corcoran." (Letter, Supt. John R. White of SNP to Director, National Park Service, March 6, 1937; copy in Farquhar files.) (SNP, INF)

Lawson Peak (13,140)   *Triple Divide Peak 15'*
In commemoration of Andrew C. Lawson (1861–1952), professor of geology at the University of California. (BGN decision, 1976.) The peak is not named on the 15-minute quad. It is on the Kaweah Peaks Ridge, one mile north by east from Black Kaweah. (SNP)

Leaning Tower   *Yosemite 15', Yosemite Valley 1:24,000*
"A tower-shaped and leaning rock, about three thousand feet in height, standing at the southwest side of the fall [Bridalveil], sometimes called the 'Leaning Tower,' nearly opposite 'Tu-tock-ah-nu-lah' [El Capitan], has on its top a number of projecting rocks that very much resemble cannon. . . . We once took the liberty of christening this 'Tu-tock-ah-nu-lah's Citadel.' " (Hutchings, *In the Heart*, 408.) (YNP)

Leavitt Peak (11,569–11,570)   *Sonora Pass 15' and 7½'*
Leavitt Creek, Meadow, Lake (9,556), **Falls, Sta** (site)   *Sonora Pass 15',*
                                                    Pickel Meadow 7½'
Hiram L. Leavitt built a hostelry in 1863 at the foot of the east end of Sonora Pass to serve the traffic between Sonora and Aurora. (Maule.) Leavitt was also an early Mono County Judge. (Farquhar from Judge Parker, Bridgeport, 1928.) "Leavitt's" (for the peak) is on Hoffmann's map of 1873 and the Wheeler Survey atlas sheet 56D, 1878–79. On the 1875 GLO plat, the creek is called "West Fork of West Walker River." The meadow is mentioned by name by Lt. Macomb in 1878. The peak, creek, and meadow have their present names on the first *Dardanelles* 30' map, 1898. The other names do not appear until the 15-minute quad, 1956. (Peak, StNF, TNF; others, TNF)

Le Conte Falls   *Tuolumne Meadows 15'*
LeConte, Mount (over 13,920)   *Mount Whitney 15' and 7½'*
Le Conte Divide   *Blackcap Mtn. 15' and 7½', Mt. Henry 7½',*
                                         Mt. Goddard 15' and 7½'
Joseph LeConte (1823–1901), professor of geology and natural history at the University of California, 1869–1901.
The falls was named in August 1892. "Cross this ledge well to the right and

gradually approach the river, which can be followed to the head of what is in many respects the most majestic cascade in the whole cañon, the Le Conte Cascade, so named by us in honor of our most esteemed Professor, Joseph Le Conte." (R. M. Price, "Through the Tuolumne Cañon," *SCB* 1, no. 6, May 1895: 204.)

"Some time ago those residents of the Lone Pine district who are interested in the mountains decided upon naming this peak Le Conte, in honor of Professor Joseph Le Conte. . . . A conical mass of rock about 150 feet high and 250 feet in diameter forms the apex of Le Conte. After careful investigation we found this utterly impossible to climb. So we placed the monument on the north side of the dome where it can be easily seen by any one approaching the summit; and in a small can we put a photograph of the Professor, with the following memorandum: 'To-day, the 14th of August, 1895, we, undersigned, hereby named this mountain Le Conte, in honor of the eminent geologist, Professor Joseph Le Conte." (A. W. de la Cour Carroll, *SCB* 1, no. 8, May 1896: 325–26.)

Farquhar (*Place Names,* 56–57) seems to assume that "Le Conte Divide" was named for the senior LeConte, but it could just as easily have been for J. N. LeConte, who explored in the Palisades and the Kings River Region. The name appears on the first edition of the *Mt. Goddard* 30' map, 1912.

See Joseph LeConte, "Ramblings Through the High Sierra," *SCB* 3, no. 1, Jan. 1900: 1–107. Memorials in *SCB* 4, no. 1, Jan. 1902: 1–11; and *SCB* 5, no. 3, Jan. 1905: 176–80. (Falls, YNP; Mount, SNP, INF; Divide, KCNP, SiNF)

Le Conte Canyon · *Mt. Goddard 15' and 7½', North Palisade 7½'*
Le Conte Point (6,410) *Hetch Hetchy Reservoir 15'*
Joseph Nisbet LeConte (1870–1950), a charter member of the Sierra Club, professor of engineering mechanics at the University of California, 1895–1937. The canyon apparently was named by the USGS during the 1907–09 survey for the *Mt. Goddard* 30' map; it is on the first edition, 1912. Le Conte Point was named by R. B. Marshall, USGS. (Farquhar: Marshall.)

Joseph N. LeConte was one of the foremost explorers of the Sierra Nevada. He hiked and climbed from 1889 to 1928, wrote extensively about his travels, compiled a number of maps, and was an expert photographer. (See the memorials in *SCB* 35, no. 6, June 1950: 1–8; and *American Alpine Journal* 7, no. 4, 1950: 484–86.) (Canyon, KCNP; point, YNP)

Lee Vining Creek *Tuolumne Meadows 15', Mono Craters 15'*
Lee Vining Peak (11,691); **Lee Vining** (town) *Mono Craters 15'*
"Leroy Vining and a few chosen companions, with one of Moore's scouts as guide, went over the Sierras to the place where the gold had been found [in 1852], and established themselves on what has since been known as Vining's Gulch or Creek." (Bunnell, *Discovery,* 1880, 278.) In the early 1860s Vining built a sawmill on the creek now named for him, and sold lumber in Aurora, Nevada.

Sometime later, Vining came to a peculiar end. "At that time the crowd of miners and gamblers used to congregate at the Exchange Saloon [in Aurora], where frequent shooting-scrapes would occur. Whenever trouble started everyone would get out of the room. On one of these occasions a gun went off in the crowd and Lee Vining went out the door . . . and started up the street toward the Odd Fellows Hall. Shortly after someone found him lying on the walk dead, and upon examination it was found that the pistol had gone off in his pocket, shooting him in the groin, from which he had bled to death." (Letter, C. F. Quimby to Maule, Sept. 1927, in *SCB* 13, no. 1, Feb. 1928: 84.)

On the A. W. Von Schmidt plat of 1857, the lower part of Lee Vining Creek, where it flows into Mono Lake, was called "Rescue Creek." Hoffmann's map of 1873 shows "Vining's Cr." The Wheeler Survey atlas sheet 56D, 1878–79, calls it "Vining Creek." All the editions of the *Mt. Lyell* 30' map, 1901 to 1948, show "Leevining Creek" and "Leevining Pk." Spelling the name as two words was put into effect on the 15-minute maps, a decision ratified by the BGN in 1957. (INF)

Lehamite Creek   *Yosemite Valley 1:24,000, Hetch Hetchy Reservoir 15'*
"The cliff along the east side of Indian Cañon was known as Le-ham-ite, and designated the place of the arrow wood, as we might say, the oaks." (Bunnell, *Report,* 1889–90, 11.) The word could have been confused with the name of one of the Indian villages, about 0.4 mile east of Indian Canyon, which was given as Le-sam'-ai-ti. (Powers, 365.)

On the Wheeler Survey map of 1883, the creek is named "Little Winkle Branch." The first five editions of the *Yosemite Valley* map (1907–29) call it "East Fork of Indian Creek." It changes to its present name on the sixth edition, 1938, and "Lehamite Falls" is added. (YNP)

Leidig Meadow   *Yosemite 15', Yosemite Valley 1:24,000*
Mr. and Mrs. George Leidig built a two-story hotel in 1869. Their son Charles was born the same year—the first white boy born in Yosemite Valley. (*YNN* 34, no. 1, Jan. 1955: 10.) Charles Leidig (1869–1956), appointed Special Forest Agent in 1898; guide and scout for the US troops in summer; one of the guides for President Theodore Roosevelt's party in May 1903. (Bingaman, *Guardians,* 87–88.)

Leidig's Hotel was torn down in 1888 by order of the Yosemite Valley Commissioners because it was "unsightly." (Sargent, *Innkeepers,* 14.) The name first appears on the *Yosemite Valley* map in 1922. (YNP)

Leighton Lake   *Pinecrest 15'*
Fred Leighton, a long-time sportsman and conservationist, had a permanent summer camp at Yellowhammer Lake. He built check-dams on many streams to improve the fishing. (DFG survey.) (StNF)

Leland Creek, Reservoir   *Pinecrest 15' and 7½'*
G. A. Leland patented several pieces of land in sec. 3, T. 4 N., R. 18 E. in 1898. (StNF files.) The reservoir was "Leland Meadow" on the 15-minute quad, 1956. (StNF)

Lembert Dome (9,450)   *Tuolumne Meadows 15'*
   John Baptist Lembert settled in Tuolumne Meadows sometime before 1882; he was visited in that year by a member of the crew surveying the original Tioga Road. Lembert was living in an eight-by-ten-foot cabin built directly atop one of the soda springs; water bubbled up in the center of the cabin. ("Surveying the Tioga Road," *YNN* 27, no. 9: 109–12.)
   Lembert raised angora goats, until he lost them in a snowstorm in the winter of 1889–90. Thereafter he made his living by collecting butterflies and botanical specimens, which he sold to museums. On June 28, 1895, he gained legal possession of the property when he homesteaded 160 acres: the southwest quarter of sec. 5, T. 1 S., R. 24 E. He was murdered at his cabin in the Merced Canyon, below Yosemite Valley, in the winter of 1896–97. The Soda Springs property was sold to the McCauley brothers in 1898 by Lembert's brother. J. J. McCauley sold it to the Sierra Club in 1912, which in turn sold it to the National Park Service in 1973. (For a detailed history of Lembert and a description of the property, see *SCB* 9, no. 1. Jan. 1913: 36–39.)
   The dome was called "Soda Spr. Dome" on the Wheeler Survey atlas sheet 56D, 1878–79. John Muir called it "Glacier Rock." (Muir, *Picturesque,* drawing on p. 18; in the reprint edition, *West of the Rocky Mountains,* p. 22.) The name was misspelled "Lambert" on many early maps and references. It is spelled that way on the first five editions of the *Mt. Lyell* 30' map, 1901–22; corrected on the edition of 1927. (YNP)

Lewis Creek,   *Merced Peak 15', Tuolumne Meadows 15'*
   Washington Bartlett Lewis (1884–1930), first civilian superintendent of Yosemite National Park 1916–28. (Bingaman, *Guardians,* 107–8.) It was under his administration that the major development of roads and trails, the construction of buildings for headquarters and personnel, and the installation of public-utility systems was accomplished—the foundation for, and often the actual structures and systems, that exist today. Obituary in *SCB* 16, no. 1, 1931: 60–62.
   The creek was called "McClure Fork" (of the Merced River) on the *Mt. Lyell* 30' maps from 1901 to 1929; changed to the present name on the edition of 1944. (YNP)

Lewis Creek, Lake   *Marion Peak 15'*
   Named for the brothers Frank M. and Jeff Lewis, pioneer stockmen, hunters, and prospectors in the Kings River region. Frank Lewis prospected over Pinchot and Cartridge passes about 1875; Cartridge Pass was known as "Lewis Pass" then. He crossed Sawmill Pass in 1878, and went to—but not down—Taboose Pass that same year. (Versteeg, from Frank Lewis, in Farquhar files.)
   "Frank and Jeff Lewis ranged sheep in the late Seventies in the upper Middle Fork of Kings River and Granite Basin region, and later about Wildman meadow and vicinity." (Winchell, 158.) (KCNP)

Lewis Fork   *Bass Lake 15'*
Jonathan Lewis homesteaded 160 acres in secs. 13 and 24, T. 6 S., R. 21 E. in 1886. (SiNF)

Lewis Lakes   *Tower Peak 15'*
Named for Bert Lewis, US Forest Service employee, who died in the First World War. (BGN decision, 1965.) (StNF)

Lewis, Mount (12,296)   *Mono Craters 15'*
Named for Washington B. Lewis. (See first **Lewis Creek**; also **Johnson, Mount.**) (INF)

Lewis Ranch   *Haiwee Reservoir 15'*
Sam N. Lewis homesteaded 160 acres in secs. 3 and 10, T. 22 S., R. 37 E. in 1922.

Liberty Cap (7,076)   *Yosemite 15', Yosemite Valley 1:24,000*
"Owing to the exalted and striking individuality of this boldly singular mountain . . . it had many godfathers in early days; who christened it Mt. Frances, Gwin's Peak, Bellows' Butte, Mt. Broderick, and others; but, when Governor Stanford . . . was in front of it with his party in 1865, and inquired its name, the above list of appellations was enumerated, and the Governor invited to take his choice of candidates. . . . he responded 'Mr. H., I cannot say that I like either of those names very much *for that magnificent mountain;* don't you think a more appropriate one could be given?' Producing an old-fashioned half-dollar with the ideal Cap of Liberty well defined upon it, the writer suggested the close resemblance in form of the mountain before us with the embossed cap on the coin; when the Governor exclaimed, 'Why! Mr. H., that would make a most excellent and appropriate name for that mountain. Let us so call it.' *Thereafter it was so called;* and as everyone preferentially respects this name, all others have been quietly renunciated." (Hutchings, *In the Heart,* 445. See also **Broderick, Mount.**)
Galen Clark gave the Indian name as Mah'-ta, said to mean "Martyr Mountain." (Clark, 108.)
"Hundreds or, for aught we could feel, thousands of feet below us thundered the river. On the far side of it rose up Mah-tah . . . two thousand feet above the fall we were climbing to reach. What patriot first called this peak 'Cap of Liberty' considerate history forgets" (Jackson, 119.)
It was called "Cap of Liberty or Mt. Broderick" on King and Gardiner's map of 1865, and "Cap of Liberty" on the Wheeler Survey atlas sheet 56D, 1878–79, and on J. N. LeConte's map of 1900. The present name has been used since then. (YNP)

Lion Rock (over 12,320), **Lake**   *Triple Divide Peak 15'*
"Looking down upon the meadow from the east was a noble peak, whose head and projecting arete cliffs had, in the descending sun, all the repose of the front of a couchant lion. It was named the Lion Rock. The Kaweah comes from the north of this peak, and its source was found in one small and one larger

lake. . . . These were named the Kaweah Lakes." (William R. Dudley in *SCB* 2, no. 3, Jan. 1898: 186.) The naming took place in July 1896. Dudley's name for the lakes did not get onto the maps. The larger lake is "Lion Lake;" the smaller is unnamed. Both the "Lion" names are on the first edition of the *Tehipite* 30' map, 1905. (SNP)

Lion Point (2,704 m.–8,866)   *Devils Postpile 15', Crystal Crag 7½'*
     May have been named by the USGS during the 1898–99 survey for the *Mt. Lyell* 30' map; it is on the first edition, 1901. (SiNF, INF)

Lippincott Mountain (12,260)   *Triple Divide Peak 15'*
     Named in 1903 for Joseph Barlow Lippincott, a hydrographer with the USGS and the US Reclamation Service, 1894–1904. The name appears on the first *Tehipite* 30' map, 1905. (Farquhar.) (SNP)

Little Bear Lake   *Mt. Abbot 15', Mt. Hilgard 7½'*
     Named in 1952 by Elden H. Vestal of the DFG. (DFG survey. See **Bear Paw Lake.**) (SiNF)

Little Claire Lake   *Mineral King 15'*
     Named in August 1900 by Ralph Hopping and Willis Linn Jepson for Hopping's daughter Claire, then about seven years old. "Here we made a mid-day camp, naming the bit of water 'Little Claire Lake,' tacking the sign to a tamarack-pine tree on the northern shore." (Jepson in *SCB* 4, no. 3, Feb. 1903: 214.)
     "One day when I was a small girl, my father and Professor Jepson returned from a trip to the mountains. Dismounting from his horse, Mr. Jepson picked me up and said, 'Well, we named a lake for you today.' " (Letter, Thomas H. Jukes to Farquhar, Aug. 30, 1939, quoting Mrs. Parker (Claire Hopping) Talbot, in Farquhar files.) (SNP)

Little Five Lakes   *Triple Divide Peak 15', Mineral King 15'*
     Probably named by the USGS in the 1920s, from their proximity to **Big Five Lakes.** The name appeared on the fourth editions of the *Kaweah* 30' map, 1926, and the *Tehipite* 30' map, 1929. It was first used in print in *SCB* 13, no. 1, Feb. 1928: photo opp. 92. (SNP)

Little French Lake (over 11,320)   *Mount Tom 7½'*
     Named in 1954 by Ralph Beck of the DFG. (See **Alsace Lake.**) (SiNF)

Little Pete Meadow   *Mt. Goddard 15', North Palisade 7½'*
     Pierre (Pete) Giraud, the "Little Pete" of Mary Austin's *The Flock* (1906, 52, 160), a well-known Inyo County sheepman. (Confirmed by letter, Mary Austin to Farquhar, May 25, 1933, in Farquhar files.)
     This might also be the same person referred to in Austin's *The Land of Little Rain* (1903), as "Petit Pete, who . . . passes year by year on the mesa trail, his thick hairy chest thrown open to all weathers, twirling his long staff, and dealing brotherly with his dogs, who are possibly as intelligent, certainly handsomer." (KCNP)

Little Round Top (9,590–9,595)   *Caples Lake 7½'*
The name was added to the map by the USGS. It apparently derives from
"Round Top," six miles southeast. The peak is not named on the *Silver Lake 15'*
quad; it is about two miles north of Caples Lake. (ENF)

Little Shot Lake   *Mt. Henry 7½'*
(See **Big Shot Lake.**) Not named on the *Blackcap Mtn.* 15' quad. It is the
first small lake just east of Devils Punchbowl. (SiNF)

Little Yosemite Valley   *Merced Peak 15', Yosemite 15',*
                                                           Yosemite Valley 1:24,000
Named on March 28, 1851, by a few men from Captain Dill's Company of
the Mariposa Battalion. (Bunnell, *Report,* 11.) "A small squad climbed above
Vernal and Nevada Falls. . . . These men were the first discoverers of Little
Yosemite Valley. . . . Their names have now passed from my memory."
(Bunnell, *Discovery,* 1880, 85.) The name is on King and Gardiner's map of
1865. (YNP)

Lloyd Meadows; Lloyd Meadows Creek   *Hockett Peak 15'*
The name was first used in 1874. For John W. *Loyd,* who ran sheep there.
(Farquhar files: Versteeg from John Loyd's son.) It is on the first edition of the
Olancha 30' map, 1907. (SeNF)

Loch Leven (10,743–10,744)   *Mt. Goddard 15', Mt. Darwin 7½'*
Loch Leven is a variety of trout, originally transplanted from Scotland. (See
SCB 7, no. 4, June 1910: 255.) Of a trip in July 1921, Chester Versteeg wrote:
"Our next camp was on the shore of an unnamed lake, popularly called 'Loch
Leven,' located on the North Fork of Bishop Creek about three miles below
Piute Pass. . . . we were rewarded with a catch of a single plump Loch Leven
trout." (*SCB* 11, no. 3, 1922: 276–77.) The name appears on the third edition of
the *Mt. Goddard* 30' map, 1923. (INF)

Log Meadow   *Triple Divide Peak 15'*
Hale D. Tharp first saw this fallen sequoia in 1858. Later he fitted the hollow
portion of it with a door and window and occupied it as a summer cabin. "This
fallen tree is 24 feet in diameter at the butt and is estimated as having been 311
feet in height when it fell. . . . The hollowed out portion of the log in which Mr.
Tharp lived consists of a room 56½ feet in length and 8 feet high in front,
tapering to 4 feet in height and width at the rear." (Walter Fry in *Nature,* No. 1,
Nov. 22, 1924.) (SNP)

Logan Meadow (campground)   *Shuteye Peak 15'*
Alexander Logan homesteaded 161 acres in sec. 34, T. 6 S., R. 24 E. and
sec. 3, T. 7 S., R. 24 E. in 1892. (SiNF)

Lone Indian, Lake of the   *Mt. Abbot 15', Graveyard Peak 7½'*
Named by J. S. and Lincoln Hutchinson and party in July 1902. "The name
was suggested to us by the very distinct profile of an Indian's face and feathery
head-gear in the mountain south of the lake. If you will look in volume IV, no. 3,
of the *Sierra Club Bulletin,* 1903, plate LXXI, opposite page 197, you will find

a photo of the lake, showing the mountain in the background, and by looking at the photo sidewise you will see the face distinctly." (Letter, J. S. Hutchinson to Farquhar, 1924.) The mountain referred to is marked as elevation 11428 on the 15-minute quad, and 11424 on the 7½-minute quad. (SiNF)

Lone Pine Meadow, Creek   *Triple Divide Peak 15'*
   The meadow was named "Heather Meadow" by William R. Dudley in July 1896, "from the large amount of *Bryanthus Breweri,* or 'Sierra Heather,' growing about." *SCB* 2, no. 3, Jan. 1898: 186.) When the first *Tehipite* 30' map was issued, in 1905, it was called "Lonepine Meadow." The creek, flowing out of Lion Lake, was named by a BGN decision in 1968; it is not named on the first edition of the 15-minute quad. (SNP)

Lone Pine Creek   *Mount Whitney 15' and 7½', Lone Pine 15',*
                                                Mt. Langley 7½'
Lone Pine Peak (3,945 m.–12,944), **Lake**   *Lone Pine 15', Mt. Langley 7½'*
   "Lone Pine Creek" and all the other "Lone Pine" names derive from a large pine tree growing at the confluence of Lone Pine and Tuttle creeks when the first white settlers came to Owens Valley in the early 1860s. (*Historic Spots,* 118.) The pine blew down in a storm in 1876. (INF)

Long Mountain (11,502), **Creek**   *Merced Peak 15'*
   Possibly named by the USGS during the 1898–99 survey for the *Mt. Lyell* 30' map; both names are on the first edition, 1901. (YNP, SiNF)

Longley Pass (over 12,400)   *Mount Whitney 15', Mt. Brewer 7½'*
   The pass was first crossed, and named, by Howard Longley and party in August 1894. "Instead of following the brook farther, we turned to the right and ascended a loose, rocky slide, perhaps 600 feet high. This brought us to a gently ascending swale, perhaps half a mile long. Upon reaching its further end, we had conquered the first divide, and were overlooking Bubb's Creek and the King's River country. . . . As the writer had been the first to reach its summit, the party concluded to call it Longley's Pass, as a means of identification in the future." (*SCB* 1, no. 6, May 1895: 190.) (KCNP)

Longley Reservoir (10,700)   *Mount Tom 7½'*
   Established by an early homesteader. Longley used the water stored behind the dam for irrigation. The reservoir was later taken over by Southern California Edison, which stores water for generating power. (USGS.) The reservoir was called "McGee Lake" on the *Mt. Tom* 15' map, because it is at the head of McGee Creek. A BGN decision in 1983 states that neither of these names is correct, and that the official name is "Longley Lake." (INF)

Lookout Mountain (11,261)   *Mt. Goddard 15', Mt. Thompson 7½'*
   Probably named by the USGS during the 1907–09 survey for the *Mt. Goddard* 30' map; it is on the first edition, 1912. (INF)

Lookout Peak (9,584)   *Markleeville 15', Ebbetts Pass 7½'*
   Probably named by the USGS during the survey for the *Markleeville* 30' map; it is on the first edition, 1891. (StNF)

Lookout Peak (8,531)   *Marion Peak 15'*
Named "Winchell's Peak" in 1868 by Elisha C. Winchell, for his cousin.
"The pyramid was now to be christened. A wicker-woven flask was produced
(its contents being tested to avoid possibility of mistake), and a generous liba-
tion poured therefrom upon the crowning block, while simultaneously was
pronounced, in honor of Alexander Winchell, LL.D., State Geologist of
Michigan, the name, 'Winchell's Peak.' " (San Francisco *Daily Morning Call,*
Sept. 11, 1872; also in *SCB* 12, no. 3, 1926: 245.)
Later, Lil Winchell, unaware of this naming, gave the name of "Mt.
Winchell" to a peak south of the Palisades. That name was moved to a peak
northwest of the Palisades by the USGS. (See **Winchell, Mount.**) J. N.
LeConte, in 1890, referred to the peak as "Grand Lookout." (*SCB* 1, no. 3, Jan.
1894: 96.) It was called "Lookout Mt." on Lt. Clark's 1899 map, and had its
present name on the first *Tehipite* 30' map, 1905. (KCNP, SeNF)

Lookout Point (3,103.8 m.–10,144)   *Mt. Pinchot 15', Aberdeen 7½'*
Possibly named by the USGS during the 1905 survey for the *Mt. Whitney*
30' map; it is on the first edition, 1907. (INF)

Looney Creek   *Pinecrest 15'*
This creek is not looney at all. Jerome *Loney* patented 160 acres in sec. 33,
T. 3 N., R. 18 E. in 1889; Joseph V. Loney, 160 acres in sec. 29 in 1890; James
Loney, Senior, 160 acres in secs. 20 and 21 in 1891. Unfortunately, the name of
the creek does not appear on the *Cherry Lake North 7½'* quad, published in
1979. (StNF)

Loope; Loope Canyon   *Topaz Lake 15', Heenan Lake 7½'*
The vanished town of Loope was originally named "Monitor" (see **Monitor
Creek, Pass**). Monitor flourished from 1858 to 1886, was completely deserted
by 1893, and was reborn as "Loope" in 1898 after a Dr. Loope, a mining
promoter. (*Historic Spots,* 26.) (TNF)

Loper Peak (10,045–10,059)   *Blackcap Mtn. 15',*
                                              Courtright Reservoir 7½'
John W. Loper, an early cattleman, was born in Ohio in 1838 and came to
Fresno County in 1883. (Vandor, vol. 1, 1264–65.) It was mistakenly called
"Soper Peak" on the 1916 SiNF map. (SiNF)

Lorraine Lake   *Mount Tom 7½'*
Named in 1954 by Ralph Beck of the DFG. (Phil Pister. See **Alsace Lake.**)
(SiNF)

Lost Arrow   *Yosemite Valley 1:24,000*
"The cliff east of the high fall, at the turn of Indian Cañon, was known as
Ham-mo, meaning the lost arrow, as it marks the place of a pretended loss of an
arrow that led to the death of Ten-ie-ya's son." (Bunnell, *Report,* 10–11.) Galen
Clark said the formation was sometimes called "The Devil's Thumb." (Clark,
100.) A 19th century guidebook had it as the "Giant's Thumb." There is also a
supposed Indian legend about what the name means and how it came about.

(See Hutchings, *In the Heart,* 370–74.) Although the name is an old one, it does not appear on the map until the eighth edition, 1958. (YNP)

Lost Bear Meadow   *Yosemite 15'*
   In June 1957 a small girl, Shirley Ann Miller, was lost for 3½ days. More than 100 men were involved in the search. When she was found, unharmed, she said, "I am not lost but the bear is lost. He went away and got lost." (YNP files; BGN decision, 1959.) The meadow is not named on the first edition of the 15-minute quad. It is near Bridalveil Creek, in sec. 30, T. 3 S., R. 22 E. (YNP)

Lost Cannon Creek, Peak (11,099) *Sonora Pass 15', Lost Cannon Peak 7½'*
   At one time it was claimed that Frémont abandoned his howitzer in the canyon of this creek in 1844, but later research has shown Frémont's route was considerably farther north. (See *SCB* 44, no. 7, Oct. 1959: 54–63.)
   It is also possible that—the issue of the cannon aside—these names may be misnomers. On the 1877 GLO plat, and in the field notes, the creek is called "Lost Cañon Creek"; it is also called "Lost Canyon Creek" on every edition of the *Bridgeport* 30' map, 1911 to 1951.
   The creek is also on the *Fales Hot Springs 15'*and *Chris Flat 7½'* quads. (TNF)

Lost Canyon   *Mineral King 15', Kern Peak 15'*
   A sheepherder was in the canyon with his sheep for six days before he was found and brought out. (Farquhar: W. F. Dean.) "Lost Cañon" is on William R. Dudley's sketch map in *SCB* 2, no. 3, 1898: plate XXV. (SNP)

Lost Keys Lakes   *Devils Postpile 15', Crystal Crag 7½', Bloody Mtn. 7½'*
   A name that commemorates a commonplace event—someone losing car keys. (BGN decision, 1970.) (SiNF)

Lost Lakes (highest, 11,911)   *Mt. Goddard 15', Mt. Darwin 7½'*
   Named by Art Schober because they were so well hidden. (Art Schober.) The upper lake may be the "Cirque Lake" named by J. S. Hutchinson. (*SCB* 5, no. 3, Jan. 1905: 160; also J. N. LeConte's map, plate XXXIII.) (SiNF)

Lost Valley   *Merced Peak 15'*
   Before modern trails were built, "Lost Valley" was difficult of access from either direction on the Merced River, especially for people with stock—which is the way everyone traveled until well into the 20th century. The first use of the name in print is in *SCB* 5, no. 4, June 1905: 316. (YNP)

Lubken Creek   *Lone Pine 15', Mt. Langley 7½'*
   John H. Lubken (1876–1973), cattle rancher, Inyo County supervisor for thirty years. (Life sketch in *Saga of Inyo County,* 153–55.) Called "Richter Creek" on the *Mt. Whitney* 30' map. Spelled "Lubkin" on the *Lone Pine* 15-minute quad. This may have been an error, but it is possible the family once spelled the name that way. The GLO records show that John *Lubkin* patented 160 acres in secs. 14 and 23, T. 14 S., R. 35 E. in 1874, about 12 miles north-northwest of Lubken Creek. Augusta M. L. Lubken patented 40 acres in sec. 17,

T. 16 S., R. 36 E. in 1894, and Albert Lubken homesteaded 120 acres in that vicinity in 1918. (INF)

Lucys Foot Pass   *Mount Whitney 15', Mt. Brewer 7½'*
Named for Lucy Fletcher Brown. She and her husband, Bolton C. Brown, crossed this pass over the Kings-Kern Divide in 1896. (See *SCB* 2, no. 1, Jan. 1897: 21; and *SCB* 3, no. 1, Jan. 1900: 109.) (KCNP, SNP)

Lukens Lake   *Hetch Hetchy Reservoir 15'*
Theodore Parker Lukens (1848–1918), a conservationist and advocate of reforestation; mayor of Pasadena, 1890–95. The lake was named by R. B. Marshall, USGS, probably in 1896. Shirley Sargent characterized Lukens as "the John Muir of Southern California." (See Sargent, *Lukens.*) (YNP)

Lundy (settlement); **Lundy Canyon, Lake**   *Bodie 15'*
Lundy Canyon; May Lundy Mine   *Matterhorn Peak 15'*
Lundy Pass   *Tuolumne Meadows 15'*
William O. Lundy began operating a sawmill in the canyon sometime before 1879. In 1881 he patented 80 acres: the N½ of the NW¼ of sec. 20, T. 2 N., R. 25 E. The mine and the lake were named for Lundy's daughter. George Montrose, an early resident of Lundy, said that the original name of the town was "Mill Creek"—which is still the name of the creek in Lundy Canyon. (Maule.) The messrs. Fox, Butterfield, Pike, and Kellogg filed on the "May Lundy Lode" in October 1881. The 1881 GLO plat shows "May Lundy Mine" and "Village of Lundy." (See *Eighth Annual Report of the State Mineralogist,* 1888, 367–71; DeDecker, 17–18; *SCB* 13, no. 1, Feb. 1928: 40–53.) (INF)

Luther Pass (7,735)   *Freel Peak 15' and 7½'*
Luther Creek   *Freel Peak 15', Woodfords 7½'*
Ira Manley Luther (1821–1890), a native of New York State, came to California in 1850. He discovered a pass from Hope Valley to Lake Valley in 1852 and took the first wagons across it in 1854. (Farquhar, *History,* 105.) Goddard's map of 1857 shows "Luther's Pass."
Luther had a ranch near Genoa, Nevada, and in the early 1860s operated a sawmill near the mouth of Fay Canyon. (Maule.) (Pass, ENF, TNF; creek, TNF)

Lyell, Mount (13,114); **Lyell Glacier, Fork** (of the Merced River)
                                                   Merced Peak 15'
Lyell Canyon, Fork (of the Tuolumne River)   *Tuolumne Meadows 15'*
Named on July 2, 1863, by William H. Brewer and Charles F. Hoffmann of the California Geological Survey. "After seven hours of hard climbing we struck the last pinnacle of rock that rises through the snow and forms the summit—only to find it inaccessible, at least from that side. . . . As we had named the other mountain Mount Dana, after the most eminent of *American* geologists, we named this Mount Lyell, after the most eminent of *English* geologists." (Brewer, *Up and Down,* 411.)
"Mount Lyell, from Sir Charles Lyell (1797–1875), whose admirable geological works have been well known to students of this branch of science, in

this country, for the past thirty years." (Whitney, *Yosemite Guide-Book*, 1870, 100.)

Mount Lyell is the highest peak in Yosemite National Park. The first ascent was by John Boies Tileston of Boston, on August 29, 1871. "I was up early the next morning, toasted some bacon, boiled my tea, and was off at six. I climbed the mountain, and reached the top of the highest pinnacle ('inaccessible,' according to the State Geological Survey), before eight. I came down the mountain, and reached camp before one, pretty tired." (*SCB* 12, no. 3, 1926: 305.) (YNP)

Maclure, Mount (over 12,960)   *Merced Peak 15'*
Maclure Creek   *Tuolumne Meadows 15'*
Named before 1868 by the Whitney Survey. "To the pioneer of American geology, William Maclure, one of the dominating peaks of the Sierra Nevada is very properly dedicated." (Whitney, *Yosemite Book*, 1869, 101.)

Maclure (1763–1840) became known as "the father of American geology" because he produced, in 1809, the first geological map of the United States. The name is on the Hoffmann and Gardiner map of 1863–67 as "Mt. Maclure." The Wheeler Survey atlas sheet 56D had it misspelled as "McClure Pk." Both the mountain and the creek, called "Fork," were spelled "McClure" on the first five editions of the *Mt. Lyell* 30' map, 1901–22; corrected to the proper spelling with the edition of 1927. The former "McClure Fork" (of the Merced River) was changed to "Lewis Creek" on the 30-minute map in 1944. The BGN in 1932 approved "Maclure Glacier" (on the north slope of Mount Maclure), and "Maclure Lake" (at the head of Maclure Creek). Neither name has thus far been on the maps. (YNP)

Macomb Ridge   *Tower Peak 15'*
Lieutenant Montgomery Meigs Macomb (1852–1924), Fourth Artillery, US Army, in charge of the Wheeler Survey field party in California, 1876, 1877, and 1878; mapped in the Yosemite region in 1878. (Wheeler Survey, *Reports*, 1877, 1878, 1879.) Portrait in *SCB* 12, no. 2, 1925: 138. The name appeared on the third edition of the *Dardanelles* 30' map, 1912. (YNP)

Maddox, Mount (over 9,680)   *Triple Divide Peak 15'*
Named for Ben M. Maddox (1859–1933) of Visalia. (Farquhar.) The name is on the first *Tehipite* 30' map, 1905. (SeNF)

Madera Peak (10,509), **Creek, Lakes,**   *Merced Peak 15'*
In 1876 the California Lumber Company built a 52-mile flume from the mountains above present-day Oakhurst to a sawmill in the San Joaquin Valley. The town that grew up around the mill was named *Madera,* the Spanish word for wood, or lumber. (Johnston, *Whistles,* 11, 87.) In 1893 the part of Fresno County north and west of the San Joaquin River was organized as a new county and named after the town. (Coy, 157.)

What is now "Madera Peak" was at first named "Black Mt.," since it appears that way on the Hoffmann and Gardiner map of 1863–67. The Wheeler Survey revised that to "Black Peak" (atlas sheet 56D, 1878–79). That name

and "Black Peak Fork" (for what is now "Madera Creek") were on the first
seven editions of the *Mt. Lyell* 30' map, 1901–29. Both features were given the
"Madera" name by a BGN decision in 1926; they appeared on the eighth edition of the 30-minute map, 1944. The lakes were first named on the 15-minute
map, 1953. (SiNF)

Maggie Mountain (10,042), **Lakes**   *Mineral King 15'*
There are two versions of how the mountain was named. One is that Frank
Knowles, who accompanied Clarence King to Mount Whitney in 1873, named
it for Maggie Kincaid, a Tulare County school teacher. (Farquhar.)

The other is that the Kincaids were on a hunting trip. A government surveyor
came by, and stayed with them. He highly praised Maggie Kincaid's biscuits,
and asked if she would like to have a mountain named for her. "Well," she
replied, "today I sat right on top of this mountain and it doesn't have a name."
So Maggie Mountain it is. (Otter, 156; see **Moses Mountain.**) The name was on
the first *Kaweah* 30' map, 1904.

The lakes were named after the peak, as suggested by Chester Versteeg in
1928. (SeNF)

Mahan Peak (9,146), **Lake**   *Tower Peak 15'*
There is strong circumstantial evidence to indicate that the peak was named
by Col. William W. Forsyth, acting superintendent of Yosemite National Park,
1909–12. During his tenure, Forsyth named a number of peaks and other features for army officers; e. g., "Kendrick," "Michie," and "Schofield." These
names, and "Mahan Peak," appeared on the map at the same time: the third edition of the *Dardanelles* 30' sheet, 1912.

Dennis H. Mahan was professor of military engineering at West Point prior
to the Civil War, and was the author of a basic textbook on strategy and tactics.
(Morison, 626.) He was the father of Adm. Alfred T. Mahan (1840–1914), the
noted naval historian.

Mahan Lake was first named on the 15-minute quad, 1956. (YNP)

Maidens Grave   *Silver Lake 15', Tragedy Spring 7½'*
Thought to be the grave of Rachel Melton, a girl from Iowa traveling with an
immigrant party, who died here in 1850. (*California Historical Landmarks*,
no. 28.) Marked simply "Grave" on the 15-minute quad. (ENF)

Major General, The (over 12,400)   *Mount Whitney 15' and 7½'*
A name suggested by Chester Versteeg in 1939, because the "Soldier
Lakes" (also suggested by Versteeg) were directly below the peak, and Army
Pass was near at hand. (SC papers in BL.) "Soldier Lakes" was not approved by
the BGN. "The Major General" was added to the 15-minute quad, 1956,
because it was in common use and not in conflict with other names. (USGS)
(SNP)

Mallard Lake (9,432)   *Mt. Abbot 15', Mt. Givens 7½'*
Named by the DFG (Charles K. Fisher, surveyor) in 1947 because a family
of mallard ducks was seen here. (DFG survey.) (SiNF)

Mallory, Mount (4,220 m.–13,850)   *Mount Whitney 15' and 7½'*
Norman Clyde made the first ascent in June 1925, and named the peak for
George H. Leigh Mallory, who was lost on the British Mount Everest Expedition in June 1924. Mallory and Irvine (see **Irvine, Mount**) attained the highest
altitude reached by mountain climbers to that time, over 28,000 feet. (*The Fight
for Everest,* 1924; *SCB* 11, no. 4, 1923: 430, 453–55; *SCB* 12, no. 2, 1925:
182–83; *SCB* 12, no. 3, 1926: 329–30.) The mountain was first named on the
sixth edition of the *Mt. Whitney* 30' map, 1927. (SNP, INF)

Malpais   *Kern Peak 15'*
French for "bad country," an apt name for an extremely rough, jumbled lava
flow about three miles long. First appeared on the 15-minute quad, 1956.
(INF)

Mamie, Lake (8,898)   *Devils Postpile 15', Crystal Crag 7½'*
Believed to be named for Mamie Clarke, Bishop superintendent of schools,
1903–22. (Smith, 20; Chalfant, 415.) One of the Mammoth Lakes. (INF)

Mammoth Mountain (11,030–11,053), **Creek**   *Devils Postpile 15',*
                                                  Mammoth Mtn. 7½'
Mammoth Lakes, Crest, Pass   *Devils Postpile 15', Crystal Crag 7½'*
Mammoth Creek; Mammoth Lakes, Old Mammoth (towns)
                                  Mt. Morrison 15', Old Mammoth 7½'
Mammoth Rock, Creek, Crest   *Mt. Morrison 15', Bloody Mtn. 7½'*
In June 1877 four men located mineral deposits at an altitude of 11,000 feet.
A mining district was formed, and the Mammoth Mining Company began work
in 1878. All other "Mammoth" names derive from the name of the principal
mine. (See *SCB* 13, no. 1, Feb. 1928: 48–49.) The town had a post office from
1879 to 1881, and again from 1896 to 1898.
    Mammoth Creek was called "South Branch of Owens River" on Von
Schmidt's plat of 1857. Mammoth Rock was called "Mammoth Mountain" on
the 1879 GLO plat. (INF)

Mammoth Peak (12,117)   *Tuolumne Meadows 15'*
The namer is unknown. It was first named on the third edition of the *Mt.
Lyell* 30' map, 1910. (YNP)

Manter Meadow   *Kernville 15'*
Manter Creek   *Kernville 15', Lamont Peak 15'*
For a sheepherder who ran sheep in the vicinity. (Crites, 269.) Both names
are on the first *Kernville* 30' map, 1908. (SeNF)

Marble Fork, Falls   *Giant Forest 15', Triple Divide Peak 15'*
The fork was named for the prominent showing of marble in the canyon.
(Tobin.) The name appears on the 1883 GLO plat. (SNP)

Marble Point (8,868–8,858)   *Huntington Lake 15', Nelson Mtn. 7½'*
Possibly named by the USGS during the 1901–02 survey for the *Kaiser* 30'
map; it is on the first edition, 1904. (SiNF)

Marie Lake (10,551–10,576)   *Mt. Abbot 15', Mt. Hilgard 7½'*
Named by R. B. Marshall, USGS, for Mary Hooper Perry, daughter of

Major William B. Hooper and sister of Selden S. Hooper, both of whom were with the USGS. (Farquhar: Marshall, Mary Hooper Perry. See also **Hooper, Mount,** and **Selden Pass.**) "Marie Lake" is on the first *Mt. Goddard* 30′ map, 1912. (SiNF)

Marion Lake, Peak (12,719)   *Marion Peak 15′*
    The lake and peak were named by J. N. LeConte in 1902 for his wife, Helen Marion Gompertz LeConte (1865–1924), who was with him on a pioneering trip up Cartridge Creek. (Farquhar: LeConte.)
    "Directly at its foot was a beautiful lake, fringed with tiny meadows on one side, and guarded on the other by fine cliffs of white granite, which could be traced far down beneath the clear waters till lost in their blue depths. Across the lake rose a splendid range of peaks of brilliant red slate and pure white granite." (*SCB* 4, no. 4, June 1903: 259.) See also a memorial in *SCB* 12, no. 2, 1925: 148–55; and *SCB* 12, no. 3, 1926: 316, photos of Helen LeConte memorial plaque at Marion Lake. (KCNP)

Mariposa Grove   *Yosemite 15′*
    The name *Mariposas* was given to an unknown location in the San Joaquin Valley in 1806. "This was called the place of the butterflies (*Llamose este Sitio de las Mariposas*), due to its great multitude especially at night and in the morning so unceasingly bothersome that they even reached the point of blocking the sun's rays, pursuing us everywhere so that one of the corporals of the expedition got one in his ear causing him much discomfort and no little trouble in extracting it." (Arch. MSB, vol. 4, Muñoz, Sept. 27, 1806.)
    The name "Mariposa" was applied to two land grants and, eventually, to the town, the county, and the grove of sequoias. The grove was discovered in May 1857 by Galen Clark and Milton Mann. "As they were in Mariposa County, I named them the Mariposa Grove of Big Trees." (Clark, *Yosemite Souvenir and Guide,* 1901, 97.) (YNP)

Marjorie, Lake (over 11,120)   *Mt. Pinchot 15′ and 7½′*
    Marjorie Mott, daughter of Mr. and Mrs. Ernest J. Mott. (Farquhar: E. J. Mott.) Appears on the fourth edition of the *Mt. Whitney* 30′ map. (See **Mott Lake.**) (KCNP)

Markleeville; Markleeville Creek   *Markleeville 15′ and 7½′*
Markleeville Peak (9,415–9,417)   *Markleeville 15′, Carson Pass 7½′*
    Jacob J. Marklee settled on the site of the later town on Sept. 12, 1861. (Maule.) The Alpine County Courthouse occupies the site of his cabin. (*California Historical Landmarks,* no. 240.) The name of the town appears on Theron Reed's map, 1864. All three features are on the Wheeler Survey atlas sheet 56D, 1878–79. (TNF)

Markwood Meadow, Creek   *Huntington Lake 15′, Dinkey Creek 7½′*
    William Markwood, a sheepman of the 1870s. (Farquhar: Versteeg, from D. C. Sample.) Markwood progressed from sheep to cattle, then grain, followed by manufacturing buggies and wagons, and meat packing; he was one of the originators of the Fresno Flume and Irrigation Company. (Vandor, vol. 1, 651–

52.) Frank Dusy, for whom several features in the higher mountains were named, patented 159 acres in the meadow and along the creek in 1882. (SiNF)

Marmot Lake   *Mt. Tom 15', Mount Tom 7½'*
   Possibly named in 1950 by Ralph Beck of the DFG. (DFG survey.) (SiNF)

Marshall Lake   *Mt. Abbot 15', Florence Lake 7½', Mt. Hilgard 7½'*
   Named in 1942 by Elden H. Vestal of the USGS, almost certainly for Robert B. Marshall, USGS, who named nearby Rose and Marie lakes, Selden Pass, and Mount Hooper. (DFG survey.) (SiNF)

Martell Flat   *Silver Lake 15', Caples Lake 7½'*
   Louis Martell homesteaded 160 acres in sec. 23, T. 9 N., R. 17 E. in 1903— less than a mile southwest of the flat, which was "Flats" on the 15-minute quad. (ENF)

Martha Lake (11,004)   *Mt. Goddard 15' and 7½'*
   George R. Davis, USGS, named the lake for his mother in 1907. (Farquhar: Davis.) (KCNP)

Martins Cow Camp   *Dardanelles Cone 15', Dardanelle 7½'*
   Joe Martin had the cattle permit in Eagle Meadow in the 1950s. (StNF files.) (StNF)

Marvin Pass (over 9,040)   *Triple Divide Peak 15'*
   S. L. N. Ellis of the Forest Service named the pass in 1899 for his son. (Farquhar files: Versteeg from Ellis.) (SeNF)

Mary, Lake   *Devils Postpile 15', Mt. Morrison 15', Crystal Crag 7½',*
                                                   Bloody Mtn. 7½'
   Named for Mary Calvert of Pine City, an old mining camp. (Smith, p. 19; but also see p. 143: a Calvert descendant denies this, and states that the lake was named for a Bodie dancehall girl. See **George, Lake.**) (INF)

Mary Austin, Mount (3,978 m.–over 13,040)   *Mt. Pinchot 15',*
                                                   Kearsarge Peak 7½'
   Mary Austin was a prominent writer, a natural historian, and a long-time resident of Independence; best known for her book *The Land of Little Rain.* Her former home in Independence is a state historical landmark. The name for the peak was suggested by Norman Clyde (Farquhar files); approved by the BGN, 1966. Not named on the first edition of the 15-minute quad; it is located one mile northeast of Black Mountain. (INF)

Marie Louise Lakes   *Mt. Goddard 15', Mt. Thompson 7½'*
   Named after Mrs. W. C. Parcher. She and her husband established "Parchers Camp" in 1922. (Schumacher, 93.) The name appears, incorrectly, as "Mary Louise Lakes" on the 15-minute quad. (INF)

Mather (community)   *Lake Eleanor 15'*
   An early sheepman pastured his flocks in the area. He painted a picture of an animal on a rock, intending to depict a sheep. His artistic talent was unequal to the task, and he admitted that the result looked more like a hog—and the area

became known as "Hog Ranch." In October 1919 it was renamed "Mather," for Stephen T. Mather, who was director of the National Park Service at that time. (Bingaman, *Guardians,* 73–74.) It was called "Hog Ranch" on Hoffmann and Gardiner's map, 1863–67, and retained that name on all the editions of the *Yosemite* 30' map, 1897–1951. (StNF)

Mather Pass (over 12,080)   *Big Pine 15', Split Mtn. 7½'*
Stephen Tyng Mather (1867–1930), first director of the National Park Service, 1917–29. Mather was a reporter on the New York *Sun* from 1887 to 1892. In 1893 he went to work for the Pacific Coast Borax Company; he was largely responsible for marketing packaged borax under the "Twenty-Mule Team Borax" trade name. In 1903 he formed an independent borax company, a business that in later years made him wealthy. He used his wealth to acquire privately owned lands within Sequoia National Park, and—with the help of friends—he purchased the Tioga Road in 1915 and donated it to the government. (*SCB* 16, no. 1, Feb. 1931: 55–59; see also *SCB* 15, no. 1, Feb. 1930: 98, 106–7.)

"To him goes the everlasting thanks of the American people, for he fathered the National Park idea through its most trying period." (Horace M. Albright and Frank J. Taylor, *Oh, Ranger!,* 1946, 186.)

J. N. LeConte, James Hutchinson, and Duncan McDuffie crossed the pass in July 1908. (*SCB* 7, no. 1, Jan. 1909: 19.) The pass was said to have been crossed by a sheepman in 1897. (*SCB* 11, no. 4, 1923: 423.) It was named by Mr. and Mrs. Chauncey J. Hamlin and party of Buffalo, New York, on August 25, 1921. (*SCB* 11, no. 3, 1922; 269–70.) The name appeared on the second edition of the *Bishop* 30' map, 1930. (KCNP)

Matlock Lake (3,218 m.)   *Mt. Pinchot 15', Kearsarge Peak 7½'*
Named for the man who first planted fish in it. (Schumacher, 88, where it is spelled "Matlack.") (INF)

Matterhorn Peak (12,264)   *Matterhorn Peak 15'*
Matterhorn Canyon   *Matterhorn Peak 15', Tuolumne Meadows 15'*
The Wheeler Survey named both features in 1878; they are shown on atlas sheet 56D, 1878–79. In 1877 John Muir gave the name "Matterhorn" to what is now Banner Peak or some other summit near it. (Muir, "Snow Banners of the California Alps," *Harper's,* July 1877.)

"That the name is a poor one there can be no doubt . . . there is only the barest suggestion of resemblance to the wonderful Swiss mountain after which it is called." (Lincoln Hutchinson in *SCB* 3, no. 2, May 1900: 162–63.) Lt. McClure, in 1894, gave the name to what are now the "Finger Peaks" because of the striking resemblance to alpine peaks; his map of 1896 thus has "Matterhorn" misplaced, even though LeConte's of 1893 has it in the right place. (Farquhar files: letter from McClure, Oct. 22, 1920.) (Peak, YNP, TNF; canyon, YNP)

Matthes Glaciers   *Mt. Henry 7½', Mt. Darwin 7½'*
François Emile Matthes, a USGS geologist for 51 years, made extensive

studies in Yosemite and elsewhere in the Sierra Nevada. (See his *The Incomparable Valley*, ed. Fritiof Fryxell, published in 1950, two years after his death.) Among nearly 100 published works, Matthes had 14 articles in various issues of the *Sierra Club Bulletin*. (Also see *SCB* 33, no. 7, July 1948: 8.)

The glaciers are not named on the *Blackcap Mtn.* and *Mt. Goddard* 15' quads. They are on the north side of Glacier Divide, from the glacier southwest of Lobe Lakes on the west to the one south of Paine Lake on the east. The name was approved by the BGN in 1972. (SiNF)

Matthes Crest (over 10,880), **Lake**   *Tuolumne Meadows 15'*
The names were first suggested for, and to, François E. Matthes in 1946; the proposal was made more formally by Reid Moran, a YNP ranger, in 1949. "Dr. Matthes was a very modest and unassuming man and would have been the last to suggest that anything be named in his honor. However, he was greatly pleased at the suggestion that this ridge bear his name, saying he knew no other unnamed feature in the Sierra which he would rather have chosen." (*SCB* 34, no. 6, June 1949: 110–11.) Matthes Crest was known informally during the 1930s as "Echo Ridge" because of its proximity to Echo Peaks and Echo Lake. (YNP)

Maul Lake   *Tuolumne Meadows 15'*
Named in 1932 by Al Gardisky for a man who was a Forest Service supervisor around 1930–32. (Spuller.) Possibly this refers to William E. Maule, and is misspelled by Gardisky and Spuller, not the USGS. (INF)

Maxson Dome (9,492–9,547), **Meadows**   *Blackcap Mtn. 15',*
        Courtright Reservoir 7½'
Big Maxson Meadow; Maxson Lake, Basin   *Blackcap Mtn. 15' and 7½'*
According to the USGS, Maxson was an early stockman; not the same person as the "Maxon" referred to by Gudde, *Place Names*, p. 196. The dome and the meadows were named first; both are on the *Mt. Goddard* 30' map, 1912. "Maxson Basin" is the most recent, having just appeared on the 7½-minute quad, 1982. (SiNF)

Maxwell Creek   *Freel Peak 15' and 7½'*
William Maxwell patented 160 acres in sec. 1, T. 10 N., R. 18 E. in 1892, and another 160 acres in 1900. (TNF)

May Lake   *Tuolumne Meadows 15'*
Charles F. Hoffmann of the Whitney Survey named the lake for Lucy Mayotta Browne, whom he married in 1870. She was the daughter of J. Ross Browne, a well-known pioneer, mining engineer, and writer. (Farquhar: Ross E. Browne.) May Lake is a mile due east of Mount Hoffmann. (YNP)

Mayfield Canyon   *Mt. Morgan 7½'*
"Colonel" Mayfield, a retired army officer leading a citizens' militia, was killed here April 9, 1862, by Indians. (Cragen, 6–8; Chalfant, 156–65.) The canyon is not named on the *Mt. Tom* 15' quad. The mouth is just northwest of Wells Meadow, a mile south of the Mono-Inyo county line. (INF)

McAdie, Mount (4,206 m.–over 13,760)   *Mount Whitney 15' and 7½'*
Alexander G. McAdie, scientist and writer; in charge of the US Weather

Bureau in San Francisco, 1903–13; professor of meteorology at Harvard, 1913–31. "Our party had the honor of naming the peak directly south of Lone Pine Pass Mt. McAdie, to commemorate your services in advancing the science of climatology." (Letter, J. E. Church, Jr. to McAdie, March 18, 1905, in *SCB* 5, no. 4, June 1905: 317.) The name did not appear on the maps until the 15-minute quad was published in 1956. (SNP, INF)

McCabe Lakes; Upper McCabe Lake *Tuolumne Meadows 15'*
McCabe Creek *Matterhorn Peak 15'*
Edward Raynsford Warner McCabe, an army officer who had no association with Yosemite National Park—except that he married Polly Forsyth, daughter of Col. W. W. Forsyth, acting superintendent of the park from 1909 to 1912. The lakes were named during that period, probably by R. B. Marshall, USGS, a close friend of Forsyth. (Farquhar files.) "McCabe Lakes" appears on the fourth *Mt. Lyell* 30' map, 1914. The creek is first named on the 15-minute quad, 1956. "Upper McCabe Lake" was ratified by the BGN in 1962 to approve what had become local usage. (YNP)

McCloud Lake *Devils Postpile 15', Crystal Crag 7½'*
Malcolm *McLeod* was a Forest Service ranger stationed at Reds Meadows from 1921 to 1929. (Smith, 15, 52–53; also USGS quad report.) On the 1879 GLO plat it was called "Blue Lake." (INF)

McClure Lake *Merced Peak 15'*
Nathaniel Fish McClure (1865–1942), Fifth Cavalry, US Army, stationed in Yosemite National Park in 1894 and 1895. He explored the northern part of the park, and compiled maps in 1895 and 1896. (Obituary in *SCB* 28, no. 3, June 1943: 96–98.) The lake probably was named by R. B. Marshall during the 1898–99 survey for the *Mt. Lyell* 30' map; it is on the first edition, 1901. (SiNF)

McClure Meadow *Mt. Goddard 15', Mt. Darwin 7½'*
Wilbur Fiske McClure (1856–1926), California State Engineer, 1912–26. McClure was in charge of selecting the final route for the John Muir Trail and overseeing the construction. (*SCB* 10, no. 1, Jan. 1916: 86–87.) The meadow was named about 1920; it is on the third edition of the *Mt. Goddard* 30' map, 1923. For a memorial to McClure, with portrait, see *SCB* 12, no. 4, 1927: 428–29. (KCNP)

McCormick Creek *Dardanelles Cone 15', Spicer Meadow Res. 7½',*
Donnell Lake 7½'
Named for an early settler. The 1879 GLO plat shows "McCormack's House" in the NE¼ of sec. 8, T. 6 N., R. 19 E. (StNF)

McDermand, Lake (over 11,520) *Mt. Goddard 15' and 7½'*
Charles K. McDermand (1902–1966), outdoorsman, writer, and authority on golden trout fishing in the High Sierra. (BGN decision, 1967.) The lake is not named on early editions of the *Mt. Goddard* 15' quad. It is on the John Muir Trail, the larger of two lakes between Wanda Lake and Muir Pass. (KCNP)

McDuffie, Mount (13,282–13,271) *Mt. Goddard 15' and 7½'*
In honor of Duncan McDuffie (1877–1951), a conservationist and early

Sierra mountaineer. With Joseph N. LeConte and James S. Hutchinson he pioneered the route across Muir Pass in 1908. (*SCB* 7, no. 1, Jan. 1909: 15–17.) He participated in the first ascents of Mount Mills, Mount Abbot, and Black Kaweah. He was a director of the Sierra Club for many years, and its president from 1928 to 1931, and again from 1943 to 1946. He was also president of the Save-the-Redwoods League from 1944 until his death, and was of prime importance in establishing the California State Park System. (Obituary and portrait in *SCB* 37, no. 10, Dec. 1952: 84–85.) The name was suggested by Walter Starr of the Sierra Club. (SC papers in BL.) (KCNP)

McGann Springs   *Mt. Pinchot 15', Kearsarge Peak 7½'*
    James McGann patented 160 acres in secs. 26 and 35, T. 12 S., R. 34 E. in 1894, and another 117 acres in sec. 35 in 1897. Peter McGann homesteaded 158 acres in sec. 35 of that township and sec. 1, T. 13 S., R. 34 E. in 1886. These properties are roughly three miles east of the springs. (INF)

McGee Creek   *Mt. Morrison 15', Mt. Abbot 15' and 7½',*
                                                           Convict Lake 7½'
McGee Mountain (10,886–10,871), **Pass**   *Mt. Morrison 15',*
                                                           Convict Lake 7½'
Big McGee Lake; Little McGee Lake   *Mt. Abbot 15' and 7½'*
    Three McGee brothers, Alney, John, and Bart, were pioneer cattlemen in Mono and Inyo counties. *This* McGee Creek was named for Alney McGee, Jr. (INF archives.) All these other "McGee" names probably are derived from the creek. The creek and mountain are named on the first *Mt. Morrison* and *Mt. Goddard* 30' maps, 1914 and 1912 respectively. (INF)

McGee Creek   *Mt. Tom 15', Mount Tom 7½', Tungsten Hills 7½'*
    Alney L. McGee homesteaded 160 acres in sec. 27, R. 6 S., T. 31 E. in 1874. (This is on Horton Creek, about five miles north of McGee Creek.) This McGee Creek was named for Alney's son John, who owned a ranch in Pleasant Valley that took its water from the creek. (INF archives.) John was sheriff of Inyo County, 1885–86. (Chalfant, *Inyo,* 413.) For the "McGee Lake" on the 15-minute quad, see **Longley Reservoir.** McGee Meadow is now a subdivision. (INF)

McGee, Mount (12,944–12,969); **McGee Lakes, Canyon**
                                   Mt. Goddard 15', Mt. Darwin 7½'
    William John McGee (1853–1912), geologist, anthropologist, and hydrologist. He joined the USGS in 1883, and was with the Bureau of American Ethnology from 1893 to 1903. The mountain probably was named by the USGS during the 1907–09 survey for the *Mt. Goddard* 30' map; it is on the first edition, 1912. The lakes and canyon are named on the third edition, 1923. (KCNP)

McGurk Meadow   *Yosemite 15'*
    John J. McGurk was the third owner of this property. The original owner filed for 160 acres, but the description in the county records indicated a claim in the next township, six miles away. McGurk built a cabin here, but he was forced

off the land by the US Army in 1897 when the invalid patent was discovered. (Robert F. Uhte, "Yosemite's Pioneer Cabins," *SCB* 36, no. 5, May 1951: 55–56.) (YNP)

McIntyre Creek, Grove   *Camp Nelson 15'*
Thomas McIntyre, a pioneer of Tulare County, who ran sheep here in the 1880s. (Farquhar: Versteeg.) (SeNF)

McKinley Grove   *Huntington Lake 15', Nelson Mtn. 7½'*
William McKinley (1843–1901), twenty-fifth president of the United States. McKinley died September 14, 1901, eight days after being shot by an assassin. The grove of sequoias was named by R. B. Marshall, USGS, who at that time was doing the topography on the *Kaiser* 30' map. (Farquhar: Marshall.) The name is on the first edition, 1904. (SiNF)

McMurry Meadows   *Big Pine 15', Fish Springs 7½'*
Samuel Jackson McMurry came to Big Pine from Illinois in 1873; he ran sheep and cattle in the area of the meadows named for him. (INF archives; *Saga,* 182–83, for sketch of family history.) According to McMurry's great great grandson, the name was originally spelled "MacMurray." Two letters were dropped to make the name fit on the timecard when he worked for a railroad before coming to Owens Valley. (USGS quad report.) (INF)

Meadow Brook   *Yosemite 15', Yosemite Valley 1:24,000*
An old name; origin unknown. It is on the first 1:24,000 map, 1907. The old Mariposa Trail entered the Yosemite Grant along this creek. (YNP files. See **Silver Strand Falls.**) (YNP)

Medley Lake   *Mt. Abbot 15', Mt. Hilgard 7½'*
William A. Dill of the DFG named the lake in 1942 "because this complex of lakelets and streams answers so well to the definition of a 'medley.' " (DFG survey.) If one assumes that Mr. Dill was not thinking of "mixture" or "jumble," but rather meant the word in its musical sense—"a piece of music combining airs or passages from various sources"—it doubtless explains the origin of the names of nearby "Flat Note Lake" and "Sharp Note Lake," which also were surveyed in 1942 by Dill. (SiNF)

Medlicott Dome   *Tuolumne Meadows 15'*
Probably named for Harry P. Medlicott, who, with H. B. Carpenter, surveyed the route of the "Great Sierra Wagon Road"—the Tioga Road—in 1882. (Keith A. Trexler, "The Tioga Road, a History," pamphlet, no date; also *YNN* 27, no. 9: 109–12.) (YNP)

Mehrten Meadow, Creek   *Triple Divide Peak 15'*
Named after James Mehrten, a pioneer cattleman of Three Rivers. (Fry and White, 179.) The name was spelled "Merten" on early editions of the *Tehipite* 30' map. The meadow was corrected to "Mehrten" on the fifth edition, 1939; the creek on the sixth, 1947. (SNP)

Mendel, Mount (13,710–13,691)   *Mt. Goddard 15', Mt. Darwin 7½'*
Johann Gregor Mendel (1822–1884), Austrian geneticist. The name was

proposed by the Sierra Club before 1942, "to add one more evolutionist to the Evolution Group. For some time the peak was informally known as Mt. Ex-Wallace." (Letter, David Brower to C. A. Ecklund, USGS, March 7, 1951, copy in Farquhar files.) The peak was mistakenly named "Mt Wallace" on the first two editions of the *Mt. Goddard* 30' map, 1912 and 1918; this name was moved to the correct location on the 1923 edition. (KCNP)

Merced River   *Merced Peak 15', Yosemite 15', El Portal 15'*
The expedition under Gabriel Moraga, including the diarist Fray Pedro Muñoz, named the river *El Rio de Nuestra Señora de la Merced* on September 29, 1806, five days after the feast day of Our Lady of Mercy. (Arch. MSB, vol. 4, Muñoz.) In 1844 Frémont referred to the river both as "Rio de la Merced" (*Expedition*, 360) and by an Indian name, "Aux-um-ne'" (*Memoir*, 17.) Preuss's 1848 map shows it as a plural: "R.d.l. Auxumnes," obviously referring to Indians living along the river.

The shortened version, "Merced River," was in use by the early 1850s. Hoffmann and Gardiner's map of 1863–67 has "So. Fork Merced River" as well. All the other "Merced" names derive from the river's name. (YNP, StNF)

Merced Grove   *El Portal 15'*
This small grove of Big Trees was probably seen by the Joseph R. Walker party in 1833. (See **Tuolumne Grove**.) It was named by Dr. John T. McLean, president of the Coulterville and Yosemite Turnpike Company, in 1871 or 1872. "While making the survey for this road a grove of big trees was discovered . . . which was named the Merced Grove by me because of its nearness to the Merced River." (Letter, McLean to Yosemite National Park Commission, 1899, in Russell, *100 Years,* 77.) (YNP)

Merced Lake (7,216)   *Merced Peak 15'*
"I first discovered this charming lake in the autumn of 1872, while on my way to the glaciers at the head of the river." (John Muir, *Scribner's Monthly,* Jan. 1879, 416.) But Muir called it "Shadow Lake," a name he first used in a letter to Mrs. Carr, Oct. 7, 1874. (Bade, vol. II, 28.) The USGS showed it as "Merced Lake" on the first edition of the *Mt. Lyell* 30' map, 1901. (YNP)

Merced Pass; Upper and **Lower Merced Pass Lake**   *Merced Peak 15'*
The pass was discovered by Corporal Ottoway while scouting for Lt. Benson in 1895, and was named by Benson. (Farquhar: Benson.) The two lakes were first named on the 15-minute quad, 1953. (YNP)

Merced Peak (11,726); **Merced Peak Fork**   *Merced Peak 15'*
The Clark Range was known as both the "Obelisk Group" and the "Merced Group" at the time of the Whitney Survey. (Whitney, *The Yosemite Book,* 1868, 97.) The present name for the peak first appears on the Wheeler Survey atlas sheet 56D, 1878–79. The fork was named on the 15-minute quad, 1953. (YNP)

Mercur Peak (over 8,000)   *Pinecrest 15'*
James Mercur (1842–1896), professor of engineering at West Point from

1884 until his death. The peak was named in 1912 by Colonel Forsyth. (Farquhar: Benson.) (YNP, StNF)

Merk Canyon   *Freel Peak 15', Woodfords 7½'*
Wendelin Merk patented 178 acres in secs. 2 and 3, T. 10 N., R. 19 E. in 1880. (TNF)

Merriam Peak (13,103–13,077), **Lake** (10,932)   *Mt. Abbot 15',*
                                                                    Mt. Hilgard 7½'
Named on December 30, 1929, by the California State Geographic Board for Dr. Clinton Hart Merriam (1855–1942), biologist and ethnologist. Merriam was the chief of the US Biological Survey, 1885–1910, in charge of the Death Valley expedition, 1890–91, and was chairman of the US Geographic Board, 1917–25. He published more than 15 books and more than 400 scientific papers.

In June 1931 the mountain was referred to by Nathan Clark as "Isosceles Mountain" because of its appearance from the northeast side. (*SCB* 17, no. 1, Feb. 1932: 123.) Lewis and Nathan Clark later successfully applied this name to a peak on the south side of Dusy Basin. The first ascent of Merriam Peak was made on July 14, 1933, by Lewis Clark, Julie Mortimer, and Ted Waller, who called it "Bastille Peak" in honor of the date, not knowing that it already had a name. (*SCB* 19, no. 3, June 1934: 93.)

The mountain is first named on the fifth edition of the *Mt. Goddard* 30' map, 1933, and the lake on the 15-minute quad, 1953. (SiNF)

Meysan Lake   *Mount Whitney 15' and 7½', Lone Pine 15', Mt. Langley 7½'*
Little Meysan Lake; Meysan Creek   *Lone Pine 15', Mt. Langley 7½'*
Felix Meysan came to Lone Pine with his family in 1869, when he was four years old. His father, Charles, born in France, had a general merchandise store in Lone Pine. Felix stocked the Meysan Lakes with fish in the 1920s. (Anecdotal family history in *Saga of Inyo County,* 169–73.) (INF)

Michie Peak (10,365)   *Tower Peak 15'*
Named by Colonel Forsyth in 1912 for Peter Smith Michie (1839–1901), professor of engineering at West Point from 1871 until his death. (Farquhar: Forsyth.) (YNP)

Midge Lake   *Kaiser Peak 15', Sharktooth Peak 7½'*
Probably named in 1953 by Elden H. Vestal of the DFG. (DFG survey.) (SiNF)

Midnight Lake (10,988)   *Mt. Goddard 15', Mt. Darwin 7½'*
Named about 1934 by Art Schober "for a large black horse we had." (Art Schober.) (INF)

Midway Mountain (4,164.8 m.–13,666)   *Mount Whitney 15',*
                                                       Mt. Brewer 7½'
The USGS added the name to the 15-minute map, 1956, because it was in common use. It is the highest point on the Great Western Divide. In 1881 the Langley party on the summit of Mount Whitney gave this mountain the name of

"Mount Michaelis," for Capt. Otho Ernest Michaelis, US Army Signal Corps, who was assigned to accompany Langley. "Captain Michaelis gave us a vivid description of the battle-ground of the Little Big Horn. He was the first white man to reach the body of General Custer on that ill-fated field." (W. B. Wallace in *MWCJ* 1, no. 1, May 1902: 5.) The name "Mount Michaelis" never made it onto the maps. (KCNP, SNP)

Miguel Meadow, Creek   *Lake Eleanor 15'*
"The ranch belongs to Mr. Miguel D. Errera, but his American friends have corrupted *Miguel* into *McGill* and by that name is his house known." (Lt. N. F. McClure in *SCB* 1, no. 5, Jan. 1895: 185.) The USGS continued the corruption, spelling the name "McGill" on the first five editions of the *Yosemite* 30' map, 1897–1911. A BGN decision corrected it to "Miguel;" it appeared that way on the sixth edition, 1929. (YNP)

Mildred Lake   *Tuolumne Meadows 15'*
Named for Mildred Sovulewski, daughter of Gabriel Sovulewski, who served as ranger and supervisor in Yosemite National Park from 1906 to 1936. He first came to Yosemite with the US Army in 1895. (YNP files.) (YNP)

Milestone Mountain (4,157 m.–13,641), **Bowl, Creek**   *Mount Whitney 15',*
Mt. Brewer 7½'
An obvious descriptive name; it first appears on Hoffmann's map of 1873. "Mount Langley . . . is known by a minaret, or obelisk, that seems to stand on the north edge of its summit. It is known among mountain prospectors as *Milestone Mountain.*" (Elliott, *Guide,* 51.) The name "Langley" was given in 1881 by someone with the Langley party on the summit of Mount Whitney, probably Capt. Michaelis. (See **Midway Mountain.**) Langley's name was later applied to the peak where it is now.
"We were soon upon a plateau, and passed from this to a bowl-shaped mountain. And since this plateau and bowl have once been parts of Milestone, Prof. Dudley named them Milestone Plateau and Milestone Bowl." (W. F. Dean in *MWCJ* 1, no. 1, May 1902: 16.) The bowl was mistakenly spelled "Bow" in articles and on the USGS *Mt. Whitney* 30' maps, 1901–21. It was changed to "Bowl" on the sixth edition, 1927. Milestone Plateau has never been named on the maps. (KCNP, SNP)

Mill City (site)   *Mt. Morrison 15', Bloody Mtn. 7½'*
The city of a 40-stamp mill built here in 1878–79 during the Mammoth gold boom. (Nadeau, *Ghost Towns,* 215–16.) (INF)

Mill Creek   *Tuolumne Meadows 15', Matterhorn Peak 15', Bodie 15'*
William O. Lundy operated a sawmill in the canyon sometime before 1879. The name is on the Wheeler Survey atlas sheet 56D, 1878–79. The "South Fork," flowing down through Lake Canyon (on the *Bodie* 15' quad), was first named in 1958. (INF)

Mill Creek   *Fales Hot Springs 15', Chris Flat 7½'*
On the 1879 plat, and in the field notes, "Boardman's Sawmill" is shown in

secs. 6 and 7, T. 7 N., R. 23 E. There are also a flume and a tramway along the creek. William Boardman patented 160 acres in secs. 6 and 7 in 1890, as well as 120 acres in secs. 29 and 30 in 1883. (TNF)

Mill Flat *Patterson Mtn. 15'*
Mill Flat Creek *Giant Forest 15', Patterson Mtn. 15'*
In 1889 the Sanger Lumber Company built two sawmills at "Millwood"—a place that no longer exists—and a 54-mile flume to Sanger. The flume paralleled Mill Flat Creek part of the way; both the creek and the flume reached the Kings River at Mill Flat. (See Johnston, *Redwoods,* and *Whistles.*) (SeNF)

Miller Crossing *Devils Postpile 15', Cattle Mtn. 7½'*
Named for William C. Miller, a pioneer sheepman. (SiNF history files.) (SiNF)

Miller Lake *Tuolumne Meadows 15'*
"I returned to the lake, and imagine my surprise to find the detachment in camp, horses unsaddled, mules unpacked, and the cook-fire blazing merrily away. The man to whom I had spoken about camping had taken my remark about its being a good camping-place in real earnest, and had told the others that my orders were to stay there until next day. His name was Miller, and, naming the lake in honor of him, I decided to remain there until the next morning." (Lt. N. F. McClure in *SCB* 1, no. 5, Jan. 1895: 174.) (YNP)

Mills, Mount (13,451–13,468); **Mills Creek, Lake** *Mt. Abbot 15' and 7½'*
Upper Mills Creek Lake (11,167); **Lower Mills Creek Lake** (10,851)
Darius Ogden Mills (1825–1910), banker and philanthropist; founder and namer of the city of Millbrae; founder of the Carson and Colorado Railroad; a charter member of the Sierra Club. (*Historic Spots,* 119, 305, 403.) The mountain was named at the suggestion of the Sierra Club after Mills' death. The mountain and creek were named on the first edition of the *Mt. Goddard* 30' map, 1912. "Upper" and "Lower Mills Creek Lake" were named in 1943 by William A. Dill of the DFG. (DFG survey.) (Peak, SiNF, INF; Mills Lake, INF; others, SiNF)

Millys Foot Pass (over 12,240) *Mount Whitney 15', Mt. Brewer 7½'*
First crossed in July 1953 by Mildred Jentsch and Sylvia Kershaw. (*Climber's Guide,* 1956, 229.) The name was added to the 15-minute map, 1956, by the USGS because it was in common use. (KCNP, SNP)

Minarets; Minaret Lake, Mine *Devils Postpile 15', Mt. Ritter 7½'*
Minaret Creek *Devils Postpile 15', Mt. Ritter 7½', Mammoth Mtn. 7½'*
Minaret Falls, Summit *Devils Postpile 15', Mammoth Mtn. 7½'*
"To the south of [Mount Ritter] are some grand pinnacles of granite, very lofty and apparently inaccessible, to which we gave the name of 'the Minarets.' " (Whitney, *The Yosemite Book,* 1868, 98.)
Seventeen of the Minarets have been given unofficial names, for those who first climbed them. The first one climbed was "Michael Minaret," on September 6, 1923. "With nothingness on one side and a sheer wall on the other, I had a feeling as I crossed the ledge that the wall might give me a little shove on the

shoulder and tip me into nothingness." (Charles W. Michael, *SCB* 12, no. 1, 1924: 31.)

Only "Minaret Creek" was on atlas sheet 56D, 1878–79. "Minarets" was on the Hoffmann and Gardiner map, 1863–67, and all other maps after sheet 56D. The other features first were named on the 15-minute quad, 1953. The Minaret Mine operated from 1928 to 1930. (Smith, 59–60.) (Minarets, SiNF, INF; others, INF)

Miner Creek   *Camp Nelson 15'*
James L. Miner patented 160 acres in sec. 7, T. 21 S., R. 31 E. in 1888. (SeNF)

Mineral King, Mineral Peak (11,550)   *Mineral King 15'*
"The first mine located in the Mineral King region was discovered in 1872. By 1879 it was a large mining settlement. . . . It was at first called Beulah, but when a mining district was organized there it was pronounced to be the king of mineral districts and given the name of Mineral King." (Farquhar: G. W. Stewart.) "Beulah" is a biblical reference, supposed to mean "the border of heaven" or "the land of promise." (*Los Tulares*, no. 66, Sept. 1965: 1–4.) Mineral King was named on the first edition of the *Kaweah* 30' map, 1904, and the peak on the fifth edition, 1934. The peak was sometimes called "The Matterhorn," since it resembles that peak from certain angles. (SNP files.) (SNP)

Mineral Lakes, Creek   *Mineral King 15'*
Named in 1956 by Elden H. Vestal of the DFG. (USGS.) (SNP)

Miningtown Meadow   *Huntington Lake 15', Dogtooth Peak 7½'*
Thomas Edward Bacon laid out "Miningtown" as a proposed silver mining town in 1879—but nothing ever came of it. (SiNF history files.) The name appears on the *Kaiser* 30' maps, 1904–50. On the 15-minute quad, the name is about a mile too far to the east. It correctly applies to the meadow area just southeast of sec. 14, T. 9 S., R. 26 E. (USGS quad report.) (SiNF)

Minnie Lake   *Mt. Abbot 15', Graveyard Peak 7½'*
Named in 1943 by William A. Dill of the DFG. "Minnie" is diminutive for *minnow*. This is one of the smaller lakes in the Minnow Creek basin. (DFG survey.) (SiNF)

Minster, The (over 12,240)   *Mount Whitney 15', Mt. Brewer 7½'*
Named by David Starr Jordan in 1899. "A gothic crag lying to the north of Stanford Brook and adjoining Deerhorn Mountain." (*SCB* 3, no. 1, Jan. 1900: 110.) "Stanford Brook" was Jordan's name for the stream flowing west from the basin south of Deerhorn Mountain; it is not on any map. (KCNP)

Mirror Lake   *Mount Whitney 15' and 7½'*
This small lake on the Mt. Whitney trail is one of the many Sierra features whose names have no specific origin. It was in common use in the 1930s or earlier, and was added to the 15-minute quad for that reason. (INF)

Mirror Lake (4,094)   *Yosemite 15', Yosemite Valley 1:24,000*
"This lake was so named by Mr. C. H. Spencer, of Utica, New York (one of my comrades). . . . The Indian name for the lake was Wai-ack, meaning the rock water, because of its nearness to Half Dome, and the perfect reflection of the rocks of peaks adjacent." (Bunnell, *Report*, 1889–90, 11.)
". . . we arrived at Lake *Ah-wi-yah*, so named and known by the Indians, but which has been newly christened by American visitors 'Lake Hiawatha,' 'Mirror Lake,' and several others, which, though pretty enough, are equally commonplace and unsuitable." (Hutchings, *Illustrated* 4, no. 5, Nov. 1859: 196.) Later on, Hutchings seems to have forgotten what he wrote in 1859. ". . . our explorations were limited to the valley, terminating at Mirror Lake— so named by our party." (Hutchings, *In the Heart*, 91.)
Whitney spelled the Indian name *Waiya*. (*Yosemite Guide-Book*, 1870, 17.) Powers has it as *A-wai'-a*. He said—in conjunction with Vernal and Nevada falls—that the word means, simply, a lake or body of water. (Powers, 365.) It is preserved in the name **Ahwiyah Point.**
". . . Lake Ah-wi-yah, known now, thanks to some American importer of looking-glasses, as Mirror Lake." (Jackson, 107.) (YNP)

Mist Falls   *Marion Peak 15'*
An obvious descriptive name, origin unknown. J. N. LeConte called it "Mist Fall" in 1890. (*A Summer*, 53.) (KCNP)

Mist Lake (10,931)   *Mt. Abbot 15' and 7½'*
Named by Bob Ehlers of the DFG on July 29, 1952, because there was a heavy mist at the time. (DFG survey.) (SiNF)

Mist Trail   *Yosemite Valley 1:24,000*
"Leaping from stone to stone, poising on slippery logs under water, clinging to Murphy's hand as to a life-preserver, blinded, choked, stifled, drenched, down into that canyon, through that steaming spray, we went. It was impossible to keep one's eyes open wide for more than half a second at a time. The spray drove and pelted, making great gusts of wind by its own weight as it fell. It seemed to whirl round and round, and wrap us, as if trying to draw us down into the black depths." (Jackson, 123.)
Although the name is an old one, it did not appear on the map until 1958. (YNP)

Mitchell Meadow   *Mineral King 15'*
Hyman Mitchell of White River, father of Susman Mitchell. (Farquhar: J. B. Agnew.) The name appears on the third edition of the *Kaweah* 30' map, 1921. (SNP)

Mitchell Peak (10,365)   *Triple Divide Peak 15'*
For Susman Mitchell of Visalia. (Farquhar: G. W. Stewart.) The name is on the first *Tehipite* 30' map, 1905. (KCNP, SeNF)

Miter, The (12,770)   *Mount Whitney 15' and 7½'*
A name suggested by Chester Versteeg in the 1930s because the mountain's

shape looks like a bishop's headdress. (SC papers in BL.) The name appears on the *Mt. Whitney* 30' map in 1937. (SNP)

Big Moccasin Lake, Little Moccasin Lake   *Mt. Abbot 15',*
Mt. Hilgard 7½'
Named in August 1951 by Elden H. Vestal of the DFG for the common American Indian footwear. (Heyward Moore, *FPP* 26, no. 2, Summer 1984: 5–6.) (SiNF)

Mogul Canyon, Peak (7,583)   *Topaz Lake 15', Heenan Lake 7½'*
Mogul was a mining camp in the 1860s and 1870s, located two miles north of Monitor. (See **Monitor Creek, Pass;** Nadeau, *Ghost Towns*, 219; *Bulletin* 193, 92.) The word "mogul" implies something important or powerful—in this case, the indication is wealth. "Mogul Dist." and "Mogul Creek" appear on Theron Reed's map, 1864. The Wheeler Survey atlas sheet 56B has "Mogul Peak" and "Mogul (abd.)." By the time of the first *Markleeville* 30' map, 1891, Mogul had a single building. The canyon was first named on the 15-minute quad. Mogul Peak was called "Markleeville LO" (lookout) on the 15-minute quad, but the name has been reinstated on the 7½-minute quad. (TNF)

Mokelumne River (North Fork)   *Silver Lake 15', Markleeville 15',*
Mokelumne Peak 7½', Pacific Valley 7½', Ebbetts Pass 7½'
Mokelumne Peak (9,334–9,332)   *Silver Lake 15', Mokelumne Peak 7½'*
Mokelumne Tetons   *Mokelumne Peak 7½'*
The names derives from a Plains Miwok village near the present town of Lockeford in San Joaquin County. It was applied to the river in 1841 by the United States Exploring Expedition under Charles Wilkes. (See Gudde, *Place Names*, 207.) On Wilkes' *Map of Upper Calfornia . . . 1841,* the name is spelled *Mogneles*. The modern spelling was first used by Frémont. (Frémont, *Memoir*, 16.)

"Mokelumne Peak" may have been named by the Wheeler Survey; it is on atlas sheet 56B, 1876–77. On the 15-minute quad, Mokelumne Tetons is the rugged northwest-southeast ridge just over a mile south of Mokelumne Peak. (StNF)

Molybdenite Creek   *Matterhorn Peak 15', Fales Hot Springs 15'*
Named for a prospect and outcrop of molybdenite. (Maule.) The name is on the first *Bridgeport* 30' map, 1911. In the 1884 GLO surveyor's field notes it is called "East Fort of East Fork of West Walker River." (TNF)

Monache Mountain (9,410), **Meadows**   *Monache Mtn. 15'*
Monache Creek   *Olancha 15', Monache Mtn. 15'*
"Monache Peak is named for the Monachi Indians, usually called Mono." (Kroeber, 48; also see **Mono Lake,** etc.) "It appears that Monachi, like most of the names of the Yokuts for their own or other tribes, no longer possesses a determinable meaning." (Kroeber, 49.)

The residents of Owens Valley petitioned the State legislature in February 1864 to create a new county south of Mono County and name it Monache.

(Chalfant, *Inyo*, 215.) That didn't come about, but it was the first attempt to use the word as a geographic name. The name "Monatchy Meadows" is on the von Leicht-Craven map, 1874. Boyd used "Monache" for both meadows and mountain in 1889. (Boyd, *A Climb.*) All three features had the name on the first *Olancha* 30' map, 1907, surveyed in 1905. The creek is also on the *Olancha* 15-minute quad. (INF)

Monarch Divide   *Tehipite Dome 15'*
Originally called "Dyke Ridge" by the Whitney Survey. "Just at the junction of the forks [Middle and South forks of the Kings River], the end of the divide is crossed by a broad red stripe. . . . This, which seemed to be a great dyke of volcanic rock, but which was afterwards found to be a vein of granite, led to giving this divide the name of 'Dyke Ridge.' " (Whitney, *Geology*, 370. See **Grand Dike.**) The name "Monarch Divide" was probably given by the USGS during the survey for the *Tehipite* 30' map; it is on the first edition, 1905. (SeNF)

Monarch Lakes, Creek   *Mineral King 15'*
"These two beautiful lakes lie at the foot of Miner's [Sawtooth] Peak." (Elliott, *History*, 235.) The lakes are named on the first *Kaweah* 30' map, 1904; the creek on the 15-minute quad, 1956. (SNP)

Monitor Creek   *Topaz Lake 15', Heenan Lake 7½'*
Monitor Pass (8,320)   *Topaz Lake 15' and 7½'*
The town of Monitor was named in 1863 for the ironclad *Monitor,* which fought the *Merrimac* at the Battle of Hampton Roads, March 9, 1862. (Clark, *Mines,* 22.) The district flourished during the 1860s and 1870s, at one time had a population of 2,000, and had a post office from 1863 to 1888. (*Bulletin* 193, 92; *Post Offices.* See also **Loope.**)
"Monitor Dist." and "Monitor Creek" are on Theron Reed's map, 1864. The pass was not named until the 15-minute quad, 1956.
Joseph LeConte had his horse shoed in Monitor in 1870. (LeConte, *Ramblings,* 129.) (TNF)

Mono Pass (10,604), **Lake, Craters, Dome** (10,614)   *Mono Craters 15'*
"Mono County and Lake are named after a wide-spread division of Shoshonean Indians on both slopes of the Southern Sierra Nevada. . . . By their Yokuts neighbors they are called Monachi. . . . The Yokuts word for 'flies' was *monoi, monai,* or *monoyi.*" (Kroeber, 48–49; see also **Monache Mountain,** etc.) "If we assume that this word forms the stem of *monachi,* it is quite certain that the name means 'fly-people' and is quite properly applied. On the shore of the otherwise barren lake are found countless millions of the pupae of a fly. . . . These pupae were not only the favorite food of these Indians, but they used them for trading with the neighboring tribes. . . . The conclusion is forced upon us that the Yokuts called these Indians *Monachi* because their wealth consisted of flies." (*CFQ* 4, no. 1, Jan. 1945: 90 ff.) "The worms are dried in the sun, the shell rubbed off, when a yellowish kernel remains, like a small yellow grain of rice. This is oily, very nutritious, and not unpleasant to the taste, and under the name of *koo-chah-bee* forms a very important article of food. The Indians gave

me some; it does not taste bad, and if one were ignorant of its origin, it would make fine soup. Gulls, ducks, snipe, frogs, and Indians fatten on it." (Brewer, *Up and Down,* 417.)

The first use of the word as a geographic name was by Lt. Tredwell Moore's party in July 1852, calling the lake "Lake Mono, after the tribe of Indians that inhabited that section." (*Daily Alta California,* Aug. 26, 1852, 2.) The lake and pass are shown on Trask's maps of 1853.

The craters were named in the 1880s. "By far the grandest display of quaternary and post-quaternary volcanic action within the Mono basin is furnished by the Mono Craters. I have given this name to the slightly crescent-shaped range of volcanic cones which commences at the southern margin of Lake Mono and extends about ten miles southward." (Russell, *Quaternary,* 378.) "Mono Dome" probably was named by the USGS during the 1898–99 survey for the *Mt. Lyell* 30' map; it is on the first edition, 1901. (INF)

Mono Creek, Pass (over 12,040), **Rock** (11,554–11,555)

Mt. Abbot 15' and 7½'
Mono Divide   *Mt. Abbot 15' and 7½', Mt. Hilgard 7½'*
The Brewer party of the Whitney Survey crossed the pass on August 2, 1864; none of the "Mono" features was named at that time. (Brewer, *Up and Down,* 539–40.) Theodore S. Solomons used the name "Mono Creek" in 1894, but does not indicate that he named it. (*SCB* 1, no. 6, May 1895: 226.) Some if not all of the other features probably were named by the USGS during the 1907–09 survey for the *Mt. Goddard* 30' map; all are named on the first edition, 1912. (Pass, SiNF, INF; others, SiNF)

Mono Creek, Meadow, Crossing, Hot Springs   *Kaiser Peak 15',*
Mt. Givens 7½'
The creek is the same as the one in the previous entry. All the features except the hot springs were named on the first *Kaiser* 30' map, 1904. The springs showed up on the fourth edition, 1923, as "Lower Hot Springs." (SiNF)

Mono Meadow   *Yosemite 15'*
The Hoffmann and Gardiner map of 1863–67 shows "Old Mono Trail" passing through the meadow. The meadow was named on the first *Yosemite* 30' map, 1897. (YNP)

Monroe Meadows   *Yosemite 15'*
Fort Monroe   *Yosemite Valley 1:24,000*
George F. Monroe was a black man who drove stage and worked as a guide for the Washburn brothers during the 1880s. The "fort" was a stage station on the old Wawona Road; it had no military connection. "It is reported that George Monroe had a flair for army life and was always talking about it, hence the name *Fort.*" (*YNN* 34, no. 1, Jan. 1955: 6.)

The site of "Fort Monroe" was named "The Hermitage" on the Wheeler Survey map of 1883. It had the name of Fort Monroe on all the *Yosemite* 30' maps, 1897–1951. It is not named on the 15-minute quad. It was named on the *Yosemite Valley* maps, 1907–70, but is not on the latest edition, 1977. It is located above the east end of the Wawona Tunnel, just where the Pohono Trail changes direction from southwest to east. Monroe Meadows was first named on the 15-minute quad. (YNP)

Montgomery Meadow *Dardanelles Cone 15', Donnell Lake 7½'*
Probably named for R. L. Montgomery of Cooperstown, who ran cattle and horses in the Dardanelle range allotment beginning about 1912. (StNF files.) The name is incorrectly located on the 15-minute quad. It belongs where it is on the 7½-minute quad, in the NE¼ of sec. 19, T. 6 N., R. 19 E. (StNF)

Monument Ridge *Matterhorn Peak 15'*
Possibly named by the USGS during the 1905–09 survey for the *Bridgeport* 30' map; it is on the first edition, 1911. (TNF)

Moonlight Lake *Mt. Goddard 15', Mt. Darwin 7½'*
Named by John Schober. (Art Schober.) (INF)

Moose Lake (10,530) *Triple Divide Peak 15'*
Named by Hale Tharp. Old-timers called big mountain bucks "moose-deer." (Col. John R. White, 1923, SNP files.) (SNP)

Moraine Ridge, Meadows, Creek *Triple Divide Peak 15'*
Probably named by the USGS during the 1903 survey for the *Tehipite* 30' map; all are on the first edition, 1905. A Sierra Club party described the ridge in 1906, but apparently didn't know it had been named. "To our left as we started was a lateral moraine, one of the largest to be seen in the Sierra, its top a thousand feet or more above the river and two or three miles long." (*SCB* 6, no. 3, June 1907: 156.) The ridge's name disappeared on the maps from 1929 to 1947, but reappeared on the 15-minute quad, 1956. (KCNP)

Moraine Dome (8,015) *Merced Peak 15', Yosemite Valley 1:24,000*
"Named for the great spiral of glacial moraine deposited on its south side." (*YNN* 34, no. 1, Jan. 1955: 12.) It appears on the first USGS map of Yosemite Valley, 1907. (YNP)

Moraine Flat *Tuolumne Meadows 15'*
Probably named by the USGS during the 1898–99 survey for the *Mt. Lyell* 30' map; it is on the first edition, 1901. (YNP)

Moraine Lake (9,290) *Kern Peak 15'*
Named in July 1897. "Moraine Lake has no visible outlet that I could discover. It was formed in the bowl of a great, gravelly, porous moraine, hence the name we gave it seemed particularly appropriate." (William R. Dudley in *SCB* 4, no. 4, June 1903: 306; also *MWCJ* 1, no. 1, May 1902: 13; on Dudley's sketch map in *SCB* 2, no. 3, Jan. 1898, plate XXV.) (SNP)

Moraine Mountain (9,754), **Meadow** *Merced Peak 15'*
The mountain may have been named by the USGS during the 1898–99 survey for the *Mt. Lyell* 30' map; it is on the first edition, 1901. The meadow is named on the third edition, 1910. (YNP)

Moran Point *Yosemite 15', Yosemite Valley 1:24,000*
The namer is unknown. Thomas Moran (1837–1926), born in England, came to the US in 1844 with his parents. His first foray into the West was with

the Hayden expedition to Yellowstone in 1871. He became famous for his large paintings of Yellowstone and the Grand Canyon. The point is on the old Four-Mile Trail, just east of Union Point. The name appears on the fifth edition of the *Yosemite Valley* map, 1929. (YNP)

Morgan, Mount (13,748); **Morgan Creek; Upper** and **Lower Morgan Lake**   *Mt. Tom 15', Mt. Morgan 7½'*
Morgan Pass   *Mt. Tom 15', Mt. Abbot 15' and 7½'*
  The mountain was named in 1878 by the Wheeler Survey for one of its members, J. H. Morgan, of Alabama. (Gudde, *Place Names*, 211; *SCB* 4, no. 4, June 1903: 290; USGS *Bulletin* 310, 161.) The mountain and creek are named on the first *Mt. Goddard* 30' map, 1912. The other names first appear on the 15-minute quads. (INF)

Moro Rock (6,725), **Creek**   *Giant Forest 15'*
  "Mr. Swanson of Three Rivers in the sixties of the last century had a blue roan mustang—the color that the Mexicans call *moro*. . . . This moro pony of Swanson's often ranged up under the rock and they called it 'Moro's Rock.' " (Farquhar: letter from Col. John R. White, 1923.) The first ascent of the rock was made in 1861 by Hale Tharp and George and John Swanson, the latter a small boy. (Fry and White, 182.) (SNP)

Morrison, Mount (3,742 m.–12,268)   *Mt. Morrison 15', Convict Lake 7½'*
  Robert Morrison, a member of a posse pursuing escaped convicts, was killed by one of them near Convict Lake on September 24, 1871. (Chalfant, *Inyo*, 251–52. See **Convict Lake**.) (INF)

Moses Mountain (9,331)   *Mineral King 15'*
  One version has it that the mountain was named during a fishing trip many years ago when an elderly member of the party was nicknamed "Moses." (Farquhar: Versteeg.) The other version is that the government surveyor who named Mount Maggie was named Moses Peabody, with the implication that he named this mountain for himself. (Otter, 156; see also **Maggie Mountain**.) (SeNF)

Moss Spring   *Yosemite 15', Yosemite Valley 1:24,000*
  ". . . the many-voiced, plant-garnished Moss Springs, and Fern Springs, gushing out at our side, temptingly invite us to drink of their transparent and ice-tempered waters." (Hutchings, *In the Heart*, 402.) The name is on the Wheeler Survey map of 1883. (YNP)

Mott Lake (over 10,040)   *Mt. Abbot 15', Graveyard Peak 7½'*
  Ernest Julian Mott (1868–1925), a conservationist, mountain explorer, and long-time member of the Sierra Club. The name was proposed by a group of Sierra Club members in 1927. (*SCB* 13, no. 1, Feb. 1928: 85.) It appears on the fourth edition of the *Mt. Goddard* 30' map, 1928. (SiNF)

Muah Mountain (11,016)   *Olancha 15'*
  "The location of the mountain and the sound of the word indicate a Shoshonean origin, probably Mono." (Kroeber, 49.) (INF)

Muglers Meadow; Mugler Creek   *Shuteye Peak 15'*
The meadow was the base camp of Christopher Mugler, a pioneer sheepman. He was born in France in 1822, came to New York when young, emigrated to Chile, emigrated again to San Francisco in 1851, and was in this area as early as 1852. (SiNF history files.) (SiNF)

Muir Gorge   *Hetch Hetchy Reservoir 15'*
John Muir (1838–1914), "born in Scotland, reared in the University of Wisconsin, by final choice a Californian, widely traveled observer of the world we dwell in, man of science and of letters, friend and protector of Nature, uniquely gifted to interpret unto other men her mind and ways." (Benjamin Ide Wheeler, President of the University of California, conferring the degree of Doctor of Laws on Muir, May 14, 1913.)

Muir was one of the four founders of the Sierra Club, and its first president, 1892–1914. He was the foremost conservationist of his time, a mountain explorer and exponent of the outdoor life. "John Muir was not a 'dreamer,' but a practical man, a faithful citizen, a scientific observer, a writer of enduring power, with vision, poetry, courage in a contest, a heart of gold, and a spirit pure and fine." (Robert Underwood Johnson in *SCB* 10, no. 1, Jan. 1916: 15. See that issue of *SCB,* 1–77.)

The gorge, in the canyon of the Tuolumne River, was named in 1894. "We named this gorge Muir Gorge, after Mr. John Muir, the first man to go through the cañon." (R. M. Price in *SCB* 1, no. 6, May 1895: 206.) (YNP)

Muir Grove   *Giant Forest 15'*
Named by R. B. Marshall, USGS, in 1909. (Farquhar: Marshall.) The name appears on the second edition of the *Tehipite* 30' map, 1912. On the first edition, 1905, it is simply called "Big Trees." (SNP)

Muir Lake   *Olancha 15', Lone Pine 15', Mt. Langley 7½'*
The name first appeared on the *Olancha* 15-minute quad, 1956. (INF)

Muir, Mount (4,271 m.–14,015)   *Mount Whitney 15' and 7½'*
The mountain was named by Alexander G. McAdie of the US Weather Bureau. (Farquhar: J. N. LeConte.) The name is on the first edition of the *Mt. Whitney* 30' map, 1907. (SNP, INF)

Muir Pass (over 11,960–11,955), **Hut**   *Mt. Goddard 15' and 7½'*
The pass was named by R. B. Marshall, USGS, and appears on the first *Mt. Goddard* 30' map, 1912. It was first crossed with pack stock by a party led by George R. Davis, USGS, in 1907. (*SCB* 7, no. 1, Jan. 1909: 4.)

The hut (not named on the maps) was dedicated in 1933. "As his work is destined to carry on through the years, so, the hope was expressed, this shelter, dedicated to him, may likewise serve for an untold period of time to offer protection and safety to storm-bound travelers." (*SCB* 19, no. 3, June 1934: 7.) (KCNP)

Muley Hole   *Huntington Lake 15', Nelson Mtn. 7½'*
A small basin where horses and mules gather to feed. (BGN name report.) The name first appears on the 15-minute quad. (SiNF)

Mulkey Meadows, Creek, Pass					*Olancha 15'*
Cyrus Mulkey, sheriff of Inyo County, 1871–74. (Chalfant, *Inyo*, 413; *SCB*
1, no. 1, Jan. 1893: 4.) (INF)

Munger Peak (12,076)					*Marion Peak 15'*
For Maynard Munger (1902–1972), local civic and business leader who was
instrumental in protecting and preserving Kings Canyon, Sequoia, and
Yosemite national parks. (BGN decision, 1978.) The peak is not named on the
existing maps. It is half a mile northwest of Goat Mountain. (KCNP)

Murdock Lake					*Tower Peak 15'*
Named by N. F. McClure in 1895 for William C. Murdock of the California
State Board of Fish Commissioners. (Farquhar: McClure.) It was shown on
McClure's map of 1896 and Benson's map of 1897, but not again after that until
the fifth edition of the *Dardanelles* 30' map, 1939. (YNP)

Muriel Lake (11,336–11,328), **Peak** (12,937–12,942)					*Mt. Goddard 15',*
						Mt. Darwin 7½'
The origin of "Muriel Lake" is a mystery, but it was probably named by
someone with the USGS during the 1907–09 survey for the *Mt. Goddard* 30'
map; it is on the first edition, 1912. The peak was named after the lake by Hervey
Voge, who made the first ascent on July 8, 1933. (Letter, David Brower to C. A.
Ecklund, USGS, March 7, 1951.) (KCNP, SiNF)

Muro Blanco					*Marion Peak 15', Mt. Pinchot 15' and 7½'*
Spanish for "white wall," an appropriate descriptive name for the northwest
side of Arrow Ridge. The name probably was applied by the USGS during the
1903 survey for the *Tehipite* 30' map; it is on the first edition, 1905. (KCNP)

Murphy Creek					*Tuolumne Meadows 15'*
Sometime before 1882 John L. Murphy built a cabin on the north shore of
Tenaya Lake—before the construction of the original Tioga Road—and catered
to travelers and campers in summer. (Robert F. Uhte, "Yosemite's Pioneer
Cabins," *SCB* 36, no. 5, May 1951: 56–57.) On the 1883 GLO plat there is a
"house" marked midway along the north shore of the lake, and at the west end is
written "Murphy's Enclosure." Murphy patented 160 acres in secs. 20 and 21,
T. 1 S., R. 23 E. in 1890.
		"But one may wish that Mr. Watkins had been denied his mountain, and Mr.
Murphy his dome if it were only for the sake of poets yet to be. What will they do
with such monsters." (Chase, 31.) Murphy did not have a nearby dome named
for him, but wound up with a creek. The name was on the first *Mt. Lyell* 30' map,
1901. (YNP)

Nance Peak (over 8,400)					*Pinecrest 15'*
Almost certainly named in 1910 by Major William W. Forsyth, for Colonel
John T. Nance, professor of military science at the University of California,
1904–27. The peak overlooks Edyth Lake, named by Forsyth for Nance's
daughter. "Nance Peak" appears on the third edition of the *Dardanelles* 30'
map, 1912. (YNP)

Neall Lake   *Hetch Hetchy Reservoir 15'*
Named by H. C. Benson for John Mitchell Neall, first lieutenant on duty with
the Fourth Cavalry in Yosemite National Park, 1892–97. (Farquhar: Benson.)
The lake was called "Rodgers Lake" on the first two editions of the *Yosemite* 30'
map; changed to "Neall Lake" in 1903. (YNP)

Needham Mountain (12,467)   *Mineral King 15'*
Named by W. F. Dean for James Carson Needham (1864–1942) of
Modesto, member of Congress from California, 1899–1913. (Farquhar: G. W.
Stewart.) Needham accompanied an inspection party on a trip to Mount
Whitney in 1899. (*MWCJ*, no. 2, 1903: 75–78.) (SNP)

Neelle Lake   *Mt. Abbot 15' and 7½'*
The name of this lake has been misspelled since it appeared on the 15-minute
quad, 1953. It was named "Needle Lake" in 1944 by William A. Dill of the
DFG because of a nearby needlelike spire. (DFG survey.) (SiNF)

Negit Lake   *Mt. Abbot 15', Mt. Hilgard 7½'*
Named by Elden H. Vestal of the DFG in August 1951; he said the word is
Piute for "night" or "darkness." Israel C. Russell, who named Negit Island in
Mono Lake in 1882, wrote that the word is Mono Indian for "blue-winged
goose." Other students of the Piute and Mono languages also dispute Vestal's
interpretation. (Heyward Moore, *FPP* 26, no. 2, Summer 1984: 6.) (SiNF)

Neil Lake (10,624)   *Mt. Abbot 15', Florence Lake 7½'*
Named in 1948 for Neil Perkins by Scott M. Soule and Jack Criqui of the
DFG. Perkins was a ranger with the US Forest Service from 1924 or 1925 to
1947. (Heyward Moore, *FPP* 25, no. 5, Spring 1984: 11.) (SiNF)

Nelder Grove, Creek   *Bass Lake 15'*
The first whites to see the grove may have been some members of the
Mariposa Battalion. (Eccleston, 66, 75.) Galen Clark discovered—or
rediscovered—the grove in the fall of 1857. (Sargent, *Clark,* 15.) The grove was
at first named "Fresno Grove" because it was in Fresno County. Madera
County—where the grove is—was not created until 1893.
John A. Nelder, a gold-miner of 1849, settled in the grove when he gave up
mining. John Muir encountered him there in 1875. "The Fresno Big Trees
covered an area of about four square miles, and while wandering about . . . I
came suddenly on a handsome log cabin . . . Strolling forward . . . I found an
old, weary-eyed, speculative, gray-haired man on a bark stool by the door,
reading a book. . . . The name of my hermit friend is John A. Nelder, a fine kind
man, who in going into the woods has at last gone home; for he loves nature truly,
and realizes that these last shadowy days with scarce a glint of gold in them are
the best of all." (Muir, *Parks,* 289–90.)
Nelder homesteaded 156 acres in secs. 5 and 6, T. 6 S., R. 22 E. in 1886.
(SiNF)

Camp Nelson; Nelson Creek   *Camp Nelson 15'*
John Milton Nelson (1830–1909) came to California from Illinois in 1850.
He settled on the land that was later named for him in 1886, and built a cabin. He

158PLACE NAMES OF THE SIERRA NEVADA

built his first hotel in the 1890s, and gradually developed a tourist resort. (*Los Tulares*, no. 73, June 1967: 1–4.)

Nelson homesteaded 160 acres in secs. 33 and 34, T. 20 S., R. 31 E. in 1901. On the same day, George D. Nelson homesteaded the NE¼ of sec. 34, and Emma N. Smith (formerly E. N. Nelson) homesteaded 160 acres in sec. 33. (SeNF)

Nelson Lake (9,636)   *Tuolumne Meadows 15'*
William Henry (Billy) Nelson (1873–1952), a colorful early-day ranger in Yosemite National Park. He served from 1917 to 1936, and 1943 to 1945. He escorted many celebrated visitors, including King Albert of Belgium. In July 1934 he accompanied Eleanor Roosevelt on a pack trip to the Young Lakes, and provided her with a hot-water bottle to keep her warm on the cold nights at 10,000 feet. (Bingaham, *Guardians,* 96.) (YNP)

Nelson Mountain (10,220–10,218), **Lakes**   *Huntington Lake 15',*
                                                    Nelson Mtn. 7½'
Nelson Creek   *Nelson Mtn. 7½', Courtright Reservoir 7½'*
Thomas P. Nelson was a sheepman in the early years, and with W. W. Shipp controlled the Laurel Creek and Bear Creek localities. (Winchell, 157–58.) The mountain was named on the first *Kaiser* 30' map, 1904. (SiNF)

Nevada Fall   *Yosemite 15', Yosemite Valley 1:24,000*
Lafayette H. Bunnell suggested the name when the fall was discovered in 1851. "The Nevada Fall was so called because it was the nearest to the Sierra Nevada, and because the name was sufficiently indicative of a wintry companion for our spring (Vernal Fall). The white, foaming water, as it dashed down Yo-wy-we from the snowy mountains, represented to my mind a vast avalanche of snow." (Bunnell, *Discovery,* 1880, 205.)

"Yo-wai-yi, Nevada Fall. In this word also we detect the root of *awaia"*— meaning a lake, or body of water. (Powers, 364.)

"A literal interpretation of the Indian name, Yo-wi-we, could not be tolerated, Yo-wi-we meaning the 'Squirming or Worm Fall,' from a twist given the water by a curving rock upon which the water strikes during its descent." (Bunnell, *Report,* 1889–90, 11.) (YNP)

New Army Pass (over 12,320)   *Olancha 15'*
Derived from "Army Pass." A trail was built over this route in 1955 to bypass the Army Pass trail, which usually is snow-clogged until late summer. (SNP, INF)

Newcomb, Mount (4,091 m.–13,410)   *Mount Whitney 15' and 7½'*
Simon Newcomb (1835–1909), born in Nova Scotia, came to the US in 1853, and became a world-renowned astronomer and political economist. He published tables of motion of stars, planets, and the moon, which are used by navigators around the world.

The name was proposed by the Sierra Club. (SC papers in BL.) It first appeared on the *Mt. Whitney* 30' map in 1937. (SNP)

Nine Lake Basin   *Triple Divide Peak 15'*
Probably named by the USGS during the 1903 survey for the *Tehipite* 30'
map; it is on the first edition, 1905. It was first used in print by a Sierra Club
party in 1908. (*SCB* 7, no. 1, Jan. 1909: 35.) (SNP)

Nipple, The (9,342–9,340)   *Markleeville 15', Carson Pass 7½'*
"Descriptive—stands out from adjacent peaks." (Maule.) Either it was
named by the USGS during the 1889 survey for the *Markleeville* 30' map, or—
as Gudde suggests (*Place Names*, 222)—it was already local usage. (TNF)

Noble Canyon, Lake   *Markleeville 15', Ebbetts Pass 7½'*
"I visited the Noble Canon Mine, first opened in 1863, in company with Mr.
Ford, one of the owners." (Arthur I. Conkling, Wheeler Survey *Report of 1878*,
170.) "Noble Mine" is on Theron Reed's map, 1864. On the 15-minute quad
these names were spelled "Nobel." They were changed to "Noble" by a BGN
decision in 1979. Nobel Creek (in the canyon) was named on the 15-minute
quad. (TNF)

Norman Clyde Peak (4,223 m.–13,920), **Glacier**   *Big Pine 15',*
                                                              Split Mtn. 7½'
Named for Norman Clyde, one of America's leading mountaineers. In 1930
he traversed the glacier and made the first ascent of the peak. (BGN decisions in
1973 and 1974.) Hervey Voge first proposed the name for the peak in 1939. (SC
papers in BL.) The BGN does not approve place names for living persons, and
thus could not make this one official until after Clyde died in 1972. The features
are not named on the *Big Pine* 15' quad. The peak is on the crest, 0.4 mile
northwest of Middle Palisade, and the glacier is just north of the peak. (Peak,
KCNP, INF; glacier, INF)

North Dome (7,542)   *Hetch Hetchy Reservoir 15',*
                                             Yosemite Valley 1:24,000
Named by the Mariposa Battalion in 1851; it was across the valley from
"South Dome," an early name for Half Dome. "The dome was known as To-co-
yah, meaning a round basket used in gathering acorns." (Bunnell, *Report*,
1889–90, 11.) "To-ko-ye, North Dome. This rock represents Tisseyak's (Half
Dome) husband. On one side of him is a huge, conical rock, which the Indians
call the acorn-basket that his wife threw at him in anger." (Powers, 364. See
Basket Dome and **Half Dome**.)
The name is on the King and Gardiner map of 1865. Two other early names
for the dome were "Capitol Rock" and "Round Tower." (YNP)

North Dome (8,717)   *Marion Peak 15'*
Named by John Muir in July 1875 on his first visit to what he termed the
"Kings River Yosemite." He named a number of features on both sides of Kings
River Canyon after their counterparts in Yosemite Valley. (San Francisco *Daily
Evening Bulletin*, Aug. 13, 1875; also in *SCB* 26, no. 1, Feb. 1941: 1–8.) In
1868 E. C. Winchell had christened the dome "Pyramid of Cheops." (San
Francisco *Daily Morning Call*, Sept. 12, 1872; also in *SCB* 12, no. 3, 1926:
247.) In 1890 J. N. LeConte called the dome "Bob Ingersoll Rock," after a

sheepherder. (LeConte, *A Summer*, 34; also in *SCB* 26, no. 1, Feb. 1941: 12.) (KCNP)

North Guard (4,062 m.–13,327); **North Guard Lake** (10,064)
Mount Whitney 15', Mt. Brewer 7½'
North Guard Creek   *Mount Whitney 15', Mt. Pinchot 15', Mt. Brewer 7½',*
Mt. Clarence King 7½'
"North Guard" and "South Guard" were named by Lt. Milton F. Davis; they are on his map of 1896. (LeConte, *Alpina*, 10.) The mountain and creek are named on the first *Mt. Whitney* 30' map, 1907. The lake was named in 1956 by J. Hoganson, a field-man for the USGS. (KCNP)

North Mountain   *Marion Peak 15'*
May have been named by the USGS during the 1903 survey for the *Tehipite* 30' map; it is on the first edition, 1905. (KCNP)

North Peak (12,242)   *Tuolumne Meadows 15'*
Possibly named by the Whitney Survey when Mount Conness was named in 1866. J. N. LeConte's "Elevations" shows "Conness, N.Pk." (YNP, INF)

Nutter Lake   *Matterhorn Peak 15'*
Edward Hoit Nutter was assistant superintendent of the Standard Consolidated Mining Co. of Bodie when this lake was named for him in 1905 by an engineer of the company. (Farquhar: Nutter. See also **Gilman Lake**.) (TNF)

Nydiver Lakes   *Devils Postpile 15', Mt. Ritter 7½'*
For David *Nidever*, a prospector in the early 1900s. (INF archives. See also **Cabin Lake**.) (INF)

Oak Creek   *Mt. Pinchot 15', Kearsarge Peak 7½'*
Undoubtedly named by early settlers. The name already existed in 1862. (Cragen, 25.) (INF)

Obelisk (9,700)   *Tehipite Dome 15'*
A descriptive name applied by the USGS during the 1903 survey for the *Tehipite* 30' map; it is on the first edition, 1905. It was called "Devils Tombstone" on Lt. Davis's map of 1896. Davis had the name "Obelisk Mt." on what is now "Crown Rock" (named "Crown Mountain" by Frank Dusy about 1870). The USGS may have borrowed the "Obelisk" name and moved it three miles south. (KCNP, SiNF)

Obelisk Lake   *Merced Peak 15'*
Mount Clark was first named the "Obelisk" by the Whitney Survey, and the Clark Range was sometimes called the "Obelisk Group." (Whitney, *Yosemite Guide-Book*, 1870, 108.) "Obelisk Lake," less than a mile northeast of Mount Clark, is the only remaining use in Yosemite of the early name. (YNP)

Observation Peak (12,362–12,322)   *Mt. Goddard 15', North Palisade 7½'*
Named in 1902 by J. N. LeConte, who used it as a triangulation point for mapping the basin of the Middle Fork of the Kings River. (Farquhar: LeConte.) In his "Elevations," LeConte calls the mountain "Panorama Point." (*SCB* 4, no. 4, June 1903: 291.) (KCNP)

Odell Lake   *Tuolumne Meadows 15'*
Al Gardisky named this lake in 1932 for a friend. (Spuller.) (INF)

Oh Ridge   *Mono Craters 15'*
Said to have acquired its name from the exclamations ("Oh!") of those who
come over the rise and get their first good look at June Lake and the mountains.
(INF)

Olaine Lake   *Devils Postpile 15', Mammoth Mtn. 7½'*
Charles Olaine prospected here about 1910. (Smith, 60.) (INF)

Olancha Peak (12,123), **Creek**   *Olancha 15'*
Olancha Pass (over 9,200)   *Monache Mtn. 15'*
The name may have derived from the Olanches Indians. (Sanchez, 297.)
"Olanche," a settlement south of Owens Lake, is shown on Farley's map of
1861. Kroeber suggests it is possible the word is a borrowing from a Yokuts tribe
west of the Sierra Nevada who called themselves "Yaudanchi," and were called
by a neighboring band "Yaulanchi." (Kroeber, 51.)
  "Olancha Peak" is on the Wheeler Survey atlas sheet 65. The pass and the
creek are named on the first *Olancha* 30' map, 1907. William Crapo told F. H.
Wales in 1881 that the word meant "sleeping beauty." From the summit of Mt.
Kaweah the reclining figure of a woman could be seen on the side of Olancha
Peak—arms across abdomen, hair flowing back of head, face and breast clearly
visible. (Farquhar files, from Versteeg.) (INF)

Old Inspiration Point   *Yosemite 15', Yosemite Valley 1:24,000*
This viewpoint was originally known as "Mount Beatitude." The *real* old
point was at an altitude of 6,802 feet, a few feet off the Pohono Trail at the top of
the hill coming west from Meadow Brook. It was the first view of Yosemite
Valley from the Mann Brothers trail. (YNP files.)
  "Almost before the gratifying fact is realized, you have reached 'Inspiration
Point,' and are standing out upon a bold promontory of rock. . . . In all my life,
let it lead me where it may . . . I think I shall see nothing else so sublime and
beautiful, till, happily, I stand within the gates of the Heavenly City."
(Hutchings, *Scenes,* 1871, 85–86; see also **Beatitude, Mount** and **Inspiration
Point.**) (YNP)

Old Squaw Lake (over 10,960)   *Mt. Abbot 15', Mt. Hilgard 7½'*
Named in August 1951 by Elden H. Vestal of the DFG, in keeping with the
Indian-associated names he applied to other lakes in this basin. (Heyward
Moore, *FPP* 26, no. 2, Summer 1984: 6.) (SiNF)

Olive Lake   *Mt. Abbot 15', Graveyard Peak 7½'*
Possibly named in 1943 by William A. Dill of the DFG. (DFG survey.)
(SiNF)

Olive Lake   *Tower Peak 15'*
Named for Olive Hall, who died in 1964, a local resident and conservationist. (BGN decision, 1965.) The lake is not named on the 15-minute quad, but
will be on the *Emigrant Lake* 7½' quad when it is published. It is about 0.6 mile
north-northwest of the southwest end of Huckleberry Lake. (StNF)

O Neals Meadow   *Bass Lake 15'*
John Ruffin O'Neal patented 160 acres in sec. 5, T. 6 S., R. 21 E. in 1884, and homesteaded 160 acres in secs. 5 and 8 in 1892. (SiNF)

Oneida Lake (9,656)   *Tuolumne Meadows 15', Mono Craters 15'*
The various "Tioga" features in this area received the name from Tioga County, New York. Perhaps a native of that state thought that one good transplant deserved another; New York State has an Oneida County and a lake and a town of that name. The Oneida Indians were one of the Five Nations of the Iroquois Confederacy. The name means "granite people" or "people of the beacon stone." (Gannett, 196.)
      The name was undoubtedly given to the lake at the time of the Lundy-Bennettville mining excitement in 1879–80. It is on the 1881 GLO plat. (INF)

Orchid Lake   *Mt. Abbot 15', Florence Lake 7½'*
The 1942 DFG survey party under William A. Dill named the lake "for the abundance of beautiful little 'Rein-orchids' in the meadow at this lake." (DFG survey.) For lack of more precise information, I presume this refers to the green rein orchid, *Habenaria sparsiflora.* (SiNF)

Ostrander Rocks, Lake   *Yosemite 15'*
The rocks were named by the Whitney Survey for Harvey J. Ostrander, who came to California during the gold rush. In the early 1860s he settled at the junction of the Glacier Point and Old Mono trails. (YNP files.) Ostrander was a sheepman; his cabin was near Bridalveil Creek. The King and Gardiner map of 1865 and the Hoffmann and Gardiner map of 1863–67 show "Ostrander's Rocks," and the latter has "Ostrander's"—the cabin.
      The lake was originally called "Pohono Lake," since it was at the headwaters of Bridalveil (Pohono) Creek. (Clark, 96.) It was ratified as "Ostrander Lake" by the BGN in 1932, and was first named on the 15-minute quad. (YNP)

Ottoway Peak (over 11,440), **Creek; Upper** and **Lower Ottoway Lake**
                                                       Merced Peak 15'
The peak was named in 1895 by Lt. N. F. McClure for a corporal in his detachment. (Farquhar: McClure.) The peak and the creek were named on the first *Mt. Lyell* 30' map, 1901. The lakes were ratified by the BGN in 1932, and appeared on the 15-minute quad, 1953. (YNP)

Ouzel Creek   *Mount Whitney 15', Mt. Brewer 7½'*
Named in 1899 by David Starr Jordan. "*Ouzel Creek,* for the brook which flows from Mount Brewer into East Lake. The water-ouzel abounds here, and it is said that John Muir's account of the water-ouzel, one of the finest bird biographies ever written, was based largely on observations made on this stream." (*SCB* 3, no. 1, Jan. 1900: 109. Also see Muir in *Scribner's Monthly,* Feb. 1878; reprinted with minor changes in *The Mountains of California,* 1894, 276–99.)
      Jordan went wild with the name "ouzel," applying it to a basin, a pool, and a camp. None of these has ever been on the maps, except on Jordan's own sketch

map. (*SCB* 3, no. 1, Jan. 1900: 111.) The creek was spelled "Ousel" on the *Mt. Whitney* 30' map, 1901–21; it was changed to "Ouzel" on the sixth edition, 1927. (KCNP)

Owens Camp *Silver Lake 15', Tragedy Spring 7½'*
Joseph F. Owen homesteaded near here in September 1904. (GLO.) (ENF)

Owens Peak (8,453) *Inyokern 15', Owens Peak 7½'*
Owens Point (3,467 m.–11,411) *Lone Pine 15', Mt. Langley 7½'*
Richard Owens was a member of John C. Frémont's third expedition (1845–46). "That Owens was a good man it is enough to say that he and Carson were friends. Cool, brave, and of good judgment; a good hunter and good shot; experienced in mountain life; he was an acquisition, and proved valuable throughout the campaign." (Frémont, *Memoirs,* 1887, 427.)
The party split up at Walker Lake, Nevada. Frémont, Carson, and Owens crossed the Sierra via Donner Pass. Walker, Kern and others went south and crossed via Walker Pass. "To one of the lakes along their route on the east side of the range I gave Owens' name." (Frémont, *Memoirs,* 1887, 455.) Thus the lake was named first. "Owens River" also appears on Preuss's map of 1848. The names of the valley, the peak, and the point are derived from the lake. The man for whom they were named never saw any of them. (Point, INF)

Pacific Creek *Dardanelles Cone 15', Markleeville 15',*
 Spicer Meadow Res. 7½', Pacific Valley 7½'
Pacific Valley, Pacific Grade Summit *Markleeville 15',*
 Pacific Valley 7½'
The name "Pacific Creek" was in use before 1870. The origin of the name is unknown, but doubtless it was given by explorers or immigrants, the implication being that they were on the Pacific side of the mountains. The valley was named on an untitled map of Alpine County, published about 1870. (StNF)

Packsaddle Lake (10,663) *Mt. Goddard 15', Mt. Darwin 7½'*
Originally called "Lovejoy Lake" by Tobe Way in 1928 or 1929, when he stocked it with fish. (Art Schober.) The present name was given by the Sierra Club. (Mrs. Art Schober.) Tobe Way was the predecessor of the Schobers in running the pack station on the North Fork of Bishop Creek. He sold out to Art and John's father in the early 1930s. (SiNF)

Page Peaks (over 10,880) *Matterhorn Peak 15'*
Page was a prospector and miner. (Farquhar files, from Judge Parker, Bridgeport, 1928.) The name is on the first *Bridgeport* 30' map, 1911. (TNF)

Paine Lake (11,216) *Mt. Goddard 15', Mt. Darwin 7½'*
Named by John Schober for Edgar Allen Paine, an Owens Valley artist. (Art Schober.) (SiNF)

Painted Lady (3,694 m.–12,126) *Mt. Pinchot 15', Mt. Clarence King 7½'*
The peak was called "The Pyramid" by Bolton C. Brown in 1899. (*SCB* 3, no. 2, May 1900: 136, 142.) By at least as early as 1910 it was known as "Colored Lady." (*SCB* 8, no. 1, Jan., 1911: photo opp. 65.) That name did not

appear on the maps. "Painted Lady" is first seen on the 15-minute quad, 1953. (KCNP)

Palisade Basin, Glacier; North Palisade (14,242)   *Mt. Goddard 15',*
North Palisade 7½'
Palisade Crest, Lakes; Middle Palisade (4,271 m.–14,040)   *Big Pine 15',*
Split Mtn. 7½'
Palisade Creek   *Mt. Goddard 15', Big Pine 15', North Palisade 7½',*
Split Mtn. 7½'

The Palisades were named by the Brewer party of the Whitney Survey in 1864. ". . . along the Main crest of the Sierra, is a range of peaks, from 13,500 to 14,000 feet high, which we called 'the Palisades.' . . . they were very grand and fantastic in shape." (Whitney, *Geology,* 393.)

The Wheeler Survey used the names "Northwest Palisade" for North Palisade and "Southeast Palisade" for Split Mountain in 1878. (Wheeler Survey, *Tables,* 19.) In 1879 Lil A. Winchell called North Palisade "Dusy's Peak." (Winchell, 160.) In 1895 Bolton C. Brown named it for David Starr Jordan, and also called the Palisades the "Saw-Tooth Mountains." (*SCB* 1, no. 8, May 1896: 296–97.) Jordan's name was later given to a peak on the Kings-Kern Divide, and J. N. LeConte prevailed over Winchell. "I have called the peak merely the North Palisade, and now ask you if you cannot . . . put Dusy's name on some less imposing mass, and give us a name to be handed down through all time." (Letter, LeConte to Winchell, Feb. 23, 1903, in SC papers in BL.)

The first ascent of North Palisade was on July 25, 1903, by LeConte, James K. Moffitt, and James S. Hutchinson. "We worked up toward the knife-edge just to the south, and instantly the stupendous panorama of precipice, glacier, and desert burst upon us. . . . The knife-edge was composed of thin blocks standing up on edge, from six to eight feet apart, and equally high. These had to be climbed over one by one, by letting down at arm's-length between two and pulling up over the thin edge of the next. At 11:30 we crawled out upon the crown, victorious at last." (*SCB* 5, no. 1, Jan. 1904: 17.)

The first ascent of the Middle Palisade was made on August 26, 1921, by Francis P. Farquhar and Ansel F. Hall. "With a shout we greeted the summit as its first visitors. . . . The summit of the mountain is an extremely narrow knife-edge. We had to use great care in moving about, as there were many large blocks just poised on the brink." (*SCB* 11, no. 3, 1922: 268.)

Palisade Creek was named by Lil Winchell. (Farquhar conversation with Winchell, Oct. 18, 1921, in Farquhar papers, BL.) All the Palisade features except the lakes and the crest were named on the first editions of the *Mt. Goddard* and *Bishop* 30' maps, 1912 and 1913 respectively. The lakes and the crest were first named on the *Big Pine* 15' quad, 1950. (KCNP, INF)

Palmer Cave   *Kaweah 15'*
Palmer Mountain (11,250)   *Triple Divide Peak 15'*
Joseph L. Palmer was a pioneer miner, hunter, and trapper. He discovered

the cave on November 12, 1872, and named it for himself. (*Nature,* no. 4, Jan. 20, 1925.) In 1882 he homesteaded 160 acres on the South Fork of the Kaweah River, in sec. 6, T. 18 S., R. 29 E.

The names of Palmer Mountain and Avalanche Peak were accidentally transposed on the first three editions of the *Tehipite* 30' map, 1905–24, and were correctly located on the fourth edition, 1929. (Cave, SNP; mtn., KCNP)

Panorama Cliff, Point (5,224), **Trail**   *Yosemite 15',*
Yosemite Valley 1:24,000

The namer is unknown, but the features were undoubtedly named for the panoramic view. They first appeared on the *Yosemite Valley* map of 1907. When the trail was constructed in 1886 it was called the "Echo Wall Trail." (*YNN* 34, no. 1, Jan. 1955: 14.) (YNP)

Panther Creek, Peak (9,046), **Gap, Meadow**   *Triple Divide Peak 15'*

The creek was named because Hale Tharp killed a panther (mountain lion) there in the early days. (Farquhar: G. W. Stewart.) The creek and the peak were named on the first *Tehipite* 30' map, 1905; the gap and the meadow on the 15-minute quad, 1956. (SNP)

Paoha or **Poacha Lake**   *Mt. Abbot 15', Mt. Hilgard 7½'*

Named "Poaha" in August 1951 by Elden H. Vestal of the DFG, who explained that the word is Piute for white or daylight—the presumed opposite meaning of "Negit Lake," to which it is adjacent. A number of students of Indian languages dispute the meaning. (Heyward Moore, *FPP* 26, no. 2, Summer 1984: 6.) No explanation is available for the change to "Poacha" on the 7½-minute quad.

The name "Paoha" was given to the large island in Mono Lake by Israel C. Russell in 1882. "In the legends of the Pa-vi-o-osi people . . . there is a story about diminutive spirits, having long, wavy hair, that are sometimes seen in the vapor wreaths ascending from hot springs. The word Pa-o-ha, by which these spirits are known, is also used to designate hot springs in general. We may therefore name the larger island Paoha Island, in remembrance, perhaps, of the children of the mist that held their revels there on moonlit nights in times long past." (Russell, *Quaternary,* 278–79.) (SiNF)

Papoose Lake   *Mt. Abbot 15', Graveyard Peak 7½'*

There is a rash of "Indian" names in this basin: Papoose, Warrior, Chief, Squaw. They apparently derive from "Lake of the Lone Indian," a name conferred in 1902. These four names appeared on the 15-minute quad, 1953. No one has ever confessed the deed, although it is possible that "Papoose Lake"—and perhaps the others—was named in 1945 by William A. Dill of the DFG. (DFG survey.) (SiNF)

Par Value Lakes   *Matterhorn Peak 15'*

The largest of three lakes was named "Par Value" after an adjacent mining claim of that name. (Maule.) The name appears on the first *Bridgeport* 30' map, 1911; it was made plural on the 15-minute quad, 1956. (TNF)

Paradise Creek   *Giant Forest 15'*
Paradise Cave, Ridge   *Kaweah 15'*
Paradise Creek, Ridge, Peak (9,362)   *Mineral King 15'*
   It is not known who first provided this common name for the features in the
area. The creek is named on the first *Kaweah* 30' map, 1904. The cave and the
ridge show up on the third edition, 1921, and the peak on the fifth edition,
1934.
   The entrance to the cave was discovered June 25, 1901, by H. R. Harmon, a
farmer. It was named on June 2, 1906, by SNP rangers Charles W. Blossom and
Walter Fry. (*Nature,* no. 4, Jan. 20, 1925.) (SNP)

Paradise Valley   *Marion Peak 15'*
   An early name, in use by 1883. (Elliott, *Guide,* 237.) It is also on J. W. A.
Wright's map, reproduced in *SCB* 32, no. 5, May 1947: 79. J. N. LeConte knew
the name in 1890. (*A Summer,* 51, *et seq.*) (KCNP)

Paris Lake (over 11,200)   *Mount Tom 7½'*
   Named in 1954 by Ralph Beck of the DFG. (Phil Pister. See **Alsace Lake.**)
It is the lake into which Puppet Lake drains, and is not named on the *Mt. Tom*
15' quad. (SiNF)

Parker Pass, Creek, Lake, Peak (12,861); **Parker Pass Lake** and **Creek**
                                                    Mono Craters 15'
   "The creek was named for an early settler of Mono County." (Farquhar:
W. L. Huber.) The name for the creek was used by Israel C. Russell in 1883. It
has been suggested that the source of all these "Parker" names was Edward A.
Parker, a student of Professor Joseph LeConte. J. N. LeConte reported on the
records he found on the summit of Mt. Lyell in 1889. The oldest was that of
Parker and another man in 1875; the next after that was Russell and Grove Karl
Gilbert of the USGS in 1883. (*SCB* 11, no. 3, 1922: 247.) All the Parker names
except the creek and the lake west of the pass are on the first *Mt. Lyell* 30' map,
1901. (YNP, INF)

Parsons Peak (over 12,080); **Parsons Memorial Lodge**
                                                Tuolumne Meadows 15'
   Edward Taylor Parsons (1861–1914), a director of the Sierra Club for nine
years; member of the outing committee for 13 years; photographer of many of
the club's early trips. The peak was named by R. B. Marshall of the USGS about
1909; it is on the third edition of the *Mt. Lyell* 30' map, 1910. It was first
climbed by Parsons' widow, Marion Randall Parsons, sometime before 1931.
In 1915 the Sierra Club built the lodge on its Soda Springs property on the north
side of Tuolumne Meadows. (*SCB* 10, no. 1, Jan. 1916: 84–85.) The lodge was
sold to the National Park Service in 1973.
   There are memorials to Parsons by John Muir and William E. Colby in *SCB*
9, no. 4, Jan. 1915: 219–24. (YNP)

Pate Valley   *Hetch Hetchy Reservoir 15'*
   An old name of uncertain origin. It may possibly have been named for a

Francis M. Pate, a resident of Indian Gulch in 1867. (YNP files.) But R. M. Price and Theodore S. Solomons spelled the name "Pait." (*SCB* 1, no. 6, May 1895: 207–8.) But also: "Pate was a sheepman from Merced Falls who ran his sheep in Pate Valley." (YNP files.) (YNP)

Pattee Rocks (4,284)   *Giant Forest 15'*
The rocks were surrounded by Pattees. Jesse G. Pattee homesteaded 160 acres in the SW and SE parts of sec. 28, T. 15 S., R. 28 E. in 1893—about two miles north of the rocks. Winthrop Pattee homesteaded 160 acres in the SW¼ of sec. 33 in 1894. Frank W. Pattee homesteaded 160 acres in sec. 8, T. 16 S., R. 28 E. in 1904—southwest of the rocks. (SeNF)

Patterson Canyon   *Fales Hot Springs 15'*
Robert Patterson operated a sawmill here in 1872. (Maule.) (TNF)

Patterson Mountain (8,167), **Bluffs**   *Patterson Mtn. 15'*
John A. and Elisha Patterson pastured sheep on the extensive mountain that is named for them. (Winchell, 158.) (SiNF)

Pavilion Dome (11,856–11,846)   *Blackcap Mtn. 15', Mt. Henry 7½'*
Named in 1879 by Lil A. Winchell. (Farquhar: Winchell.) (KCNP, SiNF)

Pear Lake (9,510)   *Triple Divide Peak 15'*
Named in the early 1920s by Col. White for its shape. (Letter from White, SNP files.) The name appears on the fourth edition of the *Tehipite* 30' map, 1929. (SNP)

Pearl Lake (10,631)   *Mt. Goddard 15' and 7½',*
Blackcap Mtn. 15' and 7½'
Stocked with fish—and apparently named—by Ted Anderson, a packer, in the early 1950s. (USGS.) It is indicative of the fragmented way in which names were once given to note that the name first appeared on the *Mt. Goddard 15'* quad, 1957, and was validated by a BGN decision in 1982. (SiNF)

Peck Cabin   *Kaweah 15'*
Julius A. Peck homesteaded 320 acres in sec. 29 and 120 acres in sec. 30, T. 18 S., R. 29 E. in 1922. (SeNF)

Peckinpah Meadow, Creek   *Shuteye Peak 15'*
Charlie Peckinpah, with several of his brothers, started a sawmill in 1884 in the NE¼ of sec. 4, T. 8 S., R. 23 E. Between then and 1896 he took ten million board feet of lumber out of 640 acres. From 1902 to 1905 he logged another 200 acres with a cut of about six million board feet. (Hurt, 19.) John W. Peckinpah patented 160 acres nearby in 1891, and five other Peckinpahs homesteaded or patented 160 acres apiece in adjacent sections during a two-day period in June 1893. (SiNF)

Pecks Canyon   *Mineral King 15'*
Peck ran sheep here about 1870. (Farquhar: Versteeg.) (SeNF)

Pee Wee Lake   *Mt. Darwin 7½'*
Art Schober named the lake when he stocked it with fish, because "it's a little

tiny bit of a thing." (Art Schober.) Not named on the *Mt. Goddard* 15' quad. It is 0.1 mile north of Topsy Turvy Lake. (INF)

Peeler Lake   *Matterhorn Peak 15'*
    Barnabas ("Barney") Peeler patented 160 acres in sec. 9, T. 4 N., R. 24 E. in 1880. (See **Barney Lake.**) (TNF)

Peep Sight Peak (9,716–9,727)   *Dardanelles Cone 15' and 7½'*
    From a certain angle a natural bridge near the top of the peak creates a window, a "peep sight." On the 15-minute quad it is called "Lookout Peak." It was changed to the present name by a BGN decision in 1975. (StNF)

Pemmican Lake   *Mt. Abbot 15', Mt. Hilgard 7½'*
    Named in August 1951 by Elden H. Vestal of the DFG, in reference to the travel food of some North American Indians. (Heyward Moore, *FPP* 26, no. 2, Summer 1984: 6–7.) (SiNF)

Pendant Lake   *Mt. Abbot 15', Mt. Hilgard 7½'*
    Elden H. Vestal of the DFG named this lake in August 1951 because its shape bore "a resemblance to an earring pendant." (Heyward Moore, *FPP* 26, no. 2, Summer 1984: 7.) (SiNF)

Pennsylvania Creek, Mine   *Markleeville 15', Ebbetts Pass 7½'*
    The claim of the Pennsylvania Gold and Silver Quartz Mine and Mill Site was filed August 19, 1875—14.21 acres in secs. 20 and 29, T. 9 N., R. 20 E. One assumes the claimants were loyal natives of Pennsylvania. The mine is not shown on the 15-minute quad. It is in the lower-right quadrant of sec. 20, just north of the northernmost bend of the creek. (TNF)

Peregoy Meadow   *Yosemite 15'*
    Charles E. Peregoy had a cattle camp on the trail between Wawona and Yosemite Valley. In 1869–70 he enlarged his log cabin into a hotel for 16, named it the "Mountain View House," and with his wife operated it until 1878. (Sargent, *Innkeepers*, 15–16: and *Pioneers*, 20–21.)
    The King and Gardiner map of 1865 shows "Trail from Peregoy's." The 1884 GLO plat has "Old Peregoy House." The first two editions of the *Yosemite* 30' map (1897 and 1900) mistakenly used the name "Paragon Meadow." It was corrected on the edition of 1903. (YNP)

Perkins, Mount (3,830 m.–12,591)   *Mt. Pinchot 15' and 7½'*
    George Clement Perkins (1839–1923), a charter member of the Sierra Club; governor of California, 1880–83; US Senator from California, 1893–1915. The peak was named in 1906 by Robert D. Pike, a Sierra Club climber. (Farquhar: J. N. LeConte.) The peak is named on the first *Mt. Whiney* 30' map, 1907. (KCNP, INF)

Perrin Creek   *Mount Whitney 15' and 7½', Kern Peak 15'*
    G. H. Perrin, who made the original survey for the General Land Office in 1884, named the creek for himself. (SNP)

Peter Pande Lake   *Mt. Abbot 15', Graveyard Peak 7½'*
The name was used informally during the 1930s and 1940s by packers and
hikers. It was called "Marilyn Lake" on the first edition of the 15-minute quad.
After Pande died in 1959, his son asked that the present name be made official,
which was done by a BGN decision in 1961. (SiNF)

Peter Peak (12,490–12,543)   *Mt. Goddard 15', Mt. Darwin 7½'*
Named by the Sierra Club for Peter Grubb, who made the first ascent on July
11, 1936. Grubb died while traveling in Europe. (Letter, David Brower to C. A.
Ecklund, USGS, Mar. 7, 1951.) (KCNP)

Lower Petite Lake; Upper Petite Lake   *Mount Tom 7½'*
Named in 1954 by Ralph Beck of the DFG. (Phil Pister. See **Alsace Lake**.)
These are not named on the *Mt. Tom 15'* quad. They are the second and third
lakes upstream from French Lake. (SiNF)

Pettit Peak (10,788)   *Tuolumne Meadows 15'*
Named by Col. W. W. Forsyth, acting superintendent of Yosemite National
Park, 1909–12, for Col. James Sumner Pettit, commander of the US Fourth
Volunteer Infantry in the Spanish-American War. (Farquhar: Forsyth.) (YNP)

Peyrone Grove   *Camp Nelson 15'*
Named after a pioneer stockman. (Fry and White, 108.) (SeNF)

Pickel Meadow   *Sonora Pass 15', Pickel Meadow 7½'*
Named for Frank Pickel, a pioneer stockman and prospector, in 1863.
(Maule.) Misspelled as "Pickle's" on the Wheeler Survey atlas sheet 56D,
1878–79, and "Pickle Meadow" on all editions of the *Dardanelles 30'* map,
1898–1947. It was corrected on the 15-minute quad, 1956. (TNF)

Pickering, Mount (4,107 m.–13,485)   *Mount Whitney 15' and 7½'*
Edward Charles Pickering (1846–1919), physicist and astronomer. He was
the founder and president of the American Astronomical Society, and director
of the Harvard University observatory for 42 years. He was recognized as the
dean of astronomical research in America. The name was suggested by the
Sierra Club, and approved by a BGN decision in 1940. (SNP)

Picket Guard Peak (3,750 m.–12,302); **Picket Creek**   *Mount Whitney 15',*
                                                            Mt. Kaweah 7½'
The peak was named in July 1897. "There is a fine pyramidal peak at the
eastern end of the third range, which was always in the background of the view as
we entered and ascended the narrow cleft of the Kern-Kaweah. This was named
the Picket Guard." (William R. Dudley in *SCB* 2, no. 3, Jan. 1898: 189; sketch
map, plate XXV.) Both features are named on the first *Mt. Whitney 30'* map,
1907. (SNP)

Pickett Peak (9,118)   *Freel Peak 15' and 7½'*
Edward M. Pickett had an early stage station, "Pickett Place," at the junction of the Luther Pass and Carson Pass roads in Hope Valley. (Maule.) The
junction is called "Picketts Jct." on some road maps, but not on the USGS topo
maps. (TNF)

Picture Puzzle (over 13,280–13,278)   *Mt. Thompson 7½'*
The name first appeared in *The Climber's Guide,* and was added to the map by the USGS because it was in common use. On the *Mt. Goddard* 15' quad it is 0.7 mile east of Saddlerock Lake, marked "13278." (INF)

Pig Chute   *Mt. Henry 7½'*
The name "refers to the chute-like appearance of the river channel, and also to the spot where the trail used to cross the river. It was a steep, dangerous crossing, and has been abandoned." (USGS.) The name is not on the *Blackcap Mtn.* 15' quad. Its location is in Goddard Canyon, about half a mile north (downstream) from where the creek from Hell For Sure Pass enters the South Fork of the San Joaquin River. (KCNP)

Pilot Knob (12,245)   *Mt. Abbot 15', Mt. Hilgard 7½'*
Probably named by the USGS during the 1907–09 survey for the *Mt. Goddard* 30' map. It is on the first edition, 1912, but is not in J. N. LeConte's "Elevations." (SiNF)

Pilot Knob (over 6,200)   *Onyx 15' and 7½'*
Possibly named by the USGS during the survey for the *Kernville* 30' map; it is on the first edition, 1908. (SeNF)

Pilot Peak (6,004)   *Lake Eleanor 15'*
"Leaving Deer Flat, the trail winds up along the side of Pilot Peak, a prominent landmark, a little over 6,000 feet above the sea-level, the summit of which may be easily reached from the trail." (Whitney, *The Yosemite Book,* 1868, 50.) (StNF)

Pinchot, Mount (4,113 m.–13,495); **Pinchot Pass** *Mt. Pinchot 15' and 7½'*
Gifford Pinchot (1865–1946), a conservationist and politician. He was chief of the Division of Forestry (later the US Forest Service) from 1898 to 1910, and was twice elected governor of Pennsylvania, in 1922 and 1930.
    The peak was named in July 1902 by J. N. LeConte from the summit of Split Mountain. "Only five miles south there stood a great rounded mass of red slate on the Main Crest, and I allowed myself to change the name Red Mountain given it by Professor Brown (*SCB* 1, no. 8, May 1896: 302, 309), and already applied to scores of the slate peaks of the Sierra, to Mt. Pinchot." (*SCB* 4, no. 4, June 1903: 262.)
    The pass was named on the fourth edition of the *Mt. Whitney* 30' map, 1919, probably in conjunction with the construction of the John Muir Trail. (KCNP)

Pincushion Peak (9,818–9,819)   *Kaiser Peak 15', Sharktooth Peak 7½'*
A round, regularly shaped peak that resembles a pincushion. The name possibly originated with sheepherders. It is on T. S. Solomons' 1896 map. (SiNF)

Pinnacle Ridge   *Mount Whitney 15' and 7½'*
The USGS added the name to the 15-minute quad because it was in common use and had appeared on other maps. (INF)

The Pinnacles; West Pinnacles Creek; East Pinnacles Creek
Mt. Abbot 15', Mt. Hilgard 7½'
The Pinnacles probably were named by the USGS during the 1907–09
survey for the *Mt. Goddard* 30' map; the name is on the first edition, 1912. The
creeks were named in August 1951 during a survey conducted by the DFG and
the Fresno County Sportsmen's Club. (Heyward Moore, *FPP* 26, no. 2,
Summer 1984: 4.) (SiNF)

Pioneer Basin; Pioneer Basin Lakes   *Mt. Abbot 15' and 7½'*
The basin was named by R. B. Marshall, USGS, during the 1907–09 survey
for the *Mt. Goddard* 30' map, when he also named four peaks for the pioneer
railroad builders, Crocker, Hopkins, Huntington, and Stanford. (Farquhar:
Marshall.) The lakes were first named on the 15-minute quad, 1953. (SiNF)

Piper Peak (2,498 m.–8,199)   *Big Pine 15', Coyote Flat 7½'*
Samuel S. Piper homesteaded 160 acres in sec. 23, T. 9 S., R. 33 E. in 1912.
The peak is two miles west of the homestead. The name appeared on the 15-
minute quad, 1950. (INF)

Pitman Creek   *Huntington Lake 15' and 7½'*
"Named for Elias Pitman, hunter, who had an early camp on its banks."
(Letter, L. A. Winchell to Farquhar, April 3, 1925, in Farquhar papers, BL.)
The creek was called "South Fork of Big Creek" on the 1885 GLO plat. (SiNF)

Piute Pass (11,423), **Lake** (10,958)   *Mt. Goddard 15', Mt. Darwin 7½'*
Piute Creek   *Mt. Goddard 15', Mt. Abbot 15', Mt. Darwin 7½',*
Mt. Henry 7½'
Piute Canyon   *Mt. Abbot 15', Blackcap Mtn. 15', Mt. Darwin 7½',*
Mt. Hilgard 7½', Mt. Henry 7½'
The Piutes (or Paiutes) are a division of Shoshonean Indians. The name has
been widely used in California, often quite indiscriminately.
The pass was named by L. A. Winchell because it was used by Owens Valley
Indians. (Farquhar: Winchell.) In 1904 J. N. LeConte applied the name of the
pass to the creek, calling it "Piute Branch" to avoid using the name of "North
Branch of the South Fork of the San Joaquin River." (*SCB* 5, no. 3, Jan. 1905:
255, plate XXXIII.)
The pass and the creek were named on the first edition of the *Mt. Goddard*
30' map, 1912. The canyon was named on the third edition, 1923. The lake was
first named on the 15-minute quad, 1948. On the *Mt. Darwin* 7½' quad appears
the name "Piute Crags," northeast of Loch Leven and southeast of Mt.
Emerson. The creek is also on the *Mt. Tom* 15' and *Mount Tom* 7½' quads.
(Pass, lake, crags, INF; pass, creek, canyon, SiNF)

Piute Lake, Creek, Meadow   *Pinecrest 15'*
Piute Meadow and Piute Creek were named by Bill Woods because Piutes
from Nevada came there to fish and hunt.
The naming of the lake is a different matter. According to Joe Ratto, an early
cattleman, Bill Woods, met a Piute on the trail at the lake. The Indian was drunk,
demanded that Woods give him the red shirt he was wearing, and was killed by

Woods in the fight that ensued. Woods is said to have weighted the Indian's body and sunk it in the lake, along with the dead man's gun. (StNF files, from Joe Ratto.) (StNF)

Piute Mountain (10,541), **Creek**   *Tower Peak 15'*
Piute Creek   *Matterhorn Peak 15'*
These names probably were given by the USGS during the 1891–96 survey for the *Dardanelles* 30' map; they are on the first edition, 1898. Lt. N. F. McClure, on his 1895 map, called the creek "Cascade Creek;" on his 1896 map it was "Slide Creek" or "Piute Creek." (YNP)

Plasse   *Silver Lake 15', Tragedy Spring 7½'*
Plasse Trading Post (Site)   *Silver Lake 15', Mokelumne Peak 7½'*
From the GLO surveyor's field notes, 1877: "Plasse's house bears North about 5.00 chains distant," from the east-west line between secs. 8 and 17, T. 9 N., R. 17 E. Peter R. Plasse homesteaded 160 acres in 1884—the southwest quarter of section 8.

The site of Plasse Trading Post was relocated about half a mile northeast on the 7½-minute quad. "There never was a permanent structure at the site. Plasse erected a lean-to, and dealt with the emigrant trains for only one season." Research by the USGS established the position of the post in its correct place: the NW¼ of the SW¼ of sec. 22, T. 9 N., R. 17 E. This was verified through Maurice Plasse of Jackson, California, great-grandson of the Plasse for whom the site is named. (USGS, Domestic Name Report.) (ENF)

Pohono Trail   *Yosemite 15', Yosemite Valley 1:24,000*
"*Pohono*. The Bridal Veil Fall, explained to signify a blast of wind, or the night-wind . . . or possibly with reference to the constant swaying of the sheet of water from one side to the other under the influence of the wind. Mr. Hutchings, more poetically, says that 'Pohono' is an evil spirit, whose breath is a blighting and fatal wind, and consequently to be dreaded and shunned." (Whitney, *Yosemite Guide-Book,* 1870, 16.)

"The whole basin drained, as well as the meadows adjacent, was known to us of the battalion, as the Pohono branch and meadows. . . . I have recently learned that Po-ho-no means a daily puffing wind, and when applied to fall, stream, or meadow, means simply the fall, stream, or meadow of the puffing wind, and when applied to the tribe of Po-ho-no-chees, who occupied the meadows in summer, indicated that they dwelled on the meadows of that stream. . . . Mr. Hutchings' interpretation is entirely fanciful, as are most of his Indian translations." (Bunnell, *Discovery,* 1911, 212–13.) (YNP)

Poison Meadow   *Giant Forest 15'*
A meadow shunned by stockmen because of the abundance of larkspur and other plants that are poisonous to stock. (Junep.) (SeNF)

Polemonium Peak (13,962 or 14,080)   *North Palisade 7½'*
Added to the map by the USGS because it was in common use and appeared in *The Climber's Guide.* (Approved by a BGN decision in 1985. The first altitude given is the one on the 7½-minute quad, published in 1982. The second

one is from the BGN's Decision List No. 8501.) The name comes from sky pilot, *Polemonium eximium,* which grows at high altitude on rock ledges and slopes. The peak is not named on the *Mt. Goddard* 15' quad. It is ½ mile southeast of North Palisade; no altitude is given. (KCNP)

Polly Dome (9,810); **Polly Dome Lakes**   *Tuolumne Meadows 15'*
Named by R. B. Marshall, USGS, for Mrs. Polly McCabe, a daughter of Col. W. W. Forsyth and the wife of Lt. McCabe. (Farquhar: Forsyth. See **McCabe Lakes.**) The name was applied to the lakes because it was in common use. (USGS.) (YNP)

Pond Lily Lake   *Devils Postpile 15', Crystal Crag 7½'*
"Famous for the mass of yellow pond lilies, usually in full bloom in late July, that cover the surface of the water near its outlet." (Smith, 14.) (SiNF)

Poopenaut Valley   *Lake Eleanor 15'*
"Named after an early settler by that name of German extraction." (Lt. McClure.) "Name applied in 1889 by Frank Elwell, who homesteaded the property." (Col. Benson.) Both those quotes are from Farquhar's files, from Chester Versteeg. The name is spelled "Poopeno" by J. N. LeConte on his Yosemite Sheet, 1900, and "Poopino" in the Report of the Acting Superintendent of Yosemite National Park, 1901. (YNP)

Porcupine Flat, Creek   *Hetch Hetchy Reservoir 15'*
The name existed when the Brewer party of the Whitney Survey camped at the flat June 23, 1863, but there is no indication that they named it. "We camped at Porcupine Flat, a pretty, grassy flat, at an elevation of 8,550 feet, surrounded by scrubby pines, and tormented by myriads of mosquitoes." (Brewer, *Up and Down,* 401.) The name is on the Hoffmann and Gardiner map, 1863–67. The creek was first named on the 15-minute quad, 1956. (YNP)

Post Peak (11,009), **Lakes; Post Peak Pass**   *Merced Peak 15'*
The peak was named for William S. Post of the USGS during the 1898–99 survey for the *Mt. Lyell* 30' map. (Farquhar: R. B. Marshall.) It is on the first edition, 1901. The pass and lakes are first named on the 15-minute quad, 1953. (Peak, lakes, SiNF; pass, SiNF, YNP)

Big Pothole Lake; Little Pothole Lake *Mt. Pinchot 15', Kearsarge Peak 7½'*
J. N. LeConte referred to Big Pothole Lake as "Devil's Pot Hole" in 1890. (*A Summer,* 65.) That lake was called simply "Pothole Lake" on all editions of the *Mt. Whitney* 30' map, 1907–39. The present names appeared on the 15-minute map, 1953. (INF)

Pothole Meadows   *Yosemite 15', Yosemite Valley 1:24,000*
Named for bowl-shaped depressions about five feet in diameter. (*Yosemite Road Guide,* 15.) The name appears on the Yosemite Valley map in 1907. (YNP)

Potluck Pass (over 12,120)   *North Palisade 7½'*
"Apparently named in 1927; perhaps because there is no obvious route

down the southeast side, and one has to take pot luck in making the descent."
(Letter, Thomas H. Jukes to Farquhar, Aug. 30, 1939.) It was added to the map
by the USGS because of its use in *The Climber's Guide*. The pass is not named
on the *Mt. Goddard* 15' quad. It is east of Palisade Basin, a bit less than ½ mile
northeast of the unnamed peak marked 12692. (KCNP)

Potter Point (10,728)   *Tuolumne Meadows 15'*
     Named in 1909 by R. B. Marshall, USGS, for Dr. Charles Potter of Boston.
(Farquhar: Marshall.) (YNP)

Potwisha   *Giant Forest 15'*
     The name was proposed by George W. Stewart for the Potwisha tribe, a
branch of the Yokuts Indians, who had a campground at the junction of the
Middle and Marble forks of the Kaweah River. (Farquhar: Stewart.) Floyd
Otter said that the Balwisha (Potwishi) were Paiutes from east of the Sierra.
(Otter, 11.) The locality was once called "Camp One" of the Mount Whitney
Power Company, the predecessor of the Southern California Edison Company.
It was also the site of a CCC camp, 1939–40. (Fry and White, 58.)
     The name first appeared as "Potwisha" on the fourth edition of the *Tehipite*
30' map, 1929. It was changed to "Potwisha Camp" on the editions of 1939 and
1947 before reverting to "Potwisha" on the 15-minute quad. (SNP)

Powell, Mount (13,356); **Powell Glacier**   *Mt. Goddard 15', Mt. Darwin 7½'*
     Named by R. B. Marshall, USGS, for John Wesley Powell (1834–1902),
explorer, scientist, and conservationist. Powell led the first two expeditions
through the Grand Canyon in 1869 and 1871–72. He was the geologist in charge
of the US Geographical and Geological Survey of the Rocky Mountain Region
(the Powell Survey), 1870–79; became first director of the Bureau of
Ethnology, 1879; second director of the US Geological Survey, 1881–94.
     The first ascent was by Walter L. Huber and James Rennie on August 1,
1925. "The very summit is an overhanging rock of enormous size. A careless
step might result in a drop to the glacial ice far below under the north face."
(*SCB* 12, no. 3, 1926: 250–51.)
     On the 15-minute quad, the peak is the one to the left of the name. The
glacier, north of the peak, is named only on the 7½-minute quad. (KCNP, INF)

Prater, Mount (4,106 m.–13,329)   *Big Pine 15', Split Mtn. 7½'*
     Named in memory of Alfred Prater and his wife, who in 1928 made what is
believed to be the first ascent. (BGN, *Sixth Report,* 618.) (KCNP, INF)

Precipice Lake (over 10,240)   *Triple Divide Peak 15'*
     A descriptive name that has been in use since before 1940. (USGS.) It was
ratified by a BGN decision in 1968. Formerly it was the upper of the three
"Hamilton Lakes." That name now applies to only the two lower lakes.
"Precipice Lake" was not named on the first edition of the 15-minute quad, but
does appear on later editions. The lake is the one just north of Eagle Scout Peak.
It has been made famous by the Ansel Adams photograph of the half-frozen lake
beneath gray and black cliffs. (Photo in *SCB* 18, no. 1, Feb. 1933: 47.) (SNP)

Price Peak (10,716)   *Tower Peak 15'*
Named for George Ehler Price, who entered the US Cavalry as a private in 1896 and retired as a lieutenant in 1912. (Farquhar: Marshall.) The namer may have been Col. W. W. Forsyth, acting superintendent of Yosemite National Park, 1909–12. The name appears on the third *Dardanelles* 30' map, 1912. (YNP)

Primrose Lake (over 11,600)   *Mount Whitney 15' and 7½'*
The name was proposed by Chester Versteeg for the abundance of wild primroses along its shores. (BGN decision, 1937–38.) The name first appeared on the *Mt. Whitney* 30' map in 1937. (SNP)

Profile Cliff   *Yosemite 15', Yosemite Valley 1:24,000*
The cliff below the fissures at Taft Point on the south rim of Yosemite Valley. In the early literature it was sometimes referred to as "Fissure Mountain." (*YNN* 34, no. 1, Jan. 1955: 14.) "The . . . appellation comes from the many faces that can be distinctly traced upon its northeastern edge at almost any hour of the day." (Hutchings, *In the Heart,* 412.) The name appeared on the first USGS *Yosemite Valley* map, 1907. (YNP)

Profile View   *Triple Divide Peak 15'*
The name may have been applied by the USGS during the 1903 survey for the *Tehipite* 30' map; it is on the first edition, 1905. (SeNF)

Pulpit Rock   *Yosemite 15', Yosemite Valley 1:24,000*
A rock formation that looks like a raised pulpit. It is on the south wall of the valley, between the Wawona Tunnel and the Merced River. (*YNN* 34, no. 1, Jan. 1955: 14.) The origin of the name is unknown; it was ratified by the BGN in 1932. (YNP)

Pumice Butte (2,912 m.–9,533)   *Devils Postpile 15', Crystal Crag 7½'*
Possibly named by the USGS during the 1898–99 survey for the *Mt. Lyell* 30' map; it is on the first edition, 1901. (SiNF, INF)

Pumice Flat   *Devils Postpile 15', Mammoth Mtn. 7½'*
"Dr. Randall arrived at old Monoville in the spring of 1861. He engaged men to accompany him to what was called Pumice Flat, now said to be eight miles north of Mammoth Canyon." (Chalfant, *Gold,* 35.) The name is on the first *Mt. Lyell* 30' map, 1901. (INF)

Purple Lake, Creek   *Mt. Morrison 15', Bloody Mtn. 7½'*
"Many-hued rocks reflect in its water, giving it a purple tint at certain times of day." (Smith, 49.) The lake is first named on the *Mt. Morrison* 30' map, 1914. The creek name appears on the 15-minute quad, 1953. (SiNF)

Putnam Canyon   *Mineral King 15'*
This name first appeared on the third edition of the *Kaweah* 30' map, 1921, misspelled "Putman." It was also spelled that way on the early editions of the 15-minute quad, but was corrected by a BGN decision in 1960. The name probably comes from Joseph Putnam, who patented 159.5 acres in sec. 6, T. 18 S., R. 29

E. in 1891. This land is about eight miles downriver from where the stream in Putnam Canyon joins the South Fork of the Kaweah River. (SNP)

Pyramid Peak (3,895 m.–12,777)   *Mt. Pinchot 15' and 7½'*
    The peak probably was named by J. N. LeConte. In June 1902, he and four others made an ascent of Arrow Peak from the south. "Immediately in front to the north were the snow-fields of Arrow Peak, and to the northeast there towered high above us an unnamed, unknown peak guarded by splendid precipices." (*SCB* 4, no. 3, Feb. 1903: 181.) Four months later, in his list of peaks in the Sierra Nevada over 12,000 feet, LeConte listed the "unnamed, unknown peak" as "Pyramid." (*SCB* 4, no. 4, June 1903: 291.) It is named on the first *Mt. Whitney* 30' map, 1907. (KCNP)

Pywiack Cascade, Dome (over 8,800)   *Tuolumne Meadows 15'*
    "The north or Ten-ie-ya branch of the Merced, which comes down the North Cañon from the glistening rocks at its source, was called Py-we-ack, 'the river of glistening rocks,' or more literally, perhaps, 'the river-smoothed rocks.' " (Bunnell, *Discovery,* 1911, 207.) Both the creek and Tenaya Lake were called "Py-we-ack" by the Indians. (See **Tenaya Lake,** etc.) The cascade also had an early name of "Slide Fall." In 1932 the BGN revoked that name and approved. "Pywiack."
    The dome was remarked on by the Whitney Survey in 1863. "At the head of Lake Tenaya is a very conspicuous conical knob of bare granite, about 800 feet high, the sides of which are everywhere finely polished and grooved by former glaciers." (Whitney, *Geology,* 425.) Various names were given to the dome, among them "Murphy's Dome" (see **Murphy Creek**), "Teapot Dome," "Matthes Dome," "Ten-ieya Dome," and "Turtle Rock." David Brower recommended "Pywiack Dome" in the early 1950s; the name first appears on the 15-minute quad, 1956. (YNP)

Qualls Camp   *Huntington Lake 15', Dogtooth Peak 7½'*
    An old cow camp, built in the early 1920s by Wesley Qualls. The last cattleman to use it was Walter Knight; thus the name was changed to "Knight Camp" on the *Dogtooth Peak* 7½' quad, published in 1982. However, the name "Qualls Camp" has been restored by a 1983 BGN decision, and therefore that name should be on future editions of the 7½-minute quad. On the 15-minute quad the camp was misplaced about ¼ mile northwest of the actual location. (BGN Name Report.) (SiNF)

Quarry Peak (11,161)   *Matterhorn Peak 15'*
    Possibly named by the USGS during the 1905–09 survey for the *Bridgeport* 30' map; the name is on the first edition, 1911. (YNP)

Quarter Domes (highest, 8,318)   *Hetch Hetchy Reservoir 15',*
                                        Yosemite Valley 1:24,000
    Named by François Matthes, famous Yosemite geologist. (*YNN* 34, no. 1, Jan. 1955: 14.) The name appeared on the first USGS *Yosemite Valley* map, 1907. (YNP)

Quartz Mountain (9,045)   *Merced Peak 15'*
Possibly named by the USGS during the 1898–99 survey for the *Mt. Lyell* 30' map; it is on the first edition, 1901. (SiNF)

Quartzite Peak (10,440)   *Merced Peak 15'*
A name suggested by François Matthes. It appeared on the ninth edition of the *Mt. Lyell* 30' map, 1948, as "Quartz Peak," even though it had been verified as "Quartzite Peak" by the BGN in 1932. (YNP)

Quinn Peak (10,168), **Ranger Station**   *Mineral King 15'*
Harry Quinn, a native of Ireland, who emigrated to Australia, and emigrated again, to California, in 1868. He was a sheep-owner in Tulare County for many years. (Farquhar.) The first use of the name was in "Quinn Horse Camp," which was on the first *Kaweah* 30' map, 1904. That name was changed to "Quinn Ranger Sta." on the fifth edition, 1934, at which time "Quinn Peak" was named. The place that was once a horse camp, and then a ranger station, is now a snow-survey cabin. (Peak, SNP, SeNF; R.S., SNP)

Rae Lake (9,889–9,894)   *Blackcap Mtn. 15', Mt. Henry 7½'*
Named for Rae Crabtree, a former Coolidge Meadow packer. It is probably the lake known earlier as "Wolverine Lake." (DFG survey.) (SiNF)

Rae Lakes   *Mt. Pinchot 15', Mt. Clarence King 7½'*
Named in 1906 by R. B. Marshall, USGS, for Rachel ("Rae") Colby, wife of William E. Colby. (Farquhar: Marshall. See **Colby Mountain,** etc.) In 1899 Bolton C. Brown named the southernmost lake for his wife—"Lake Lucy." (*SCB* 3, no. 2, May 1900: 136.) Marshall also named just that one lake. It appeared as "Rae Lake" on all editions of the *Mt. Whitney* 30' map, 1907–39. It was changed to "Rae Lakes" on the 15-minute quad, 1953. (KCNP)

Rafferty Peak (over 11,120), **Creek**   *Tuolumne Meadows 15'*
Captain Ogden Rafferty (1860–1922), US Army Medical Corps. The names were given in 1895 by Lt. N. F. McClure, when he was accompanied by Rafferty on a patrol of Yosemite National Park. (Farquhar: McClure.) (YNP)

Ragged Peak (10,912)   *Tuolumne Meadows 15'*
"July 6 [1863] Hoffmann and I visited a peak about four miles north of camp [at Tuolumne Meadows], to complete our bearing for this region. It is a naked granite ridge, about 10,500 feet high, and like all the rest commands a sublime view." (Brewer, *Up and Down,* 415.) The peak probably was named by the Wheeler Survey; it appears on atlas sheet 56D, 1878–79. (YNP)

Ragged Spur   *Mt. Goddard 15' and 7½'*
Probably named by the USGS during the 1907–09 survey for the *Mt. Goddard* 30' map. It is on the first edition, 1912. The spur has two summits over 12,000 feet, neither of which is in J. N. LeConte's 1903 list of peaks in the Sierra over 12,000 feet. (*SCB* 4, no. 4, June 1903: 285–91.) (KCNP)

Rainbow Falls   *Devils Postpile 15', Crystal Crag 7½'*
Probably named by the USGS during the 1898–99 survey for the *Mt. Lyell* 30' map; the name is on the first edition, 1901. (Devils Postpile National Monument)

Rainbow Lakes   *Mt. Goddard 15', North Palisade 7½'*
Named by one Halladay, an early packer on the South Fork of Bishop Creek.
(Art Schober.) (KCNP)

Rainbow Mountain (over 12,000)   *Mineral King 15'*
Named for the different shades of coloring in the rocks, with a "rainbow oval
crest." (Guy Hopping, SNP files.) The name appears on the fifth edition of the
Kaweah 30' map, 1934. (SNP)

Rainbow View (4,953)   *Yosemite 15', Yosemite Valley 1:24,000*
A viewpoint on the Old Big Oak Flat Road opposite the east end of the
Wawona Tunnel. It got its name from the rainbow which sometimes may be seen
in Bridalveil Fall during summer midafternoons. (*YNN* 34, no. 1, Jan. 1955:
14.) The name appeared on the fourth edition of the *Yosemite Valley* map,
1927. (YNP)

Ram Lake   *Blackcap Mtn. 15' and 7½', Mt. Goddard 7½'*
Named in 1948 by William A. Dill of the DFG because it is close to Bighorn
Lake. (DFG survey.) (SiNF)

Rambaud Peak (11,044), **Creek**   *Mt. Goddard 15', North Palisade 7½'*
Pete Rambaud was a Basque sheepman. In 1877 he brought the first sheep
into the region of the Middle Fork of the Kings River, coming from the east side
of the mountains via Bishop Pass. (Farquhar: L. A. Winchell.) Both names are
on the first *Mt. Goddard* 30' map, 1912. (KCNP)

Ramshaw Meadows   *Kern Peak 15', Olancha 15'*
Named for Peter Ramshaw, a stockman in this region from 1861 to 1880.
(Farquhar: Versteeg.) (INF)

Rancheria Creek   *Hetch Hetchy Reservoir 15', Tower Peak 15',
                                        Matterhorn Peak 15'*
Rancheria Mountain (8,995), **Falls**   *Hetch Hetchy Reservoir 15'*
The Spanish word "rancheria" originally meant a collection of crude
dwellings, but in Spanish California it was used to mean Indian villages in
general. Several sites have been located on the slopes of Rancheria Mountain.
(YNP files.) "Rancheria Creek" is on the Wheeler Survey atlas sheet 56D,
1878–79. The mountain is named on the first edition of the *Yosemite* 30' map,
1897, and the falls is named on the fifth edition, 1911. (YNP)

Randall Creek   *Markleeville 15' and 7½'*
Franklin Randall homesteaded 160 acres in sec. 6, T. 10 N., R. 20 E. in
1895. (TNF)

Raymond Peak (10,014–10,011), **Lake** (8,994), **Meadows;**
Raymond Meadows Creek   *Markleeville 15', Ebbetts Pass 7½'*
Raymond Canyon Creek   *Markleeville 15' and 7½', Ebbetts Pass 7½'*
The Whitney Survey named the peak in 1865 for Rossiter W. Raymond, a
US mineral examiner and commissioner of mining statistics in the Treasury
Department. (Maule; Gudde, *Gold,* 417.) He also surveyed and wrote reports
on the mines in Alpine County. (*Alpine Heritage,* 29.) Theron Reed's map of the

Silver Mountain Mining District, 1864, shows "Raymond Dist." and "Raymond," a settlement. The lake, meadows, and two creeks were first named on the 15-minute quad, 1956. (TNF)

Raymond Mountain (8,712) *Yosemite 15'*
Israel Ward Raymond (1811–1887) was influential in securing the grant of the Yosemite Valley and the Mariposa Grove to California in 1864. He was appointed as one of the first commissioners to manage the park, and served until 1886. (Farquhar; *SCB* 33, no. 3, March 1948: 66–69.) The name was given by the Whitney Survey; it is on the Hoffmann and Gardiner map of 1863–67 as "Mt. Raymond." (SiNF)

Reba, Mount (8,755–8,758) *Silver Lake 15', Mokelumne Peak 7½'*
Named for Reba Blood, daughter of Harvey S. Blood. (Wood, 60; see **Bloods Toll Station**, etc.) (StNF)

Recess Peak (12,813–12,836); **First Recess, Lakes; Second Recess; Third Recess, Lake** (10,531); **Fourth Recess, Lake** (10,132)
Mt. Abbot 15' and 7½'
Theodore S. Solomons discovered and named the four recesses in 1894, and named the peak because of its proximity to the First Recess. (Farquhar: Solomons.) The lakes are first named on the 15-minute quad, 1953. (SiNF)

Red and White Mountain (12,816–12,850), **Lake** *Mt. Abbot 15' and 7½'*
Named by Theodore S. Solomons in 1894. (Farquhar: Solomons.) The first ascent was made on July 18, 1902, by Lincoln and James Hutchinson and Charles A. Noble. Once on top, they thought of renaming it. "Being the first to set foot on its summit, it seemed our right to name it as we chose. . . . In the end, however, it seemed wiser to make no change. The name has gained a place in the maps, and it is peculiarly descriptive of the great peak of red slate fantastically streaked with seams of white granite. The name identifies the mountain." (*SCB* 4, no. 3, Feb. 1903: 200–201.) The lake was first named on the 15-minute quad, 1953. (Mtn., SiNF, INF; lake, SiNF)

Red Lake; Red Lake Peak (10,063–10,061), **Creek** *Markleeville 15', Carson Pass 7½'*
On February 14, 1844, John C. Frémont and Charles Preuss climbed Red Lake Peak, the first ascent by white men of an identifiable mountain in the Sierra Nevada. From the summit they were the first to see and describe Lake Tahoe. (Vincent P. Gianella, "Where Frémont Crossed the Sierra Nevada in 1844," *SCB* 44, no. 7, Oct. 1959: 54–63.)
The lake and the mountain acquired names at the same time. "Red Lake at the foot of Red Peak is a small marshy lake apparently drying up." (Goddard, *Report,* 105.) "Red Lake" appears on Theron Reed's map of the Silver Mountain Mining District, 1864. Later, in a reversal of the normal pattern, the mountain was renamed from the lake, and became "Red Lake Peak" on the first *Markleeville* 30' map, 1891. The creek was first named on the 15-minute quad. (TNF)

Red Mountain (11,963–11,951); **Red Mountain Basin**
Blackcap Mtn. 15', Mt. Henry 7½'
J. N. LeConte and Clarence L. Cory made the first ascent of the mountain on July 12, 1898, and first used the name in print but did not claim to have named it. (*SCB* 2, no. 5, Jan. 1899: 260–61.)
    The USGS probably named the basin; both names are on the first *Mt. Goddard* 30' map, 1912. As will be seen on the 7½-minute quad, the basin now includes the total area at the headwaters of Fleming Creek, west of Red Mountain, containing more than 20 lakes. (Mtn., SiNF, KCNP; basin, SiNF)

Red Peak (11,699), **Creek; Red Peak Fork; Red Devil Lake**
Merced Peak 15'
The peak probably was named by the Wheeler Survey; it is on atlas sheet 56D, 1878–79. The other names derive from the peak. All of them were first named on the 15-minute quad, 1953. (YNP)

Red Peak (10,009–10,021)   *Sonora Pass 15', Disaster Peak 7½'*
Possibly named by the USGS during the 1891–96 survey for the *Dardanelles* 30' map; it is on the first edition, 1898. (StNF)

Red Point (over 11,840)   *Marion Peak 15'*
Possibly named by the USGS during the 1903 survey for the *Tehipite* 30' map; it is on the first edition, 1905. (KCNP)

Red Slate Mountain (13,163)   *Mt. Morrison 15', Convict Lake 7½'*
Named by the Whitney Survey in 1864. This mountain and several others of similar coloring were called "Red Slate Peaks." The present name is on Hoffmann's map of 1873, but it is not clear whether it applies to this peak or to Red and White Mountain. (SiNF, INF)

Red Spur; Red Spur Creek   *Mount Whitney 15', Mt. Kaweah 7½'*
"From Mt. Kaweah, this chain continues east to near the Kern, in a long, reddish sloping ridge, seen from many places in the Kern River Cañon. We named it the Red Spur." (William R. Dudley in *SCB* 2, no 3, Jan. 1898: 189, and sketch map, plate XXV.) The USGS probably named the creek during the 1905 survey for the *Mt. Whitney* 30' map; both features are on the first edition, 1907. (SNP)

Red Top (9,977)   *Merced Peak 15'*
Possibly named by the USGS during the 1898–99 survey for the *Mt. Lyell* 30' map; it is on all editions of the map, 1901–48, as "Redtop." (YNP, SiNF)

Red Top Mountain (3,184 m.–10,279) *Devils Postpile 15', Mt. Ritter 7½'*
The name was approved by the BGN in 1976, but with no explanation of who proposed it. The mountain is not named on the 15-minute quad. It is 1.9 miles southeast of the outlet of Minaret Lake, marked "10279." (INF)

Reds Meadow, Creek   *Devils Postpile 15', Crystal Crag 7½'*
Reds Lake   *Devils Postpile 15', Mammoth Mtn. 7½'*
Named for "Red" Sotcher, who came to the area in 1879 as a sheepherder. (Smith, *Mammoth*, 14.) A stockman with a red beard. (Farquhar.) "Reds

Meadows" and the creek were named on the first *Mt. Lyell* 30' map, 1901. The lake appears on the 15-minute quad. On that map the creek flows west from near the lake. On the 7½-minute quad the name "Reds Creek" has been placed on the creek heading on the southwest side of Mammoth Mountain and flowing into Reds Meadow. (INF)

Redwood Meadow; Redwood Meadow Grove　　*Triple Divide Peak 15'*
The meadow was named in 1877 by W. B. Wallace, T. J. Witt, and N. B. Witt. (Farquhar: G. W. Stewart.) The land was privately owned. In 1921 Stephen T. Mather purchased it from the heirs of James Hamilton and placed it in trust to become part of Sequoia National Park. Title to the land was conveyed to the United States in 1927. (Farquhar; see **Hamilton Lakes, Creek.**) The grove was first named on the 15-minute map, 1956. (SNP)

Reflection, Lake (3,057 m.–10,005)　　　　　*Mount Whitney 15',*
Mt. Brewer 7½'
Named by Howard Longley and party in August 1894. (*SCB* 1, no. 6, May 1895: 192.) (KCNP)

Register Creek　　*Hetch Hetchy Reservoir 15', Tuolumne Meadows 15'*
The origin of the name is unknown, "but possibly because of some sort of registration book along the creek." (YNP files.) The name was not used by travelers down the Grand Canyon of the Tuolumne River in 1894 and 1897, but it is on the first edition of the *Mt. Lyell* 30' map, 1901. Thus one must assume that the creek was named either by army patrols or by USGS surveyors in the late 1890s. (YNP)

Regulation Peak (over 10,560), **Creek**　　*Tuolumne Meadows 15'*
In 1895 Lt. Harry C. Benson and a trumpeter named McBride placed copies of Yosemite National Park regulations on trees throughout the park. McBride suggested the name "Regulation Peak" for a mountain between Smedberg Lake and Rodgers Lake. Benson put the name on his map of 1897. Lt. McClure, on his map of 1896, put the name in an ambiguous position. When the USGS 30' maps were published, the name was put on the wrong peak. The true "Regulation Peak" was given the name "Volunteer Peak" on the first *Bridgeport* 30' map, a name it has had ever since. (Farquhar: Benson.)
On the first *Mt. Lyell* 30' map, 1901, "Regulation Peak" was on a summit a mile south of Rodgers Lake. On the 1905 edition it had disappeared. The 1910 edition moved it north to its present position, and gave the name "West Peak" to the former "Regulation Peak."
"Regulation Creek" was named "West Fork Return Creek" on the *Mt. Lyell* 30' maps, 1901–29. It acquired its present name on the eighth edition, 1944. (YNP)

Reinstein, Mount (12,586–12,604)　　*Mt. Goddard 15' and 7½'*
Named by R. B. Marshall, USGS, for Jacob Bert Reinstein, a charter member of the Sierra Club. (Farquhar: Marshall.) The peak is named on the first *Mt. Goddard* 30' map, 1912. (SiNF, KCNP)

Upper Relief Valley   *Pinecrest 15'*
Lower Relief Valley   *Pinecrest 15', Dardanelles Cone 15', Dardanelle 7½'*
Relief Creek   *Pinecrest 15', Tower Peak 15'*
Relief Peak (10,808)   *Tower Peak 15'*
Relief Reservoir   *Sonora Pass 15' and 7½'*
This seeming complexity and profusion of names arises only because the
named features cluster around the spot where four quadrangles have a common
corner. The name "Relief Valley" comes from an episode in 1852 when a party
of emigrants were caught in an early snowstorm on the east side of the
mountains. They abandoned their wagons, crossed the summit on foot to a
sheltered spot on the west side, and sent some of their number for help. (*Historic
Spots*, 566.)
   "This valley takes its very appropriate name from the fact that it was here
that relief was brought to the emigrants in their almost starving condition, from
the generous-hearted citizens of Sonora and Columbia." (Hutchings,
Illustrated 2, May 1858: 494.)
   "Relief Valley" is on Goddard's *Map of Sonora Pass*, 1853. Apparently
this was what is now the site of "Relief Reservoir." It was called "Lower Relief
Valley" on the 1883 GLO plat and in the field notes of the surveyor. The creek
was called "Relief Valley Creek" in those same documents. The peak, creek,
and "Relief Valley" are on the Wheeler Survey atlas sheet 56D, 1878–79. The
present array of names came into being on the four 15-minute quads in 1956.

Return Creek   *Matterhorn Peak 15', Tuolumne Meadows 15'*
   The name first appeared on the Wheeler Survey atlas sheet 56D, 1878–79. I
find no explanation for its origin. (YNP)

Reversed Creek, Peak (9,473)   *Mono Craters 15'*
   "The ancient drainage has been reversed by the deposition of morainal
debris; we have therefore called the stream draining June and Gull lakes,
Reversed Creek. The drainage before the site of June Lake was occupied by a
glacier must have been northward." (Russell, *Quaternary*, 343.) The peak was
named for the creek by USGS surveyors; both names are on the first *Mt. Lyell*
30' map, 1901. (INF)

Reymann Lake   *Tuolumne Meadows 15'*
   Named for William M. Reymann (1883–1938), a Yosemite National Park
ranger. (Bingaman, *Guardians*, 115.) (YNP)

Reynolds Peak (9,679–9,690)   *Markleeville 15', Ebbetts Pass 7½'*
   Named in 1929 on the recommendation of the USGS for G. Elmer
Reynolds, an advocate of forest conservation and for many years the managing
editor of the Stockton *Record*. (BGN, *Sixth Report*, 640.) (ENF, TNF)

Rex Montis Mine   *Mt. Pinchot 15'*
   At 12,000 feet, the highest mine of the Kearsarge Mining District; it has not
been worked since 1883. (DeDecker, 54–56.) (INF)

Ribbon Fall, Meadow   *Yosemite 15', Yosemite Valley 1:24,000*
Ribbon Creek   *Hetch Hetchy Reservoir 15', Yosemite 15',*
Yosemite Valley 1:24,000

"The Indians call this Lung-oo-too-koo-yah, or the graceful and slender one; while a lady, whose name shall be nameless, once christened it 'Virgin's Tears.' " (Hutchings, *In the Heart,* 398.)

"The name for the little fall to which the name of 'Virgin's Tears' has been applied, was known to us as 'Pigeon Creek Fall.' The Indian name is 'Lung-yo-to-co-ya;' its literal meaning is 'Pigeon Basket,' probably signifying to them 'Pigeon Nests,' or *Roost.* In explanation of the name for the creek, I was told that west of El Capitan, in the valley of the stream, and upon the southern slopes, pigeons were at times quite numerous." (Bunnell, *Discovery,* 1911, 213–14.) "Mr. Hutchings has named the fall 'The Ribbon Fall,' as an English name was desirable." (Bunnell, *Report,* 9–10.)

The Whitney Survey maps showed "Virgin Tear's Fall" and "Virgin Tears Creek." "Ribbon Falls" is on the first *Yosemite* 30' map, 1897. The creek is named on the USGS *Yosemite Valley* map in 1907; the meadow on the 15-minute quad, 1956. (YNP)

Richardson Peak (9,884)   *Tower Peak 15'*
Named in June 1879 by Lt. M. M. Macomb of the Wheeler Survey. "I was accompanied by Mr. Thomas Richardson, who has a sheep range in Cherry Valley and vicinity, and who is perfectly familiar with the rugged country south of the Relief trail." (Macomb, *Annual Report of the Chief of Engineers, U.S. Army, for 1879,* Appendix F of Appendix 00, 257.) The name is on atlas sheet 56D as "Richardson's." It was changed to "Richardson Peak" on the first *Dardanelles* 30' map, 1898. (YNP)

Rickey Peak (10,126), **Cabin**   *Fales Hot Springs 15' and 7½'*
Named for Tom Rickey, an early settler who became a large landowner and cattle rancher. In the 1890s the Rickey Land and Cattle Company owned 12,000 acres in Bridgeport Valley. "The other farmers used to say that Tom Rickey started his holdings with one bull and a branding iron." (Cain, 37.)

The names are on the Wheeler Survey atlas sheet 56D as "Rickey's Pk." and "Rickey's." The 1884 GLO plat shows "Rickey's House" exactly where the cabin is, in sec. 15, T. 5 N., R. 23 E. (TNF)

Ritter, Mount (4,006 m.–13,157); **Ritter Lakes, Pass**
Devils Postpile 15', Mt. Ritter 7½'
Ritter Range   *Devils Postpile 15', Mt. Ritter 7½', Cattle Mtn. 7½'*
The mountain was named by the Whitney Survey in 1864. "Ritter is the name of the great German geographer, the founder of the science of modern comparative geography." (Whitney, *Yosemite Guide-Book,* 1870, 101.) Karl Ritter (1779–1859) was professor of history at the University of Berlin when Whitney was a student there during the 1840s.

John Muir made the first ascent in October 1872. "I was suddenly brought to a dead stop, with arms outspread, clinging close to the face of the rock, unable to move hand or foot either up or down. My doom appeared fixed. I *must* fall. There would be a moment of bewilderment, and then a lifeless rumble down the one general precipice to the glacier below. When this final danger flashed upon me, I became nerve-shaken for the first time since setting foot on the mountain, and my mind seemed to fill with a stifling smoke. But . . . life blazed forth again with preternatural clearness. I seemed suddenly to become possessed of a new sense. . . . Then my trembling muscles became firm again, every rift and flaw in the rock was seen as through a microscope, and my limbs moved with a positiveness and precision with which I seemed to have nothing at all to do. Had I been borne aloft upon wings, my deliverance could not have been more complete. . . . I found a way without effort, and soon stood upon the topmost crag in the blessed light." (Muir, *Mountains,* 64–65.)

The mountain is named on Hoffmann and Gardiner's map, 1863–67. "Ritter Range" appears on the fifth edition of the *Mt. Lyell* 30' map, 1922. Neither the lakes nor the pass are named on the 15-minute quad. There are four lakes, two large and two small, west of Mt. Ritter and south of Lake Catherine. The pass is over the range 1.2 miles south-southeast of Mt. Ritter. (Lakes, SiNF; others, SiNF, INF)

River Spring   *Kern Peak 15'*
A strong flow of water bubbles up from beneath a rock formation. The name is on the first *Olancha* 30' map, 1907. (INF)

River Valley   *Triple Divide Peak 15'*
The name for the canyon of the upper Middle Fork of the Kaweah River is one of those that just grew. When it got to be in common use, the USGS put it on the map—the fourth edition of the *Tehipite* 30' map, 1929. (SNP)

Rixford, Mount (3,928 m.–12,890)   *Mt. Pinchot 15',*
                                              Mt. Clarence King 7½'
Named by Vernon L. Kellogg in 1899. "On climbing this peak I found records of but two previous ascents . . . the first in time being that of Dr. Emmet Rixford. Dr. Rixford's name became especially familiar to us last summer through finding it at the top of almost every peak we got up. . . . At my suggestion we have called the hitherto unnamed peak in the Gardner-Kearsarge Divide 'Mt. Rixford.' " (*SCB* 3, no. 2, May 1900: 168–69.) Rixford was professor of surgery at Stanford. (KCNP)

Roaring River   *Triple Divide Peak 15', Marion Peak 15'*
Named by Frank M. Lewis in the 1870s. (Farquhar: Lewis. See **Lewis Creek, Lake.**) E. C. Winchell gave it a different name in 1868. "A mile above the ford we passed the mouth of 'Kettle Brook,' which leaps into the gorge from the southeast, down a slope of 45 degrees, through an impassable ravine." (San Francisco *Daily Morning Call,* Sept. 12, 1872; also in *SCB* 12, no. 3, 1926: 247.)

"The Roaring River came down its narrow cañon in a series of rapids for a mile, and then plunged down 40 feet into the pool, filling the air with driving spray. It was a wild scene, to look up that gorge. So narrow was it that a man could not possibly get a foothold anywhere along the river, for the walls sloped in some places at an angle of from 60 to 70 degrees." (LeConte, *A Summer*, 33.) (KCNP)

Robinson Creek, Peak (10,806)   *Matterhorn Peak 15'*
Moses Robinson operated a sawmill on this stream in 1861. (Maule.) In the GLO surveyor's field notes and on the plat of 1877 it is called "Robison Creek." In sec. 15, T. 4 N., R. 24 E., just where the road bends west and touches the edge of sec. 16, is the legend "Robison's Mill." The 1882 plat of T. 3 N., R. 24 E. calls it "Robinson Creek." That name is on the Wheeler Survey atlas sheet 56D, 1878–79. The peak is named on the first *Bridgeport* 30' map, 1911. (TNF)

Robinson, Mount (12,967)   *North Palisade 7½'*
Named for Douglas Robinson, who spent 30 years with the US Forest Service. (*Saga*, 200.) The name came into use informally in *The Climber's Guide*, and was added to the map by the USGS because it was in common use. On the *Mt. Goddard* 15' quad it is an unnamed and unmarked peak ¾ mile west by north from the northern tip of Sam Mack Lake. (INF)

Rock Creek   *Kern Peak 15', Mount Whitney 15' and 7½'*
The name probably was given by sheepmen, who were the first to enter this region. It was already in use in 1890. (LeConte, *A Summer*, 79.) (SNP)

Rock Creek; Rock Creek Lake   *Casa Diablo Mtn. 15', Mt. Tom 15',*
Mt. Morgan 7½'
On A. W. Von Schmidt's township plat of 1855 the creek was shown as the "West Branch of Owens River." Later, because of its extremely rocky bed, it was named "Rock Creek." Both names are on the first *Mt. Goddard* 30' map, 1912. (INF)

Rock Island Lake, Pass; Rock Canyon, Creek   *Matterhorn Peak 15'*
"I named the stream Rock Creek, and the lake Rock Island Lake, from a large granite island that was visible near the northern end." (Lt. N. F. McClure in *SCB* 1, no. 5, Jan. 1895: 178.) In the same article McClure used "Rock Cañon" as though it were an existing name; thus he was extending it to other features. The canyon, lake, and pass are named on the first *Bridgeport* 30' map, 1911, but the creek name doesn't appear until the 15-minute quad, 1956. (YNP; pass also TNF)

Rockhouse Meadow, Basin   *Lamont Peak 15'*
On the 1881 GLO plat the name "Rock House Meadow" is in the N½ of the NW¼ of sec. 34, T. 23 S., R. 35 E. The house is marked just below the meadow at the left edge of the section. The meadow and the basin are named on the first *Kernville* 30' map, 1908. (SeNF)

Rockslide Lake   *Mount Whitney 15', Mt. Kaweah 7½'*
Apparently named by William R. Dudley in July 1897. (Sketch map in *SCB* 2, no. 3, Jan. 1898: plate XXV.) (SNP)

Rockslides   *Yosemite 15', Yosemite Valley 1:24,000*
An early BGN decision designated the area "Rockslides Slope," but that

name was never on the maps. In October 1942, rockslides wiped out the
"Zigzags" on the Old Big Oak Flat Road—and that put the name on the maps.
(YNP)

Rocky Basin Lakes (largest, 10,745)   *Kern Peak 15'*
   A GLO surveyor provided the name simply by describing the area as a
"Rocky Basin Containing Five Lakes" on the 1873 plat. Thereafter the name
did not appear on maps until the 15-minute quad was published in 1956. (INF)

Rocky Point   *Yosemite 15', Yosemite Valley 1:24,000*
   "Rocky Point . . . is just under the lowest shoulder of the 'Three Brothers,'
and is formed by large blocks of rocky talus that once peeled from its side."
(Hutchings, *In the Heart,* 394.) Ansel Hall gave the Indian name as "We-ack,"
meaning "the rocks," the place where Chief Tenaya's three sons were captured
in 1851. (Hall, *Yosemite,* 16; also *YNN* 34, no. 1, Jan. 1955: 14.) (YNP)

Rodeo Meadow   *Dogtooth Peak 7½'*
   A meadow where three cattle outfits used to separate their cattle in the fall.
The resulting melees gave rise to the name. (USGS.) The name is not on the
Huntington Lake 15' quad. It is the large meadow ½ mile southeast of Long
Meadow. (SiNF)

Rodgers Canyon, Meadow   *Hetch Hetchy Reservoir 15'*
Rodgers Lake   *Tuolumne Meadows 15'*
Rodgers Peak (12,978)   *Merced Peak 15'*
   These four features are named for Capt. Alexander Rodgers, Fourth
Cavalry, US Army, acting superintendent of Yosemite National Park in 1895
and 1897.
   The peak was named in 1895 by Lt. N. F. McClure. That same year, Lt.
H. C. Benson gave Rodgers' name to the lake and the peak just south of it. To
avoid duplication, the USGS gave the name "Regulation Peak" to the second
"Rodgers Peak." (See **Regulation Peak, Creek.** Farquhar: McClure,
Benson.)
   The first edition of the *Yosemite* 30' map had "Rodgers Canyon" and
"Rodgers Lake." This lake (which is not the present one) had its name changed
to "Neall Lake" on the third edition of the map, 1903. The present "Rodgers
Lake" was on the first *Mt. Lyell* 30' map, 1901. The meadow was first named
on the 15-minute map, 1956.
   At about the time that Lt. McClure named it "Rodgers Peak," J. N. LeConte
named it "Mount Kellogg," for Vernon L. Kellogg, professor of entomology at
Stanford. (LeConte, *Alpina,* 10.) He had the name on his 1896 map. Neither
name was on the USGS 30-minute maps, although "Rodgers Peak" had been
ratified by the BGN in 1932. It finally showed up on the 15-minute quad, where
an early edition had it misspelled "Rodger Peak." (Peak, YNP, INF, SiNF;
others, YNP)

Rogers Camp   *Camp Nelson 15'*
   Henry C. Rogers patented 160 acres in the SW¼ and the SE¼ of sec. 9, T.
21 S., R. 31 E. in 1890. (SeNF)

Roget Lake   *Mount Tom 7½'*
Named in 1954 by Ralph Beck of the DFG. (Phil Pister. See **Alsace Lake.**)
Not named on the *Mt. Tom* 15' quad. It is the crescent-shaped lake, with neither
inlet nor outlet, ¼ mile south-southeast of the east end of Puppet Lake. (SiNF)

Roman Four Lake   *Blackcap Mtn. 15' and 7½'*
Named in 1948 by William A. Dill of the DFG because of a fancied
resemblance to a Roman *IV*, the brand of Ted Anderson, former Dinkey Creek
packer. (DFG survey.) (SiNF)

Roosevelt Lake (10,184)   *Tuolumne Meadows 15'*
Named for Eleanor Roosevelt, to commemorate a visit she made to
Yosemite National Park in July 1934. (Bingaman, *Guardians,* 40.) (YNP)

Rosasco Lake   *Pinecrest 15'*
Named for Dave Rosasco, an early cattleman. (DFG files.) (StNF)

Rose Lake (10,495)   *Mt. Abbot 15', Florence Lake 7½'*
Named about 1910 by R. B. Marshall, USGS, for Rosa Hooper, a sister of
Selden S. Hooper, an assistant with the USGS, and daughter of William B.
Hooper. (Farquhar: Marshall, Mary Hooper Perry. See **Selden Pass** and
Hooper, Mount.) The name is on the first *Mt. Goddard* 30' map, 1912. (SiNF)

Rosebud Lake   *Mt. Abbot 15', Florence Lake 7½'*
Possibly named by Elden H. Vestal of the DFG. It may take its name from
the nearby, much larger, Rose Lake. (SiNF)

Rosemarie Meadow   *Mt. Abbot 15', Mt. Hilgard 7½'*
This apparently is a composite name, drawn from nearby "Rose Lake" and
"Marie Lake," both of which were named about 1910 by R. B. Marshall of the
USGS. "Rosemarie Meadow" appeared on the 15-minute quad, 1953.
(SiNF)

Ross Creek   *Shuteye Peak 15'*
Jesse B. Ross homesteaded 160 acres in secs. 8 and 9, T. 8 S., R. 24 E. in
1900. (SiNF)

Rosy Finch Lake (10,791)   *Mt. Abbot 15' and 7½'*
Named in 1943 by William A. Dill of the DFG when it was surveyed for fish
planting. (*SCB* 36, no. 4, April 1951: 11.) (SiNF)

Round Mountain (3,410.1 m.–11,188)   *Big Pine 15', Coyote Flat 7½'*
Probably named by the USGS during the 1910–11 survey for the *Bishop* 30'
map; it is on the first edition, 1913. (INF)

Round Mountain (9,884)   *Monache Mtn. 15'*
Probably named by the USGS during the 1905 survey for the *Olancha* 30'
map; it is on the first edition, 1907. (INF)

Round Top (10,381–10,380)   *Markleeville 15', Silver Lake 15',*
                                       Carson Pass 7½', Caples Lake 7½'
Round Top Lake   *Silver Lake 15', Caples Lake 7½'*
For the field season of 1877, Lt. M. M. Macomb wrote that "we made a

triangulation station on what is locally known as Silver Era Peak, but which is called by the United States Coast Survey 'Round Top.' " (Wheeler Survey, *Report,* 1878, 141.) The lake was first named on the 15-minute quad, 1956. (ENF)

Round Valley   *Mt. Tom 15', Rovana 7½'*
Round Valley Peak (over 11,960–11,943)   *Mt. Tom 15', Mt. Morgan 7½'*
The name "Round Valley" came into existence when the first white settlers arrived in the region in the 1860s. The peak probably was named by the USGS during the 1907–09 survey for the *Mt. Goddard* 30' map; it is on the first edition, 1912. (INF)

Roush Creek   *Shuteye Peak 15'*
Charley Roush operated a sawmill, 1920–24, in the NE¼ of sec. 3, T. 8 S., R. 23 E. During that time he cut 6,000,000 feet of lumber from 240 acres. (Hurt, 22.) (SiNF)

Rowell Meadow   *Triple Divide Peak 15'*
Chester Rowell (1844–1912), born in New Hampshire, grew up in Illinois, came to California in 1866. He was a physician, newspaper publisher, banker, state senator, mayor of Fresno, and regent of the University of California, 1891–1912. (Winchell, *Fresno County,* 169, and Vandor, vol. 1, 237–39.)
"Doctor Chester Rowell and his brother George were owners of sheep in the middle Seventies, that were ranged on the western slopes of the Kings-Kaweah divide. Rowell Meadow was one of their camps." (Winchell, 158.) (SeNF)

Royal Arches; Royal Arch Cascade   *Yosemite 15',*
                                            Yosemite Valley 1:24,000
Royal Arch Creek   *Hetch Hetchy Reservoir 15', Yosemite 15',*
                                            Yosemite Valley 1:24,000
"The name given to the rocks now known as 'The Royal Arches' is Scho-ko-ya when alluding to the fall, and means 'Basket Fall,' as coming from To-ko-ya, and when referring to the rock itself it was called Scho-ko-ni, meaning the movable shade to a cradle, which, when in position, formed an arched shade over the infant's head. The name of 'The Royal Arch' was given to it [in 1851] by a comrade who was a member of the Masonic Fraternity, and it has since been called 'The Royal Arches.' " (Bunnell, *Discovery,* 1880, 212.)
"Cho-ko-nip'-o-deh (baby basket), Royal Arches. This curved and overhanging canopy-rock bears no little resemblance to an Indian baby-basket. Another form is *cho-ko'-ni;* and either one means literally 'dog-place' or 'dog-house.' " (Powers, 364.)
There has also been a contention that the Indian name was "Hunto." "From an Indian word for eye." (Sanchez, 278.) *Huntu* is "eye" in Southern Sierra Miwok. (Kroeber, 43.) "Shun'-ta, Hun'-ta (the eye), the Watching Eye." (Powers, 365.)
"Owing to the curve of these wing-like arches, stretching as they do from a kind of lion-like head . . . a gentleman resident of Philadelphia suggested that 'The Winged Lion' (one of the sculptures found by Layard in the ruined cities of

the Euphrates Valley) would be a more expressive and suitable name for it than 'Royal Arches.' " (Hutchings, *In the Heart,* 383; Layard was the excavator of Nineveh.)

"Royal Arches" appears on the King and Gardiner map of 1865. The creek and cascade are first named on the fourth *Yosemite Valley* map, 1927. (YNP)

Royce Peak (over 13,280–13,253), **Lakes**   *Mt. Abbot 15', Mt. Hilgard 7½'*
Josiah Royce (1855–1916), philosopher and educator, a native of Grass Valley, California. He taught English for four years at the University of California, and was a professor of philosophy at Harvard, 1882–1916.

The name for the peak was proposed by the California State Geographic Board in 1929; the name appeared on the fifth edition of the *Mt. Goddard* 30' map, 1933. The lakes were first named on the 15-minute quad, 1953. (SiNF)

Rush Creek   *Mono Craters 15', Devils Postpile 15', Mt. Ritter 7½'*
This is one of the older names on the east side of the Sierra, yet its origin is unknown. It appears on the Hoffmann and Gardiner map of 1863–67 and in Whitney's *Yosemite Book,* 1868. On A. W. Von Schmidt's plat of 1857 it is called "Lake Creek," possibly because of the many lakes at its headwaters. This name was still used on GLO plats as late as 1895, even though the Wheeler Survey called it "Rush Creek" on atlas sheet 56D, 1878–79. (INF)

Ruskin, Mount (3,938 m.–12,920)   *Mt. Pinchot 15' and 7½'*
Named in 1895 by Bolton C. Brown for John Ruskin (1819–1900), English writer and critic. (Farquhar: J. N. LeConte.) Brown describes making the first ascent of the peak in 1895, but does not mention the naming in the text. (*SCB* 1, no. 8, May 1896: 304–5.) (KCNP)

Russell, Mount (4,294 m.–14,086)   *Mount Whitney 15' and 7½'*
Named for Israel Cook Russell (1852–1906), geologist with the Wheeler Survey and the USGS, and professor of geology at the University of Michigan, 1892–1906. (Farquhar: R. B. Marshall. See the bibliography.) (SNP, INF)

Rust Lake   *Mount Tom 7½'*
Named by Scott M. Soule of the DFG, sometime after the 1951 survey. (DFG survey.) It is not named on the *Mt. Tom* 15' quad; it is the larger of two lakes south-southeast of Steelhead Lake, in sec. 32, T. 7 S., R. 30 E. (SiNF)

Ruth Lake   *Merced Peak 15'*
According to warden Herb Black of the DFG, the lake was named by the 1934 DFG-USFS survey party for the wife of A. E. Burghduff of the DFG. Earlier names for the lake were "Hidden Lake," "Nutcracker Lake," and "Hideaway Lake." (DFG survey.) (SiNF)

Rutherford Lake   *Merced Peak 15'*
Named for Lt. Samuel McPherson Rutherford, Fourth Cavalry, US Army, on duty in Yosemite National Park in 1896. (Farquhar.) (SiNF)

Ruwau Lake   *Mt. Goddard 15', Mt. Thompson 7½'*
The name is a combination of the names of two power-company engineers, Clarence H. Rhudy and E. J. Waugh. (Schumacher, 94.) Rhudy was also a

climber. He made the first ascent of Mt. Thompson, in 1909 (*SCB* 27, no. 4, Aug. 1942: 96), and one of the early ascents of Mt. Humphreys. (*SCB* 11, no. 2, Jan. 1921: 203–4). (INF)

Sabrina, Lake (9,132)   *Mt. Goddard 15', Mt. Thompson 7½'*
Named for Sabrina Hobbs, whose husband, Charles M. Hobbs, was the first general manager of the Nevada California Power Company, which dammed the lake during 1907–08. (Farquhar: W. L. Huber.) The name was spelled "Sebrina" on the first three editions of the *Mt. Goddard* 30' map, 1912–23. It was corrected in 1928. "Camp Sabrina," ½ mile below the lake on the 15-minute quad, is no longer in existence. It is now a USGS campground. (INF)

Sacatar Meadow, Canyon, Trail   *Lamont Peak 15'*
Sacratone Flat   *Hockett Peak 15'*
The word "sacatar" is Spanish for a place where a certain bunchgrass—sacaton—grows. "Sacratone" is probably a misspelling of the word. (*Los Tulares,* no. 60, March 1964: 3.) The meadow and canyon were named on the first *Kernville* 30' map, 1908. "Sacratone Flat" appeared on the 15-minute quad, 1956. (Flat, SeNF)

Sachse Monument (9,405)   *Tower Peak 15'*
Sachse was a cowboy for Bill Woods (or Wood). He was credited with locating many routes through the Emigrant Basin area which later became trails. (StNF files, from Joe Ratto.) (StNF)

Saddle Horse Lake   *Hetch Hetchy Reservoir 15'*
The origin is unknown. This lake and "Irwin Bright Lake" switched names due to a BGN decision in 1960. (YNP)

Saddle Mountain (11,189–11,192)   *Kaiser Peak 15',*
                    Sharktooth Peak 7½'
Upper Saddle Lake; Lower Saddle Lake   *Sharktooth Peak 7½'*
The mountain probably was named by the USGS during the 1901–02 survey for the *Kaiser* 30' map; it is on the first edition, 1904. The two lakes were named in 1949 by Charles K. Fisher of the DFG because of their proximity to the mountain. (DFG survey.) On the 15-minute quad, they are the first two small lakes just north of the mountain. (SiNF)

Saddlebag Lake   *Tuolumne Meadows 15'*
On the 1895 GLO plat (surveyed in 1883), the lake was called "Lee Vinings Lake," since it is at the head of Lee Vining Creek. The first two editions of the *Mt. Lyell* 30' map, 1901 and 1905, called it "Saddleback Lake." It was changed to "Saddlebag Lake" beginnning with the edition of 1910. (INF)

Saddlerock Lake   *Mt. Goddard 15', Mt. Thompson 7½'*
Named by one Halladay, a South Fork packer, for a funny-shaped rock on its far shore. (Art Schober.) (INF)

Sadler Peak (10,567), **Lake** (9,345)   *Merced Peak 15'*
Named in 1895 by Lt. N. F. McClure for a corporal in his detachment. (Farquhar: McClure; see also *SCB* 1, no. 8, May 1896: 334.) The name was

mistakenly spelled "Sadlier" on McClure's map of 1896, and on the first four editions of the *Mt. Lyell* 30' map, 1901–14. It was corrected beginning with the fifth edition, 1922. (SiNF)

Sailor Lake   *Mt. Goddard 15', Mt. Darwin 7½'*
"There was an old sailor who hung out around the Lake Sabrina lodge. When the packers went up to this little lake to stock it with fish they found the sailor there, sleeping off the effects of too much drink." (Mrs. Art Schober.) On the 7½-minute quad, 1983, the lake is called "Drunken Sailor Lake," but also in 1983 a BGN decision changed the name back to "Sailor Lake," which is how it should appear on future editions. (INF)

Sallie (Sally) Keyes Lakes   *Mt. Abbot 15', Mt. Hilgard 7½',*
                                                                              Florence Lake 7½'
Sallie (Sally) Keyes Creek   *Florence Lake 7½', Ward Mountain 7½'*
"Sallie" is the correct spelling. Maps published before 1983 still have it spelled "Sally." (BGN decision, 1983.)

Sallie Keyes Shipp McCray was the daughter of John and Maud (Sample) Shipp, the principal owners of Blayney Meadows from the 1890s to 1940. Maud named her daughter after a school chum. An aspen tree in Blayney Meadows still bears her carved name: "Sallie Keyes Shipp." The name was verified in 1983 by her aunt, Mrs. Ruth Beveridge, and Fred Ross, an area packer since 1932. The name for the creek was submitted by Ross. (USGS.) (SiNF)

Sample Meadow   *Kaiser Peak 15' and 7½'*
D. C. Sample was an early sheepman. He ranged over the mountains from lower Crown Valley to the brink of Tehipite Valley, and between Deer Creek and the North Fork of the Kings River. (Winchell, 158.) The name is plural— "Meadows"—on the 15-minute quad. (SiNF)

San Joaquin River
San Joaquin Mountain (3535.7 m.–11,600)   *Devils Postpile 15',*
                                                                              Mammoth Mtn. 7½'
Gabriel Moraga named the river in 1805 or 1806 for San Joaquin (Saint Joachim), the father of the Virgin Mary. (Arch. MSB, vol. 4, Muñoz, Sept. 24, 1806.) The name spread up the river into the mountains, where it became North, Middle, and South forks. The mountain probably was named by the USGS during the 1898–99 survey for the *Mt. Lyell* 30' map, simply because it was a convenient name to borrow for a triangulation point. It is on the first edition, 1901. (River, INF, SiNF; mtn., INF)

Sand Meadows   *Mineral King 15'*
"Named for a smoothly rounded hill of very white sand, evidently deposited in former ages by action of water." (Guy Hopping, SNP files, 1928.) (SNP)

Sandpiper Lake   *Mt. Abbot 15', Mt. Hilgard 7½'*
Named by a DFG survey party in 1942 because of the many little sandpipers that nest in the basin of the South Fork of Bear Creek. (DFG survey.) (SiNF)

Sanger Meadow   *Big Pine 15', Coyote Flat 7½'*
Probably named for Gustave Sanger, a wealthy rancher and mine owner.
(INF archives.) The name is on the first *Bishop* 30' map, 1913. (INF)

Sapphire Lake (10,966)   *Mt. Goddard 15', Mt. Darwin 7½'*
"Here it was desirable to cross the creek and follow the west bank to the next
shelf above, where another large lake lies like a jewel in its circular rock
setting. . . . So I took my way around the shores of these Crystal Lakes. . . ."
(J. N. LeConte in *SCB* 5, no. 3, Jan. 1905: 235–37.) There is no record of
anyone claiming to have named "Sapphire Lake." The name appears on the
third *Mt. Goddard* 30' map, 1923. (KCNP)

Sardella Lake   *Tower Peak 15'*
Named for Giovanni Domenico Sardella (1879–1955), a noted local
resident. (BGN decision, 1965.) The lake is not named on early printings of the
map. It is small and round, and is about 0.7 mile northeast of Granite Dome.
(StNF)

Sardine Lake, Lower and **Upper**   *Mono Craters 15'*
"I hailed Bodie with an inquiry as to the reason for the name, and received
his illuminating reply in one word, 'Canned.' I later learned that years ago an ill-
fated mule bearing a cargo of the delicacy consigned to a merchant in some
mining-camp of the Walker River region had fallen off the trail, and after a series
of spectacular revolutions had vanished in the icy waters." (Chase, 299.)
"Sardine Lake" (the lower one) is named on the first *Mt. Lyell* 30' map, 1901.
That lake was called "Red Lake" by John Muir in 1869. (Muir, *Mountains,* 85.)
(INF)

Saurian Crest (11,095)   *Tower Peak 15'*
Named in 1911 by William E. Colby because of its resemblance to an
ancient monster. (Farquhar: Colby; see also *SCB* 8, no. 3, Jan. 1912: photo opp.
157.) The name appeared on the fourth *Dardanelles* 30' map, 1924. (YNP)

Savage, Mount (5,745)   *Yosemite 15'*
Named for Major James D. Savage, leader of the Mariposa Battalion, whose
members explored Yosemite Valley in 1851 and named many of the features.
The name was suggested by Chester Versteeg in the early 1950s. The mountain
was formerly known in the Wawona area as "Twin Peaks" and "Mt. Adeline."
(YNP files.) (YNP)

Sawmill Creek, Pass (3,458.7 m.–11,347), **Point** (2,874 m.–9,416),
Lake, Meadow   *Mt. Pinchot 15', Aberdeen 7½'*
James W. Smith had a sawmill on the creek in the 1870s. Frank M. Lewis, a
sheepman, came up to Sawmill Pass from the west in 1875, and crossed it in
1878. (Farquhar: Versteeg. See **Lewis Creek, Lake.**) The creek, pass, and
point were named on the first *Mt. Whitney* 30' map, 1907. The lake and
meadow were added to the 15-minute quad, 1953. (Pass, KCNP, INF; others,
INF)

Sawmill Ridge   *Matterhorn Peak 15'*
The ridge overlooks Twin Lakes and Robinson Creek. There was a sawmill on the creek as early as 1861. (See **Robinson Creek, Peak.**) The USGS may have applied the name; it is on the first *Bridgeport* 30' map, 1911. (TNF)

Sawtooth Peak (12,343), **Pass**   *Mineral King 15'*
The early name for the mountain was "Miners' Peak," a name used by J. W. A. Wright in 1881 and on his 1883 map. (San Francisco *Daily Evening Post,* Sept. 3, 1881; *SCB* 32, no. 5, May 1947: 79.) Wright also gave "Saw Tooth" as an alternative name in the 1881 article. William R. Dudley, in July 1896, called it "Miner's Peak," but added that it was "locally known at present as 'Sawtooth,' from its peculiar beak-like form." (*SCB* 2, no. 3, Jan. 1898: 185.) It was "Sawtooth Pk" on the first *Kaweah* 30' map, 1904. The pass was first named on the 15-minute quad, 1956. (SNP)

Sawtooth Ridge   *Matterhorn Peak 15'*
A descriptive name, in use since about 1880. It is also known locally as "The Crags." (USGS.) (YNP, TNF)

Scaffold Meadows   *Triple Divide Peak 15'*
Early sheepherders built a scaffold to protect their food from bears and other animals. (Farquhar; also *SCB* 6, no. 3, June 1907: 156.) (KCNP)

Scenic Meadow   *Triple Divide Peak 15'*
The name was in use by local cattlemen before 1925. (Farquhar: Jim Barton. See **Barton Peak, Creek.**) In a reversal of the usual pattern, the name first appeared in Farquhar's *Place Names,* 1926, and then turned up on the fourth edition of the *Tehipite* 30' map, 1929. (KCNP)

Schober Holes (Lakes)   *Mt. Goddard 15', Mt. Darwin 7½'*
Art and John Schober named them when stocking them with fish in the 1930s. "Schober Holes" was the name they used. This was changed to "Schober Lakes" at the request of the Sierra Club. (Mr. and Mrs. Art Schober.) The name "Schober Holes" has been reinstated on the 7½-minute quad. (INF)

Schober Mine   *Mt. Goddard 15', Mt. Thompson 7½'*
"It started about 1942—tungsten was all the go during the war. My brother John and I did assessment work, but we finally sold it—and packed in the equipment for the two buyers. They worked it for a year and took out $372,000 in that time. Then they let it go, so John refiled on it and still has it." (Art Schober.) (INF)

Schofield Peak (9,935)   *Tower Peak 15'*
General John McAllister Schofield (1831–1906), Secretary of War, 1868–69; superintendent at West Point, 1876–81; commander-in-chief of the US Army, 1888–95. The peak was named by Major W. W. Forsyth, acting superintendent of Yosemite National Park, 1909–12. (Farquhar: H. C. Benson.) The name is on the third edition of the *Dardanelles* 30' map, 1912. (YNP)

Scossa Canyon   *Freel Peak 15', Woodfords 7½'*
Joseph Scossa homesteaded 160 acres in sec. 18, T. 11 N., R. 20 E. in 1892.
(TNF)

Scotts Lake (8,012)   *Freel Peak 15' and 7½'*
Named for J. B. Scott, an early dairyman in Hope Valley. (Maule.) The
name is on the Wheeler Survey atlas sheet 56B, 1876–77. (TNF)

Scylla (12,956–12,939)   *Mt. Goddard 15' and 7½'*
Named in 1895 by Theodore S. Solomons and Ernest C. Bonner. "At half-
past one this gorge lay directly south of us, and in an hour we had descended to
its head, which we found was guarded by a nearly frozen lake, whose sheer, ice-
smoothed walls arose on either side, up and up, seemingly into the very sky, their
crowns two sharp black peaks of most majestic form. A Scylla and a Charybdis
they seemed to us, as we stood at the margin of the lake and wondered how we
might pass the dangerous portal." (Solomons in *Appalachia* 8, no. 1, 1896: 55.)
The mountain was called "Scylla Peak" on the first three editions of the *Mt.
Goddard* 30' map, 1912–23. It was changed to "Scylla" in 1928, which is what
Solomons intended in the first place. (See **Charybdis**.) (KCNP)

Seavey Pass   *Tower Peak 15'*
Named by R. B. Marshall for Clyde L. Seavey, a member—at different
times—of the State Board of Control, the State Civil Service Commission, the
State Railroad Commission, and the Federal Power Commission. (Farquhar:
Marshall.) The name appeared on the third *Dardanelles* 30' map, 1912. (YNP)

Selden Pass (over 10,880)   *Mt. Abbot 15', Mt. Hilgard 7½'*
R. B. Marshall, USGS, named the pass for Selden Stuart Hooper, an
assistant with the USGS from 1891 to 1898. (Farquhar: Marshall.) When
Marshall submitted the name to the BGN in 1911, he erroneously spelled it
"Seldon." (Heyward Moore, *FPP* 25, no. 5, Spring 1984: 9.) It appeared that
way on the first three editions of the *Mt. Goddard* 30' map, 1912–23, and was
corrected on the edition of 1928. (See also **Rose Lake** and **Hooper, Mount**.)
(SiNF)

Senger, Mount (12,286–12,271)   *Mt. Abbot 15', Mt. Hilgard 7½'*
Senger Creek   *Mt. Abbot 15', Mt. Hilgard 7½', Blackcap Mtn. 15',*
                Mt. Henry 7½', Ward Mountain 7½'
The mountain was named in 1894 by Theodore S. Solomons for Joachim
Henry Senger (1848–1926), one of the four founders of the Sierra Club.
(Farquhar: Solomons. The other three were John Muir, Warren Olney, and
William D. Armes. See *SCB* 10, no. 2, Jan. 1917: 135–45.) Born in Prussia,
Senger came to California in 1882, and was later professor of German and
Greek at the University of California. (Memorial by J. N. LeConte in *SCB* 12,
no. 4, 1927: 428.) Both the mountain and the creek are named on the first *Mt.
Goddard* 30' map, 1912. (SiNF)

Sentinel Rock (7,038), **Dome** (8,122), **Creek, Fall**   *Yosemite 15',*
Yosemite Valley 1:24,000
"Opposite the Three Brothers is a prominent point, which . . . from its
fancied likeness to a gigantic watch-tower, is called "Sentinel Rock.' "
(Whitney, *Geology*, 412. This was the first "Sentinel" feature named; the
others derive from it.) "The present 'Sentinel' they [mission Indian guides]
called 'Loya,' a corruption of Olla (Oya), Spanish for an earthen water-pot."
(Bunnell, *Discovery*, 1880, 212.) "If the name comes from the Spanish word
Ho-yas, holes in rocks, the sentinel designated the place of the acorn mortar
mills; or, perhaps, the obelisk form was supposed to resemble the stone pestle
for pulverizing the acorns used by the Indians as food." (Bunnell, *Report*, 12.)
"The peak called by us the 'South Dome' has since been given the name of
'Sentinel Dome.' " (Bunnell, *Discovery*, 1880, 212.)
The creek was called "Lola Brook" on the Wheeler Survey map of 1883.
The rock and the dome were named on the King and Gardiner map of 1865. The
creek acquired its present name on the first USGS map of the valley, 1907, and
the fall on the fourth edition, 1927. (YNP)

Sentinel Dome (9,115)   *Marion Peak 15'*
Sentinel Ridge   *Triple Divide Peak 15', Marion Peak 15'*
The dome was named because of its "likeness to a gigantic watchtower."
(Fry and White, 180.) J. N. LeConte on his Kings-Kern map of 1893 calls the
dome "Sentinel Rock." (*SCB* 1, no. 1, Jan. 1893.) The dome and ridge were
both named on the first *Tehipite* 30' map, 1905. (KCNP)

Sequoia National Park, National Forest
Sequoia Lake, Creek   *Giant Forest 15'*
In 1847 an Austrian scholar, Stephen Endlicher, gave the names *Sequoia
sempervirens* and *Sequoia gigantea* for what he thought were two species of the
same giant California tree. These were later determined to be two stages of
growth of the same species, the coast redwood. The French botanist, J.
Decaisne, transferred the latter name to the "Big Trees" of the Sierra Nevada in
1854.
"Although we have no documentary evidence, there does not seem to be any
question that Endlicher named the newly established genus in honor of
Sequoyah, the Cherokee Indian." (Erwin G. Gudde, "The Two Sequoias,"
Names 1, June 1953: 119–20.) Sequoyah (c. 1770–1843), the native name of
George Gist (or Guess). He created a syllabary of 86 characters for the
Cherokee language, making it possible to put that language into a written form
for the first time.
When the national park was created in 1890, it was given its name by John
W. Noble, Secretary of the Interior, at the suggestion of George W. Stewart.
The national forest was established in 1908 by executive order of President
Theodore Roosevelt. (Farquhar.)
Sequoia Lake was created in 1889 when the Kings River Lumber Company
dammed Mill Flat Creek to create a source of water to operate the

company's flume, which transported lumber 54 miles to a mill at Sanger. (Johnston, *Redwoods,* 30.) In 1890 J. N. LeConte called the lake "Flooded Meadow." (*SCB* 1, no. 3, Jan. 1894: 95.) The present name for the lake is on the first *Tehipite* 30' map, 1905. The creek is first named on the 15-minute quad. (Lake, SeNF; creek, SNP)

Seven Gables (over 13,080–13,075); **Seven Gables Lakes**   *Mt. Abbot 15', Mt. Hilgard 7½'*
     The peak was named September 20, 1894, by Theodore S. Solomons and Leigh Bierce. "The south wall of the gap we found to be the side of a peak, the eccentric shape of which is suggested in the name Seven Gables, which we hastened to fasten upon it." (*SCB* 1, no. 6, May 1895: 230.) The lakes were first named on the 15-minute quad. (SiNF)

77 Corral   *Cattle Mtn. 7½'*
     Named for a corral constructed here in 1877. (See **Corral Meadow.**) (SiNF)

Shadow Lake, Creek   *Devils Postpile 15', Mt. Ritter 7½'*
     Origin unknown. On Solomons' map of 1896 it is called "Garnet Lake," and the name "Shadow Lake" is on what is now Rosalie Lake. (INF)

Shakspere, Mount (12,174–12,151)   *Mt. Goddard 15', North Palisade 7½'*
     In a USGS quad report, a letter from Charles Locker dated August 13, 1951, states that the mountain was named in 1920 by those who made the first ascent. Francis P. Farquhar was one of those, but in his notes he spelled the name "Shakespeare." (Farquhar files.) The name first appeared on the 15-minute quad. (KCNP)

Shamrock Lake   *Matterhorn Peak 15'*
     On the map, it appears to have three lobes—like a shamrock. (YNP files.) It was probably named by the USGS during the 1905–09 survey for the *Bridgeport* 30' map; it is on the first edition, 1911. (YNP)

Shamrock Lake   *Tuolumne Meadows 15'*
     Al Gardisky named the lake in 1932 because of its shape. (Spuller.) (INF)

Sharktooth Peak (over 11,640), **Lake**   *Kaiser Peak 15', Sharktooth Peak 7½'*
Sharktooth Creek   *Devils Postpile 15', Crystal Crag 7½'*
     The peak was named by Theodore S. Solomons in 1892 for its shape. (Farquhar: Solomons.) "Sharktooth Peak" was mislocated on the 15-minute quad. The peak it was applied to is now named "Cockscomb." On the 15-minute quad, the correct Sharktooth Peak is 0.8 mile north-northwest of Silver Peak, on the Silver Divide. (BGN decisions, 1969.) The lake and creek were first named on the 15-minute quads. (SiNF)

Sharp Creek   *Courtright Reservoir 7½'*
     Named for Kenneth Sharp (1921–1972), a civil engineer for the Pacific Gas and Electric Company who died in a diving accident while working on the Helms Pumped Storage Project. (BGN decision, 1975.) (SiNF)

Sharp Note Lake   *Mt. Abbot 15', Mt. Hilgard 7½'*
See **Medley Lake**. (SiNF)

Shelf Lake   *Mt. Abbot 15', Graveyard Peak 7½'*
Named in 1949 by Charles K. Fisher of the DFG "because it lies on a shelf above Cold Creek." (DFG survey.) (SiNF)

Shell Lake   *Tuolumne Meadows 15'*
For years Al Gardisky sold Shell products (at the Tioga Pass lodge), and the seashell insignia appealed to him so much he felt that he had to have a lake named "Shell." (Spuller.) (INF)

Shell Mountain (9,594)   *Giant Forest 15'*
The namer is unknown. A description by Chester Versteeg, who climbed the mountain in 1931, indicates a possible reason for the name. "There is a row of rock formations extending over halfway along the top that looked like ruined fortress walls, due to weathering of a dike different from the native rock." (Farquhar files.) The name is on the first *Tehipite* 30' map, 1905. (SeNF)

Shepherd Creek   *Mount Whitney 15', Lone Pine 15', Mt. Williamson 7½',*
                                                        Manzanar 7½'
Shepherd Pass   *Mount Whitney 15', Mt. Williamson 7½'*
John Shepherd (1833–1908), born in Illinois, came to California in 1852 and to Owens Valley in 1863. (INF archives.) In 1873 he built a house ½ mile west of the Manzanar crossroads; it was said to be the first two-story frame dwelling in Owens Valley. (*Historic Spots,* 116.) James Shepherd patented 160 acres in secs. 10 and 15, T. 14 S., R. 35 E. in 1872, and John patented 160 acres in sec. 10 in 1874.
The name for the creek was mistakenly spelled "Shepard" on the first five editions of the *Mt. Whitney* 30' map, 1907–1921. It was corrected in 1927, at which time the pass was named from the creek at the recommendation of the Sierra Club. (BGN.) (Pass, SNP, INF; creek, INF)

Shepherd Crest, Lake   *Matterhorn Peak 15'*
Origin uncertain, but probably named after the sheepherders of the late 19th and early 20th centuries. (YNP files.) The crest is named on the first *Bridgeport* 30' map, 1911; the lake appears on the 15-minute quad. (YNP)

Sherman Canyon   *Silver Lake 15', Tragedy Spring 7½'*
The GLO surveyor's field notes in 1876 read: "Sherman Dairy House and Barn in this valley." The name is a misspelling. George *Shearman* filed homestead papers on 160 acres in secs. 4 and 9, T. 9 N., R. 16 E. in 1893, a homestead encompassing the present Willow Flat. (ENF)

Shinn, Mount (over 10,960–11,020); **Mount Shinn Lake**
                        Blackcap Mtn. 15', Ward Mountain 7½'
The USFS named the peak in 1925 for Charles Howard Shinn (1852–1924), a charter member of the Sierra Club and a long-time forester and conservationist. (Farquhar; memorial and portrait in *SCB* 12, no. 2, 1925: 163–

64.) The peak was first named on the 1928 *Mt. Goddard* 30' map, and the lake on the 15-minute quad. (SiNF)

Shuteye Peak (8,351), **Pass, Creek; Little Shuteye Peak** (8,362), **Pass**
Shuteye Peak 15'
Old Shuteye was an Indian who was blind in one eye. One of the major trails to the east side of the Sierra passed through his rancheria. (Farquhar: L. A. Winchell.) The two peaks were named on the first *Kaiser* 30' map, 1904; the two passes on the fourth edition, 1923; the creek on the 15-minute quad. (SiNF)

Siberian Outpost, Pass, Pass Creek   *Kern Peak 15'*
J. N. LeConte and party crossed the pass in 1890, before it was named. "The summit was an immense flat area covered with loose slabs of granite piled on top of one another in sharp pinnacles. Many dead pines stood around. Still more lay prostrate, all barkless, limbless, and bleached by the winds and snow, but not a living tree in sight." (LeConte, *A Summer*, 78.)
The name "Siberian Outpost" was given in 1895 by a Harvey Corbett, for the area's bleak appearance. (Farquhar: LeConte.) In 1899 G. W. Stewart referred to it as "Cossack Outpost," but that name was never in general use. (Farquhar files.) The pass was called "Rampart Pass" by Wallace, Wales, and Wright in 1881. (*MWCJ* 1, no. 1, May 1902: 2.) It was named "Siberian Pass" on the first *Olancha* 30' map, 1907. On the first four editions of that map, 1907–1927, the creek was called "S. Fork Rock Creek." It was changed to the present name in 1931. (Pass, SNP, INF; others, SNP)

Sierra Nevada
Spanish for "snowy mountain range." *Sierra* is the word for "saw," and when used in this way means a jagged range of mountains—the teeth of the saw being similar to a row of mountain peaks. The Spanish used the name *Sierra Nevada* with abandon—any time they saw a mountain range with snow on it. As early as 1542, Juan Rodriguez Cabrillo gave that name to what we now know as the "Santa Lucia Range," south of Big Sur. Our present Sierra Nevada received its name from Fray Pedro Font, who saw it from a hill east of the contemporary town of Antioch in April 1776.
"If we looked to the east we saw on the other side of the plain at a distance of some thirty leagues a great Sierra Nevada, white from the summit to the skirts, and running diagonally almost from south-southeast to north-northwest." (Bolton, 386; see also Farquhar, *History*, 15–20.)

Sierra Point   *Yosemite 15', Yosemite Valley 1:24,000*
A point sought for, and discovered, by Charles A. Bailey, from where one can see Illilouette, Vernal, Nevada, and Upper and Lower Yosemite falls. "That this point might no longer remain incognito, but be known to all lovers of Yosemite, on June 14, 1897, accompanied by Walter E. Magee and Warren Cheney, of Berkeley . . . I deposited thereon Register Box of the Sierra Club, No. 15, and took the liberty of naming it Sierra Point, in honor of the Sierra Club, and raised a flag bearing the name." (*SCB* 2, no. 4, June 1898: 217.) The name appeared on the second *Yosemite Valley* map, 1918. (YNP)

Sill, Mount (14,153–14,162)   *Mt. Goddard 15', North Palisade 7½'*
Edward Rowland Sill (1841–1887), poet, teacher of English in the Oakland public schools, professor of literature and chairman of the English Department at the University of California, 1874–82. (*DAB.*) This second highest peak in the Palisades was named by J. N. LeConte in 1896. (*SCB* 5, no. 1, Jan. 1904: 3.) (KCNP, INF)

Silliman, Mount (11,188); **Silliman Creek, Crest, Lake, Meadow, Pass**
Triple Divide Peak 15'
Named by Brewer's party of the Whitney Survey in 1864. "Tuesday, June 28, we had a fine clear morning, and four of us started to visit a peak a few miles distant. We had a rough trail, over sharp ridges, and finally up a very steep pile of granite rocks, perhaps a thousand feet high, to the peak . . . which we called Mount Silliman, in honor of Professor Silliman, Junior." (Brewer, *Up and Down*, 523.)
Benjamin Silliman, Jr. (1816–1885), professor of chemistry at Yale, 1847–85. Brewer had studied agricultural chemistry under Silliman.
The mountain, creek, and crest were named on the first *Tehipite* 30' map, 1905. The lake appeared on the fourth edition, 1929, and the meadow and the pass on the fifth edition, 1939. The meadow was called "Cahoon Meadow" on the first four editions. (See **Cahoon Meadow,** etc.) (Peak, pass, crest, SNP, KCNP; others, SNP)

Silver Apron   *Yosemite Valley 1:24,000*
The name originated in the 19th century, but the namer is unknown. It was called the "Silver Chain" in one early guidebook. (*YNN* 34, no. 1, Jan. 1955: 16.) ". . . the whole river is scurrying over smooth, bare granite, at the rate of a fast express train on the best of railroads." (Hutchings, *In the Heart,* 450.) (YNP)

Silver City   *Mineral King 15'*
Never a city, but rather a mining camp founded and named in March 1874 by miners en route to the reputed rich silver strike at Mineral King. (Harper, 22.) The name did not appear on the *Kaweah* 30' map until the sixth edition, 1942. (SNP)

Silver Creek   *Camp Nelson 15', Mineral King 15'*
This may be the only "silver" name in the Sierra Nevada that doesn't have anything to do with silver. Frank Silvers patented 160 acres in the SW¼ of sec. 20, the NW¼ of sec. 29, and the SE¼ of sec. 30, T. 19 S., R. 31 E. in 1891. This includes the land where Silver Creek joins the North Fork of the Middle Fork of the Tule River. (SeNF)

Silver Creek   *Kaiser Peak 15', Sharktooth Peak 7½', Devils Postpile 15',*
Crystal Crag 7½'
Silver Peak (11,878)   *Kaiser Peak 15', Sharktooth Peak 7½'*
Silver Pass; Silver Pass Lake, Creek   *Mt. Abbot 15', Graveyard Peak 7½'*
Silver Divide   *Mt. Abbot 7½', and all the above quadrangles*
Theodore S. Solomons named Silver Creek in 1892 for its silvery

appearance, and he later named the peak from the stream. (Farquhar: Solomons.) The creek is the only one of these features to appear on Solomons' map of 1896. The pass and the divide apparently were named by the USGS during the 1907–09 survey for the *Mt. Goddard* 30' map, 1912. The other features were first named on the 15-minute map, 1953. (SiNF)

Silver Mountain (site), **Creek, Peak** (10,772–10,774)   *Markleeville 15', Ebbetts Pass 7½'*
The original name of the town was "Kongsberg," named by John Johnson, Halver Oleson, and 14 others—mostly Norwegians—about 1860, after Köngsberg, Norway, famous for its silver mines. (Wood, 53.) In May 1863 a post office under the name "Konigsberg" was opened. The name was changed to "Silver Mountain" in 1865, although that name was in use in 1863 when William H. Brewer and the Whitney Survey party passed through. (Brewer, *Up and Down,* 432–33.) The town was the first county seat of Alpine County, 1864–75. The post office was closed in 1883, and the place was abandoned by 1886. (TNF)

Silver King Valley   *Topaz Lake 15', Wolf Creek 7½'*
Silver King Creek   *Topaz Lake 15'*
The Silver King District saw some mining during the 1860s. (*Bull.* 193, 120.) Joseph LeConte and his party of collegians passed through the deserted town of Silver King in 1870. "There are several rather pretentious but unfinished buildings—hotels, stores, etc. The lots are all staked out, and a few years ago were held at high prices. . . . We took possession of the hotel; used the bar-room as our dining-room, and the bar-counter as our table. Made a hearty dinner, the young men all the while playing hotel life, laughing and calling 'Waitaw! roast beef! Waitaw! bottle of champagne!' " (LeConte, *Ramblings,* 127.) (TNF)

Silver Lake   *Silver Lake 15', Caples Lake 7½', Tragedy Spring 7½'*
The origin is unknown, but probably named by early travelers or miners. The name existed at least as early as 1863. "Here we descended into the valley of Silver Lake, a lovely little sheet of water, very deep and blue. . . ." (Brewer, *Up and Down,* 436.) (ENF)

Silver Lake   *Mono Craters 15'*
The lake takes its name "from the silver-gray color of its water on overcast days." (Smith, 25.) On the 1879 and 1885 GLO plats it is called "Goose Lake," and the name "Silver Lake" was applied to what is now June Lake. (INF)

Silver Spray Falls   *Tehipite Dome 15'*
"The falls descend in three sections. The water of the last is separated into misty spray before reaching the bottom, and adds much to its beauty; hence its name, 'Silver Spray.' " (Elliott, *Guide,* 15.) John Muir called it "Tehipite Fall" in his *Century Magazine* article, November 1891. Theodore S. Solomons, on his map of 1896, used that name, spelling it "Tehipitee Fall." But on his map of Tehipite Valley, Jan. 1897, "assisted by L. A. Winchell, who gave many of the names," it is called "Silver Spray Falls." (*SCB* 12, no. 2, 1925: 127.) The

implication is that the name originated with Winchell or with his contemporary, Frank Dusy, who discovered Tehipite Valley in 1869. (KCNP)

Silver Creek, Spur   *Marion Peak 15', Tehipite Dome 15'*
The namer is unknown. The creek name is on Solomons' map of 1896, and is used as an existing name by another traveler that same year. (*SCB* 2, no. 1, Jan. 1897: 45.) Both names are on the first *Tehipite* 30' map, 1905. (Spur, KCNP, SiNF; creek, SiNF)

Silver Strand Falls   *Yosemite 15', Yosemite Valley 1:24,000*
The falls is on Meadow Brook, which drains a small area and thus quickly runs dry once the snow has melted. Its earlier name was "Widow's Tears Falls," because—as early stage drivers told tourists—it lasted only two weeks. (*YNN* 34, no. 1, Jan. 1955: 16.) It appeared that way on the Wheeler Survey map of 1883 and on the *Yosemite Valley* maps from 1907 to 1922. The present name was given at the suggestion of François E. Matthes, and appeared on the 1927 edition of the map. (BGN.) (YNP)

Simmons Peak (12,503)   *Tuolumne Meadows 15'*
Named in 1909 by R. B. Marshall, USGS, for Dr. Samuel E. Simmons of Sacramento. (Farquhar: Marshall.) (YNP)

Simpson Meadow   *Marion Peak 15'*
Members of the Simpson family ran sheep here in the 1880s, and patented the land in 1900. Earlier, it was called "Dougherty Meadow," for Bill and Bob Dougherty, who pastured horses here. (Farquhar: Versteeg. See **Dougherty Peak**, etc.) (KCNP)

Sing Peak (10,552)   *Merced Peak 15'*
Named in 1899 by R. B. Marshall, USGS, for Tie Sing, a Chinese cook with the Geological Survey from 1888 until 1918, when he was killed by an accident in the field. (Farquhar: Marshall.) (YNP, SiNF)

Sinnamon Meadow   *Bodie 15'*
James Sinnamon was a successful miner at Monoville in 1859, and later a rancher at Bridgeport Valley. (Cain, 6–7.)

Sister Lake   *Matterhorn Peak 15'*
Possibly named by Lt. H. C. Benson in 1895. All the named features in the vicinity appeared on the first *Bridgeport* 30' map, 1911; several of them are known to have been named by Benson. (YNP)

Sivels Ranch, Mountain (5,813)   *Bass Lake 15'*
The name is misspelled. Thomas *Sivils* patented the SE¼ of sec. 20, T. 6 S., R. 22 E. in 1891. (SiNF)

Six Shooter Lake   *Blackcap Mtn. 15' and 7½'*
Probably named in 1948 by Charles K. Fisher of the DFG. (DFG survey.) (SiNF)

Sixty Lake Basin   *Mt. Pinchot 15', Mt. Clarence King 7½'*
Bolton C. Brown visited the basin in 1899, and *almost* named it—but not

quite. ". . . ah, the *lakes!*—in every variety, form, and position—fifty of them if there is one. . . ." (*SCB* 3, no. 2, May 1900: 139.) The name probably was given by the USGS during the 1905 survey for the *Mt. Whitney* 30' map; it is on the first edition, 1907. (KCNP)

Skelton Lake   *Mt. Morrison 15', Bloody Mtn. 7½'*
Named for the "Skelton boys," early prospectors who had a 3-stamp mill below the lake. (Smith, 49.) (INF)

Skelton Lakes   *Tuolumne Meadows 15'*
Henry A. Skelton (1869–1955). He was hired in June 1898 as a forest agent to protect the north end of Yosemite National Park during the absence that summer of the army troops, due to the Spanish-American War. After that he worked for the General Land Office, and was a YNP ranger from 1916 to 1932. (YNP files; Bingaman, *Guardians,* 92–93.) (YNP)

Sky-Blue Lake   *Mount Whitney 15' and 7½'*
Named for its azure color—a name in common use. (BGN decision, 1937.) It appeared on the eighth *Mt. Whitney* 30' map, 1937. (SNP)

Sky Haven (over 12,840–12,834)   *Mt. Thompson 7½'*
The name was added to the map by the USGS because it was in common use by climbers. On the *Mt. Goddard* 15' quad it is one mile north of the outlet of Fifth Lake, marked "12834." (INF)

Sky High Lake (11,861–11,869)   *Mt. Darwin 7½'*
Named by the Forest Service, according to Art Schober. The altitude given on the 7½-minute quad as "11661" is obviously incorrect. Not named on the *Mt. Goddard* 15-minute quad. It is 0.8 mile north of Mt. Lamarck. (INF)

Sky Parlor Meadow   *Kern Peak 15'*
The name apparently came into general use in the Sierra Club in the early 1920s. It was called "Funston's Kaweah Meadow" on William R. Dudley's sketch map. (*SCB* 2, no. 3, Jan. 1898: plate XXV.) On the first three editions of the *Olancha* 30' map it was "Upper Funston Meadow." The present name appeared on the edition of 1927. (SNP)

Slide Canyon, Mountain (northern), **Mountain** (southern, 10,479);
The Slide; Little Slide Canyon   *Matterhorn Peak 15'*
Lt. N. F. McClure used the name "Slide Cañon" in 1894, but in such a way that it seems the name already existed—perhaps applied by sheepherders after its salient feature. "I came to the most wonderful natural object that I ever beheld. A vast granite cliff, two thousand feet in height, had literally tumbled from the bluff on the right-hand side of the stream with such force that it had not only made a mighty dam across the cañon, but many large stones had rolled far up on the opposite side." (McClure in *SCB* 1, no. 5, Jan. 1895: 175–76.) The canyon is named on McClure's map of 1895, the northern mountain and the little canyon on the first *Bridgeport* 30' map, 1911, and "The Slide" and the southern mountain on the 15-minute quad. (Little Slide Canyon, TNF; north mtn., YNP, TNF; others, YNP)

Slide Creek, Peak (10,915), **Bluffs, Lakes**   *Marion Peak 15'*
"Slide-Foot Creek" is on Theodore S. Solomons' map of 1896, and was probably named by Solomons in 1895, or perhaps earlier by Lil Winchell. The USGS borrowed the "Slide" name during the 1903 survey for the *Tehipite 30'* map; all the features except the lakes are on the first edition, 1905. (KCNP)

Slinkard Creek, Valley   *Topaz Lake 15'*
A. James Slinkard, road supervisor of Douglas County, Nevada, 1862–65. He later built a road up the creek and into the valley that are named for him. (Maule.)

Smedberg Lake   *Matterhorn Peak 15'*
Lt. H. C. Benson named the lake in 1895 for Lt. William Renwick Smedberg, Jr., Fourth Cavalry, US Army, who was on duty in Yosemite National Park that year. (Farquhar: Benson.) (YNP)

Smith Meadow   *Lake Eleanor 15', Hetch Hetchy Reservoir 15'*
Smith Peak (7,751)   *Hetch Hetchy Reservoir 15'*
"Hetch-Hetchy is claimed by a sheep-owner, named Smith, who drives stock into it every summer, by a trail which was built by Joseph Screech. It is often called Smith's Valley." (John Muir in *Overland Monthly,* July 1873: 49–50.) Cyril C. Smith, originally from Maine, built a cabin in the meadow in 1885. (*SCB* 36, no. 5, May 1951: 64.) (YNP)

Smoky Jack Campground   *Hetch Hetchy Reservoir 15'*
". . . one of the sheep-men of the neighborhood, Mr. John Connell, nicknamed Smoky Jack, begged me to take care of one of his bands of sheep. . . . Smoky Jack was known far and wide, and I soon learned that he was a queer character. . . . He lived mostly on beans. In the morning after his bean breakfast he filled his pockets from the pot with dripping beans for luncheon, which he ate in handfuls as he followed the flock. His overalls and boots soon . . . became thoroughly saturated, and instead of wearing thin, wore thicker and stouter, and by sitting down to rest from time to time, parts of all the vegetation, leaves, petals, etc., were embedded in them, together with wood fibers, butterfly wings, mica crystals, fragments of nearly everything that the world contained—rubbed in, embedded and coarsely stratified, so that these wonderful garments grew to have a rich geological and biological significance. . . ." (Badè, 195–96.) (YNP)

Snow Creek   *Hetch Hetchy Reservoir 15', Tuolumne Meadows 15'*
Snow Creek Falls   *Hetch Hetchy Reservoir 15'*
Snow Flat   *Tuolumne Meadows 15'*
The creek was called "Glacier Brook" on the King and Gardiner map of 1865. "This stream was called Glacier Brook, from the abundant traces of former glacial action in its vicinity." (Whitney, *The Yosemite Guide-Book,* 1870, 117.) John Muir called it "Dome Creek" in 1869. (Muir, *First Summer,* 200.) It was "Glacier Creek" on atlas sheet 56D, 1878–79; "Glacier Brook" on the Wheeler Survey map of Yosemite Valley, 1883; and finally achieved "Snow Creek" on the first *Yosemite 30'* map, 1897. The falls and the flat were first named on their respective 15-minute quads. (YNP)

Soda Creek   *Mineral King 15', Kern Peak 15'*
Probably named by William R. Dudley in 1897. (Sketch map in *SCB* 2, no. 3, Jan. 1898: plate XXV.) (SNP)

Soda Spring   *Kern Peak 15'*
Named by a camping party from Inyo County in 1873. Among the party were Charley Begole, Johnny Lucas, and Al Johnson, who made the first ascent of Mt. Whitney, from this camp, on August 18, 1873. (*Inyo Independent*, Sept. 20, 1873.) (SNP)

Soda Springs   *Tuolumne Meadows 15'*
"The Soda Springs cover quite an extensive area, and have a copious flow of water, which, at the time of our visit, July, 1863, had a temperature of 46° to 47°. There is a continual escape of carbonic acid gas over the surface, the water resembling in taste that of the 'Congress Spring,' at Saratoga." (Whitney, *Geology*, 428.) (YNP)

Soldier Lake (10,624)   *Matterhorn Peak 15'*
The origin is uncertain, but probably named for soldiers of the US Army, which administered Yosemite National Park from 1890 until creation of the National Park Service in 1916. (YNP files.) (YNP)

Soldier Meadow   *Merced Peak 15', Devils Postpile 15', Cattle Mtn. 7½'*
The area was used as a patrol camp during the years when the US Army administered Yosemite National Park. (YNP files.) This region was part of the park from 1890 to 1905. The meadow was called "Little Jackass Meadow" on the first four editions of the *Mt. Lyell* 30' map, 1901–14, and was changed to the present name in 1922. (SiNF)

Solomons, Mount (13,034–13,016)   *Mt. Goddard 15' and 7½'*
Named for Theodore Seixas Solomons (1870–1947). (BGN decision, 1968.) In three extensive mountain trips from 1892 to 1895 Solomons explored, mapped, and established a route in the Sierra Nevada that now constitutes the northern half of the John Muir Trail. Of particular interest are two articles in volume 1 of the *SCB;* six articles in *Overland Monthly* in 1896–97; "The Beginnings of the John Muir Trail," *SCB* 25, no. 1, Feb. 1940: 28–40; and a memorial by Farquhar in *SCB* 33, no. 3, March 1948: 117–18. The peak is not named on early editions of the 15-minute quad. It is just southwest of Muir Pass, marked "13016." (See also **John Muir Trail.**) (KCNP)

Sonora Pass (9,643–9,628), **Peak** (11,459–11,462)
                                                    Sonora Pass 15' and 7½'
The pass took its name from the town of Sonora, established in 1848 by Mexican miners from the state of Sonora. (Gudde, *Place Names*, 316–17.) The first printed record of the name "Sonora Pass" is in the report of the Pacific Railroad Survey of 1853 under Lt. Tredwell Moore. This is shown on Goddard's map of 1857 as being about eight miles south of the present Sonora Pass, in the NW¼ of sec. 12, T. 4 N., R. 21 E.—"Emigrant Pass" on the *Tower Peak* 15-minute quad. William H. Brewer was probably the first to use "Sonora Pass" in

reference to its present location, in 1863. "July 17 we came on up the pass and camped at a little grassy flat, near the summit of Sonora Pass, at the altitude of 9,450 feet. . . ." (Brewer, *Up and Down,* 423.) The peak probably was named by the Wheeler Survey; it is on atlas sheet 56D, 1878–79. (StNF, TNF)

Soquel Meadow   *Bass Lake 15'*
Smith Comstock moved his sawmill to this area in 1881 from the town of Soquel in Santa Cruz County—and brought the name with him, too. (Hurt, 18.) For the origin of the name "Soquel," see Gudde, *Place Names,* 317. (SiNF)

Sotcher Lake (7,616)   *Devils Postpile 15', Mammoth Mtn. 7½',*
                                                      Crystal Crag 7½'
Named for "Red" Sotcher. (See **Reds Meadow,** etc.) The name was spelled as it is now on the first five editions of the *Mt. Lyell* 30' map, 1901–22. It was changed to "Satcher" from 1927 to 1948, and back again to "Sotcher" on the 15-minute quad, 1953. The change to "Satcher" was apparently due to that spelling being used in Farquhar's *Place Names* (1926) on the authority of W. A. Chalfant. The USGS investigated further, and stated that "Sotcher" is correct. (USGS quad report, 1953.) (INF)

South America, Lake (3,641 m.–11,941)   *Mount Whitney 15',*
                                                      Mt. Brewer 7½'
Named in 1896 by Bolton C. Brown. ". . . we came around the southern end of the last lake against the eastern basin-wall, shaped just like South America. . . ." (*SCB* 2, no. 1, Jan. 1897: 21; also sketch maps opp. 22 and 23.) (SNP)

South Guard (4,033 m–13,224); **South Guard Lake** (3,548 m.–11,630)
                                          Mount Whitney 15', Mt. Brewer 7½'
South Guard and North Guard were named by Lt. Milton F. Davis; they are on his map of 1896. (LeConte, *Alpina,* 10.) Both features are named on the *Mt. Whitney* 30' map, 1907. On all editions of that map, through 1939, the name "South Guard" was on peak 12964, about 1 mile east by south from Mt. Brewer. The 15-minute quad located it correctly, on what was peak 13232 on the 30-minute map. (KCNP)

Southfork Pass   *Big Pine 15', Split Mtn. 7½'*
A knapsack route between the south fork of Big Pine Creek and the John Muir Trail above Palisade Lakes. The name first appeared in print in *SCB* 24, no. 3, June 1939: 48. It was added to the maps by the USGS because it was in common use. (KCNP, INF)

Spanish Mountain (10,051), **Meadow, Lake; Little Spanish Lake**
                                                      Tehipite Dome 15'
"The Spanish mined there years ago. The actual existence of a mine was more or less legendary. The mountain was named by Silas Bennett, a pioneer of the '70s, in 1879." (Farquhar files: S. L. N. Ellis, interviewed by Versteeg before 1925.) All the features except Little Spanish Lake are named on the first *Tehipite* 30' map, 1905. (SiNF)

Spearhead Lake   *Mt. Goddard 15', Mt. Thompson 7½'*
A descriptive name for a long, narrow lake. Probably named by Halladay, a
packer on the South Fork of Bishop Creek in the 1930s. (Art Schober.) (INF)

Spearpoint Lake   *Mt. Abbot 15', Mt. Hilgard 7½'*
Named in August 1951 by Elden H. Vestal of the DFG because of its shape
and for the "Piute large game-hunting head or spearpoint." (Heyward Moore,
FPP 26, no. 2, Summer 1984: 2.) (SiNF)

Speckerman Mountain (7,137)   *Bass Lake 15'*
Named for Thomas Speckerman, an early settler. (SiNF history files.)
(SiNF)

Spencer, Mount (12,431)   *Mt. Goddard 15', Mt. Darwin 7½'*
One of the "Evolution Group," named in 1895 by Theodore S. Solomons for
Herbert Spencer (1820–1903), English philosopher and evolutionist.
(*Appalachia* 8, no. 1, 1896: 48.) (KCNP)

Sphinx, The (9,146); **Sphinx Creek**   *Marion Peak 15'*
Sphinx Creek, Lakes, Crest   *Triple Divide Peak 15'*
John Muir named The Sphinx in 1891. (Map in *Century Magazine* 43, no.
1, Nov. 1891.) It was called "The Watch Tower" by Hutchings in 1875. (*Inyo
Independent,* Oct. 23, 1875.) J. N. LeConte had "The Sphinx" on his 1893
map. The creek and lakes were named on the first *Tehipite* 30' map, 1905. The
crest was first named on the 15-minute quad. (KCNP)

Spiller Creek, Lake (10,696)   *Matterhorn Peak 15'*
J. Calvert Spiller was a topographical assistant with Lt. Macomb's party of
the Wheeler Survey in 1878–79. (*SCB* 10, no. 3, Jan. 1918: photo opp. 369.)
The name "Spiller's Cañon" is on atlas sheet 56D. "Spiller Creek" is on Lt.
McClure's sketch map of 1894. (*SCB* 1, no. 5, Jan. 1895: 173.) Both creek and
lake are on the first *Bridgeport* 30' map, 1911. (YNP)

Split Mountain (14,058)   *Big Pine 15', Split Mtn. 7½'*
"To the north of this gap the crest rises into a huge mountain with a double
summit . . . which I called Split Mountain." (Bolton C. Brown, 1895, in *SCB* 1,
no. 8, May 1896: 309.) The Wheeler Survey called it "Southeast Palisade," and
it was also known as "South Palisade," although it is not actually part of the
Palisades. Theodore Solomons used the latter name on his 1896 map. (KCNP,
INF)

Split Pinnacle   *Yosemite 15', Yosemite Valley 1:24,000*
The name came into use among Sierra Club climbers in the 1930s. (USGS.)
It appeared on the 15-minute quad, 1956. (YNP)

Spotted Lakes   *Merced Peak 15'*
A cluster of small lakes, possibly named because of their spotty appearance
on the map. (YNP files.) The name was ratified by the BGN in 1932, and
appeared on the final edition of the *Mt. Lyell* 30' map, 1948. (YNP)

Spring Lake   *Mineral King 15'*
The spring forms a miniature lake at a higher level than the main lake. (Guy

Hopping, 1927, SNP files.) The name appears on the fifth *Kaweah* 30' map, 1934. (SNP)

Spuller Lake   *Tuolumne Meadows 15'*
Everett Spuller named it for himself in 1932. "Al [Gardisky] did not know a lake was there, and I was the first one ever to plant it." (Spuller.) (INF)

Square Lake   *Mt. Tom 15', Mount Tom 7½'*
Probably named in 1950 by Elden H. Vestal and Scott M. Soule of the DFG, for its shape. (DFG survey.) (SiNF)

Squaw Creek   *Kaweah 15', Mineral King 15'*
Named about 60 years after a Mexican murdered his wife at the old trail crossing. (Guy Hopping, SNP files, 1927.) The name appears on the fifth *Kaweah* 30' map, 1934. (SNP)

Squaw Lake   *Graveyard Peak 7½'*
This was called "Helen Lake" on the *Mt. Abbot* 15' quad. The name change was made by a BGN decision in 1969, apparently to make it agree with the other "Indian" names: Papoose, Chief, Warrior. (SiNF)

Squaw Dome (7,818)   *Shuteye Peak 15'*
Origin unknown, but it is an old name. It was on the first *Kaiser* 30' map, 1904. On the 1895 GLO plat—surveyed in 1885—it is called "Squaw Nipple Peak." (SiNF)

Staircase Falls   *Yosemite 15', Yosemite Valley 1:24,000*
A series of small falls coming down the south valley wall just west of Camp Curry, giving the appearance of a large staircase. (*YNN* 34, no. 1, Jan. 1955: 17.) It was first named on the 1927 *Yosemite Valley* map. (YNP)

Stanford Lakes   *Merced Peak 15'*
A misspelled name. The lakes were named in the late teens or early twenties by Billy Brown, a local packer, for the Kenneth J. *Staniford* family of Fresno. (Letter from Barton A. Brown, M.D., November 7, 1983.) (SiNF)

Stanford, Mount (4,259 m.–13,963)   *Mount Whitney 15', Mt. Brewer 7½'*
Bolton C. Brown named the mountain for Stanford University when he made the first ascent in August 1896. (*SCB* 2, no. 2, May 1897: 91–94.) (KCNP)

Stanford, Mount (12,838–12,851); **Stanford Lake** (11,436)
Mt. Abbot 15' and 7½'
Leland Stanford (1824–1893), one of the "Big Four" who built the Central Pacific Railroad; governor of California and US Senator; founder of Stanford University. Named by R. B. Marshall, USGS, during the 1907–09 survey for the *Mt. Goddard* 30' map. The lake was first named on the 15-minute quad. (Mtn., SiNF, INF; lake, INF)

Stanford Point   *Yosemite 15', Yosemite Valley 1:24,000*
Probably named for Leland Stanford. (See **Stanford, Mount.**) (*YNN* 34, no. 1, Jan. 1955: 17.) It appeared on the first USGS *Yosemite Valley* map, 1907. (YNP)

Stanislaus River
Stanislaus Peak (11,233–11,220)   *Sonora Pass 15', Disaster Peak 7½'*
An expedition under Gabriel Moraga discovered the river in October 1806 and named it *Rio de Nuestra Senora de Guadalupe.* (Arch. MSB, vol. 4, Muñoz, Oct. 2, 1806.) It was on this river, the next day, that they found the rancheria of the "Taulámne" Indians, but the name "Tuolumne" wound up on the next river to the south.

Estanislao was an Indian, born at Mission San Jose, baptised, and given a saint's name—probably for one of the two Polish saints called Saint Stanislas. Estanislao ran away from the mission—inducing some other converted Indians to leave with him—and became a rebel. The Mexicans, under Gen. Vallejo, defeated Estanislao in two battles in May and June of 1829. (Gudde, *Place Names,* 320; *Historic Spots,* 368, 539.) The river later became known as *Rio Estanislao,* and was anglicized into "Stanislaus River" by Frémont in 1844. (Frémont, *Expedition,* 359.)

The peak was named in the middle 1870s. In 1877 Lt. Macomb climbed it and found "a fine monument erected by a reconnaisance party of the Coast Survey." (Wheeler Survey, *Report,* May 1, 1878, 143.) The name is on atlas sheet 56D, 1878–79. Thus, by a series of unlikely events, the name of a Polish saint was given to a mountain in Alpine County, California. (StNF, TNF)

Starkweather Lake   *Devils Postpile 15', Mammoth Mtn. 7½'*
Named for a prospector who had claims on the slopes above the lake in the 1920s. He was referred to by some as "the human gopher." (Smith, 13.) (INF)

Starr, Mount (12,835–12,870)   *Mt. Abbot 15' and 7½'*
Named by the Sierra Club in honor of Walter A. Starr, Jr., a renowned mountain climber and author of *Guide to the John Muir Trail and the High Sierra Region.* (BGN decision, 1939.) Starr was killed in August 1933 while climbing in the Minarets. (See *SCB* 19, no. 3, June 1934: 81–85.)

The first ascent of the mountain was on July 16, 1896, by Walter A. Starr, Sr. and Allen L. Chickering, who gave it a name of their own. ". . . a large cloud passed over us. Suddenly everything began to buzz like an electric car in motion. The camera tripod, our fingertips, and even our hair, which stood out straight, seemed to exude electricity. We were badly frightened, and got off the peak as rapidly as possible. We called this point Electric Peak." (*SCB* 20, no. 1, Feb. 1935: 62.) (SiNF, INF)

Starr King, Mount (9,092)   *Yosemite 15', Yosemite Valley 1:24,000*
Starr King Meadow   *Merced Peak 15', Yosemite 15',*
                                        Yosemite Valley 1:24,000
Starr King Lake   *Yosemite 15'*
Thomas Starr King (1824–1864), famous preacher and lecturer; pastor of the Hollis Street Unitarian Church in Boston at age 24; came to San Francisco Unitarian Church, 1860; visited Yosemite, the Big Trees, and Lake Tahoe; orator for the Union cause during the Civil War. The dome-shaped mountain was named during the war years; it is on King and Gardiner's map of 1865.

In May 1862 the Brewer party of the Whitney Survey gave the name "Mount King" to the northeast peak of Mount Diablo; it is now simply named "North Peak." Brewer characterized King as "the most eloquent divine and, at the same time, one of the best fellows in the state." (Brewer, *Up and Down*, 263, 267.)

The meadow was named on the first USGS *Yosemite Valley* map, 1907. The lake was named "Helen Lake" on the editions from 1918 to 1929, "Starr King Lake" in 1938 and 1947, and no name at all beginning with the edition of 1958. "A former lake, now a mosquito-infested swamp." (YNP files.) (YNP)

State Peak (12,620), **Lakes**   *Marion Peak 15'*
Named by R. B. Marshall, USGS, during the 1903 survey for the *Tehipite* 30' map; both names are on the first edition, 1905. (Farquhar: Marshall.) (KCNP)

Statum Meadow, Creek   *Tehipite Dome 15'*
The odd name apparently is a misspelling for A. H. *Statham,* an early sheepman. As early as 1871 he had a range between Dinkey and Deer creeks. He later pastured his sheep on a large range east of Rancheria Creek, an area including the meadow and creek named for him. (Winchell, 158.) Both names are on the first *Tehipite* 30' map, 1905. (SiNF)

Steelhead Lake   *Tuolumne Meadows 15'*
Al Gardisky planted steelhead trout in the lake in 1929 and 1930, and named it in 1932. (Spuller.) (INF)

Steelhead Lake (11,361)   *Mt. Tom 15', Mount Tom 7½'*
Probably named by Ralph Beck of the DFG, who surveyed the lake in 1951. (DFG survey.) (SiNF)

Stevens Lake   *Freel Peak 15', Woodfords 7½'*
David Stevens homesteaded 160 acres in sec. 4, T. 10 N., R. 20 E. in 1883.

Stevens Peak (10,059–10,061)   *Markleeville 15', Carson Pass 7½'*
J. M. Stevens, a supervisor of Alpine County, operated a stage station in nearby Hope Valley from 1864 to 1866. (Maule.) The name appears on the first *Markleeville* 30' map, 1891. (TNF)

Stewart, Mount (12,205)   *Triple Divide Peak 15'*
George W. Stewart (1857–1931), the "Father of Sequoia Park." As editor of *The Visalia Delta* in the late 1880s, Stewart was the chief promoter of the plan to create Sequoia and General Grant national parks. He was a staunch conservationist, a learned amateur anthropologist, and registrar of the General Land Office in Visalia, 1898–1914. (Memorial by Farquhar in *SCB* 17, no. 1, Feb. 1932: 49–52.)

The name was proposed by the Visalia Kiwanis Club in April 1929, and appeared on the fifth edition of the *Tehipite* 30' map, 1939. (SNP)

Stoneman Meadow, Bridge   *Yosemite Valley 1:24,000*
The Stoneman House, a four-story hotel built by the state of California in 1885, was named for the then-governor, George Stoneman, and was located at

the east end of the meadow. It burned in 1896. (*YNN* 34, no. 1, Jan. 1955: 17.) The meadow was first named on the third *Yosemite Valley* map, 1922. (YNP)

String Meadows					*Devils Postpile 15', Kaiser Peak 15',*
Crystal Crag 7½', Sharktooth Peak 7½'
The name derives from the fact that the three meadows are more or less in line. (USGS quad report.) (SiNF)

Striped Mountain (4,017 m.–over 13,120)			*Mt. Pinchot 15' and 7½'*
Bolton C. Brown named it in July 1895. "That nearest the pass is strikingly barred across its steep craggy summit with light streaks. As this is an unusually marked case of this peculiarity and as it seems well occasionally to have a mountain whose name bears some relation to its visible character, I called it Striped Mountain." (*SCB* 1, no. 8, May 1896: 309; sketch map, 302.) (KCNP, INF)

Stuard Canyon				*Freel Peak 15', Woodfords 7½'*
James A. Stuard homesteaded 160 acres in secs. 17 and 18, T. 11 N., R. 20 E. in 1898. (TNF)

Stub Lake					*Mt. Abbot 15', Mt. Hilgard 7½'*
The lake is in a moraine basin at the foot of high talus slopes. It was probably named in 1952 by V. D. Volkinburg of the DFG. (DFG survey.) (SiNF)

Stubblefield Canyon					*Tower Peak 15'*
The name was first used by Lt. N. F. McClure on his explorations in 1894, and is probably the name of an early sheepman. (*SCB* 1, no. 5, Jan. 1895: 179, sketch map; also *SCB* 1, no. 8, May 1896: 330–32.) (YNP)

Sugar Pine					*Bass Lake 15'*
The Madera Sugar Pine Company established a sawmill here in 1899 and named the place "Sugar Pine." (Hurt, 18.) (SiNF)

Sugarbowl Dome (over 7,600)				*Triple Divide Peak 15'*
A depression on top retains snow most of the summer, giving the appearance of a sugar-filled bowl. The name appears on Lt. Davis's map of 1896. (SNP)

Sugarloaf (8,002); **Sugarloaf Creek, Meadow, Valley**
Triple Divide Peak 15'
Sugarloaf was named "Sugar Loaf Rock" by the Brewer party of the Whitney Survey in June 1864. "This camp (No. 170) was situated behind a sharp granite knob which rises from the valley like a sugar-loaf, as seen from below. . . ." (Whitney, *Geology,* 377.) All four features were named on the first *Tehipite* 30' map, 1905. (KCNP)

Sugarloaf (3,362 m.–11,026)			*Big Pine 15', Coyote Flat 7½'*
Probably named by the USGS during the 1910–11 survey for the *Bishop* 30' map; it is on the first edition, 1913. (INF)

Summers Creek, Meadows (Upper and **Lower)**			*Matterhorn Peak 15',*
Bodie 15'
Jesse A. Summers operated a butcher shop in the area in the early 1860s,

and grazed cattle in the meadows. (Maule.) Summers homesteaded 160 acres in secs. 19 and 20, T. 4 N., R. 25 E. in 1876. (Creek, upper mdws., TNF)

Summit City Creek   *Markleeville 15', Silver Lake 15', Carson Pass 7½',*
Caples Lake 7½', Mokelumne Peak 7½'
Summit City is long gone; the name remains on the creek. The town appears on Theron Reed's map of the Silver Mountain Mining District, 1864, at which time it had a population of nearly 600.
"A mining hamlet, now abandoned, on the ridge between Williams's and the lakes [Blue Lakes], bears the name of Summit City." (Wheeler Survey, *Report of Lt. Macomb*, 1878, 142.) (ENF)

Sunset Lake   *Mt. Goddard 15', Mt. Thompson 7½'*
"I named it. The sun set on the high pinnacles around there." (Art Schober.) (INF)

Swauger Creek   *Fales Hot Springs 15'*
Samuel A. Swauger patented 160 acres in sec. 28, T. 6 N., R. 24 E. in 1881, and another 200 acres in secs. 21 and 22 in 1886. The name was misspelled "Swager" on the *Bridgeport* 30' maps. (TNF)

Switchback Peak (5,016)   *Giant Forest 15'*
"Called thus since the Mt. Whitney Power & Electric Company built a zigzag trail up its side. The route is now the Generals Highway." (Visalia *Times Delta*, Dec. 8, 1928.) The name appeared on the second *Tehipite* 30' map, 1912. (SNP)

Symmes Creek   *Mount Whitney 15', Mt. Pinchot 15',*
Independence 15' and 7½', Mt. Williamson 7½', Kearsarge Peak 7½'
Named for J. W. Symmes, a pioneer settler near Independence, who appropriated the water from the creek for his ranch. (Farquhar files, from Versteeg.) Symmes was the Inyo County superintendent of schools, 1870–73 and 1876–82. (Chalfant, *Inyo*, 415.) (INF)

Table Lake   *Hetch Hetchy Reservoir 15'*
Probably named by the USGS during the 1893–94 survey for the *Yosemite* 30' map; it is on the first edition, 1897. The lake is in a flat area, about a mile west of a flat-topped mountain that was used as a triangulation point. (YNP)

Table Mountain (4,155.1 m.–13,630)   *Mount Whitney 15',*
Mt. Brewer 7½'

Table Creek   *Triple Divide Peak 15', Mount Whitney 15', Mt. Brewer 7½'*
This flat-topped mountain was briefly described—and almost named—by Clarence King when he and Richard Cotter made the first ascent of Mt. Tyndall in July 1864. "At one place the ridge [the Great Western Divide] forms a level table." (Whitney, *Geology*, 386.) The name "Table" was on Hoffmann's map of 1873.
In 1881 the mountain was named "Mt. Hazen" in honor of General Hazen, Chief Signal Officer of the US Army, by Captain Michaelis, the officer in command of the signal service on the scientific expedition to Mt. Whitney. (J. W. A. Wright, *Mining and Scientific Press*, Nov. 3, 1883.) "Table

Mountain" and "Table Creek" were on the first editions of the *Mt. Whitney* and *Tehipite* 30' maps, 1907 and 1905, respectively. (Mtn., SNP, KCNP; creek, KCNP)

Taboose Pass (over 11,360)   *Mt. Pinchot 15' and 7½'*
Taboose Creek   *Mt. Pinchot 15' and 7½', Big Pine 15', Aberdeen 7½',*
Fish Spring 7½'
    Taboose is the Piute Indian word for a small edible groundnut found in Owens Valley. (Farquhar.) There was a "Taboose Ranch" about 12 miles north of Independence in the 1870s. (Cragen, 136.) Apparently the USGS surveyors borrowed the word for the pass and creek; both names are on the first *Mt. Whitney* 30' map, 1907.
    Bolton C. Brown called the pass "Wide Gap" in July 1895. (*SCB* 1, no. 8, May 1896: 309; map, 302; sketch, 308. The view in the sketch is northeast, not northwest as the caption says.) (Pass, KCNP, INF; creek, INF.)

Taft Point   *Yosemite 15', Yosemite Valley 1:24,000*
    Named by R. B. Marshall, USGS, for William Howard Taft (1857–1930), 27th president of the United States, 1909–13, and chief justice of the Supreme Court, 1921–30. (Farquhar: Marshall.) Taft visited Yosemite National Park in the fall of 1909. (YNP)

Tallulah Lake   *Matterhorn Peak 15'*
    David Brower speculated that it may have been named for Tallulah LeConte. (Gudde, *Place Names,* 330.) The name is on the first *Bridgeport* 30' map, 1911. (YNP)

Tamarack (a settlement)   *Big Meadow 15', Tamarack 7½'*
    The area was known as "Onion Valley" since about the 1880s due to the profusion of wild onions growing there. W. H. Hutchins built the first store there, in the early 1920s, and changed the name to "Camp Tamarack." (Wood, 43.) The "Camp" was from a cow camp once located there. (USGS.) The name "Onion Valley" was on the 15-minute quad, but has been omitted on the 7½-minute quad. (StNF)

Tamarack Flat   *Hetch Hetchy Reservoir 15'*
Tamarack Creek   *Yosemite 15', Hetch Hetchy Reservoir 15'*
    The flat was named by Bunnell, probably in 1851, using the common (but incorrect) name for the lodgepole pine. "We came to what I finally called 'Tamarack Flat,' although the appealing looks of the grizzlies we met on their way through this pass to the Tuolumne, caused me to hesitate before deciding upon the final baptism." (Bunnell, *Discovery,* 1880, 316.)
    "The flat is named after the two-leaved pine, common here, especially around the cool margin of the meadow." (Muir, *First Summer,* 131.) "Tamarack Creek is icy cold, delicious, exhilarating champagne water. It is flowing bank full in the meadow with silent speed. . . ." (ibid., 133.) (YNP)

Tar Gap   *Mineral King 15'*
    "Named by Mineral King miners in 1879, probably due to pitch on pines there." (John R. White, SNP files.) (SNP, SeNF)

Tawny Point (12,332)   *Mount Whitney 15', Mt. Brewer 7½'*
The name "Tawny Boy" was suggested by Chester Versteeg in 1953. (SC papers in BL.) The USGS added "Tawny Point" to the map in 1956 because it was in common use. (SNP)

Taylor Canyon   *Fales Hot Springs 15', Chris Flat 7½'*
"Black" Taylor was one of the discoverers of the Bodie mines. (INF archives.) (TNF)

Taylor Creek   *Lamont Peak 15', Kernville 15'*
Taylor Meadow   *Kernville 15'*
Named after Charlie Taylor, who for many years was manager of the A. Brown interests at Kernville. (Crites, 269.) (SeNF)

Teddy Bear Lake   *Mt. Abbot 15', Mt. Hilgard 7½'*
Probably named by the DFG in 1952. (See **Bear Paw Lake**.) (SiNF)

Tehipite Valley, Dome (7,708); **Little Tehipite Valley**   *Tehipite Dome 15'*
"*Tehipite* was an Indian word, and by these people was applied to the massive granite tower. Its interpretation is 'high rock.' " (L. A. Winchell, manuscript, 1896, in Farquhar papers, BL.)
Frank Dusy discovered Tehipite Valley in 1869, and in 1879 took the first photographs of the area. (See **Dusy Branch,** etc.) The valley, the dome, and a falls (now "Silver Spray Falls") are on Solomons' map of 1896; he spelled the name "Tehipitee." (KCNP)

Temple Crag (3,955 m.–12,999)   *Big Pine 15', Split Mtn. 7½ᵃ*
Originally named "Mount Alice" for Mrs. Alice Ober of Big Pine, who chaperoned a group of young people to the region. (Gudde, *Place Names,* 334.) The name appeared as "Mt Alice" only on the first *Bishop* 30' map, 1913. It was changed to "Temple Crag" before 1930. (BGN, *Sixth Report,* 748.) (INF)

Templeton Meadows, Mountain (9,932)   *Olancha 15'*
Benjamin Stuart Templeton ran sheep in the area, 1877–85. (Farquhar.) (INF)

Ten Lakes   *Hetch Hetchy Reservoir 15'*
"A glacier basin with ten glassy lakes set all near together like eggs in a nest." (John Muir, letter to Mrs. Carr, October 8, 1872, in Badè, vol. 1, 344.) The name first appears on a small map in Whitney, *Yosemite Guide-Book,* pocket edition, 1874. (YNP)

Tenaya Lake (8,149), **Peak** (10,301)   *Tuolumne Meadows 15'*
Tenaya Creek   *Tuolumne Meadows 15', Hetch Hetchy Reservoir 15',*
                    Yosemite 15', Yosemite Valley 1:24,000
Tenaya Canyon   *Yosemite Valley 1:24,000*
Lafayette H. Bunnell of the Mariposa Battalion named the lake on May 22, 1851. "Looking back to the lovely little lake, where we had been encamped during the night, and watching Ten-ie-ya as he ascended to our group, I suggested . . . that we name the lake after the old chief, and call it 'Lake Ten-ie-ya'. . . . At first, he seemed unable to comprehend our purpose, and pointing to

the group of glistening peaks, near the head of the lake, said: 'It already has a name; we call it Py-we-ack.' Upon my telling him that we had named it Ten-ie-ya, because it was upon the shores of the lake that we had found his people, who would never return to it to live, his countenance fell and he at once left our group and joined his own family circle. His countenance as he left us indicated that he thought the naming of the lake no equivalent for the loss of his territory." (Bunnell, *Discovery,* 1880, 236–37.)

"The Ten-ie-ya Cañon was known as Py-we-ack, meaning the stream of the glistening rocks, from the dazzling brightness of the glacial ground peaks at Lake Ten-ie-ya, its source." (Bunnell, *Report,* 11. See **Pywiack Cascade, Dome.**)

"Looking back from the trail soon after leaving the lake, we saw a conspicuous and very picturesque peak . . . to the north filled with a grand mass of snow. . . . We called this *Coliseum Peak.* So let it be called hereafter, to the end of time." (LeConte, *Ramblings,* 76–77.) That name did not appear on maps. T. S. Solomons called it "Tenaya Peak" on his 1896 map, although it did not appear on the *Mt. Lyell* 30' map until the fifth edition, 1922.

The Hoffmann and Gardiner map of 1863–67 had "L. Tenaya" and "Tenaya Fork." "Tenaya Creek" and "Tenaya Canyon" were on the Wheeler Survey atlas sheet 56D, 1878–79. (YNP)

Lower and **Upper Tent Meadow**   *Marion Peak 15'*
A large block of granite, in the lower meadow, resembles a white tent when seen from a distance. (Farquhar.) (KCNP)

Tether Lake   *Mt. Abbot 15', Mt. Hilgard 7½'*
Named in August 1951 by Elden H. Vestal of the DFG after the buckskin or braided hide rope used by Indians, because the lake is tethered, or tied, to two adjacent lakes. (Heyward Moore, *FPP* 26, no. 2, Summer 1984: 2.) (SiNF)

Tharps Log, Rock   *Triple Divide Peak 15'*
Hale D. Tharp (1828–1912), a native of Michigan, settled in the Three Rivers region in 1856. In 1858 he was the first white man to explore the Giant Forest area. On the day he arrived at what is now "Log Meadow" he carved his name and the year on the hollow sequoia log that he later converted into a summer camp—"Tharps Log." (Walter Fry in *Nature,* no. 1, Nov. 22, 1924.) The present Alta Peak was once known as "Tharp's Peak." (See **Alta Meadow, Peak.**) (SNP)

Thibaut Creek   *Independence 15', Mt. Pinchot 15', Kearsarge Peak 7½', Aberdeen 7½', Black Rock Springs 7½'*
Named for a French family who in the 1890s lived where the old county road crossed the creek. (INF archives.) The name is on the first *Mt. Whitney* 30' map, 1907. (INF)

Thimble Peak (9,805–9,827)   *Silver Lake 15', Caples Lake 7½'*
"On its [Silver Lake's] east rises a lofty range of dark volcanic mountains . . . which terminate to the north at the two remarkable thimble-looking obelisks of black rock. . . ." (Goddard, *Report,* 100.) Goddard later

refers to "the Thimbal Rocks, before named." (101.) The name has its present form on atlas sheet 56B, 1876–77. (ENF)

Thompson Canyon   *Tower Peak 15', Matterhorn Peak 15'*
The name was used by Lt. N. F. McClure in 1894, as though it already existed; thus it may have been named for an early sheepherder. (*SCB* 1, no. 5, Jan. 1895: 179.) (YNP)

Thompson, Mount (13,494); **Thompson Ridge, Lake**   *Mt. Goddard 15',*
Mt. Thompson 7½'
The mountain and ridge were named about 1908 by R. B. Marshall, USGS, for Almon Harris Thompson (1839–1906). Thompson was associated with John Wesley Powell in exploration of the Colorado River and the surrounding plateau country, 1870–78, and was a geographer with the USGS, 1882–1906. (Farquhar: Marshall.) (KCNP, INF)

Thompson Peak (9,340)   *Freel Peak 15' and 7½'*
Named for John A. "Snow-shoe" Thompson (or Thomson), who carried the mail across the Sierra Nevada in winter for 20 years, 1856–76. (Farquhar, *History*, 99–101; *Historic Spots*, 25–26.) (ENF, TNF)

Thor Peak (3,751 m.–12,300)   *Mount Whitney 15' and 7½'*
The name was proposed by the Sierra Club in 1937. (*SCB* 23, no. 2, April 1938: 105.) Thor is the god of thunder in Scandinavian mythology. As applied to a mountain in California, it is a classic example of bad naming. (INF)

Thousand Island Lake (9,834)   *Devils Postpile 15', Mt. Ritter 7½'*
Probably named by Theodore S. Solomons; the name is on his map of 1896. "Next morning we passed down the slope of the mountain to the lake, with its hundred islets. . . ." (Solomons in *SCB* 1, no. 2, Jan. 1894: 70.) John Muir called it "Islet Lake" in August 1873. (Muir, *Writings*, 31.) (INF)

Three Brothers; Middle Brother; Lower Brother   *Yosemite 15',*
Yosemite Valley 1:24,000
"These remarkable peaks were so named by the writer from their number coinciding with the three brothers captured by us while hidden among the rocks of the peaks. Young Ten-ie-ya, a son of the chief, was subsequently killed while attempting to escape.

"The Indians called the peaks Kom-po-pai-ses, meaning the Frog Mountains, because of their complete resemblance to the heads of those amatory reptiles. The attempts made to translate the Indian name into mountains playing 'leap frog' are as absurd as they are amusing. . . ." (Bunnell, *Report*, 10.)

". . . three points which the Indians know as 'Eleacha,' named after a plant much used for food, but which some lackadaisical person has given the commonplace name of 'The Three Brothers.' " (Hutchings, *Scenes*, 1860, 94.)

"The common idea is that the Indians imagined the mountains to be playing 'Leap Frog.' It would remain, in that case, to show that the Indians practiced that, to us, familiar game; we have never caught them at it." (Whitney, *The Yosemite Book,* 1868, 17.) (YNP)

Three Island Lake (10,568)   *Mt. Abbot 15', Mt. Hilgard 7½'*
   A descriptive name, given in 1942 by a DFG survey party under William A. Dill. (DFG survey.) (SiNF)

Three Sirens, The   *Mt. Goddard 15' and 7½'*
   A cluster of three peaks, just east of Scylla, so named because of their location between Scylla and Charybdis. The name came into use among climbers, and was ratified by a BGN decision in 1964. It does not appear on early editions of the 15-minute quad.
   "First you will come to the Sirens, who bewitch every one who comes near them. If any man draws near in his innocence and listens to their voice, he never sees home again. . . . There in the meadow they sit, and all around is a great heap of bones, mouldering bodies and withering skins." (Homer, 129.) (KCNP)

Three Sisters   *Huntington Lake 15', Dogtooth Peak 7½'*
   Possibly named by the USGS during the 1901–02 survey for the *Kaiser* 30' map; the name is on the first edition, 1904. (SiNF)

Three Springs   *Tehipite Dome 15'*
   The springs could have been named by early sheepherders or by the USGS during the 1903 survey for the *Tehipite* 30' map; the name is on the first edition, 1905. (SiNF)

Thumb, The (13,388)   *Big Pine 15', Split Mtn. 7½'*
   Named by Windsor B. Putnam, who made the first ascent, December 12, 1921. ". . . the familiar profile was revealed in astonishing boldness—a gigantic thumb, placed horizontally, with the tip held aloft!" (*SCB* 11, no. 3, 1922: 274.) The name appeared on the second *Bishop* 30' map, 1930. (INF)

Thunder and Lightning Lake (11,717)   *Mt. Goddard 15',*
                                                          Mt. Thompson 7½'
   Probably named by Halladay, a South Fork packer, who got caught in a storm while planting fish in the lake—sometime during the 1920s. (Art Schober.) (INF)

Thunder Mountain (13,558)   *Mount Whitney 15', Mt. Brewer 7½'*
   Named by George R. Davis, USGS, in August 1905, when he made the first ascent and placed a bench mark on the summit. (Farquhar: letter from Davis to W. L. Huber, Sept. 14, 1916.) (KCNP, SNP)

Thunder Mountain (9,408 and 9,410)   *Caples Lake 7½'*
   Named by USFS personnel because "thunderheads appear to build up in that area." (BGN decision, 1980.) Not named on the *Silver Lake* 15' quad. It is the peak with a double summit two miles south-southwest of Kirkwood, marked "9402." (ENF)

Thunderbolt Peak (14,003)   *Mt. Goddard 15', North Palisade 7½'*
   Named by Francis P. Farquhar and six others when they made the first ascent on August 13, 1931. ". . . shortly after the party reached the summit a

violent thunder-storm drove all precipitately to a place of safety. So rapidly did the storm gather that Eichorn, last man to leave the ridge, was dangerously close to a lightning flash that appeared to strike the mountain. The importance of immediate retreat as soon as the rocks begin to 'sing' was strongly impressed upon the members of the party." (*SCB* 17, no. 1, Feb. 1932: 125.) (KCNP, INF)

Tilden Lake, Canyon, Creek   *Tower Peak 15'*
The lake and canyon probably were named by Lt. N. F. McClure, but for whom is not known; both names are on McClure's map of 1895. On Hoffmann's map of 1873 the lake is called "Lake Nina," a name probably given by Hoffmann and Alfred Craven in 1870 when they made the first ascent of Tower Peak. Nina Florence Browne, Hoffmann's sister-in-law, married Craven in 1871. (Farquhar.) (YNP)

Tiltill Valley   *Hetch Hetchy Reservoir 15'*
Tiltill Creek   *Hetch Hetchy Reservoir 15', Tower Peak 15'*
Tiltill Mountain (9,005)   *Tower Peak 15'*
The valley was named "in 1887 by Eugene Y. Ellwell, who homesteaded this meadow." (Farquhar files: Versteeg, from Col. Benson.) There is no mention of what the word means. The valley is first named on Lt. N. F. McClure's map of 1895, the creek on the 1897 *Yosemite* and 1898 *Dardanelles* 30' maps, and the mountain on the 15-minute quad. (YNP)

Timber Gap   *Mineral King 15'*
The name is first seen on J. W. A. Wright's map of 1883. The origin is uncertain, but it may be due to the fact that during the 1870s the slopes between Mineral King valley and the ridge were largely denuded of timber—creating quite a "gap"—by the demands of the silver-mining excitement. (Harper, 27.) (SNP)

Timberline Lake   *Mount Whitney 15' and 7½'*
A lake at timberline on the John Muir Trail between Crabtree Meadow and Trail Crest. The name was added to the 7½-minute quad by the USGS because it has been in common use and had appeared on other maps. It is not named on the 15-minute quad. (SNP)

Tinemaha, Mount (3,816 m.–12,561); **Tinemaha Creek, Lake**
                                        Big Pine 15', Split Mtn 7½'
Named in honor of the legendary Paiute chief, Tinemaha. The creek was named first; it appeared on the *Bishop* 30' map, 1913. The peak was known by this name to early prospectors and cattlemen of Owens Valley. The name was proposed formally by Chester Versteeg in 1935. (Farquhar files.) (INF)

Tioga Pass (9,945), **Crest**   *Tuolumne Meadows 15'*
Tioga Peak (11,513)   *Mono Craters 15'*
Tioga Lake (9,651)   *Tuolumne Meadows 15', Mono Craters 15'*
Tioga is an Iroquois name meaning "where it forks" (Farquhar), "at the forks," "swift current," or "a gate" (Gannett, 253). The name has been preserved in counties, towns, and a river in Pennsylvania and New York.

The Tioga mining district was organized in 1878, and one can only assume that one or more of the promoters was from Pennsylvania or New York. The Tioga Mine was known as "The Sheepherder" when it was located in 1860. The site marked "Bennettville" on the map was briefly called "Tioga," and had a post office under that name from May 1880 to June 1881. Before the "Tioga" name became rampant, the pass was called "MacLane's Pass." (Whitney, *Geology*, 434.) Tioga Lake was originally named "Lake Jessie," for Jessie Montrose of Lundy. (YNP files.) The crest had an early name of "Mount Warren Ridge." (Russell, *100 Years*, 131; also *SCB* 13, no. 1, Feb. 1928: 45.) The Tioga Road, first known as "The Great Sierra Wagon Road," was built in 1882 and 1883. (Pass, YNP, INF; others, INF)

T J Lake   *Devils Postpile 15', Crystal Crag 7½'*
Named for Tom Jones, one of the first supervisors of Inyo National Forest. (Smith, 51.) (INF)

Tocher Lake (8,775)   *Huntington Lake 15', Dogtooth Peak 7½'*
Named for Dr. Lloyd Tocher of Fresno. (DFG survey.) (SiNF)

Toe Lake   *Mt. Abbot 15', Mt. Hilgard 7½'*
Probably named by a DFG survey party about 1952. (DFG survey.) The lake is at the toe of boot-shaped Lake Italy. (SiNF)

Tokopah Valley, Falls   *Triple Divide Peak 15'*
The name is Yokut Indian for "high mountain valley." (White, 51.) It was suggested to White by George W. Stewart about 1923. The valley is named on the fourth *Tehipite* 30' map, 1929. The name was extended to the falls on the 15-minute quad, 1956. (SNP)

Tom, Mount (13,652)   *Mt. Tom 15', Mount Tom 7½'*
Named for Thomas Clark, a resident of the pioneer town of Owensville, who is credited with having made the first ascent, in the 1860s. He said he was guided to the top by Indians. (*Inyo*, 147.) (INF)

Tomahawk Lake (11,145–11,146)   *Mt. Tom 15', Mount Tom 7½'*
Named in 1950 by Elden H. Vestal of the DFG because from the air the lake's outline looks like the head of a tomahawk. (DFG survey.) (SiNF)

Tombstone, The; Tombstone Creek   *Mt. Abbot 15', Florence Lake 7½'*
"The Tombstone" probably was named by the USGS for its shape, during the 1907–09 survey for the *Mt. Goddard* 30' map; it is on the first edition, 1912. The creek name appears on the 15-minute quad. (SiNF)

Tombstone Ridge, Creek   *Tehipite Dome 15'*
Probably named by the USGS during the 1903 survey for the *Tehipite* 30' map; the names are on the first edition, 1905. (Ridge, KCNP, SiNF; creek, SiNF)

Tooth Lake   *Mt. Abbot 15', Mt. Hilgard 7½'*
Probably named by the DFG in 1952. (See **Bear Paw Lake.**) (SiNF)

Toowa Range   *Kern Peak 15', Olancha 15'*
"Unknown, but a Shoshonean, probably Mono, origin is indicated."
(Kroeber, 63.) The name is on the first *Olancha* 30' map, 1907. (INF)

Topsy Turvy Lake   *Mt. Goddard 15', Mt. Darwin 7½'*
Named in the 1930s by Art Schober "for the huge boulders scattered every
which way." (Art Schober.) (INF)

Tower Peak (11,755), Lake, Canyon   *Tower Peak 15'*
"I recognized also several other well known peaks, one of which was a lofty
castellated peak south of the Sonora and Walker River Immigrant Road, named
the Castle Peak, and whose position I had determined when on the Railway
Exploration under Lieut. Moore, U.S.A., in 1853." (Goddard, *Report,* 101.)
"The grand mass of Tower Peak is a prominent and most remarkably picturesque object. This is one of the three points in the Sierra to which the name of
'Castle Peak' has been given, and is the first and original one of that name,
having been called so by Mr. G. H. Goddard.... By some unaccountable
mistake the name was transferred to a rounded, and not at all castellated, mass
about eighteen miles a little south of east from the original 'Castle Peak,' where it
has become firmly fixed. Hence we have been obliged to give a new name to Mr.
Goddard's peak, which we now call 'Tower Peak.' " (Whitney, *Yosemite Guide-
Book,* 1874, 131–32. See also **Dunderberg Peak** and **Warren, Mount.**)
The lake and canyon were first named on the 15-minute quad. (Peak, YNP,
TNF; others, TNF)

Tower Rock (8,469)   *Kern Peak 15'*
The name was used by the Sierra Club in 1903. (*SCB* 5, no. 1, Jan. 1904:
59–60; photo, plate XVI.) J. W. A. Wright labelled that area "Basalt
Columns" on his map of 1883. (INF)

Townsley Lake   *Tuolumne Meadows 15'*
Forest Sanford Townsley (1882–43), chief ranger in Yosemite National
Park, 1916–43. The lake was named for him when he planted golden trout in
it. Prior to that time it was called "Upper Fletcher Lake." (Bingaman,
Guardians, 88–89; obituary in *YNN* 22, no. 9, Sept. 1943: 75.) (YNP)

Tragedy Spring; North Tragedy Creek   *Silver Lake 15',*
                                                    Tragedy Spring 7½'
Tragedy Creek   *Silver Lake 15', Tragedy Spring 7½',*
                                            Bear River Reservoir 7½'
July 19, 1848. "Made only five or six miles and encamped at the spring near
the fresh grave; determining to satisfy ourselves, it was soon opened. We were
shocked at the sight. There lay the three murdered men robbed of every stitch of
clothing, lying promiscuously in one hole about two feet deep.... The blood
seemed fresh still oozing from their wounds."
July 20, 1848. "We cut the following inscription on a balsam fir that stood
near the grave: 'To the memory of Daniel Browett, Ezrah H. Allen, and
Henderson Cox, who were supposed to have been murdered and buried by

Indians on the twenty-seventh of June, A.D. 1848.' We called this place
Tragedy Spring." (Gudde, *Bigler,* 115–16.) Bigler, his companions, and the
murdered men were members of the disbanded Mormon Battalion, on their way
back to Great Salt Lake. (ENF)

Trail Crest   *Mount Whitney 15' and 7½'*
   When a new Mt. Whitney trail was built in the early 1930s, the place where
it crossed the Sierra crest—north of Whitney Pass on the old trail—was named
"Trail Crest." (BGN.) The name first appeared on the 1937 *Mt. Whitney 30'*
map. (SNP, INF)

Trail Peak (11,623), **Pass**   *Olancha 15'*
   The peak probably was named by the USGS during the 1905 survey for the
Olancha 30' map; it is on the first edition, 1907, and was not mentioned by any
travelers before that time. The pass was on the route of the old Hockett Trail,
built in 1862–64. It was first named on the 15-minute quad. (INF)

Treasure Lakes   *Mt. Abbot 15' and 7½'*
   A name that was in common use, and was promoted as an official name by
Chester Versteeg in 1936. The lakes had been planted with golden trout. (INF
archives.) (INF)

Treasure Lakes   *Mt. Goddard 15', Mt. Thompson 7½'*
   "Named by the Parchers [of Parcher's camp]. My youngest brother was in
on that. They stocked them with golden trout, which is how they got the name."
(Art Schober.) (INF)

Tresidder Peak (over 10,560)   *Tuolumne Meadows 15'*
   Donald B. Tressider, husband of Mary Curry Tressider, was president of the
Yosemite Park & Curry Co., 1925–48, and president of Stanford University,
1943–48. During Tressider's reign as head of the Curry Company, he built the
Ahwahnee Hotel, the cafeteria and dining room at Camp Curry, and the Big
Trees Lodge in the Mariposa Grove. He was also responsible for beginning a
skiing program in Yosemite and for constructing the High Sierra Camps. (BGN
decision, 1959.) (YNP)

Triple Divide Peak (12,634)   *Triple Divide Peak 15'*
   Called "The Keystone" by William R. Dudley in 1902. (*SCB* 4, no. 4, June
1903: 304.) It was undoubtedly given its present name by the USGS during the
survey for the *Tehipite 30'* map in 1903; it is on the first edition, 1905. (KCNP,
SNP)

Triple Divide Peak (11,607); **Triple Peak Fork**   *Merced Peak 15'*
   Almost certainly named by the USGS during the 1898–99 survey for the
Mt. Lyell 30' map; both names are on the first edition, 1901. (Peak, YNP, SiNF;
fork, YNP)

Triple Falls   *Marion Peak 15'*
   "The river divides into two streams which approach within fifty feet of each
other, and each then falls 200 feet . . . both fall into one basin about 100 feet in
diameter; then the united waters . . . drop 400 feet." (Elliott, *Guide,* 16.)

Considering that this was published in 1883, the information probably came from either Frank Dusy or L. A. Winchell. The description is inaccurate. There are two streams, rather than one that divides and then reunites. Winchell used the name "Triple Falls" in a letter to T. S. Solomons, March 20, 1896. (Farquhar papers, BL.) (KCNP)

Trojan Peak (4,251 m.–13,950) *Mount Whitney 15', Mt. Williamson 7½'*
The name was suggested by Chester Versteeg and Ralph A. Chase to honor the University of Southern California "Trojans"—the athletic teams. The namers had wanted to call it "Southern California Peak," but the BGN favored the shorter name. (Los Angeles *Times*, Oct. 7, 1951.) The name appeared on the *Mt. Whitney* 30' map, 1937. (INF)

True Meadow *Kernville 15'*
Henry B. True patented 120 acres in secs. 27, 33, and 34, T. 24 S., R. 34 E. in 1891. (SeNF)

Trumbull Lake *Matterhorn Peak 15'*
A misspelled name. John S. *Trumble* patented land close to the lake in 1881: 160 acres in secs. 5, 6, and 8, T. 2 N., R. 25 E. The name has been spelled "Trumbull" since it appeared on the *Bridgeport* 30' map in 1911. (TNF)

Tryon Peak (9,970), **Meadow** *Markleeville 15', Ebbetts Pass 7½'*
Named for Charles Tryon, who ran stock in the area. (StNF files.) (Peak, StNF, TNF; meadow, StNF)

Tub Lake *Sharktooth Peak 7½'*
Probably named by Elden H. Vestal of the DFG, who surveyed the lake in 1953. (DFG survey.) Not named on the *Kaiser Peak* 15' quad. It is the tiny lake at the south end of Reef Lake. (SiNF)

Tueeulala Falls *Lake Eleanor 15'*
"It's Indian name is *Tu-ee-u-lá-la*. . . . From the brow of the cliff it leaps, clear and free, for a thousand feet; then half disappears in a rage of spattering cascades among the bowlders of an earthquake talus." (John Muir, "Hetch-Hetchy Valley," *Overland Monthly* 6, no. 1, July 1873: 46.) There is no explanation of what the name means. Despite its early use by Muir, the name did not get onto a map until publication of the 15-minute quad in 1956. (YNP)

Tulainyo Lake (3,908 m.–12,802) *Mount Whitney 15' and 7½'*
A composite name, created out of *Tulare* and *Inyo*, coined by R. B. Marshall, USGS, during the 1905 survey for the *Mt. Whitney* 30' map. It is on the first edition, 1907. It is a snow-melt lake, in a depression, with neither inlet nor outlet; and, although close to the county line, is entirely within Tulare County. (SNP)

Tule Lake *Mt. Henry 7½'*
A descriptive name, possibly given by William A. Dill of the DFG when he surveyed the lake in 1947. "The shore is about five-sixths bulrushes in water." (DFG survey.) Not named on the *Blackcap Mtn.* 15' quad. It is the swampy area near the John Muir Trail in sec. 24, T. 8 S., R. 28 E. (SiNF)

Tule Lake (6,780)   *Kaiser Peak 15', Mt. Givens 7½'*
Probably named in 1949 by Charles K. Fisher of the DFG. There is an "extensive bed of tules at the south end; hence the name." (DFG survey.) (SiNF)

Tule River   *Kaweah 15', Mineral King 15', Camp Nelson 15'*
A *tule* is a common bulrush or cattail, and a place where *tules* grow is a *tular*. The present Tule River was named "Rio de San Pedro" by Moraga's expedition in 1806. (Arch. MSB, vol. 4, Muñoz, Oct. 21, 1806.)
On Derby's map of 1850 it appears as "Tule River or Rio San Pedro." This name for a reed that flourishes in swampy places at low altitudes has been extended far back into the mountains. There are North, Middle, and South forks of the river, and even a "South Fork of Middle Fork." For a detailed discussion of the words *tule* and *tulare* and of the evolution of the names, see Gudde, *Place Names*, 346–47. (SeNF)

Tully Hole   *Mt. Morrison 15', Bloody Mtn. 7½'*
Tully Lake   *Mt. Abbot 15', Graveyard Peak 7½'*
Gene Tully was one of the original 60 rangers in the US Forest Service. He helped rid Yosemite National Park of sheep during 1905–07, and was intermittently a forest ranger until 1938. Tully Hole was where he used to rest his stock during a six-week patrol of the mountains. (*FPP* 9, no. 5, Dec. 1967: 1–2.) (SiNF)

Tunemah Peak (11,894)   *Marion Peak 15'*
Tunemah Lake (11,131–11,122)   *Mt. Goddard 15' and 7½'*
There was once a "Tunemah Pass" (on the *Tehipite* 30' maps, 1905–47), and a "Tunemah Trail"—long abandoned. It was the latter that gave birth to the dreadful name, as a herd of sheep belonging to Frank Dusy and Bill Coolidge was forced down a precipitous trail into Simpson Meadow, in 1878.
"Two Chinese herders—appalled by the awful chasm confronting them—worked to a point of exhaustion by their desperate efforts to force the massed and balking sheep onward—cursed the sheep, the dogs, the trail and all other related factors, in the most forcible epithets known to the celestial vocabulary. Above the bleating of the sheep and the barking of the frantic dogs, from the enveloping clouds of dust, there repeatedly and wrathfully resounded 'Teu-na-mah-ne! muck-a-hai! Yeu-nicky-shee-fut! Teu-na-mah-ne! Teu-na-mah-ne!'—a thousand times. . . . Peck and Nye (Dusy's head packers) agreed to call the sheep plunge 'Teu-na-mah-ne.' " (Winchell, 159.)
And what does it mean? It means something as horrible as "You sleep with your grandmother." It might even mean something worse than that. Consult your local authority. (KCNP)

Tunnabora Peak (4,134 m.–13,565)   *Mount Whitney 15' and 7½'*
George R. Davis, USGS, made the first ascent in August 1905 during the survey for the *Mt. Whitney* 30' map. (*SCB* 10, no. 2, Jan. 1917: 231.) He apparently named the peak at this time. There is no explanation of the meaning

of the Indian-sounding name. The name appears on the map in 1907, but is not in J. N. LeConte's "Elevations." (*SCB* 4, no. 4, June 1903: 290–91.) (SNP, INF)

Tunnel Meadow, Air Camp, Guard Station *Kern Peak 15'*
Golden Trout Creek and the South Fork of the Kern River come within a few hundred feet of each other near a trail junction north of the guard station. About 1883 or 1884 some enterprising South Fork ranchers dug a diversion tunnel to take water from the creek to irrigate their meadows lower down the river. The tunnel was plagued by cave-ins, and was converted into an open cut about 1891. That too had a cave-in problem, and the project was abandoned about 1899. (*Los Tulares,* no. 144, August 1984: LeConte, *A Summer,* 77.)
The name "The Tunnel" is on the *Olancha* 30' maps, 1907–47. The meadow was named "South Fork Meadows" from 1907 through 1931, and was changed to "Tunnel Meadows" on the sixth edition of the map, 1939. The air camp is a fly-in resort for fisherman and hunters. (INF)

Tuohy Meadow, Creek *Mineral King 15'*
John Tuohy (1828–1916), born in Ireland, came to San Francisco in 1850 and to Tulare County in 1868. In 1870 he took 6,000 sheep to what is now the meadow named for him, but he never tried to own the land. He was one of the prime movers for establishment of Sequoia National Park. (*Los Tulares,* no. 32, Sept. 1957: 1–2.) (SNP)

Turf Lakes *Blackcap Mtn. 15', Mt. Henry 7½'*
Named in 1947 by a DFG survey party under Charles K. Fisher. Both lakes are partly bordered by meadows. (DFG survey.) (SiNF)

Tuolumne River *Tuolumne Meadows 15', Hetch Hetchy Reservoir 15',*
Lake Eleanor 15'
Tuolumne Meadows, Peak (10,845), **Falls, Pass** *Tuolumne Meadows 15'*
Tuolumne Grove *Lake Eleanor 15'*
The name is from a tribe of Indians that lived on the banks of the lower Tuolumne and Stanislaus rivers, in the vicinity of Knights Ferry. (Kroeber, 64.) The tribe was called *Taulámne*—and also *Tahualamne*—by Padre Muñoz. (Arch. MSB, vol. 4, Oct. 3, 1806, ff.) The Moraga-Muñoz party named the Tuolumne River the *Delores,* from the time of its discovery, October 1, the "Dolores of September," but that name did not prevail.
Frémont and Preuss, on their 1845 map, mistakenly called the Tuolumne River the "Rio de los Merced." On the 1848 map, they corrected it to "Rio de los Towalumnes." The modern spelling is on Derby's 1849 map. It is said that the Indians pronounced the word *Tu-ah-lum'-ne*. (Sanchez, 222.)
The Whitney Survey named "Tuolumne Meadows;" it is on Hoffmann and Gardiner's map, 1863–67. The falls is first named on Hoffmann's 1873 map, the peak on the Wheeler Survey atlas sheet 56D, 1878–79, and the pass on the first *Mt. Lyell* 30' map, 1901. The grove was not named on USGS maps until publication of the 15-minute quad in 1956. (YNP)

Turner Lake   *Merced Peak 15'*
Henry Ward Turner (1857–1937), USGS; he pioneered some of the geologic mapping in Yosemite National Park. (BGN decision, 1963.) (YNP)

Turner Meadows   *Yosemite 15'*
The name is on Lt. N. F. McClure's 1896 map. Will Turner, grandfather of Arthur L. Gallison (see **Gallison Lake**), a park ranger for 37 years. Turner ran cattle in the area in the 1880s, before it was part of the park. (Bingaman, *Guardians,* 93.) (YNP)

Turret Peak (12,091), **Lakes** (**Upper, Middle** and **Lower**)   *Mt. Abbot 15',*
                                                              Mt. Hilgard 7½'
Turret Creek   *Blackcap Mtn. 15', Mt. Henry 7½', Mt. Hilgard 7½'*
The peak probably was named, for its shape, by J. N. LeConte when he was in the region in 1898; it appears on his map of 1899. The other "Turret" names first appeared on the 15-minute quads. (SiNF)

Turtleback Dome   *Yosemite 15', Yosemite Valley 1:24,000*
A descriptive name; it is thought that François Matthes named it. (*YNN* 34, no. 1, Jan. 1955: 18.) It appears on the first USGS *Yosemite Valley* map, 1907. (YNP)

Tuttle Creek   *Lone Pine 15' and 7½', Mt. Langley 7½'*
Lyman Tuttle, born in Ohio in 1821, died at Cerro Gordo in 1885. He was a civil engineer, one of the organizers of Inyo County in 1866, and the first county surveyor, 1866–72. (INF archives.) (INF)

Twin Lake (8,145)   *Markleeville 15', Pacific Valley 7½'*
So named because it is a twin to Lower Blue Lake. (USGS Domestic Name Report.) (ENF)

Twin Lakes (7,092 and 7,081)   *Matterhorn Peak 15'*
Probably named by early settlers in the 1860s. The name is on the Wheeler Survey atlas sheet 56D, 1878–79. (TNF)

Twin Lakes   *Tehipite Dome 15'*
Probably named by Scott M. Soule of the DFG in 1948. The northern lake was originally called "Long Twin Lake;" the other, "Round Twin Lake." (DFG survey.) (SiNF)

Twin Peaks   *Matterhorn Peak 15'*
Probably named by the Wheeler Survey; they are on atlas sheet 56D, 1878–79. (YNP, TNF)

Twin Peaks (10,485 and 10,268)   *Triple Divide Peak 15'*
Probably named by the USGS; the name appears on the second *Tehipite* 30' map, 1912. (SNP, KCNP)

Two Eagle Peak (12,966)   *Mt. Thompson 7½'*
The name first came into use in *The Climber's Guide.* It was placed on the map by the USGS because it was in common use. Not named on the *Mt. Goddard* 15' map. It is about 0.6 mile west of Fifth Lake. (INF)

Two Teats (11,387)   *Devils Postpile 15', Mammoth Mtn. 7½'*
Probably named by the USGS during the 1898–99 survey for the *Mt. Lyell* 30' map. The name is on the first edition, 1901, but is not on T. S. Solomons' map of 1896. (INF)

Tyee Lakes   *Mt. Goddard 15', Mt. Thompson 7½'*
"Tyee" was a famed brand of salmon eggs. The name came into common use, and was suggested for approval by Chester Versteeg in 1936. (INF archives.) A man named Brown stocked the lower lake about 1920, and it was then known as "Brown Lake" until the new name came along. (Art Schober.) The name "Tyee Lakes" appeared on the sixth edition of the *Mt. Goddard* 30' map, 1940. (INF)

Tyndall, Mount (4,272.8 m.–14,018)   *Mount Whitney 15',*
Mt. Williamson 7½'
Tyndall Creek   *Mount Whitney 15', Mt. Williamson 7½',*
Mt. Brewer 7½', Mt. Kaweah 7½'
The mountain was named by Clarence King when he and Richard Cotter made the first ascent, July 1864. "We had now an easy slope to the summit, and hurried up over rocks and ice, reaching the crest at exactly twelve o'clock. I rang my hammer upon the topmost rock; we grasped hands, and I reverently named the grand peak **Mount Tyndall.**" (King, 75.)
John Tyndall (1820–1893), British professor of natural philosophy, scientist, and explorer in the Alps.
The creek was first named on the 15-minute quad. (Mtn., SNP, INF; creek, SNP)

Unicorn Peak (over 10,880), **Creek**   *Tuolumne Meadows 15'*
The peak was named by the Whitney Survey in 1863. "A very prominent peak, with a peculiar horn-shaped outline, was called 'Unicorn Peak.'" (Whitney, *Geology,* 427.) But then Whitney added an apologetic footnote for the romantic/mythical name. "Names are frequently given to prominent objects, by parties like ours, for convenience; as where peaks are used for topographical stations. If not named, they would have to be numbered, which would be both awkward and inconvenient."
The creek was named on the first *Mt. Lyell* 30' map, 1901. (YNP)

Union Point (6,314)   *Yosemite 15', Yosemite Valley 1:24,000*
A point on the Four-Mile Trail, probably named when the trail was built, in 1871, or shortly thereafter. "Union" was a frequently used patriotic name during and after the Civil War. "On our way down we stopped for a few moments to rest on Union Point, half way between Glacier Point and the valley. Here we found an Irishman living in a sort of pine-plank wigwam, from the top of which waved the United States flag." (Jackson, 133.) The name was on the USGS maps of the valley from 1907 through 1970, but was omitted from the 1977 edition. (YNP)

University Peak (4,142 m.–13,632)   *Mount Whitney 15',*
Mt. Williamson 7½'
Named by J. N. LeConte and party on July 12, 1896, when they made the
first ascent. The name, in honor of the University of California, had been given
to a different peak by LeConte in 1890. At this same time he renamed that
summit "Mount Gould." (*SCB* 2, no. 2, May 1897: 84; see **Gould, Mount.**)
(KCNP, INF)

Upper Basin   *Mt. Pinchot 15', Big Pine 15', Split Mtn. 7½'*
The upper basin of the South Fork of the Kings River. It was probably named
by the USGS during the 1905 survey for the *Mt. Whitney* 30' map; it is on the
first edition, 1907, and also on the first *Bishop* 30' map, 1913. (KCNP)

Ursa Lake   *Mt. Abbot 15', Mt. Hilgard 7½'*
Named in 1952 by Elden H. Vestal of the DFG. (DFG survey. See **Bear
Paw Lake.**) (SiNF)

Useless Lake   *Sharktooth Peak 7½'*
Named in 1949 by William A. Dill of the DFG because the lake appeared to
be "useless for anything—even for frogs." (DFG survey.) Not named on the
Kaiser Peak 15' quad. It is the tiny lake just west of Sedge Lake and south of
Shorty Lake. (SiNF)

Vacation Pass (over 12,640)   *Mount Whitney 15' and 7½'*
A name that first appeared in *The Climber's Guide,* and was added to the
map by the USGS because it was in common use. (SNP, INF)

Valor Lake   *Mt. Goddard 15' and 7½'*
Named in 1948 by William A. Dill of the DFG. The reason for the name was
not given. (DFG survey.) (SiNF)

Vandever Mountain (11,947)   *Mineral King 15'*
William Vandever (1817–1893), a general in the Civil War, member of
Congress from Iowa, 1859–61, and from the sixth district of California, 1887–
91. In 1890 he introduced the bills establishing Yosemite, Sequoia, and General
Grant national parks. (Farquhar; *MWCJ* 1, no. 2, May 1903: 35.) (SNP,
SeNF)

Vee Lake (11,163)   *Mt. Abbott 15', Mt. Hilgard 7½'*
Named in 1942 for its shape by William A. Dill of the DFG. (DFG survey.)
(SiNF)

Vermilion Cliffs, Lake   *Mt. Abbot 15', Graveyard Peak 7½'*
The name was given in September 1894 by Theodore S. Solomons and
Leigh Bierce for a valley that is now under the waters of Lake Thomas A.
Edison. "This flat is at least five miles long by a mile in average width. From the
color of its soil, we christened it Vermilion Valley." (Solomons in *SCB* 1, no. 6,
May 1895: 227.) Vermilion Cliffs were named at the same time by Solomons.
(Solomons' annotated copy of Farquhar's *Place Names,* in Farquhar Papers,
BL.) The lake was first named on the 15-minute quad. (SiNF)

Vernal Fall *Yosemite 15', Yosemite Valley 1:24,000*
Named in 1851 by Lafayette Bunnell. "The Vernal Fall I so named because of the cool, vernal spray in contrast at midday with summer heat, reminding me of an April shower, and because of the blue grass curiously growing among dark rocks and gay, dripping flowers, making it an eternal April to the ground. The Indian name is Yan-o-pah, meaning a little cloud, because of the spray through which the old trail passed, and because of the circular rainbow, nowhere else seen in the mountains." (Bunnell, *Report,* 12.)

"While gazing at its beauties, let us, now and forever, earnestly protest against the perpetuation of any other nomenclature to this wonder than *Pi-wy-ack,* the name which is given to it by the Indians, and means *a shower of sparkling crystals. . . .*" (Hutchings, *Illustrated* 4, no. 6, Dec. 1859: 249.)

"Mr. Hutchings . . . has misstated the Indian name for this fall, furnished him by myself. . . . The name given by the Yosemites to the Ten-ie-ya branch of the Merced was unmistakably Py-we-ack. This name has been transferred from its original locality by some *romantic* preserver of Indian names. . . . It is indeed a laughable idea for me to even suppose a worm- and acorn-eating Indian would ever attempt to construct a name to mean '*a shower of sparkling crystals;*' his diet must have been improved by *modern* intelligent culture." (Bunnell, *Discovery,* 1911, 211.) (YNP)

Vernon, Lake *Tower Peak 15'*
Origin unknown. When Lt. N. F. McClure came to the lake in 1894 it was already named; his sketch map showed a cabin in the meadow just north of the lake, and thus one assumes that it was named by or for a sheepherder. (*SCB* 1, no. 5, Jan. 1895: 182–86.) (YNP)

Versteeg, Mount (13,470) *Mount Whitney 15', Mt. Williamson 7½'*
Chester Versteeg (1887–1963), lawyer, businessman, lecturer, and author, who devoted much of his life to furthering interest in the Sierra Nevada. (BGN decision, 1964.) Versteeg had a strong interest in place names. He did much original research on the origin of Sierra Nevada names. Many of the names he suggested are now on the maps; many more were rejected by the US Board on Geographic Names. The first edition of the 15-minute quad, 1956, does not have the name on it. The peak is on the crest, just west of "Lake Helen of Troy"—which was named by Versteeg. (SNP, INF)

West Vidette (over 12,560); **East Vidette** (3,766 m.–12,350); **Vidette Lakes**
Mount Whitney 15', Mt. Brewer 7½'
Vidette Creek *Mount Whitney 15', Mt. Pinchot 15', Mt. Brewer 7½',*
Mt. Clarence King 7½'
Vidette Meadow *Mt. Pinchot 15', Mt. Clarence King 7½'*
"Two of these promontories, standing guard, as it were, the one at the entrance to the valley and the other just within it, form a striking pair, and we named them the Videttes." (C. B. Bradley in *SCB* 2, no. 5, Jan. 1899: 272.) The more common spelling is "vedette," meaning "a mounted sentry in advance of the outposts of an army."

Bradley, on his sketch map, gave the name "Deerhorn Creek"—because it flowed from the base of Deerhorn Mountain—to Vidette Creek. The creek had its present name on the first *Mt. Whitney* 30′ map, 1907. J. N. LeConte used the name "Vidette Meadow" in 1900 (*Sunset Magazine* 5, no. 6, Oct. 1900: 280), but it didn't get on the USGS maps until 1953. The lakes are first named on the 15-minute quad, 1956. (KCNP)

Virginia Creek   *Bodie 15′*
Virginia Lakes, Peak (12,001), **Pass, Canyon**   *Matterhorn Peak 15′*
Virginia Canyon, Lake (9,230)   *Tuolumne Meadows 15′*
The name probably originates from early miners from Virginia. Virginia Creek was the first feature to be named. It is on Hoffmann's map of 1873, and was used by Joseph LeConte in 1870. (LeConte, *Ramblings,* 118.)

"Virginia" obviously had a nice ring to the surveyors, who were generous in its use. The other names all appeared on the 1910 *Mt. Lyell* or 1911 *Bridgeport* 30′ maps, except "Virginia Peak," which was called "Red Peak" at that time. The Park Service recommended changing the name to "Virginia Peak," since there already was another "Red Peak" (in the Clark Range) within the park. (BGN decision, 1932.) (Peak, canyon, lake, pass, YNP; creek, lakes, pass, TNF)

Vogelsang Peak (11,516), **Lake** (10,341)   *Tuolumne Meadows 15′*
Farquhar (*Place Names,* p. 99) stated that Col. Benson named these features for Alexander Theodore Vogelsang, president of the California State Board of Fish and Game Commissioners, 1896–1901. However, Charles Adolphus Vogelsang (a brother) wrote Farquhar that Benson named the peak for him, in 1907. He was the executive officer of Fish and Game, 1901–10, 1919–22. (Letter, Oct. 20, 1930, in Farquhar files.) "My recollection is that Col. Benson gave the name for ATV, but CAV may be right." (Farquhar files.) In 1932 the BGN ratified these names and also "Vogelsang Pass," which is generally known by that name but is not on the map. It is ½ mile south of Vogelsang Lake.

"Although named for a man, the name is singularly fitting to the beautiful place; it means in older German 'a meadow in which birds sing.' " (Gudde, *Place Names,* 356.) (YNP)

Voight Canyon   *Freel Peak 15′, Woodfords 7½′*
Frederick Voight homesteaded 160 acres in sec. 26, T. 11 N., R. 19 E. in 1894. (TNF)

Volcanic Butte (8,607)   *Fales Hot Springs 15′ and 7½′*
Possibly named by the USGS during the 1905–09 survey for the *Bridgeport* 30′ map; it is on the first edition, 1911. (TNF)

Volcanic Cone   *Tehipite Dome 15′*
Probably named by the USGS during the 1903 survey for the *Tehipite* 30′ map. The name is on the first edition, 1905, but is not on Lt. Davis's map of 1896. (SiNF)

Volcanic Knob (11,140–11,168)   *Mt. Abbot 15', Graveyard Peak 7½'*
Named by Theodore S. Solomons in 1894. (Farquhar: Solomons.) (SiNF)

Volcanic Lakes   *Marion Peak 15'*
Probably named by the USGS during the 1903 survey for the *Tehipite* 30'
map. The name is on the first edition, 1905, but is not on Lt. Davis's map of
1896. (KCNP)

Volcanic Ridge   *Devils Postpile 15', Mt. Ritter 7½'*
Probably named by the USGS during the 1898–99 survey for the *Mt. Lyell*
30' map. The name is on the first edition, 1901, but is not on Solomons' map of
1896. (INF)

Volcano Falls, Meadow   *Kern Peak 15'*
"The third day we camped on Whitney Creek, upon which we tried
unsuccessfully to impress the name 'Volcano Creek,' as that stream does not rise
in the vicinity of Mt. Whitney. We lay over a day at this point to explore the
craters of two extinct volcanoes and to feast on rainbow trout." (W. B. Wallace
in *MWCJ* 1, no. 1, May 1902: 2.)
Lt. Davis used the name "Volcano Creek" on his 1896 map, and called the
falls "Whitney Falls." On the first edition of the *Olancha* 30' map, 1907, the
USGS named the creek "Golden Trout Creek" and the falls "Volcanic Falls."
The latter name was changed to "Volcano Falls" on the fourth edition, 1927.
The meadow was first named on the 15-minute quad, 1956. (See also **Golden
Trout Creek** and **Whitney Creek**.) (INF)

Volunteer Peak (10,479)   *Matterhorn Peak 15'*
See **Regulation Peak**. (YNP)

W Lake   *Tower Peak 15'*
The name was approved by a BGN decision in 1965. On the DFG's Lake
Survey report it is called "Wilson Lake," probably for Malcolm E. Wilson, who
did the survey in 1963. Not named on early editions of the 15-minute quad. It is
a small lake ½ mile southeast of the east end of Emigrant Lake. (StNF)

Wade Canyon   *Freel Peak 15', Woodfords 7½'*
William B. Wade bought 40 acres in the NW¼ of sec. 35, T. 11 N., R. 19 E.
in 1879, and Clarissa S. Wade homesteaded 120 acres in secs. 26 and 35 in
1890. (TNF)

Wah Hoo Lake   *Blackcap Mtn. 15' and 7½'*
Possibly named in 1948 by Jack Criqui of the DFG. No reason is given for
the name. (DFG survey.) (SiNF)

Wahoo Lakes   *Mt. Goddard 15', Mt. Darwin 7½'*
Named by Art Schober. There was a man named "Hobby" Hobson who
used to come to Parcher's resort. Whenever he caught a fish he would holler out
"Wahoo!" (Art Schober.) (SiNF)

Wales Lake (3,573 m.–11,700)   *Mount Whitney 15' and 7½'*
Frederick Henry Wales (1845–1925), a minister, editor, and farmer,

residing in Tulare County. In 1881, Wales, W. B. Wallace, and J. W. A. Wright made a 200-mile exploring trip to the Kern River Canyon and Mount Whitney, and made the first ascent of Mount Kaweah. (Farquhar.) The name was suggested by the Sierra Club in 1925, and appeared on the sixth edition of the *Mt. Whitney* 30' map, 1927. (SNP)

Walker Creek   *Monache Mtn. 15'*
In the early days it was known as "Gus Walker's Creek." Walker was a native of Germany. He passed through the region in 1859 on his way to the San Joaquin Valley. In 1864 he returned, took up land at Olancha, and raised hay to sell to Remi Nadeau's teamsters. He later started a cattle business, which he ran until his death in 1923 at age 95. (INF archives.) (INF)

Walker Creek, Lake (7,935)   *Mono Craters 15'*
William J. Walker patented 159 acres in secs. 6 and 7, T. 1 S., R. 26 E. in 1883—the land just east of the lake outlet. In 1869 John Muir called the lake "Moraine Lake," from "the large lateral moraines which extend out into the desert." (Muir, *First Summer,* 301.) He named the creek "Cañon Creek;" the upper part of the creek is in Bloody Canyon, which was already named. (Muir, *Mountains,* 87.) (INF)

Walker Pass (5,246)   *Onyx 15', Walker Pass 7½'*
West Walker River; Little Walker River
Walker Mountain (11,563)   *Matterhorn Peak 15'*
Joseph R. Walker (1798–1876), leading a party of Bonneville's men, made the first east-to-west crossing of the Sierra Nevada, in 1833. On the return journey, in 1834, he crossed via the pass that is now named for him. Walker was a guide on Frémont's third expedition, 1845–46; it was Frémont who named the pass. (*Memoirs,* vol. 1, 354.) He also named the river and Walker Lake, Nevada. Walker Mountain was first named on the 1911 *Bridgeport* 30' map. It is at the headwaters of the Little Walker River. (Pass, SeNF; others, TNF)

Wallace Lake (3,497 m.–11,450), **Creek**   *Mount Whitney 15' and 7½'*
Judge William B. Wallace (1849–1926), a mountaineer and explorer of the sourthern Sierra Nevada. Wallace "spent twenty consecutive summers in the mountains. . . . He climbed Mount Whitney and other high peaks, traversed wild cañons, discovered passes, blazed trails, traveled through trackless forests, and named several streams, lakes, meadows, and mountains." (George W. Stewart in *SCB* 12, no. 4, 1927; 430–31.)
The names were proposed by the Sierra Club in 1925, and approved by the BGN. They appeared on the sixth edition of the *Mt. Whitney* 30' map, 1927. Prior to that, the creek was named "East Fork" of the Kern River. (SNP)

Wallace, Mount (13,377)   *Mt. Goddard 15', Mt. Darwin 7½'*
Alfred Russel Wallace (1823–1913), British naturalist, who developed the theory of evolution contemporaneously with Darwin. The mountain is one of the so-called "Evolution Group," named by Theodore S. Solomons in 1895. (*Appalachia* 8, no. 1, 1896: 48–50.) On the first two editions of the *Mt. Goddard* 30' map (1912 and 1918) the name was mistakenly placed on the

western ridge of Mount Darwin. It was moved to the correct location in 1923. (KCNP, INF)

Walton Lake   *Merced Peak 15'*
Charles K. Fisher of the DFG reported in 1948 that the name was given in 1940 by John Handley, formerly at the DFG's Madera hatchery. (DFG survey.) No reason was given for the name, but one might guess it was for Izaak Walton, author of *The Compleat Angler.* (SiNF)

Wampum Lake   *Mt. Abbot 15', Mt. Hilgard 7½'*
Named in August 1951 by Elden H. Vestal of the DFG "after bead money as one of several means of exchange among Indians." (Heyward Moore, *FPP* 26, no. 2, Summer 1984: 7.) (SiNF)

Wanda Lake (11,426–11,453)   *Mt. Goddard 15' and 7½'*
Named by R. B. Marshall, USGS, for Wanda Muir Hanna, one of John Muir's daughters. (Farquhar: Marshall.) Described by J. N. LeConte in 1904 as one of the "Crystal Lakes." (*SCB* 5, no. 3, Jan. 1905: 236.) (KCNP)

Wapama Falls   *Lake Eleanor 15'*
Origin unknown. It is called "Hetch Hetchy Fall" on Hoffmann and Gardiner's map, 1863–67. On Benson's map of 1896 it is "Macomb Falls." The present name appeared on the fifth edition of the *Yosemite* 30' map, 1911. (YNP)

Ward Mountain; Ward Mountain Lake   *Blackcap Mtn. 15',*
Ward Mountain 7½'
Ward Lake   *Mt. Abbot 15', Florence Lake 7½'*
Named for Dr. George C. Ward, a former president of Southern California Edison, who was the chief engineer in charge of developing the hydroelectric projects at Shaver, Huntington, and Florence lakes. (Los Angeles *Times,* March 20, 1938.) Ward Tunnel, 13.5 miles long, from Florence Lake to Huntington Lake, was also named for him. Ward Mountain Lake was named by a DFG survey party in 1946. (DFG survey.) (SiNF)

Warlow, Mount (13,206–13,231)   *Mt. Goddard 15', Mt. Darwin 7½'*
Chester Harvey Warlow (1889–1963), a civic leader and conservationist who played an important role in the creation of Kings Canyon National Park. (BGN decision, 1969.) The mountain is not named on early editions of the 15-minute quad. It is 0.7 mile southeast of Mt. Huxley. (KCNP)

Warren Bench   *Big Pine 15' and 7½'*
George Warren was Big Pine's representative on the Owens Valley Irrigation District during the "Water Wars" of the 1920s. (Nadeau, *Water Seekers,* 72–74, 78, 102.) The name was suggested by Paul Bateman, a geologist with the USGS.

Warren, Mount (12,327); **Warren Fork** (of Lee Vining Creek)
Mono Craters 15'
Gouverneur Kemble Warren (1820–1882), army officer and topographical engineer. He collaborated with A. A. Humphreys (for whom Mt. Humphreys

is named) in compiling a map of the trans-Mississippi West and publishing reports of the Pacific railroad surveys. (Lamar, 1238.)

The peak was named by the Whitney Survey; it is on Hoffmann and Gardiner's map, 1863–67. For a brief period it was thought that the local name of "Castle Peak" referred to "Mount Warren," but it was actually being applied to "Dunderberg Peak"—which left the name "Mount Warren" undisturbed. (See **Dunderberg Peak** and **Tower Peak.**) (INF)

Warrior Lake   *Mt. Abbot 15', Graveyard Peak 7½'*
This was named "Bobs Lake" on the Mt. Abbot 15' map; changed to "Warrior Lake" by a BGN decision in 1969. The former "Warrior Lake" was changed to "Chief Lake." The reason for the changes was not explained. (SiNF)

Wasco Lake   *Tuolumne Meadows 15'*
Named by Al Gardisky in 1932 after the town in which a close friend of his lived. (Spuller.) (INF)

Washburn Lake   *Merced Peak 15'*
Washburn Point, Slide   *Yosemite 15', Yosemite Valley 1:24,000*
Albert Henry Washburn operated the Yosemite Stage & Turnpike Co. in the 1870s and later. In December 1874 he and two partners bought Clark and Moore's Station on the South Fork, and developed the Wawona Hotel Company. (Sargent, *Wawona*, 22 ff.)

The lake was named in 1895 by Lt. N. F. McClure. (Farquhar: McClure.) On his 1896 map he called it "Lake A. H. Washburn." The other "Washburn" names appeared on the *Yosemite Valley* map in 1947. (YNP)

Washington Column   *Yosemite 15', Yosemite Valley 1:24,000*
The name dates from the early days in Yosemite, although the namer is unknown; it is on King and Gardiner's map of 1865. From the right place on the south rim of the valley, the rock formation is said to look like a gigantic sculpture of George Washington. It has also been called "Washington Tower." (Hutchings, *In the Heart*, 383–84.) (YNP)

Waterhouse Peak (9,497)   *Freel Peak 15' and 7½'*
Named by the Forest Service in memory of Clark Waterhouse, who had been in charge of the Angora Lookout. He was killed in the First World War. (Gudde, *Place Names*, 359.) (ENF, TNF)

Waterwheel Falls   *Tuolumne Meadows 15'*
"The lowest set of cascades in this group we called the 'Rocket Cascades,' because the water, striking the edges of the great plates of granite . . . was continually thrown off in great arches. . . ." (Whitney, *The Yosemite Guide-Book*, pocket edition, 1874, 155–56.)

"The water dashes 600 or 700 feet down a surface inclined at an angle of 50 to 55 degrees, a mass of foam and spray. At intervals . . . the water is thrown out in columns fifteen to twenty feet high, and in huge water-wheels of fantastic forms." (R. M. Price, "Through the Tuolumne Cañon," *SCB* 1, no. 6, May 1895: 204.) (YNP)

Watkins, Mount (8,500)   *Hetch Hetchy Reservoir 15',*
Yosemite Valley 1:24,000
Watkins Pinnacles   *Yosemite Valley 1:24,000*
". . . a noble overhanging mass of rock, to which the name of Mount Watkins has been given, as a compliment to the photographer who has done so much to attract attention to this region." (Whitney, *The Yosemite Book,* 1868, 63.)

Carleton E. Watkins (1829–1916), one of the earliest photographers of Yosemite. He provided illustrations for the publications of the Whitney Survey. His view of Mirror Lake, with "Mount Watkins" reflected in it, is doubtless what led to his name being affixed to the peak.

"*Waijau.* Mount Watkins; meaning the Pine Mountain." (Whitney, *The Yosemite Guide-Book,* 1870, 17.)

"Wei-yow', meaning 'Juniper Mountain.' " (Clark, 108.)

The mountain is named on King and Gardiner's map of 1865. The pinnacles are first named on the *Yosemite Valley* map in 1958. (YNP)

Waugh Lake (9,424)   *Mono Craters 15', Devils Postpile 15', Mt. Ritter 7½'*
An artificial lake, created in 1918, and named for E. J. Waugh, the engineer in charge of constructing the dam. (Farquhar: W. L. Huber.) (INF)

Wawona; Wawona Dome, Point, Tunnel   *Yosemite 15'*
". . . Crane Flat—so named by us, as one of our party shot a large crane there while going over, but it is now known as Wawona." (Stephen F. Grover's narrative, May 1852, in Russell, *100 Years,* 57.)

"The Indians' name for the area was *Pallahchun* (a good place to stop)." (Sargent, *Wawona,* 11.)

Galen Clark built a cabin in the meadow on the South Fork of the Merced in April 1857. This became known as "Clark's Station." When Edwin Moore acquired a half interest in 1869 it got the name of "Clark and Moore's." The Washburn brothers purchased the property in December 1874, and renamed it "Big Tree Station." In 1882 Jean Bruce Washburn suggested a more appropriate name—*Wah-wo-nah.* (Sargent, *Wawona,* 12–16, 39.)

Galen Clark said that the word meant "Big Tree." (Clark, 109.) Stephen Powers was of the same opinion. "The California big tree is also in a manner sacred to them, and they call it *woh-woh'-nau,* a word formed in imitation of the hoot of the owl, which is the guardian spirit and diety of this great monarch of the forest." (Powers, 398.)

"Wawona Meadows themselves might be called the Sleepy Hollow of the West. It is the most peaceful place that I know in America, and comes near being the most idyllic spot I have seen anywhere (which is a considerable admission for an Englishman to make)." (Chase, 165.)

Wawona Dome was earlier known as "Granite Dome" and "Capitol Dome." The dome and Wawona Point were named on the first *Yosemite 30'* map, 1897.

The Wawona Tunnel, completed in 1933, replaced a portion of the old Wawona Road that went high across the shoulder of the hill. (YNP)

Wegner Lake   *Hetch Hetchy Reservoir 15'*
Named for John H. Wegner, a Yosemite National Park ranger from 1916 to
1944, and chief ranger at Sequoia National Park, 1944–49. (Bingaman,
Guardians, 94–95.) (YNP)

Wells Peak (11,118)   *Tower Peak 15'*
Named by R. B. Marshall, USGS, for Rush Spencer Wells, an army officer.
(Farquhar: Marshall.) The name appeared on the third *Dardanelles* 30' map,
1912. (YNP)

Wells Peak (10,833)   *Sonora Pass 15', Lost Cannon Peak 7½'*
Named for John C. Wells (1844–1922), a ranger and supervisor in Mono
National Forest (now Toiyabe NF), 1901–22. (BGN, *Sixth Report,* 807.)
(TNF)

West Lake (8,764)   *Huntington Lake 15' and 7½'*
So named because it is west of Red Mountain. Earlier it had a variety of
informal names: "Lost Lake," "China Lake," "Wheaton Lake," "Red
Mountain Lake," and "George Lake." (DFG survey.) (SiNF)

West Peak (over 10,480)   *Tuolumne Meadows 15'*
The name appeared on the third edition of the *Mt. Lyell* 30' map, 1910. On
the 1905 map it was unnamed. On the 1901 map it was called "Regulation
Peak." The origin of the present name is unknown. (See **Regulation Peak.**)
(YNP)

Westfall Creek   *Shuteye Peak 15', Kaiser Peak 15' and 7½'*
Named after Eldridge Westfall, one of the first forest rangers in this area.
(USGS.) (SiNF)

Westfall Meadows   *Yosemite 15'*
". . . follow along Alder Creek to its source in a large meadow, known as
Westfall's. . . . Here are two houses, Westfall's and Ostrander's, sometimes
occupied during the summer by herders of sheep, and which have often afforded
a kind of shelter, poor, but better than none, to persons overtaken by night, or too
much fatigued to go farther." (Whitney, *The Yosemite Book,* 1868, 53–54.)
(YNP)

Westfall Campground, Ranger Station   *Bass Lake 15'*
Sampson W. Westfall patented 160 acres in sec. 26, T. 5 S., R. 21 E. in
1887. (SiNF)

Weston Meadow   *Giant Forest 15'*
Austin J. Weston, from near Visalia, made his headquarters and pastured his
stock in this meadow during the summer. (Farquhar: George W. Stewart.)
Weston patented 160 acres in secs. 1, 2, and 11, T. 14 S., R. 28 E. in 1888, and
another 160 acres in sec. 12—where the meadow is—in 1891. (SNP)

Wet Meadow   *Tehipite Dome 15'*
The name probably was given by the USGS during the 1903 survey for the
Tehipite 30' map. It is on the first edition, 1905, but is on neither Lt. Davis's nor
Theodore Solomons' maps of 1896. (SiNF)

Wet Meadows   *Mineral King 15'*
The name derived from the swampy character of the meadows in the early days. (Junep.) The name is on the first *Kaweah* 30' map, 1904. (SeNF)

Whaleback (11,726)   *Triple Divide Peak 15'*
Probably named by the USGS during the 1903 survey for the *Tehipite* 30' map; it is on the first edition, 1905. (KCNP)

Wheats Meadow, Cow Camp   *Dardanelles Cone 15', Donnell Lake 7½'*
Wheats Meadow Creek   *Dardanelles Cone 15', Donnell Lake 7½',*
                                                         Spicer Meadow Res. 7½'
Wheat was an early settler. The legend "Wheat's house" is on the 1879 GLO plat and in the surveyor's field notes. (StNF)

Wheel Mountain (12,774–12,781)   *Mt. Goddard 15' and 7½'*
Lewis Clark, Marjory Bridge, John Poindexter, and John Cahill made the first ascent of the peak on July 26, 1933, and named the mountain "because of the peculiar structure of the summit, which consists of four steep buttresses radiating symetrically from a hub like the spokes of a wheel." (*SCB* 19, no. 3, June 1934: 94.) (KCNP)

Wheeler Ridge   *Mt. Tom 15', Mt. Morgan 7½'*
Probably named for Lt. George Montague Wheeler (1842–1905), engineer and surveyor, head of the army's United States Geographical Surveys West of the One Hundredth Meridian—the Wheeler Survey—from its inception in 1872 until the creation of the US Geological Survey in 1879.
The name was approved as "Wheeler Ridge" by the BGN in 1911, but appeared as "Wheeler Crest" on all editions of the *Mt. Goddard* 30' map and on the *Mt. Tom* 15' quad. It was not until publication of the 7½-minute quad in 1982 that the name finally became "Wheeler Ridge." (INF)

Wheeler Peak (9,001)   *Tower Peak 15'*
Probably named about 1910 for an army officer. Col. W. W. Forsyth, acting superintendent of Yosemite National Park, 1909–12, named a number of features in the northern part of the park for army officers. The names all appeared on the third *Dardanelles* 30' map, 1912. One might speculate that this peak was named for Joseph Wheeler (1836–1906), a Confederate general during the Civil War. In 1898, at the outbreak of the Spanish-American war, he was commissioned a major general of volunteers. He served in Cuba and the Philippines, and was made a brigadier general in the regular army in 1900. (EB.) (YNP, StNF)

White Bear Lake   *Mt. Abbot 15', Mt. Hilgard 7½'*
Probably named in 1952 by Elden H. Vestal of the DFG. (DFG survey. See **Bear Paw Lake**.) (SiNF)

White Cascade   *Tuolumne Meadows 15'*
Named by the Whitney Survey in 1866. "Just at the crossing is a charming group of shelving rapids, in which the Tuolumne River falls about 80 feet perpendicular, in a mass of white foam; to this we gave the name of the 'White Cascades.' " (Whitney, *The Yosemite Guide-Book,* 1874, 155.) (YNP)

White Divide   *Marion Peak 15', Mt. Goddard 15' and 7½'*
Probably named by the USGS during the 1907–09 survey for the *Mt. Goddard* 30' map; it is on the first edition, 1912. (KCNP)

White Dome (7,555)   *Lamont Peak 15'*
Probably named by the USGS during the survey for the *Kernville* 30' map; it is on the first edition, 1908. (SeNF)

White Meadow   *Camp Nelson 15'*
Possibly named for Huffman White, a Mountain Home sheepman during the 1860s, or for his brother, Harrison White, a Forest Service supervisor, 1899–1900. (Otter, 37, 42, 48, 109.) (SeNF)

White Mountain (over 8,720)   *Kern Peak 15'*
Probably named by the USGS during the 1905 survey for the *Olancha* 30' map; it is on the first edition, 1907. (SeNF)

White Mountain (11,398)   *Sonora Pass 15', Lost Cannon Peak 7½'*
Probably named by the USGS during the 1891–96 survey for the *Dardanelles* 30' map; it is on the first edition, 1898. (TNF)

White Mountain (over 12,000)   *Tuolumne Meadows 15'*
Probably named by the USGS during the 1898–99 survey for the *Mt. Lyell* 30' map; it is on the first edition, 1901. (YNP, INF)

White Wolf   *Hetch Hetchy Reservoir 15'*
Said to have been named by John Meyer, a native of Germany, who, with his two brothers, had a cattle ranch near Groveland. While chasing Indians who had stolen some of their horses, they came to a temporary Indian camp in an alpine meadow, and called it White Wolf, for the Indian chief. (Paden, 153.) (YNP)

Whitecliff Peak (over 10,800–10,833)   *Sonora Pass 15',*
                                                          Disaster Peak 7½'
Whitecliff Lake   *Disaster Peak 7½'*
The peak probably was named by the USGS during the 1891–96 survey for the *Dardanelles* 30' map; it is on the first edition, 1898. The lake's name was added to the map by the USGS because it was in local use. (TNF)

Whitman Creek   *Mineral King 15'*
Named by troopers after their commanding officer, Capt. William Whitman, First Cavalry, US Army, acting superintendent of Sequoia National Park in 1912. (Junep.) The name appeared on the third edition of the *Olancha* 30' map, 1922. (SNP)

Whitney, Mount (4,416.9 m.–14,494); **Whitney Pass**
                                      Mount Whitney 15' and 7½'
Whitney Creek   *Mount Whitney 15' and 7½', Mt. Brewer 7½'*
Big Whitney Meadow; Little Whitney Meadow   *Kern Peak 15'*
Whitney Portal   *Lone Pine 15', Mt. Langley 7½'*
Josiah Dwight Whitney (1819–1896), state geologist and chief of the California State Geological Survey ("Whitney Survey"), 1860–74; professor

of geology at Harvard, 1865–96. (Brewster; portrait in *SCB* 12, no. 2, 1925: opp. 126.)

The mountain was named in July 1864 by Clarence King and Richard Cotter of the Whitney Survey from the summit of Mount Tyndall when they made the first ascent of Tyndall. "On setting the level, it was seen at once that there were two peaks equally high in sight, and two still more elevated, all within a distance of seven miles. Of the two highest, one rose close by. . . . The other, which we called Mount Whitney, appeared equally inaccessible from any point on the north or west side. . . ." (Whitney, *Geology,* 386.)

"Whitney had forbidden his subordinates to name for him the mountain which is now called after the Rev. Lorentine Hamilton. This time, in their chief's absence, they stood upon their rights of discovery, and called their great peak, Mt. Whitney." (Brewster, 238.)

"For years our chief, Professor Whitney, has made brave campaigns into the unknown realm of Nature. Against low prejudice and dull indifference he has led the survey of California onward to success. There stand for him two monuments,—one a great report made by his own hand; another the loftiest peak in the Union, begun for him in the planet's youth and sculptured of enduring granite by the slow hand of Time." (King, 280–81.)

In 1871 King climbed what he thought was Mount Whitney, but he was actually on Mount Langley—then known as "Sheep Mountain," a name applied by King himself in 1864. The real first ascent of Whitney was made on August 18, 1873, by John Lucas, Charles D. Begole, and Albert H. Johnson, all of Lone Pine, who made the climb from a summer camp on the Kern River. "Charley Begole, Johnny Lucas and Al Johnson took a trip to the summit of the highest mountain in the range, and christened it 'Fisherman's Peak.' Some people are now trying to take the credit of their being the first there away from them, but they won't succeed. Prof. Whitney's agent has just returned from the mountain, and finds fault with the people here for their lack of romance in calling it 'Fisherman's Peak.' Ain't it as romantic as 'Whitney?' The fishermen who found it looked mighty romantic on their return to Soda Springs. Wonder who that old earthquake sharp thinks is running this country, anyhow?" (*Inyo Independent,* September 20, 1873.) For a detailed account of the name controversy and of early ascents of the mountain, see Francis P. Farquhar, "The Story of Mount Whitney," *SCB* 14, no. 1, Feb. 1929: 39–52.)

The name "Whitney Creek" was at first applied to what is now named "Golden Trout Creek," because the creek arose near Mt. Langley, which had been thought to be Mt. Whitney. Those who discovered the error tried—in 1881—to correct it. "The third day we camped on Whitney Creek, upon which we tried unsuccessfully to impress the name 'Volcano Creek,' as that stream does not rise in the vicinity of Mt. Whitney." But later on, the same party applied the name to the correct stream, where it is today. "We were at an altitude of about 11,500 feet, in a little meadow, through which flows the clear, cold water of a creek heading at the foot of the mountain. This is the stream which we thought should have been named Whitney Creek." (W. B. Wallace in *MWCJ* 1, no. 1, May 1902: 2–3. See **Volcano Falls; Golden Trout Creek.**)

When Joseph N. LeConte passed through Big Whitney Meadow in 1890 he referred to it as "Whitney Creek Meadows." It became simply "Whitney Meadow" on the 1907 *Olancha* 30' sheet; the word "Big" was added with publication of the 1956 *Kern Peak* 15' map. Little Whitney Meadow was called "Long Meadow" on early editions of the *Olancha* 30' sheet; it was changed to its present name in 1938 by a BGN decision because the name was in common use.

"Whitney Pass" was the route of the first trail built to the summit of Mt. Whitney from Owens Valley, in 1904, and probably was named at that time.

The original name of Whitney Portal was "Hunter Flat" or "Hunter's Camp," given many years ago for William L. Hunter, an early pioneer of Owens Valley and one of the two men who made the first ascent of Mt. Williamson, in 1884. The name "Whitney Portal" was applied at the official opening of the new automobile road to the flat in June 1936. (USGS.) For a biographical sketch and portrait of Hunter (1842–1902), see *Saga of Inyo County*, 163–64.

(Mtn. and pass, SNP, INF; creek, SNP; mdws. and portal, INF)

Whorl Mountain (12,029)   *Matterhorn Peak 15'*
Probably named by the USGS during the 1905–09 survey for the *Bridgeport* 30' map; it is on the first edition, 1911. It has been suggested that the name "Whorl" is meant in its botanical sense: several leaves or branches growing out of the same place. (YNP files.) The mountain has three closely associated peaks; the name applies to the middle one. (YNP)

Wildcat Creek, Falls   *Yosemite 15', Yosemite Valley 1:24,000*
Probably named for the local species of bobcat. (*YNN* 34, no. 1, Jan. 1955: 20.) Both names appeared on the *Yosemite Valley* map in 1927. (YNP)

Wildcat Point (9,455)   *Tuolumne Meadows 15'*
Possibly named by the USGS during the 1898 survey for the *Mt. Lyell* 30' map; it is on the first edition, 1901. (YNP)

Wildman Meadow   *Marion Peak 15'*
"About 1881 brother Jeff and I camped there with a band of sheep. After dark we were startled by a lot of unearthly yells like someone in distress. After spending a large part of the night we were unable to locate anyone and finally concluded that it must have been a wild man, and so named the meadow. Later we found the noise was caused by a peculiar-looking owl." (Letter, Frank Lewis to Farquhar, February 12, 1926.) (SeNF)

Williams Butte (8,431)   *Mono Craters 15'*
Thomas Williams patented 160 acres in secs. 32 and 33, T. 1 N., R. 26 E. in 1882. The land is about a mile south of the butte. (INF)

Williamson, Mount (14,375); **Williamson Creek**   *Mount Whitney 15',*
                                                        Mt. Williamson 7½'
Williamson Bowl   *Mt. Williamson 7½'*
"Farther observations, by Mr. King, showed that a point about two miles northeast of Mount Tyndall was a little higher than this mountain; it was named

in honor of Major R. S. Williamson, of the United States Engineers, so well known by his topographical labors on the Pacific coast, especially in connection with the United States railroad surveys." (Whitney, *Geology,* 382.)

Robert Stockton Williamson (1824–1882) led an expedition in 1853 to explore the passes across the southern Sierra Nevada to find a suitable route for a railroad. (Pacific Railroad *Reports,* vol. V.) (INF)

Wilma Lake *Tower Peak 15'*
Named by R. B. Marshall, USGS, for Wilma Seavey, daughter of Clyde L. Seavey. (Farquhar: Marshall. See **Seavey Pass.**) The name was mistakenly given as "Wilmer" in Farquhar's *Place Names* and on the *Dardanelles 30'* maps, 1912–47. It was changed to "Wilma" on the 15-minute quad, 1956. That spelling was ratified by a BGN decision in 1964. (YNP)

Wilson Creek *Matterhorn Peak 15'*
Named by Lt. H. C. Benson for his friend Mountford Wilson, of San Francisco. (Farquhar.) (YNP)

Wilson Meadow *Lake Eleanor 15'*
William B. Wilson patented 159 acres in this vicinity in 1892. (StNF)

Wilsonia *Giant Forest 15'*
Daniel M. Perry patented 160 acres in 1891: the exact center of sec. 5, T. 14 S., R. 28 E. (BGN.) The timber was cut during the 1880s. The land was later sold to Andy Ferguson, who subdivided it in 1918 to create a colony of summer homes. (*Los Tulares,* no. 53, Aug. 1962: 4.) Another source gives the date as 1921, and states that it was named for Woodrow Wilson. (White, 98.) Wilsonia is private land within Kings Canyon National Park.

Winchell, Mount (13,775–13,768) *Mt. Goddard 15', North Palisade 7½'*
Alexander Winchell (1824–1891), for many years the state geologist of Michigan and professor of geology at the University of Michigan. (Farquhar.)

In 1868 Elisha C. Winchell, Alexander's cousin, honored him by giving the name "Mount Winchell" to what is now named "Lookout Point." (See the second **Lookout Point.**) Unaware of that naming, Lil A. Winchell, the son of Elisha, in 1879 gave the same name to a peak south of the Palisades. (Letter, L. A. Winchell to T. S. Solomons, 1896, in Farquhar papers, BL.) The name "Mount Winchell" apparently was transferred to its present location by the USGS during the survey for the *Mt. Goddard 30'* map, although J. N. LeConte contradicts L. A. Winchell by saying that it was Winchell who applied the name to the present Mount Winchell. (*SCB* 5, no. 1, Jan. 1904: 3.) (KCNP, INF)

Window Cliffs *Kern Peak 15'*
"These cliffs are perforated with a window-like opening at the head of a gorge dropping into Kern Canyon, through which inspiring views of the [Sequoia National] park may be obtained." (BGN, *Sixth Report,* 821.) (SNP, INF)

Window Peak (3,684 m.–12,085) *Mt. Pinchot 15' and 7½'*
The peak probably was named by the USGS during the 1905 survey for the *Mt. Whitney 30'* map. It is on the first edition, 1907, but is not in LeConte's

"Elevations," 1903. There is a "window" through the rocks near the summit. (See *SCB* 26, no. 1, Feb. 1941: 127.) (KCNP)

Windy Cliff   *Mt. Goddard 15', North Palisade 7½'*
Probably named by the USGS during the 1907–09 survey for the *Mt. Goddard* 30' map; it is on the first edition, 1912. (KCNP)

Windy Cliffs, Gulch; Windy Gulch Grove   *Tehipite Dome 15'*
The cliffs and gulch probably were named by the USGS during the 1903 survey for the *Tehipite* 30' map; both names are on the first edition, 1905. The grove was named on the 15-minute quad. (SeNF)

Windy Peak (8,867), **Canyon, Ridge**   *Marion Peak 15'*
Probably named by the USGS during the 1903 survey for the *Tehipite* 30' map; all the names are on the first edition, 1905. (KCNP)

Winnemucca Lake (8,980)   *Markleeville 15', Carson Pass 7½'*
Maule speculated that the name was brought here by a resident of Nevada, where the town and a mining district were named in the 1860s for a Paiute chief. The name appeared on the *Markleeville* 30' map in 1936. In 1875 the GLO surveyor called it "Summit Lake" in his field notes. (ENF)

Wishbone Lake   *Mt. Darwin 7½'*
Named for its shape by the Forest Service. (Art Schober.) Not named on the *Mt. Goddard* 15' quad. It is the first lake upstream from Upper Lamarck Lake. (INF)

Wishon Reservoir, Dam   *Tehipite Dome 15', Blackcap Mtn. 15',*
                                              Courtright Reservoir 7½'
A. Emory Wishon of the San Joaquin Light and Power Corp, which merged with the Pacific Gas and Electric Company in 1930. The dam was completed in 1958. (SiNF)

Wolverton Creek   *Triple Divide Peak 15'*
James Wolverton, an early trapper and hunter, discovered and named the General Sherman Tree on August 7, 1879. He had served as a lieutenant under Sherman during the Civil War. (White, 30.) (SNP)

Wonder Lakes   *Mt. Goddard 15', Mt. Darwin 7½'*
Named by Art Schober in the 1930s when he planted fish in the lakes. He had a terribly difficult time getting there with his stock, and once there he wondered how he had done it. (Art Schober.) (INF)

Wood Lake   *Pinecrest 15'*
Named for Bill Wood, an early cattleman in the Piute-Emigrant-Huckleberry area. (StNF files, from Joe Ratto.) (StNF)

Wood, Mount (12,637)   *Mono Craters 15'*
Named in 1894 by Lt. N. F. McClure for Capt. Abram Epperson Wood, acting superintendent of Yosemite National Park, 1891–93. (Farquhar: McClure.) Wood commanded the first troops assigned to Yosemite: companies I

and K of the Fourth Cavalry. They arrived on May 19, 1891, and set up camp at Wawona. (Bingaman, *Guardians,* 83.) (INF)

Woodfords   *Freel Peak 15', Woodfords 7½'*
In 1847 Sam Brannan, leader of the Mormons in California, left two men here to establish the first white settlement in the area. The place became known as "Brannan Springs," even though Brannan's outpost was abandoned. John Cary (or Carey) settled here in 1851 and built a sawmill, and the place then was called "Cary's Mill." Daniel Woodford had arrived in 1849 and built the first permanent building, a hotel known as the "Sign of the Elephant." Woodford bought the mill in 1869, and thereafter the name of the place was "Woodfords." (*Historic Spots,* 26; Wood, 29; *Alpine Heritage,* 19; Maule.) (TNF)

Woods Creek   *Marion Peak 15', Mt. Pinchot 15' and 7½'*
Woods Lake   *Mt. Pinchot 15' and 7½'*
Named by J. N. LeConte for Robert Martin Woods, a sheepman of the Kings River region, who spent most summers between 1871 and 1900 in the Sierra. (Farquhar: LeConte and Versteeg.) On his 1890 trip LeConte met "two fellows from Visalia, and a shepherd and wife out on a fishing tour." The latter two were Bob and Em Woods. (LeConte, *A Summer,* 32.) (KCNP)

Woods Gulch   *Dardanelles Cone 15' and 7½'*
Named for Bill Wood, an early cattleman, the same person for whom Wood Lake on the *Pinecrest* 15' quad was named. (StNF files, from Joe Ratto.) (StNF)

Woodworth, Mount (12,219)   *Mt. Goddard 15', North Palisade 7½'*
Named about 1888 for Benjamin R. Woodworth, a resident of Fresno, who was with a camping party in Simpson Meadow at the time. (Farquhar: L. A. Winchell.) (KCNP)

Wotans Throne (over 12,720)   *Mount Whitney 15' and 7½'*
The name was suggested by Chester Versteeg in 1936. (SC papers in BL.) It is not known whether he was borrowing from the peak of the same name in Grand Canyon National Park. (INF)

Wren Peak (9,450)   *Tehipite Dome 15'*
Wren Creek   *Tehipite Dome 15', Marion Peak 15'*
Probably named by the USGS during the 1903 survey for the *Tehipite* 30' map; both names are on the first edition, 1905. (SeNF)

Wright Lakes   *Mount Whitney 15' and 7½', Mt. Williamson 7½'*
Wright Creek   *Mount Whitney 15' and 7½', Mt. Williamson 7½',*
                                                Mt. Kaweah 7½'
James William Albert Wright accompanied F. H. Wales and W. B. Wallace on a memorable trip to the Kern River and Mount Whitney in 1881. (See **Wales Lake** and **Wallace Lake;** also *SCB* 32, no. 5, May 1947: 78–81.) Wright drew the first good map of the southern Sierra Nevada. It was published in Elliott's *Guide* and Winchell's *History of Fresno County,* and reprinted in part in *SCB* 32, above.

242   PLACE NAMES OF THE SIERRA NEVADA

"Captain Wright was the only fleshy member of our party. His ribs were encased in such thick layers of fatty tissue that, knowing his inability to freeze, we elected that he should sleep on the windward side of the camp." (W. B. Wallace in *MWCJ* 1, no. 1, May 1902: 2.)

The name for the lakes was proposed by the Sierra Club in 1925, and appeared on the sixth edition of the *Mt. Whitney* 30' map, 1927. On that same map the former "East Fork Kern River" was changed to "Wright Creek." (SNP)

Wynne, Mount (4,017 m.–13,179)   *Mt. Pinchot 15' and 7½'*
Named for Sedman W. Wynne, former supervisor of Sequoia National Forest, who lost his life while on duty. (BGN, *Sixth Report,* 826.) The name appeared on the seventh edition of the *Mt. Whitney* 30' map, 1933. (KCNP)

Yaney Canyon   *Fales Hot Springs 15'*
Yaney operated a sawmill here in the early 1860s, supplying lumber to Aurora, Nevada. (Maule, 9.) (TNF)

Yosemite Valley   *Yosemite 15', Yosemite Valley 1:24,000*
Yosemite Creek, Falls, Point (6,936)   *Hetch Hetchy Reservoir 15',*
                     Yosemite Valley 1:24,000
"Here we began to encounter in our path, many small streams which would shoot out from under these high snow-banks, and after running a short distance in deep chasms which they have through ages cut in the rocks, precipitate themselves from one lofty precipice to another, until they are exhausted in rain below. Some of these precipices appeared to us to be more than a mile high." (Leonard, 174.) Zenas Leonard was a member of the Joseph R. Walker party that crossed the Sierra Nevada in 1833. Francis P. Farquhar, and others, take this to be a description of Yosemite Valley by the first whites to see it, but there are dissenting views.

"Ten-ie-ya said that a small party of white men once crossed the mountains on the North side, but were so guided as not to see it." (Bunnell, *Discovery,* 1911, 78.) Paden and Schlichtmann argue that Leonard was describing Cascade, Tamarack, Coyote, and Wildcat creeks, and provide a persuasive description of the route most likely taken by Walker's party. (Paden, 259–64.)

At least two white men saw—but did not enter—Yosemite Valley as early as 1849. "While at Savage's Reamer and I saw grizzly bear tracks and went out to hunt him down getting lost in the mountains and not returning until the following evening found our way to camp over an Indian trail that lead past a valley inclosed by stupendous cliffs arising perhaps 3000 feet from their base and which gave us cause for wonder. Not far off a waterfall dropped from a cliff below three jagged peaks into the valley while farther beyond a rounded mountain stood the valley side of which looked as though it had been sliced with a knife as one would slice a loaf of bread and which Reamer and I called the Rock of Ages." (Diary of William Penn Abrams, BL.) Clearly Abrams saw Bridalveil Fall, the three Cathedral Rocks, and Half Dome. The author of an article in the Modesto *Stanislaus News* of January 22, 1875, claimed that James Savage had been in Yosemite Valley as early as June 1849, but this cannot be substantiated.

The first white men *known* to have entered Yosemite Valley were members of Major Savage's Mariposa Battalion. The date was March 27, 1851. (Eccleston, 48, 58–60.) The valley and many of the major features in or near it were named by these men during the first four or five days.

"Some romantic and foreign names were offered . . . a very large number were canonical and scripture names. As I did not take a fancy to any of the names proposed, I remarked that . . . 'I could not see any necessity for going to a foreign country for a name for American scenery—the grandest that had ever yet been looked upon. . . . that the name of the tribe who had occupied it, would be more appropriate than any I had heard suggested.' I then proposed 'that we give the valley the name of Yo-sem-i-ty, as it was suggestive, euphonious, and certainly *American;* that by so doing, the name of the tribe of Indians which we met leaving their homes in this valley, perhaps never to return, would be perpetuated.' I was here interrupted by Mr. Tunnehill, who impatiently exclaimed: 'Devil take the Indians and their names! Why should we honor these vagabond murderers by perpetuating their name?' Another said: 'I agree with Tunnehill:——the Indians and their names. Let's call this "Paradise Valley.' " The question of giving it the name of Yo-sem-i-ty was then explained, and upon a *viva voce* vote being taken, it was almost unanimously adopted.

"Lieutenant Moore, of the U.S.A., in his report of an expedition to the Valley in 1852, substituted *e* as the terminal letter, in place of *y*, in use by us; no doubt thinking the use of *e* more scholarly, or perhaps supposing Yosemite to be of Spanish derivation. . . . Sometime after the name had been adopted, I learned from Major Savage that Ten-ie-ya repudiated the name for the Valley, but proudly acknowledged it as the designation of his band, claiming that 'when he was a young chief, this name had been selected because they occupied the mountains and valleys which were the favorite resort of the Grizzly Bears, and because his people were expert in killing them. That his tribe had adopted the name because those who had bestowed it were afraid of 'the Grizzlies' and feared his band." (Bunnell, *Discovery,* 1880, 61–64.)

"While we most willingly acquiesce in the name of Yo-Semite . . . as neither that nor Yo-Ham-i-te, but *Ah-wah-ne,* is said to be the *pure Indian* name, we confess that our preferences still are in favor of the pure Indian being given; but until that is determined upon (which we do not ever expect to see done now), Yo-Semite, we think, has the preference." (Hutchings, *Scenes,* 1876, 95.)

"In the first place the aborigines never knew of any such locality as Yosemite Valley. Second, there is not now and there has not been anything in the valley which they call Yosemite. Third, they never called 'Old Ephraim' himself Yosemite, nor is there any such word in the Miwok language. The valley has always been known to them, and is to this day, when speaking among themselves, as A-wa'-ni." (Powers, 361.)

Bunnell named the falls and the creek, stating that the Indians called the falls

"Choolook" or "Schoolook," meaning "The Fall," and the creek "Scho-tal-lo-wi," which he interpreted to mean "the creek of the fall." (Bunnell, *Discovery,* 1880, 201–2.)

Yosemite Point was first named on the USGS *Yosemite Valley* map of 1907, although it had been described long before that. (Whitney, *Geology,* 414.) (YNP)

Young Lakes   *Tuolumne Meadows 15'*
General Samuel Baldwin Marks Young (1840–1924), acting superintendent of Yosemite National Park in 1896, and of Yellowstone National Park, 1907–08. Young was a veteran of the Civil War, some campaigns against the Indians, and the Spanish-American War, and was Chief of Staff of the US Army, 1903–04. (Farquhar.) The name is on the first *Mt. Lyell* 30' map, 1901. (YNP)

Young, Mount (4,016 m.–13,177)   *Mount Whitney 15' and 7½'*
"Know all men! that I hereby on the 7th day of September 1881 do name this Mountain '*Young*' in honor of Prof. *Charles Young* now of Princeton and formerly Prof. at Dartmouth College—in witness whereof I have hereon erected this monument as a perpetual memorial. Situation—N.W. of Mt. Whitney, Distance about 3 miles. About N. of Mt. Hitchcock and about two miles distant. Fred H. Wales." (Inscription on a piece of paper in a tin can found on the summit of the mountain on July 24, 1934, by Sierra Club members; see *SCB* 20, no. 1, Feb. 1935: 108. See also **Wales Lake.**)

Charles Augustus Young (1834–1908), professor of mathematics at Western Reserve, 1857–66; professor of natural philosophy and astronomy at Dartmouth, 1866–77; professor of astronomy at Princeton, 1877–1908. (Farquhar.) (SNP)

"Z" Lake   *Tuolumne Meadows 15'*
Named in 1932 by Al Gardisky for its shape. (Spuller.) (INF)

Zumwalt Meadows   *Marion Peak 15'*
Daniel Kindle Zumwalt (1845–1904), land agent and attorney for the Southern Pacific Railroad. Zumwalt was one of the important figures in the creation of Sequoia and General Grant national parks in 1890. (Farquhar; see *SCB* 47, no. 9, Dec. 1962: 68–82.) Zumwalt patented 160 acres in sec. 17, T. 13 S., R. 31 E. on April 4, 1891; the land is about two miles west of Zumwalt Meadows. On that same day, however, Abraham Agnew patented 80 acres in the S½ of the NW¼ of sec. 15, which included most or all of the meadows. Thus Agnew either sold the land to Zumwalt at some later time, or was acting as Zumwalt's agent in 1891. The meadow was first named on the fourth edition of the *Tehipite* 30' map, 1929. (KCNP)

Bibliography

Alpine Heritage. Centennial Book Committee. *One Hundred Years of History . . . in Alpine County, California, 1864–1964.* Campbell, California: Craftsman Typographers, 1964.

Arch. MSB. Archivo de la Mision de Santa Barbara: *Muñoz, Diario de la Expedicion hecha por Don Gabriel Moraga, Alférez de la Compañia de San Francisco, á los Nuevos Descubrimientos del Tular, 1806.* (Transcript, Bancroft Library, Berkeley.)

Badè. Badè, William Frederic. *The Life and Letters of John Muir.* Boston and New York: Houghton Mifflin Co., 1924.

Benson's 1896 map. *Yosemite National Park, 1896,* by 1st Lt. H. C. Benson, Fourth Cavalry, US Army. (In *Report of the Acting Superintendent of the Yosemite National Park, 1896.* Reprinted in *Report* for 1897.)

BGN. US Board on Geographic Names.

BGN, *Sixth Report.* *Sixth Report of the United States Geographic Board, 1890 to 1932.* Washington: Government Printing Office, 1933.

Bingaman, *Guardians.* Bingaman, John W. *Guardians of the Yosemite.* Privately printed, 1961.

Bingaman, *Pathways.* Bingaman, John W. *Pathways, A Story of Trails and Men.* Lodi, California: End-kian Publishing Co., 1968.

BL. Bancroft Library, Berkeley.

Bolton. Bolton, Herbert Eugene, trans. and ed. *Font's Complete Diary: A Chronicle of the Founding of San Francisco.* Berkeley: University of California Press, 1933.

Boyd. Boyd, William Harland. *A Climb Through History: from Caliente to Mount Whitney in 1889.* Richardson, Texas: Havilah Press, 1973.

Brewer, *Up and Down.* Brewer, William Henry. *Up and Down California in 1860–1864: the Journal of William H. Brewer.* Edited by Francis P. Farquhar. 3d ed. Berkeley and Los Angeles: University of California Press, 1966.

Brewer's diary. The field diary kept by William H. Brewer during his five seasons with the first California Geological Survey, in the Bancroft Library, Berkeley.

Brewster. Brewster, Edwin Tenney. *Life and Letters of Josiah Dwight Whitney.* Boston and New York: Houghton Mifflin Co., 1909.

Bull. 193. Clark, William B. *Gold Districts of California, Bulletin no. 193.* San Francisco: Division of Mines and Geology, 1970. Includes map of California showing the locations of gold districts.

Bunnell, *Discovery*. Bunnell, Lafayette Houghton. *Discovery of the Yosemite, and the Indian War of 1851, which led to that event.* 2d ed., Chicago: F. H. Revell, 1880; 3d ed., 1892; 4th ed., Los Angeles: G. W. Gerlicher, 1911.

Bunnell, *Report*. *Biennial Report of the Commissioners to Manage Yosemite Valley,* 1889–90.

Cain. Cain, Ella M. *The Story of Early Mono County.* San Francisco: Fearon Publishers, Inc., 1961.

Carpenter and Gilcrist Map. *Map of Homer Mining District in Mono County, California.* H. B. Carpenter and J. Gilcrist, 1880.

CAS. California Academy of Sciences.

CFQ. *California Folklore Quarterly.*

Chalfant, *Gold*. Chalfant, W. A. *Gold, Guns, & Ghost Towns.* Stanford: Stanford University Press, 1947.

Chalfant, *Inyo*. Chalfant, W. A. *The Story of Inyo.* Rev. ed. Bishop, California: Pinon Book Store, 1933.

Chase. Chase, Joseph Smeaton. *Yosemite Trails.* Boston and New York: Houghton Mifflin Co., 1911.

Clark. Clark, Galen. *Indians of the Yosemite Valley. . . .* Yosemite Valley: Galen Clark, 1904.

Clark's map. *Reconnaissance sketch of Sequoia National Park and vicinity.* 2nd Lt. Henry B. Clark, 3rd U.S. Art'y, 1899.

Clark, *Mines*. Clark, William B. *Mines and Mineral Resources of Alpine County, California.* Sacramento: California Division of Mines and Geology, 1977.

***Climber's Guide*.** Roper, Steve. *The Climber's Guide to the High Sierra.* San Francisco: Sierra Club Books, 1976.

Coy. Coy, Owen Cochran. *California County Boundaries.* Rev. ed. Fresno: Valley Publishers, 1973.

Cragen. Cragen, Dorothy Clora. *The Boys in the Sky-Blue Pants.* Fresno: Pioneer Publishing Co., 1975.

Crites. Crites, Arthur S. *Pioneer Days in Kern County.* Los Angeles: The Ward Ritchie Press, 1951.

DAB. *Dictionary of American Biography.*

Davis's map. *Sketch of that portion of the Sierra Nevadas adjacent to The [Sequoia] National Park.* 2nd Lieut. Milton F. Davis, 4th Cavalry, U.S.A., 1896.

DeDecker. DeDecker, Mary. *Mines of the Eastern Sierra.* Glendale: La Siesta Press, 1966.

Derby's maps. Lt. George H. Derby of the Topographical Engineers (known in literature as John Phoenix). *Sketch of Gen. Riley's Route through the Mining Districts,* 1849; *Reconnaissance of the Tulares Valley,* 1850.

DFG. California Department of Fish and Game. "DFG survey" refers to Lake Survey reports on file at the DFG offices in Fresno and Bishop.

EB. *Encyclopedia Britannica.*

Eccleston. *The Mariposa Indian War, 1850–1851. Diaries of Robert Eccleston: The California Gold Rush. Yosemite, and the High Sierra.* Edited by C. Gregory Crampton. Salt Lake City: University of Utah Press, 1957.

Elliott, *Guide.* *A Guide to the grand and sublime scenery of the Sierra Nevada in the region about Mount Whitney.* San Francisco: W. W. Elliott & Co., 1883.

Elliott, *History.* *History of Fresno County.* San Francisco: W. W. Elliott & Co., 1882.

ENF. Eldorado National Forest.

Farley's map. *Farley's Map of the Newly Discovered Tramontane Silver Mines in Southern California and Western New Mexico,* 1861. Minard H. Farley.

Farquhar. Francis P. Farquhar. The name standing alone or followed by another name indicates that the source of the information is Farquhar's 1926 place-names book.

Farquhar, *History.* Farquhar, Francis P. *History of the Sierra Nevada.* Berkeley and Los Angeles: University of California Press, 1965.

Farquhar, *Place Names.* Farquhar, Francis P. *Place Names of the High Sierra.* San Francisco: Sierra Club, 1926.

FPP. *Fresno, Past & Present.* Quarterly publication of the Fresno City and County Historical Society, Fresno, California.

Frémont, *Expedition.* Frémont, John Charles. *Report of the Exploring Expedition to the Rocky Mountains in the year 1842, and to Oregon and north California in the years 1843–44.* Washington, 1845. (U.S. 28th Cong., 2d sess. House. Ex. doc. no. 166.)

Frémont, *Memoir.* Frémont, John Charles. *Geographical Memoir Upon Upper California.* Washington, 1848. (U.S. 30th Cong., 1st sess. Senate. Misc. doc. no. 148.)

Frémont, *Memoirs.* Frémont, John Charles. *Memoirs of My Life.* Chicago and New York: Belford, Clarke & Co., 1887.

Fry and White. Fry, Walter, and White, John R. *Big Trees.* London: Oxford University Press, 1930.

Gannett. Gannett, Henry. *The Origin of Certain Place Names in the United States.* (U.S. Geological Survey, Bulletin 197.) Washington: Government Printing Office, 1902.

Garcés. Garcés, Francisco. *On the Trail of a Spanish Pioneer: The Diary and Itinerary of Francisco Garces . . . 1775–1776.* Translated and edited by Elliott Coues. 2 vols. New York: Francis P. Harper, 1900.

GLO. The General Land Office was created in 1812, as a branch of the Treasury Department, to administer the public lands. It was transferred to the Department of the Interior when that agency was created in 1849. In 1946 the GLO was combined with the Grazing Service to create the Bureau of Land Management. The patent and homestead records cited are from the Bureau of Land Management's "Control Document Index" microfilm files in Sacramento.

Goddard's maps. George H. Goddard's *Map of Sonora Pass, 1853; Britton and Rey's Map of the State of California, 1857.*

Goddard, *Report*. Goddard, George H. *Report of a Survey of a portion of the Eastern Boundary of California, and a Reconnaissance of the old Carson and Johnson Immigrant Roads over the Sierra Nevada.* To the Honorable S. H. Marlette, Surveyor-General, December 15, 1855.

Gudde, *Bigler*. Gudde, Erwin G. *Bigler's Chronicle of the West.* Berkeley and Los Angeles: University of California Press, 1962.

Gudde, *Gold*. Gudde, Erwin G. *California Gold Camps.* Edited by Elizabeth K. Gudde. Berkeley and Los Angeles: University of California Press, 1975.

Gudde, *Place Names*. Gudde, Erwin G. *California Place Names.* 3d ed., rev. Berkeley and Los Angeles: University of California Press, 1969.

Hall, *Sequoia*. Hall, Ansel F. *A Guide to Sequoia and General Grant National Parks.* Berkeley: National Parks Publishing House, 1930.

Hall, *Yosemite*. Hall, Ansel F. *Guide to Yosemite.* San Francisco: Sunset Publishing House, 1920.

Harper. Harper, John L. *Mineral King: Public Concern with Government Policy.* Arcata: Pacifica Publishing Co., 1982.

Heitman. Heitman, Francis B. *Historical Register and Dictionary of the United States Army, 1789–1903.* vol. 1. Washington: Government Printing Office, 1903.

Historic Spots. Hoover, Mildred Brooke; Rensch, Hero Eugene; and Rensch, Ethel Grace. *Historic Spots in California.* 3d ed. Revised by William N. Abeloe. Stanford: Stanford University Press, 1966.

Hoffmann and Gardiner map. *Map of a portion of the Sierra Nevada adjacent to the Yosemite Valley.* From surveys made by Chs. F. Hoffmann and J. T. Gardner, 1863–1867. Geological Survey of California.

Hoffmann's 1873 map. *Topographical map of Central California, together with a part of Nevada,* 1873. State Geological Survey of California.

Homer. Homer. *The Odyssey.* Translated by W. H. D. Rouse. New York: The New American Library, Mentor Books, 1950.

Hubbard. Hubbard, Douglass. *Ghost Mines of Yosemite.* Fresno: Awani Press, 1971.

Hurt. Hurt, Bert. *A Sawmill History of the Sierra National Forest, 1852–1940.* Typed copy, Bancroft Library, Berkeley.

Hutchings, *Illustrated*. Hutchings, James Mason. *Hutchings' California Magazine (Illustrated).* Published from July 1856 to June 1861.

Hutchings, *In the Heart*. Hutchings, James Mason. *In the Heart of the Sierras.* . . . Oakland: Pacific Press Publishing House, 1886.

Hutchings, *Scenes*. Hutchings, James Mason. *Scenes of Wonder and Curiosity in California.* San Francisco: Hutchings and Rosenfield, 1860, 1861; 2d ed., San Francisco: J. M. Hutchings, 1862; 3d ed., London: Chapman and Hall, 1865; 4th ed., New York and San Francisco: A. Roman and Co., 1870, 1871, 1872, 1876.

INF. Inyo National Forest.

Inyo. *Saga of Inyo County.* Southern Inyo American Association of Retired Persons, 1977. A compilation of historic vignettes, family histories, personal anecdotes, and historic and family photographs.

Jackson. Jackson, Helen Hunt. *Bits of Travel at Home.* Boston: Roberts Brothers, 1878.

Johnston, *Redwoods*. Johnston, Hank. *They Felled the Redwoods.* 3d ed., rev. Los Angeles: Trans-Anglo Books, 1969.

Johnston, *Thunder*. Johnston, Hank. *Thunder in the Mountains.* Los Angeles: Trans-Anglo Books, 1968.

Johnston, *Whistles*. Johnston, Hank. *The Whistles Blow No More.* Glendale: Trans-Anglo Books, 1984.

Junep. Junep, Herbert L. *A Chronological History of the Sequoia National Park and Vicinity.* Manuscript, 1937, Sequoia National Park files.

KCNP. Kings Canyon National Park.

King. King, Clarence. *Mountaineering in the Sierra Nevada.* Lincoln: University of Nebraska Press, Bison Book, 1970. (First published in 1872.)

King and Gardiner map. *Map of the Yosemite Valley,* 1865. By C. King and J. T. Gardner. Geological Survey of California.

Kroeber. Kroeber, Alfred Louis, "California Place Names of Indian Origin," *University of California Publications in American Archaeology and Ethnology* 12, no. 2, June 15, 1916: 31–69.

Lamar. *The Reader's Encyclopedia of the American West.* Edited by Howard R. Lamar. New York: Thomas Y. Crowell Co., 1977.

LeConte, *Alpina*. LeConte, Joseph N. "The High Sierra of California," *Alpina Americana,* no. 1, 1907. (Only one issue published.)

LeConte, "Elevations." LeConte, Joseph N. "Table of Elevations of Peaks in the Sierra Nevada Mountains over 12,000 feet above Sea-Level," *Sierra Club Bulletin* 4, no. 4, June 1903: 285–91.

LeConte, *Ramblings*. LeConte, Joseph. *A Journal of Ramblings through the High Sierra of California.* San Francisco: Sierra Club, 1960. (Page references are to this volume. The journal also is in *SCB* 3, no. 1, Jan. 1900: 1–107.)

LeConte, *A Summer*. LeConte, Joseph N. *A Summer of Travel in the High Sierra.* Ashland, Oregon: Lewis Osborne, 1972.

LeConte maps. Joseph N. LeConte compiled five important maps, based on his own original surveys and information gathered from other early travelers in the mountains and from the US Geological Survey. *Map of a portion of the Sierra Nevada adjacent to the Yosemite and Hetch Hetchy Valleys*, 1893; *Map of a portion of the Sierra Nevada adjacent to the King's River*, 1893; *Map of the Sierra Nevada Mountains of Central California*, 1896; *Portion of the Sierra Nevada Mountains of Central California*, 1899–1904, in three sheets; and *Outline map of the southern Sierra Nevada*, 1906, published in *Alpina Americana*, no. 1, 1907.

Leonard. Leonard, Zenas. *Adventures of Zenas Leonard, Fur Trader.* Edited by John C. Ewers. Norman: University of Oklahoma Press, 1959. (First published in 1839 as the *Narrative of the Adventures of Zenas Leonard, written by himself.*)

Los Tulares. The quarterly bulletin of the Tulare County Historical Society. Lindsay, California.

Maule. Maule, William M. *A Contribution to the Geographic and Economic History of the Carson, Walker, and Mono Basins in Nevada and California.* San Francisco: US Forest Service, 1938.

McClure's maps. 1st Lieut. N. F. McClure, *Map of the Yosemite National Park*, 1895, in *Report of the Acting Superintendent of the Yosemite National Park, 1895. Map of the Yosemite National Park*, 1896, in the *Report* for 1900, 1902, 1903, and 1904.

Moore, Heyward. Professor of Political Science at California State University at Fresno. He has done intensive research on the origin of High Sierra lake and stream names in Fresno County.

Morison. Morison, Samuel Eliot. *The Oxford History of the American People.* New York: Oxford University Press, 1965.

Muir, *First Summer*. Muir, John. *My First Summer in the Sierra.* Boston and New York: Houghton Mifflin Co., 1911.

Muir, *Mountains*. Muir, John. *The Mountains of California.* New York: The Century Co., 1894.

Muir, *Parks*. Muir, John. *Our National Parks.* Boston and New York: Houghton Mifflin and Co., 1901.

Muir, *Picturesque*. *Picturesque California; the Rocky Mountains and the Pacific Slope.* Edited by John Muir. New York and San Francisco: J. Dewing Publishing Co., 1889–91. (Reprint edition under the title *West of the Rocky Mountains.* Philadelphia: Running Press, c. 1976.)

Muir, *Writings*. *South of Yosemite: Selected Writings of John Muir.* Edited by Frederic R. Gunsky. Garden City: The Natural History Press, 1968.

Muir, *The Yosemite*. Muir, John. *The Yosemite.* New York: Century Publishing Co., 1912.

MWCJ. *Mount Whitney Club Journal.* Three numbers issued: vol. 1, nos. 1, 2 and 3 (1902–1904), total of 134 pages.

Nadeau, *Ghost Towns*. Nadeau, Remi. *Ghost Towns and Mining Camps of California.* Los Angeles: The Ward Ritchie Press, 1965.

Nadeau, *Water Seekers*. Nadeau, Remi A. *The Water Seekers*. Garden City: Doubleday & Co., Inc., 1950.

***Nature*.** *Sequoia Nature Guide Service Bulletin*. Sequoia National Park. From June 1922 to December 1931.

***Newsletter*.** An irregular publication of the Tulare County Historical Society.

Otter. Otter, Floyd Leslie. *The Men of Mammoth Forest*. Ann Arbor: Edwards Brothers, Inc., 1963.

Paden. Paden, Irene, and Schlichtmann, Margaret E. *The Old Big Oak Flat Road: an account of freighting from Stockton to Yosemite Valley*. Yosemite: Yosemite Natural History Association, 1959.

***Post Offices*.** Salley, H. E. *History of California Post Offices, 1849–1976*. La Mesa, California: Postal History Associates, Inc., 1977.

Powers. Powers, Stephen. *Tribes of California*, in *Contributions to North American Ethnology*, vol. 3, US Geographical and Geological Survey of the Rocky Mountain Region. Washington: Government Printing Office, 1877.

Preuss's maps. Charles Preuss was the cartographer on Frémont's first, second, and fourth expeditions to the Far West. The Preuss and Frémont map of 1845 shows the routes of the first two expeditions. The map of 1848, although entitled *Map of Oregon and Upper California*, covers all the territory of the United States west of the 105th meridian.

Quad. The quadrangle topographic maps published by the US Geological Survey. Each covers either 15 minutes or 7½ minutes of latitude and longitude. The scale of the former is 1:62,500, and of the latter, 1:24,000.

Reed's map. *Map of the Silver Mountain Mining District*, 1864. Theron Reed.

Russell, *100 Years*. Russell, Carl Parcher. *One Hundred Years in Yosemite*. Stanford: Stanford University Press, 1931.

Russell, *Quaternary*. Russell, Israel Cook. *Quaternary History of Mono Valley, California*. Washington: Government Printing Office, 1889. (In *Eighth Annual Report of the director of the U.S. Geological Survey*, 1886–87, pt. 1.)

Sanchez. Sanchez, Nellie Van de Grift. *Spanish and Indian Place Names of California*. 1930. Reprint. New York: Arno Press, 1976.

Sargent, *Clark*. Sargent, Shirley. *Galen Clark: Yosemite Guardian*. Yosemite: Flying Spur Press, 1981.

Sargent, *Innkeepers*. Sargent, Shirley. *Yosemite & Its Innkeepers*. Yosemite: Flying Spur Press, 1975.

Sargent, *Lukens*. Sargent, Shirley. *Theodore Parker Lukens, father of forestry*. Los Angeles: Dawson's Book Shop, 1969.

Sargent, *Pioneers*. Sargent, Shirley. *Pioneers in Petticoats*. Los Angeles: Trans-Anglo Books, 1966.

SC. The Sierra Club.

***SCB*.** *Sierra Club Bulletin*, published in San Francisco since January 1893.

Schober. Art Schober's father bought the pack outfit on the North Fork of Bishop Creek in the early 1930s. Art and his brother John stocked many lakes with fish, naming them at the same time, in the North Fork and Middle Fork basins, and in Humphreys Basin, west of Piute Pass.

Schumacher. Schumacher, Genny. *Deepest Valley: Guide to Owens Valley....* San Francisco: Sierra Club, 1962.

SeNF. Sequoia National Forest.

SiNF. Sierra National Forest.

Smith. Smith, Genny Schumacher. *The Mammoth Lakes Sierra.* 4th ed. Palo Alto: Genny Smith Books, 1976.

SNP. Sequoia National Park.

Spuller. The Rev. Everett L. Spuller of Oxnard, California, and his wife spent the summer of 1932 helping Al Gardisky manage the Tioga Pass Resort. Mrs. Spuller and Al named more than 20 lakes that summer in what is now the Hoover Wilderness, at the headwaters of Lee Vining Creek. The information and a sketch map are in a letter from Spuller to Will Neely, a naturalist at Yosemite National Park, July 2, 1956, in the park's research library.

StNF. Stanislaus National Forest.

Taylor. Taylor, Benjamin F. *Between the Gates.* Chicago: S. C. Griggs and Co., 1878.

TNF. Toiyabe National Forest.

Tobin. Tobin, Daniel F. *A Brief History of Sequoia National Park.* Typed copy in SNP files.

Trask's maps. *Map of the State of California* and *Topographical Map of the Mineral Districts of California,* 1853. John B. Trask.

USFS. United States Forest Service.

USGS. United States Geological Survey.

VABM. Vertical Angle Bench Mark.

Vandor. Vandor, Paul E. *History of Fresno County.* 2 vols. Los Angeles: Historic Record Co., 1919.

Von Leicht and Craven map. *Map of California and Nevada.* drawn by F. v. Leicht and A. Craven. 3d ed. State Geological Survey of California, 1878.

Wheeler Survey, *Report*. Wheeler, George M. *Report Upon United States Geographical Surveys West of the 100th Meridian.* Washington, 1889. See the *Annual Report* for the specified year. Atlas sheet 56B, *Parts of Eastern California and Western Nevada,* expeditions of 1876 and 1877 under the command of 2nd Lieut. M. M. Macomb, 4th Artillery, U.S. Army. Atlas sheet 56D, *Parts of Central California,* 1878 and 1879, 1st Lieut. M. M. Macomb. Atlas sheet 65, *Parts of Eastern California and Southern Nevada.* Expedition of 1871, no date.

Wheeler Survey, *Tables*. Wheeler, George M. *Tables of Geographic Positions, Azimuths, and Distances ... and itineraries of important Routes,* prepared principally by 1st Lieut. M. M. Macomb. Washington, 1885.

White. White, John R., and Pusateri, Samuel J. *Sequoia and Kings Canyon National Parks*. Stanford: Stanford University Press, 1949.

Whitney, *Geology*. Whitney, Josiah Dwight. *Geology*. Vol. 1. Philadelphia: Caxton Press of Sherman & Co., 1865.

Whitney, *The Yosemite Book*. Whitney, Josiah Dwight. *The Yosemite Book*. New York: J. Bien, 1868.

Whitney, *The Yosemite Guide-Book*. Whitney, Josiah Dwight. *The Yosemite Guide-Book*. Cambridge, Mass.: University Press, 1869, 1870, 1871, and 1874.

Williamson, *Report*. Williamson, Lieut. Robert S. *Report of Explorations in California for Railroad Routes, to connect with the route near the 35th and 32d parallels of North Latitude*. (Vol. 5 of *Pacific Railroad Reports*.) Washington, 1856. Volume 11, part 2 contains Williamson's *Map of Passes in the Sierra Nevada, From Walker's Pass to the Coast Range*, 1853.

Winchell. Winchell, Lilbourne Alsip. *History of Fresno County and the San Joaquin Valley, Narrative and Biographical*. Fresno: A. W. Cawston, 1933. Winchell (1855–1939) spent five months in the High Sierra in 1879. He went to Tehipite Valley with Frank Dusy, explored the Palisade region, and with Louis Davis made the first ascent of Mount Goddard. He made other exploring trips in the Sierra over a period of many years, was acquainted with the early sheepmen and hunters, and gave names to a number of features.

Wood. Wood, Richard Coke. *Big Tree-Carson Valley Turnpike. Ebbetts Pass and Highway Four*. Murphys, Calfornia: Old Timers Museum, 1968.

Wright's map of 1883. *Guide to the scenery of the Sierra Nevada*, drawn by J. W. A. Wright for W. W. Elliott & Co., 1883. See **Wright Lakes, Creek.**

YNN. *Yosemite Nature Notes*, published by the Yosemite Natural History Association from 1922 to 1961.

YNP. Yosemite National Park.

Yosemite Road Guide. Yosemite: Yosemite Natural History Association, 1981.